"A wish-I'd-thought-of-it premise, beautifully executed. Mike Carey and Peter Gross are both doing the very best work of their lives. Highly recommended for anyone who thinks that fantasy can do more than just help you escape the real world."

— **Brian K. Vaughan**
(Eisner-winning writer of Y: THE LAST MAN)

"Fascinating. . . . With casual yet deeply informed writing from Mike Carey and accessible art from Peter Gross. . . One of the brainiest and most interesting comics of the year."

— **WIRED / UNDERWIRE**

"By the first page of the first issue of THE UNWRITTEN, I was intrigued. By page 3, I knew I'd be finishing the issue. Two pages later, and I knew I'd be a fan and loyal reader of this new series for its entire run. A comic series that I wish I had created, it's obvious that the adult adventures of (possible) child star Tommy Taylor were written specifically for my enjoyment, but I suppose they won't mind if you read along as well."

— **Bill Willingham**
(Eisner-winning writer of FABLES)

"One of the more intriguing comics on the horizon… a fantasy series that… soars off into its own unexpected directions. . . . There's a lot of promise in its pages."

— **THE LOS ANGELES TIMES / HERO COMPLEX**

"Carey and Gross perfectly capture the zeitgeist of our *Harry Potter*-obsessed-chaotic-apocalyptic times with a depth and whimsy that makes me jealous, and I can't wait to read more of THE UNWRITTEN."

— **Ed Brubaker**
(Eisner-winning writer of *Captain America*)

"To say that I can't wait to see what the future unfolds for this title would be an understatement… This book is not only entertaining, it has become a genre lifeline."

— **AIN'T IT COOL NEWS**

"A tremendous story about stories, need, and the emptiness of the world. This could be Mike Carey's masterpiece."

— **Paul Cornell**
(Hugo-nominated writer for BBC's *Doctor Who*)

"A single taste will hook readers right off… ambitious, exciting… A-"

— **THE ONION**

"About ten times as smart as anything else in comics right now, THE UNWRITTEN has deft story-telling grace, abruptly eerie imagining and quiet razor wit. Outstanding!"

— **Richard Morgan**
(Philip K. Dick Award-winning sci-fi novelist)

"Impeccably good creative team... You're definitely going to want to pick this up."
— **Blair Butler, G4TV**

"Magical... 4.5 / 5.0 stars"
— **AM NY**

"Clever [and] engrossing."
— **CREATIVE LOAFING**

"Reality-bending. . . .
THE UNWRITTEN may be just what you're looking for."
— **io9**

"A literary mystery? I'm so there."
— **PINK RAYGUN**

"Engrossing... Particularly suited for fans of stories that revisit literature past, such as
THE SANDMAN, FABLES, and THE LEAGUE OF EXTRAORDINARY GENTLEMEN,
and fans of conspiracy thrillers such as *The Da Vinci Code*."
— **NASHVILLE EXAMINER**

"Reading THE UNWRITTEN feels like getting in on the ground floor of the next big
thing. . . I don't think it's too early to call the series an unqualified success."
— **IGN**

"Compelling."
— **THE STRANGER**

"An interesting mind-twisting beginning of a series...
Anyone with a love of all things books will want to give it a try."
— **NEWS and SENTINEL**

"This series has hooked me from the first issue."
— **TOLEDO FREE PRESS**

"This book is easily one of the best on the market now."
— **NEWSARAMA**

"An analysis of the power of fiction... Expect post-modern twists galore."
— **PASTE Magazine**

"I can't remember the last time I was this excited to see what happens next in a comic."
— **MONDO MAGAZINE, Book of the Month**

WITHDRAWN

the unwritten

Tommy Taylor and the Bogus Identity

Mike Carey & Peter Gross Script - Story - Art
Chris Chuckry Jeanne McGee Colorists
Todd Klein Letterer
Yuko Shimizu Original series covers
THE UNWRITTEN created by Gross and Carey

Karen Berger   SVP-Executive Editor
Pornsak Pichetshote   Editor-Original Series
Georg Brewer   VP-Design & DC Direct Creative
Bob Harras   Group Editor-Collected Editions
Robbin Brosterman   Design Director-Books
Louis Prandi   Art Director

DC COMICS
Paul Levitz   President & Publisher
Richard Bruning   SVP-Creative Director
Patrick Caldon   EVP-Finance & Operations
Amy Genkins   SVP-Business & Legal Affairs
Jim Lee   Editorial Director-WildStorm
Gregory Noveck   SVP-Creative Affairs
Steve Rotterdam   SVP-Sales & Marketing
Cheryl Rubin   SVP-Brand Management

Cover by Yuko Shimizu

The Land of LAF

I believe it may be a movement. I even nurse a grudging suspicion that it might be the early days of a new age.

Beginning a bit more than half a century ago, superhero stories began to dominate the comic publishing business, and they're still going strong. Good. More power to them. We do, we have, and we will always need stories about heroes fighting the good fight, doing what's right, often in the face of an indifferent or even antagonistic populace. So we'll call the second half of the previous century the Superhero Age of Comics. That's an easy call to make.

But along comes a new century, a new millennium in fact, and look at this: Another modest and humble movement within comics has pushed its way quietly above the soil in our comics garden. Small but hardy, it seems to be gaining ground (acreage in fact) more rapidly and more vigorously with each passing year. Call it the LAF Triumvirate, which of course must stand for: Literature-based fantasy; Animal fantasy; and Fairy tale fantasy — grouped together because they belong together. They're inseparably part of the same new movement.

It starts in the woods. In fact it's all about the woods. Over in that deep and dark patch of woods a doughty young mouse named Karic is thrust on a quest to restore the honor and past glories of the fallen Order of the Mice Templar. And in another part of the forest, perhaps just down the way, the fearless and dedicated Mouse Guard patrols their realm, keeping the innocent and unwary safe from all manner of beast and monster. And then, in the Farm's Great Forest there are the Mouse Police (or Mounted Police as they're more properly named), tiny men and women, FABLES all, mounted on their valiant mouse destriers, keeping the peace in Smalltown.

But it's not just about the mice, or the talking owls and badgers, goats and mallards. They're but one part of the new modern fairytale landscape, a place where the Big Bad Wolf is surprised to recognize his one true love in Snow White, and the title character from a bit of doggerel rhyme fights for life and love against his wicked brother, dressed all in pied, conjuring terrible curses with his pipe. It's a haunted HOUSE OF MYSTERY, which is still an inescapable part of the magical forest, being a stand of woods, cut and hammered together. It's also a place where The Invisible Man, and Mr. Hyde, and Captain Nemo have to leave the familiar comfort of their individual books, to write an end to evil conquerors from the orient, or cold alien invaders from distant, martial Mars. It's an often mad Boschian world, where our very dreams take form and insist on writing their own Endless stories.

It's the merry and disturbing and frightening Land of LAF.

And it's growing.

By way of illustration, let's take a look at one small and wonderful new series, in our new comics landscape. It's called THE UNWRITTEN, this very book you hold in your hands. Like most of the others, it takes place under the restless, rustling leaves. But these leaves happen to be the pages of a book — a series of books, 13 in number, or possibly 14, which is part of the mystery. I won't talk about that — about the particulars of the story you're about to read. Why spoil it? But I will go on a bit about how delightful the story is, and how dearly I wish I could have every new issue as soon as I finish the previous one. And, in the interests of tidy housekeeping, I should note where THE UNWRITTEN finds its place in the LAF

Triumvirate. It's about storybook characters dumped unceremoniously into the real world, which places it squarely in the "L" column. L for Literature-based fantasy. But of course, a few issues in, there's already a bit of the Animal tale and Fairy tale in there too. You can't separate the three pillars of LAF, which is why it's all part of a single, marvelous whole.

Contrary to its discomforting title, THE UNWRITTEN happens to be written quite well, by Mike Carey. I can't tell you much about the man, other than he seems a good bloke at conventions, and he's constantly writing stories I want to read – that I wish I'd written in fact.

I know the other guy a bit better. Mike is teamed with Peter Gross, who draws the series. I first met him more than twenty years back, when he was doing an odd and delightfully idiosyncratic comic series for Comico (while I was there doing *Elementals*) about a group of heroic fantasy characters who sort of fell into our modern mundane world – specifically into a bowling alley. *Empire Lanes* was the name of the series (and the bowling alley). It was a fine story that ended too soon. Apparently heroic fantasy bowling tales were not the new thing coming. Or maybe it was just ahead of its time. I believe *Empire Lanes* was Peter's first comics work, which is impressive, because he started right out drawing and writing like an accomplished veteran of many years in the business. At the same time I wasn't quite so adept in my craft, but I promise I didn't let the disparity in our skills keep me from liking the affable fellow from the start. I've been a fan of him and his work ever since.

That said, with the full knowledge that both Mike and Peter have toiled in our comic book fields for many years, and produced truly lovely stories along the way, I suspect, without any fear of hyperbole, that THE UNWRITTEN may be their masterwork. From the first issue, from just the third or fourth page in, I knew that this comic was important – that this story was going to be exactly what I needed it to be, and that I'd be a faithful reader of every issue, for as long as the series lasts (and please let that be for a long time to come). The fact that it's part of the LAF community of books, wherein I live and work, makes it all the better. Good for us. So here we are then. With a simple turn of a friendly page, you're about to start reading THE UNWRITTEN, perhaps for the first time, in this collected edition of the first five monthly issues. If so, lucky you. I'm about to start reading it again, because what good is a story you only want to read once?

It takes place somewhere in the vast and ever growing Land of LAF, a bizarre pancommunity of fallen princesses and acerbic talking ravens, itinerant storybook heroes and exiled FABLES, of mice and men, battling for life, love and virtue, among the leaves of cursed books or enchanted woods. Let us welcome our new (but hardly newest) residents. It's a grand thing that they came along when they did, so that we don't have to leave THE UNWRITTEN unread.

Bill Willingham
From somewhere in the Minnesota woods

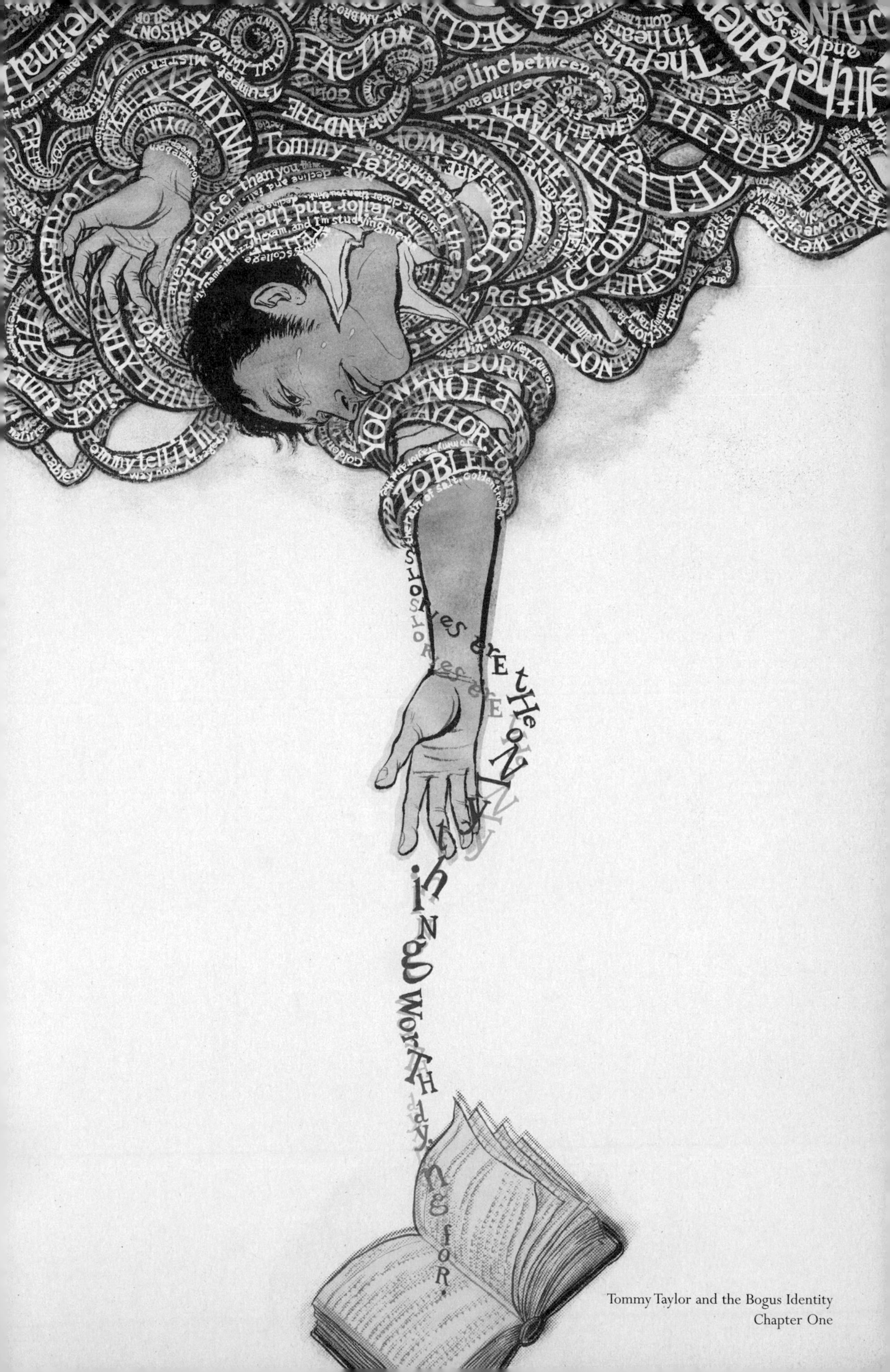
FACTION
The line between
Tommy Taylor
YOU WERE BORN
TELL THE WOMEN
THE PURE
WILSON
Stories are the only thing worth dying for.

Tommy Taylor and the Bogus Identity
Chapter One

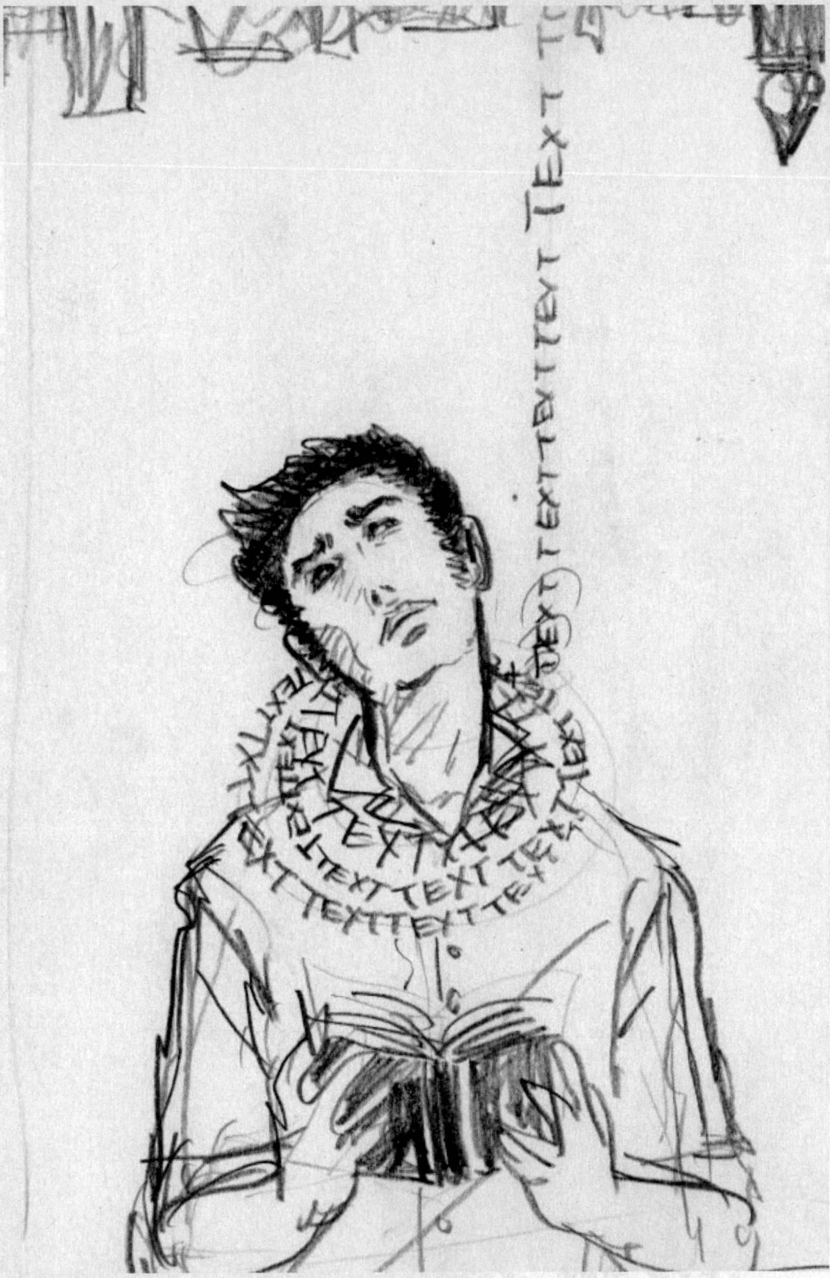
TEXT TEXT TEXT TEXT TEXT

Sketch by Yuko Shimizu

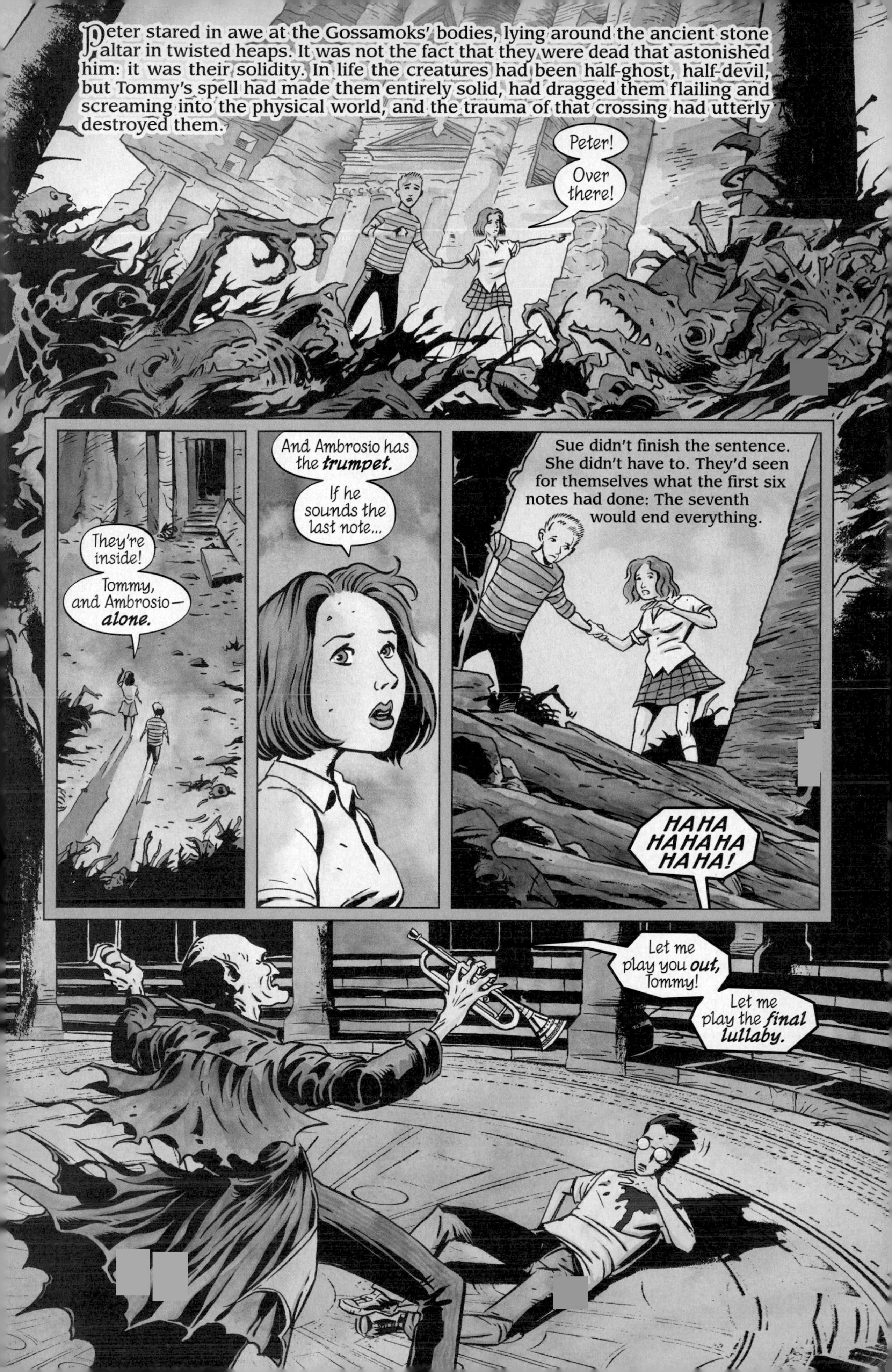

Peter stared in awe at the Gossamoks' bodies, lying around the ancient stone altar in twisted heaps. It was not the fact that they were dead that astonished him: it was their solidity. In life the creatures had been half-ghost, half-devil, but Tommy's spell had made them entirely solid, had dragged them flailing and screaming into the physical world, and the trauma of that crossing had utterly destroyed them.
Peter!
Over there!
They're inside!
Tommy, and Ambrosio— *alone.*
And Ambrosio has the *trumpet.*
If he sounds the last note...
Sue didn't finish the sentence. She didn't have to. They'd seen for themselves what the first six notes had done: The seventh would end everything.
HAHA HAHAHA HAHA!
Let me play you *out,* Tommy!
Let me play the *final lullaby.*

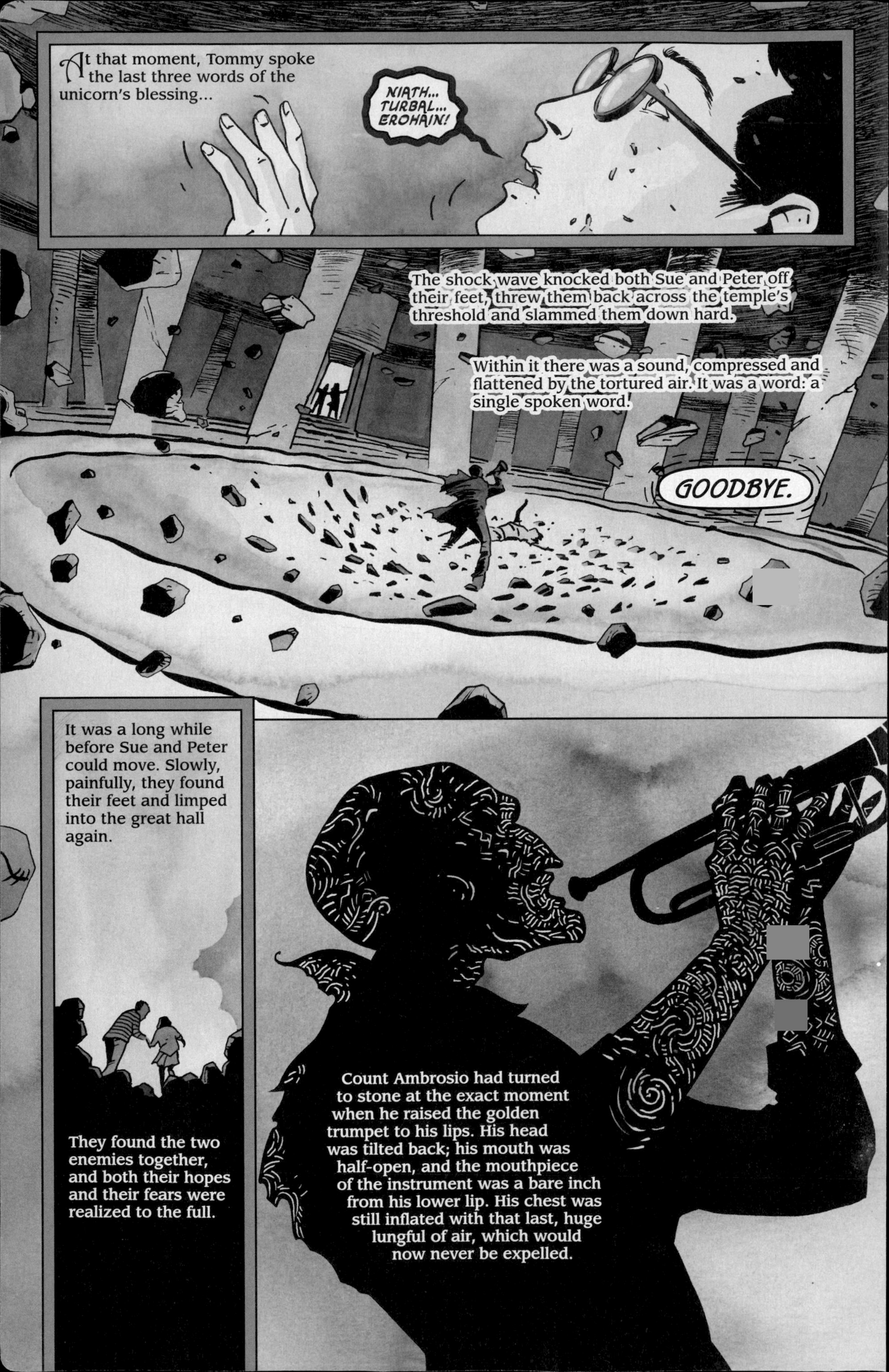
At that moment, Tommy spoke the last three words of the unicorn's blessing...
NIATH... TURBAL... EROHAIN!
The shock wave knocked both Sue and Peter off their feet, threw them back across the temple's threshold and slammed them down hard.
Within it there was a sound, compressed and flattened by the tortured air. It was a word: a single spoken word.
GOODBYE.
It was a long while before Sue and Peter could move. Slowly, painfully, they found their feet and limped into the great hall again.
They found the two enemies together, and both their hopes and their fears were realized to the full.
Count Ambrosio had turned to stone at the exact moment when he raised the golden trumpet to his lips. His head was tilted back; his mouth was half-open, and the mouthpiece of the instrument was a bare inch from his lower lip. His chest was still inflated with that last, huge lungful of air, which would now never be expelled.

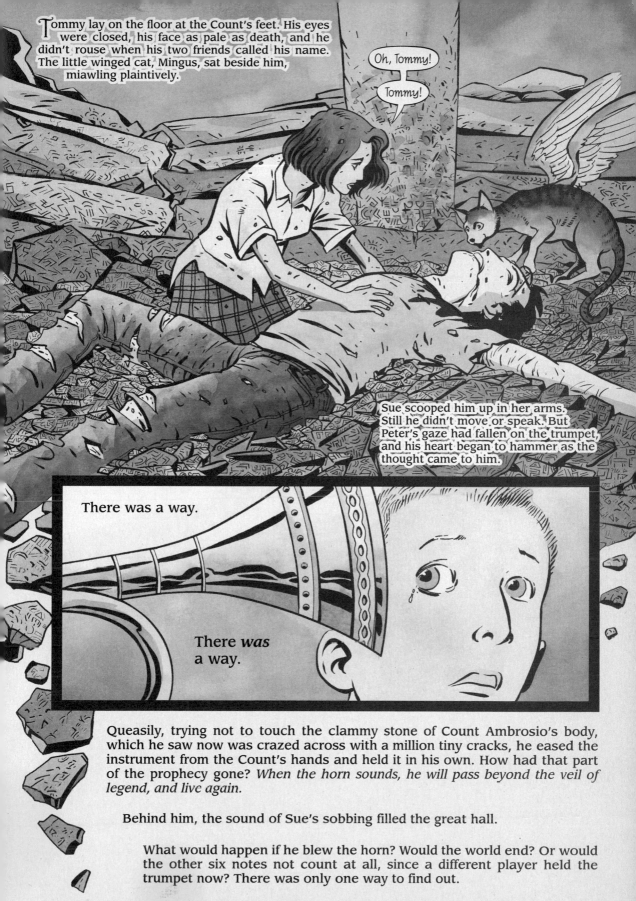

Tommy lay on the floor at the Count's feet. His eyes were closed, his face as pale as death, and he didn't rouse when his two friends called his name. The little winged cat, Mingus, sat beside him, miawling plaintively.

Oh, Tommy!

Tommy!

Sue scooped him up in her arms. Still he didn't move or speak. But Peter's gaze had fallen on the trumpet, and his heart began to hammer as the thought came to him.

There was a way.

There *was* a way.

Queasily, trying not to touch the clammy stone of Count Ambrosio's body, which he saw now was crazed across with a million tiny cracks, he eased the instrument from the Count's hands and held it in his own. How had that part of the prophecy gone? *When the horn sounds, he will pass beyond the veil of legend, and live again.*

Behind him, the sound of Sue's sobbing filled the great hall.

What would happen if he blew the horn? Would the world end? Or would the other six notes not count at all, since a different player held the trumpet now? There was only one way to find out.

Peter Price lifted the golden trumpet to his lips and blew the final, irrevocable note.

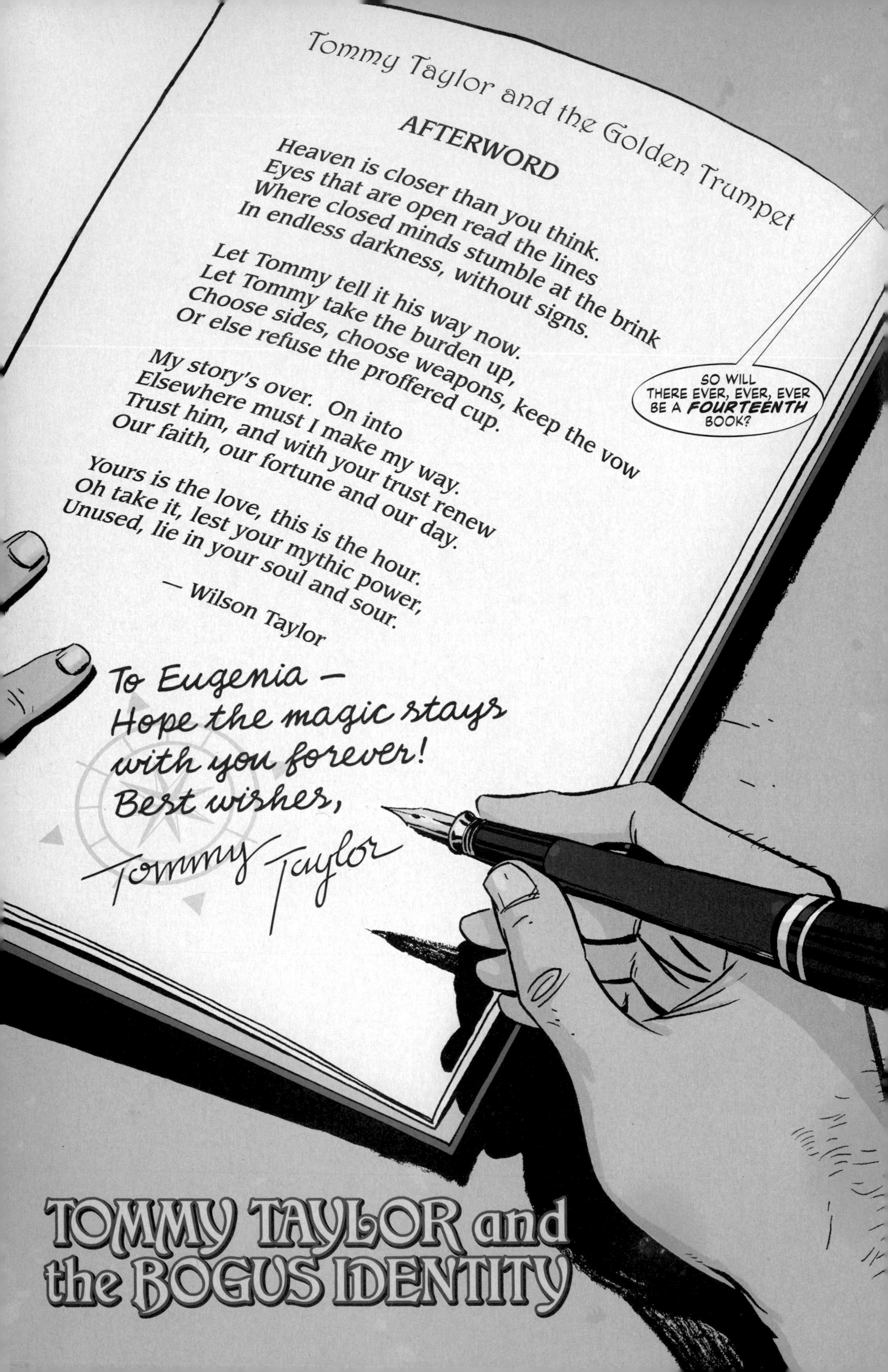
Tommy Taylor and the Golden Trumpet
AFTERWORD
Heaven is closer than you think.
Eyes that are open read the lines
Where closed minds stumble at the brink
In endless darkness, without signs.
Let Tommy tell it his way now.
Let Tommy take the burden up,
Choose sides, choose weapons, keep the vow
Or else refuse the proffered cup.
My story's over. On into
Elsewhere must I make my way.
Trust him, and with your trust renew
Our faith, our fortune and our day.
Yours is the love, this is the hour.
Oh take it, lest your mythic power,
Unused, lie in your soul and sour.
— Wilson Taylor
SO WILL THERE EVER, EVER, EVER BE A FOURTEENTH BOOK?
To Eugenia –
Hope the magic stays
with you forever!
Best wishes,
Tommy Taylor
TOMMY TAYLOR and the BOGUS IDENTITY

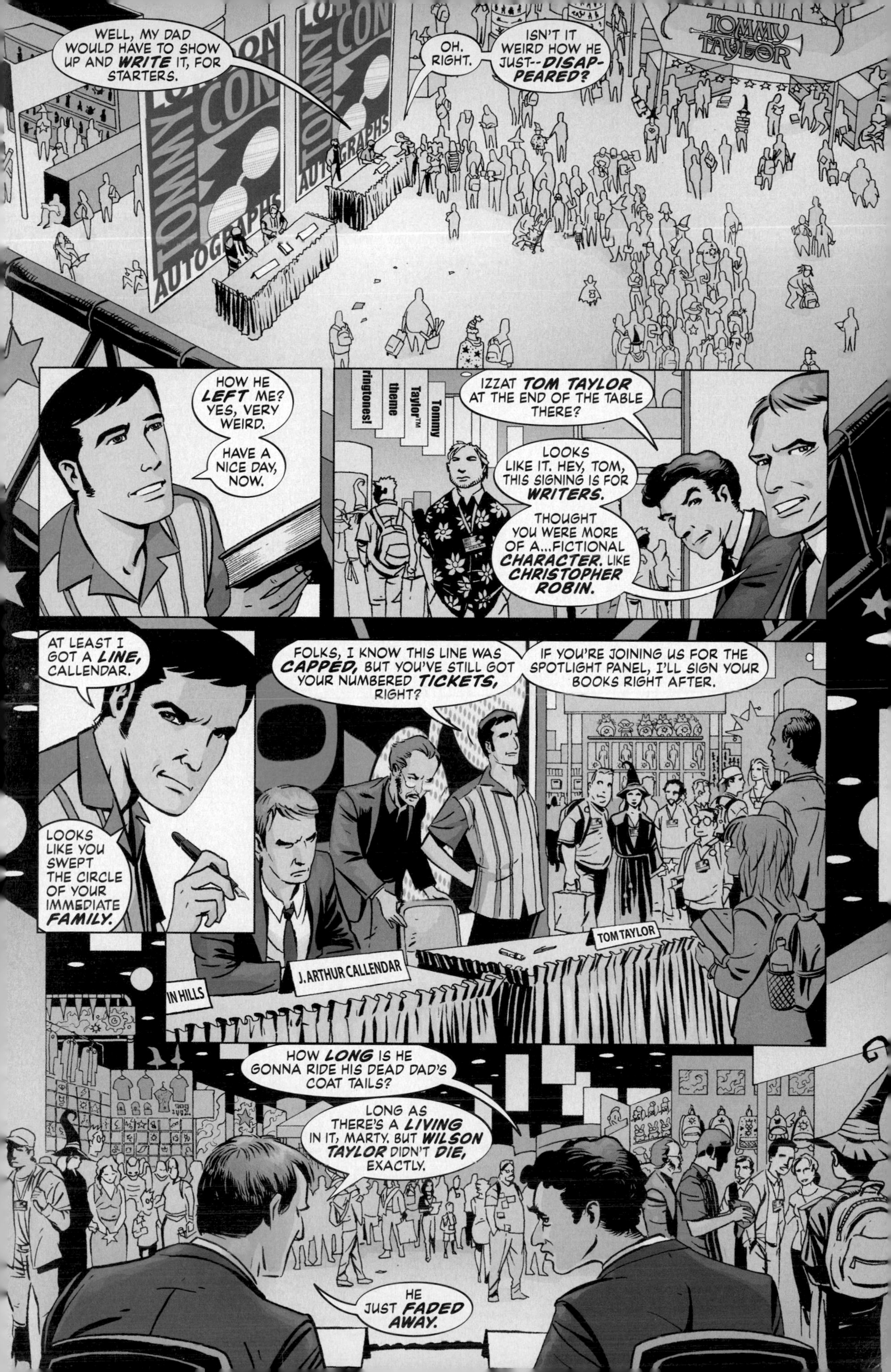

TOMMY TAYLOR
AUTOGRAPHS
WELL, MY DAD WOULD HAVE TO SHOW UP AND WRITE IT, FOR STARTERS.
OH. RIGHT.
ISN'T IT WEIRD HOW HE JUST--DISAPPEARED?
HOW HE LEFT ME? YES, VERY WEIRD.
HAVE A NICE DAY, NOW.
Tommy Taylor™ theme ringtones!
IZZAT TOM TAYLOR AT THE END OF THE TABLE THERE?
LOOKS LIKE IT. HEY, TOM, THIS SIGNING IS FOR WRITERS.
THOUGHT YOU WERE MORE OF A...FICTIONAL CHARACTER. LIKE CHRISTOPHER ROBIN.
AT LEAST I GOT A LINE, CALLENDAR.
LOOKS LIKE YOU SWEPT THE CIRCLE OF YOUR IMMEDIATE FAMILY.
FOLKS, I KNOW THIS LINE WAS CAPPED, BUT YOU'VE STILL GOT YOUR NUMBERED TICKETS, RIGHT?
IF YOU'RE JOINING US FOR THE SPOTLIGHT PANEL, I'LL SIGN YOUR BOOKS RIGHT AFTER.
J. ARTHUR CALLENDAR
TOM TAYLOR
HOW LONG IS HE GONNA RIDE HIS DEAD DAD'S COAT TAILS?
LONG AS THERE'S A LIVING IN IT, MARTY. BUT WILSON TAYLOR DIDN'T DIE, EXACTLY.
HE JUST FADED AWAY.

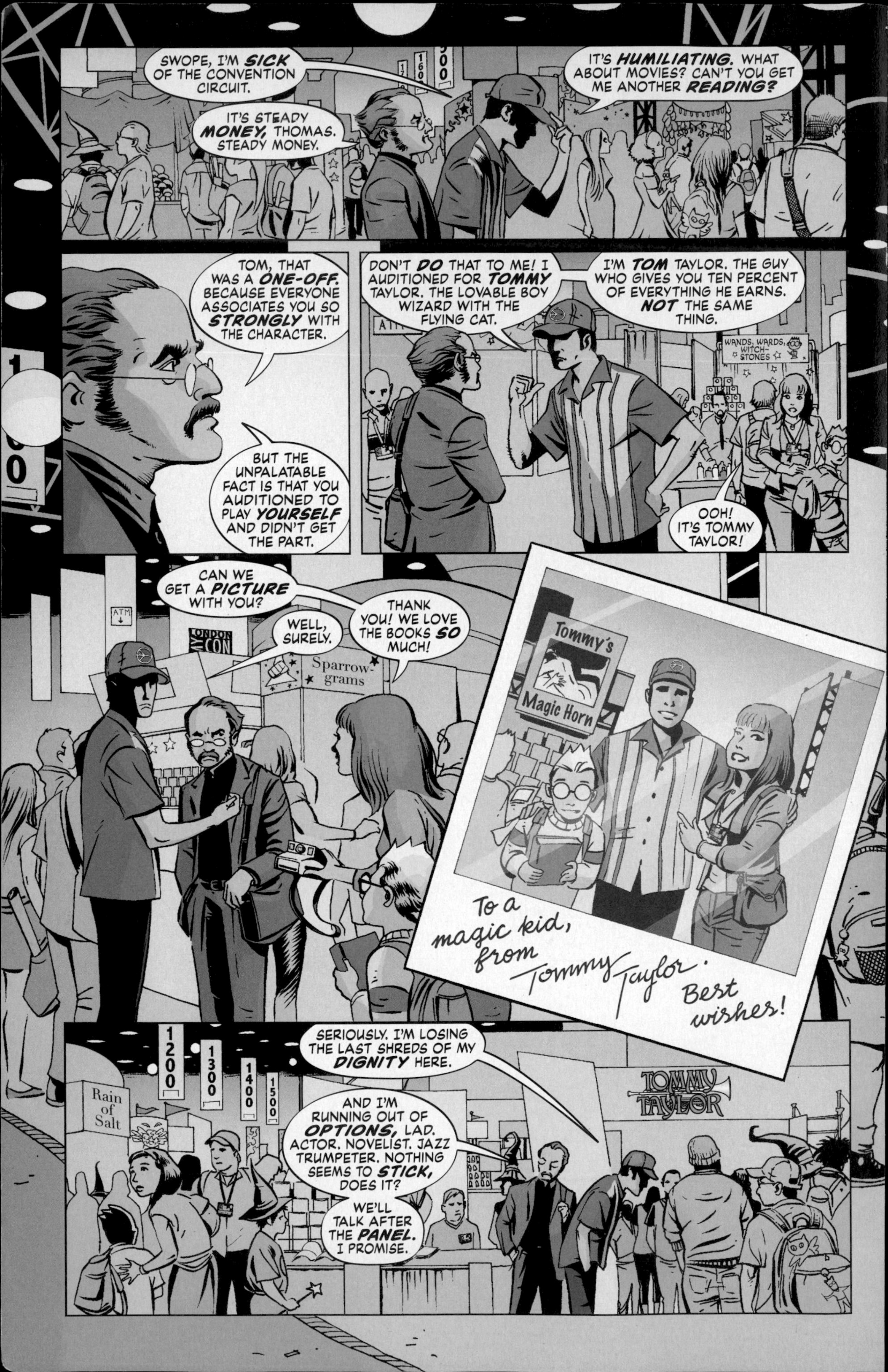
SWOPE, I'M SICK OF THE CONVENTION CIRCUIT.
IT'S HUMILIATING. WHAT ABOUT MOVIES? CAN'T YOU GET ME ANOTHER READING?
IT'S STEADY MONEY, THOMAS. STEADY MONEY.
TOM, THAT WAS A ONE-OFF. BECAUSE EVERYONE ASSOCIATES YOU SO STRONGLY WITH THE CHARACTER.
BUT THE UNPALATABLE FACT IS THAT YOU AUDITIONED TO PLAY YOURSELF AND DIDN'T GET THE PART.
DON'T DO THAT TO ME! I AUDITIONED FOR TOMMY TAYLOR. THE LOVABLE BOY WIZARD WITH THE FLYING CAT.
I'M TOM TAYLOR. THE GUY WHO GIVES YOU TEN PERCENT OF EVERYTHING HE EARNS. NOT THE SAME THING.
WANDS, WARDS, WITCH-STONES
OOH! IT'S TOMMY TAYLOR!
CAN WE GET A PICTURE WITH YOU?
WELL, SURELY.
THANK YOU! WE LOVE THE BOOKS SO MUCH!
ATM
LONDON CON
Sparrow-grams
Tommy's Magic Horn
To a magic kid, from Tommy Taylor. Best wishes!
SERIOUSLY. I'M LOSING THE LAST SHREDS OF MY DIGNITY HERE.
AND I'M RUNNING OUT OF OPTIONS, LAD. ACTOR. NOVELIST. JAZZ TRUMPETER. NOTHING SEEMS TO STICK, DOES IT?
WE'LL TALK AFTER THE PANEL. I PROMISE.
1200
1300
1400
1500
Rain of Salt
TOMMY TAYLOR

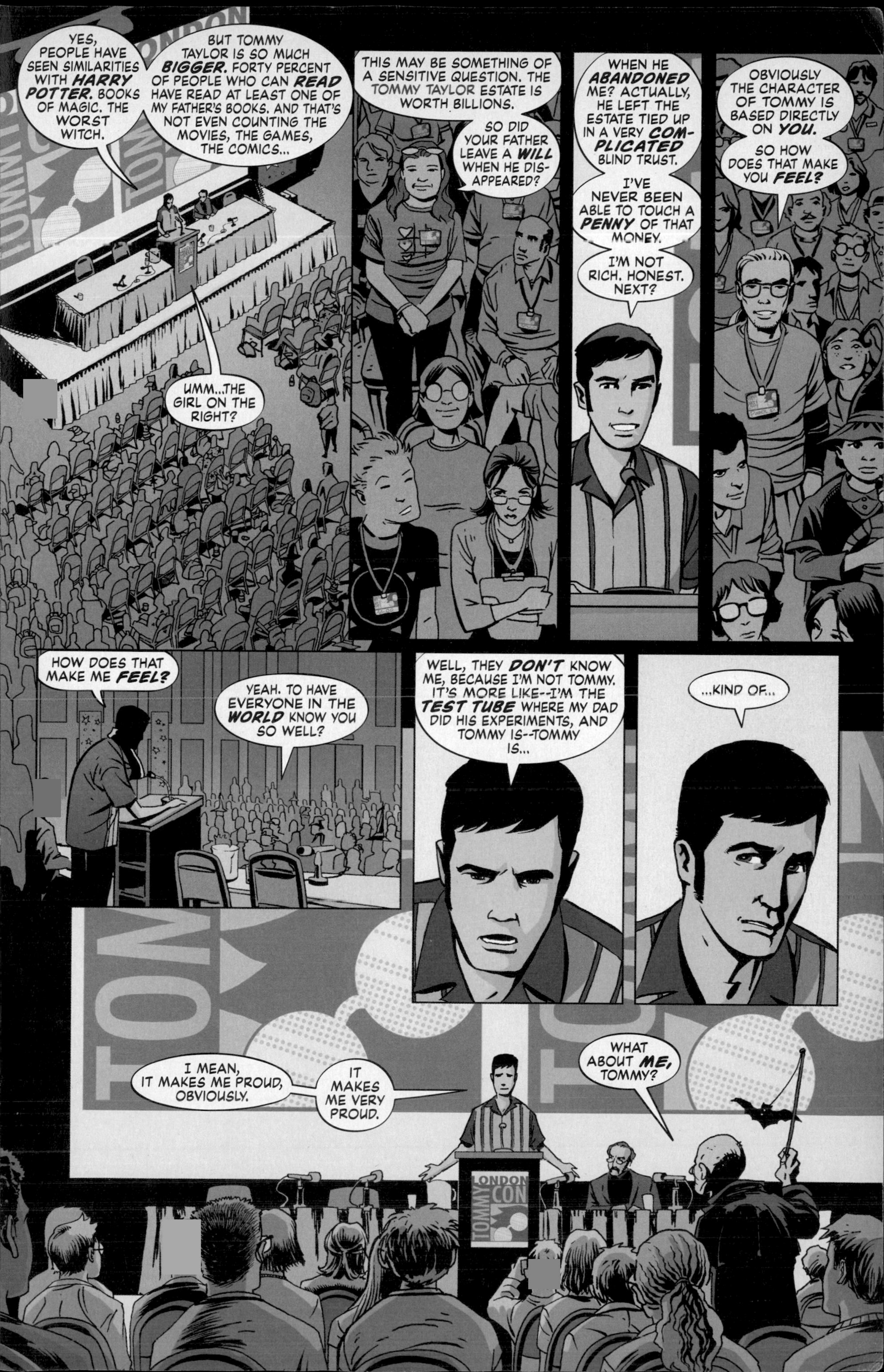
YES, PEOPLE HAVE SEEN SIMILARITIES WITH HARRY POTTER. BOOKS OF MAGIC. THE WORST WITCH.
BUT TOMMY TAYLOR IS SO MUCH BIGGER. FORTY PERCENT OF PEOPLE WHO CAN READ HAVE READ AT LEAST ONE OF MY FATHER'S BOOKS. AND THAT'S NOT EVEN COUNTING THE MOVIES, THE GAMES, THE COMICS...
UMM...THE GIRL ON THE RIGHT?
THIS MAY BE SOMETHING OF A SENSITIVE QUESTION. THE TOMMY TAYLOR ESTATE IS WORTH BILLIONS.
SO DID YOUR FATHER LEAVE A WILL WHEN HE DISAPPEARED?
WHEN HE ABANDONED ME? ACTUALLY, HE LEFT THE ESTATE TIED UP IN A VERY COMPLICATED BLIND TRUST.
I'VE NEVER BEEN ABLE TO TOUCH A PENNY OF THAT MONEY.
I'M NOT RICH. HONEST. NEXT?
OBVIOUSLY THE CHARACTER OF TOMMY IS BASED DIRECTLY ON YOU.
SO HOW DOES THAT MAKE YOU FEEL?
HOW DOES THAT MAKE ME FEEL?
YEAH. TO HAVE EVERYONE IN THE WORLD KNOW YOU SO WELL?
WELL, THEY DON'T KNOW ME, BECAUSE I'M NOT TOMMY. IT'S MORE LIKE--I'M THE TEST TUBE WHERE MY DAD DID HIS EXPERIMENTS, AND TOMMY IS--TOMMY IS...
...KIND OF...
I MEAN, IT MAKES ME PROUD, OBVIOUSLY.
IT MAKES ME VERY PROUD.
WHAT ABOUT ME, TOMMY?
LONDON TOMMY CON

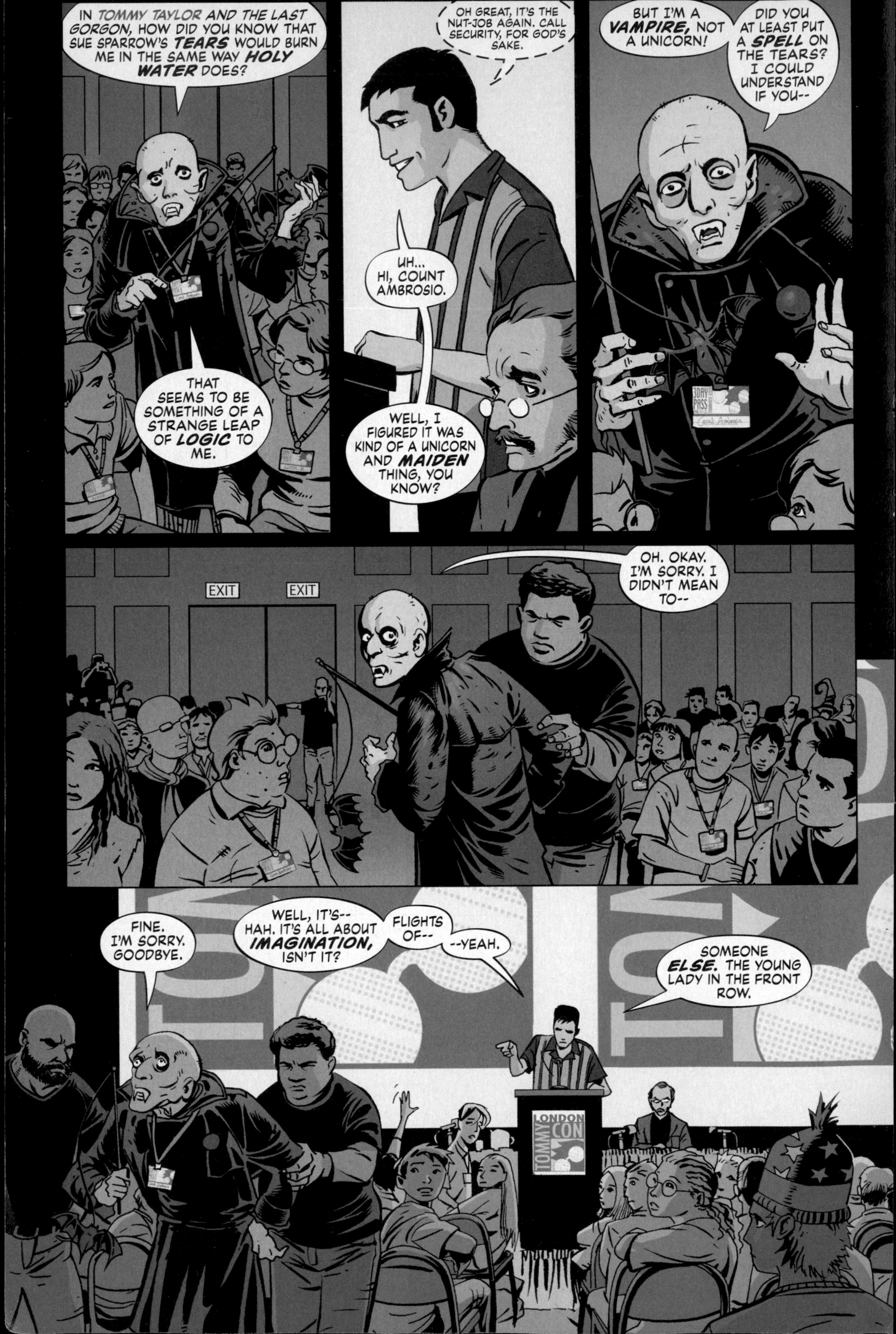
IN TOMMY TAYLOR AND THE LAST GORGON, HOW DID YOU KNOW THAT SUE SPARROW'S TEARS WOULD BURN ME IN THE SAME WAY HOLY WATER DOES?
THAT SEEMS TO BE SOMETHING OF A STRANGE LEAP OF LOGIC TO ME.
OH GREAT, IT'S THE NUT-JOB AGAIN. CALL SECURITY, FOR GOD'S SAKE.
UH... HI, COUNT AMBROSIO.
WELL, I FIGURED IT WAS KIND OF A UNICORN AND MAIDEN THING, YOU KNOW?
BUT I'M A VAMPIRE, NOT A UNICORN!
DID YOU AT LEAST PUT A SPELL ON THE TEARS? I COULD UNDERSTAND IF YOU--
3DAY PASS
EXIT
EXIT
OH. OKAY. I'M SORRY. I DIDN'T MEAN TO--
FINE. I'M SORRY. GOODBYE.
WELL, IT'S-- HAH. IT'S ALL ABOUT IMAGINATION, ISN'T IT?
FLIGHTS OF--
--YEAH.
SOMEONE ELSE. THE YOUNG LADY IN THE FRONT ROW.
LONDON TOMMY CON

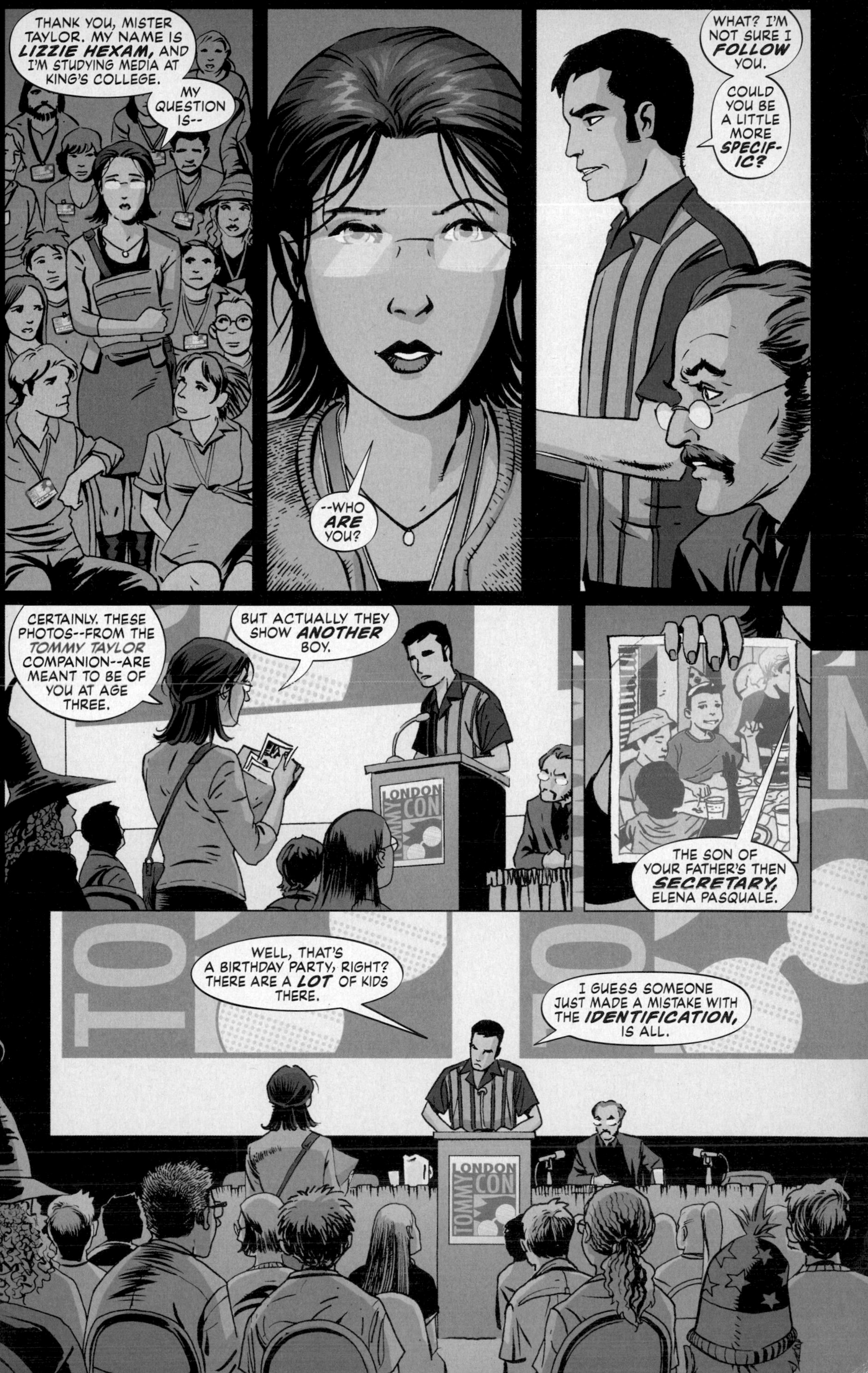
THANK YOU, MISTER TAYLOR. MY NAME IS LIZZIE HEXAM, AND I'M STUDYING MEDIA AT KING'S COLLEGE.
MY QUESTION IS--
--WHO ARE YOU?
WHAT? I'M NOT SURE I FOLLOW YOU.
COULD YOU BE A LITTLE MORE SPECIFIC?
CERTAINLY. THESE PHOTOS--FROM THE TOMMY TAYLOR COMPANION--ARE MEANT TO BE OF YOU AT AGE THREE.
BUT ACTUALLY THEY SHOW ANOTHER BOY.
LONDON TOMMY CON
THE SON OF YOUR FATHER'S THEN SECRETARY, ELENA PASQUALE.
WELL, THAT'S A BIRTHDAY PARTY, RIGHT? THERE ARE A LOT OF KIDS THERE.
I GUESS SOMEONE JUST MADE A MISTAKE WITH THE IDENTIFICATION, IS ALL.
LONDON TOMMY CON

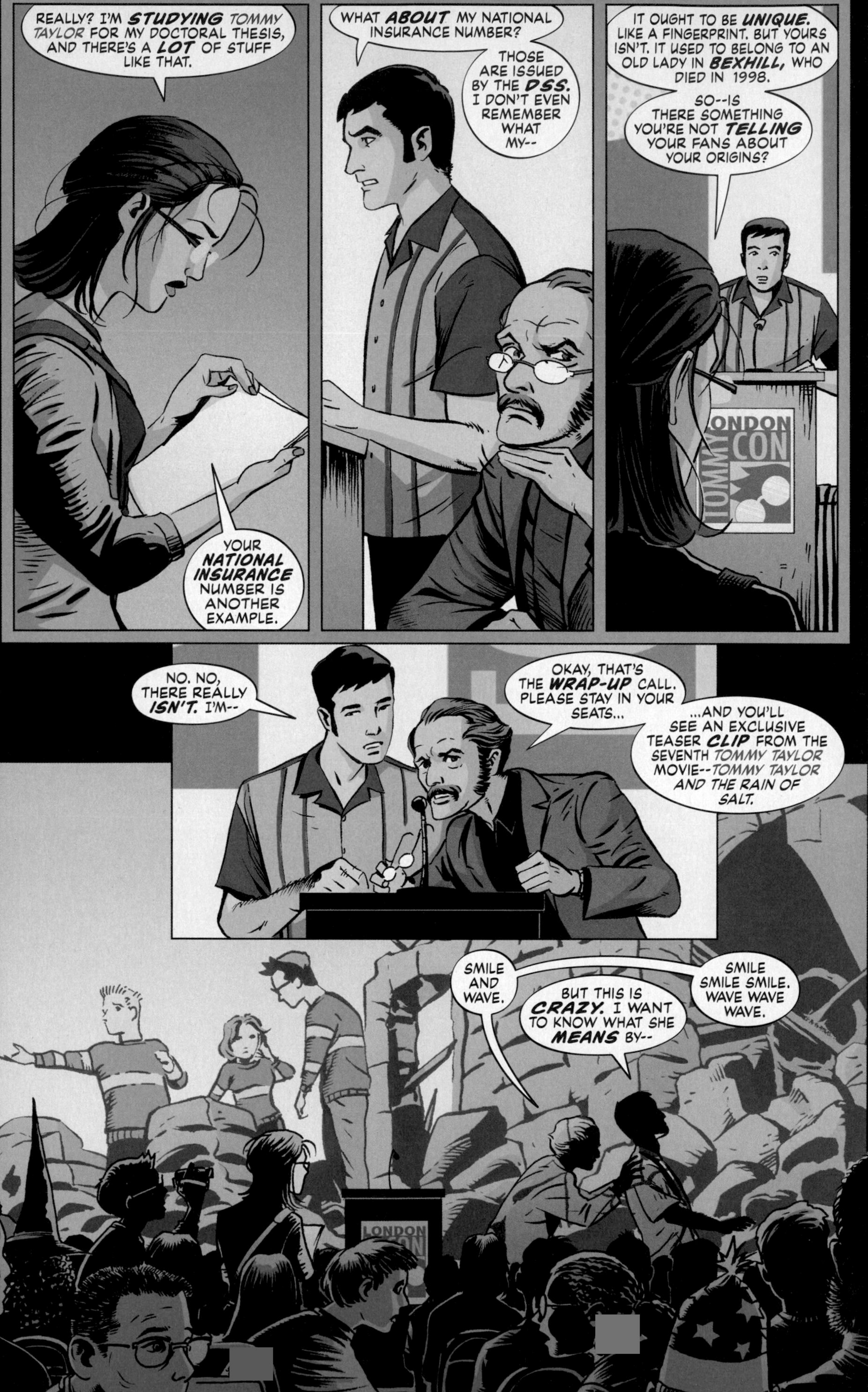
REALLY? I'M STUDYING TOMMY TAYLOR FOR MY DOCTORAL THESIS, AND THERE'S A LOT OF STUFF LIKE THAT.
YOUR NATIONAL INSURANCE NUMBER IS ANOTHER EXAMPLE.
WHAT ABOUT MY NATIONAL INSURANCE NUMBER?
THOSE ARE ISSUED BY THE DSS. I DON'T EVEN REMEMBER WHAT MY--
IT OUGHT TO BE UNIQUE. LIKE A FINGERPRINT. BUT YOURS ISN'T. IT USED TO BELONG TO AN OLD LADY IN BEXHILL, WHO DIED IN 1998.
SO--IS THERE SOMETHING YOU'RE NOT TELLING YOUR FANS ABOUT YOUR ORIGINS?
LONDON TOMMY CON
NO. NO, THERE REALLY ISN'T. I'M--
OKAY, THAT'S THE WRAP-UP CALL. PLEASE STAY IN YOUR SEATS...
...AND YOU'LL SEE AN EXCLUSIVE TEASER CLIP FROM THE SEVENTH TOMMY TAYLOR MOVIE--TOMMY TAYLOR AND THE RAIN OF SALT.
SMILE AND WAVE.
SMILE SMILE SMILE. WAVE WAVE WAVE.
BUT THIS IS CRAZY. I WANT TO KNOW WHAT SHE MEANS BY--
LONDON

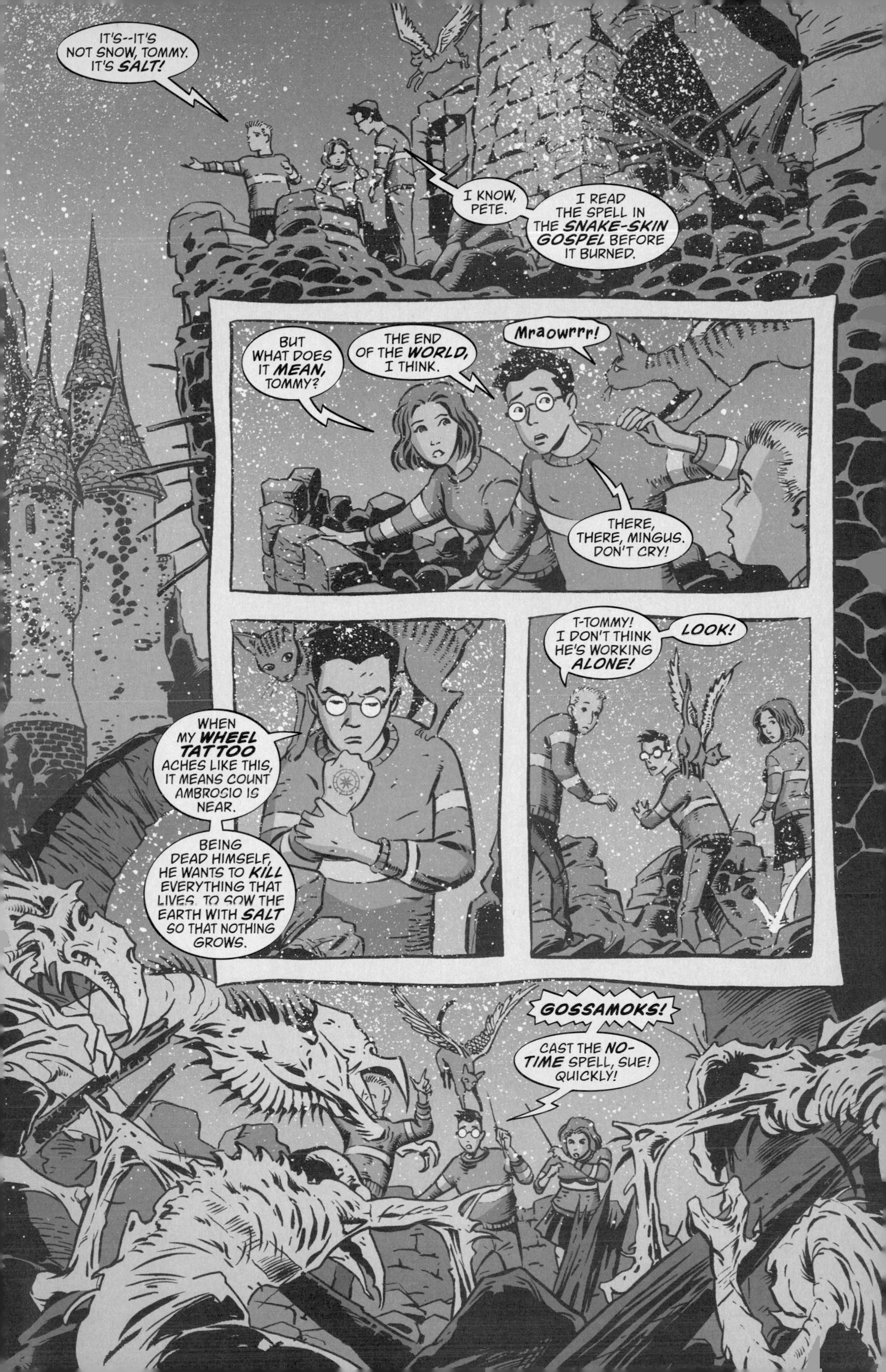
IT'S--IT'S NOT SNOW, TOMMY. IT'S SALT!
I KNOW, PETE.
I READ THE SPELL IN THE SNAKE-SKIN GOSPEL BEFORE IT BURNED.
BUT WHAT DOES IT MEAN, TOMMY?
THE END OF THE WORLD, I THINK.
Mraowrrr!
THERE, THERE, MINGUS. DON'T CRY!
WHEN MY WHEEL TATTOO ACHES LIKE THIS, IT MEANS COUNT AMBROSIO IS NEAR.
BEING DEAD HIMSELF, HE WANTS TO KILL EVERYTHING THAT LIVES. TO SOW THE EARTH WITH SALT SO THAT NOTHING GROWS.
T-TOMMY! I DON'T THINK HE'S WORKING ALONE!
LOOK!
GOSSAMOKS!
CAST THE NO-TIME SPELL, SUE! QUICKLY!

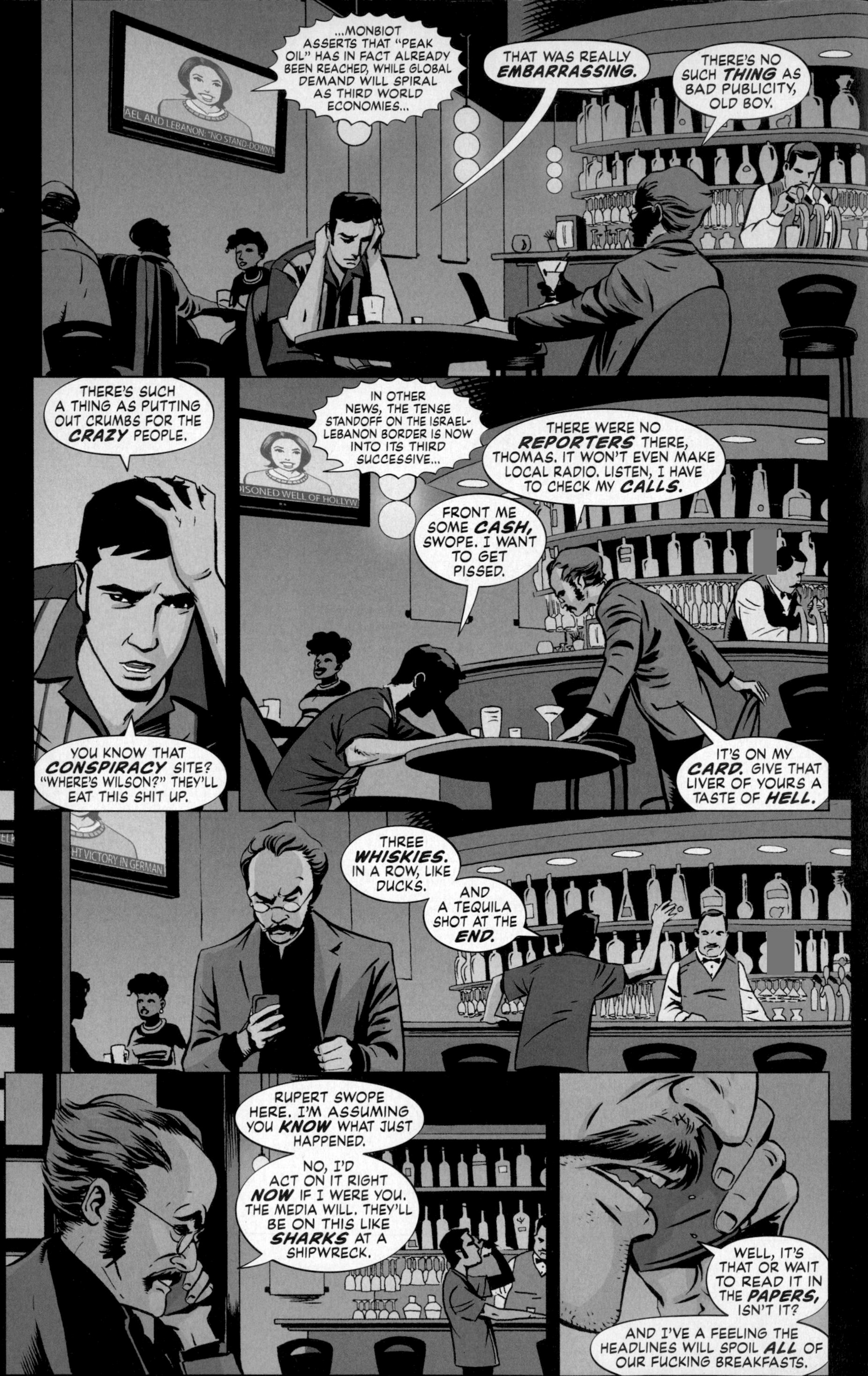
...MONBIOT ASSERTS THAT "PEAK OIL" HAS IN FACT ALREADY BEEN REACHED, WHILE GLOBAL DEMAND WILL SPIRAL AS THIRD WORLD ECONOMIES...
AEL AND LEBANON: "NO STAND-DOWN
THAT WAS REALLY EMBARRASSING.
THERE'S NO SUCH THING AS BAD PUBLICITY, OLD BOY.
THERE'S SUCH A THING AS PUTTING OUT CRUMBS FOR THE CRAZY PEOPLE.
YOU KNOW THAT CONSPIRACY SITE? "WHERE'S WILSON?" THEY'LL EAT THIS SHIT UP.
IN OTHER NEWS, THE TENSE STANDOFF ON THE ISRAEL-LEBANON BORDER IS NOW INTO ITS THIRD SUCCESSIVE...
OISONED WELL OF HOLLYW
THERE WERE NO REPORTERS THERE, THOMAS. IT WON'T EVEN MAKE LOCAL RADIO. LISTEN, I HAVE TO CHECK MY CALLS.
FRONT ME SOME CASH, SWOPE. I WANT TO GET PISSED.
IT'S ON MY CARD. GIVE THAT LIVER OF YOURS A TASTE OF HELL.
HT VICTORY IN GERMAN
THREE WHISKIES. IN A ROW, LIKE DUCKS.
AND A TEQUILA SHOT AT THE END.
RUPERT SWOPE HERE. I'M ASSUMING YOU KNOW WHAT JUST HAPPENED.
NO, I'D ACT ON IT RIGHT NOW IF I WERE YOU. THE MEDIA WILL. THEY'LL BE ON THIS LIKE SHARKS AT A SHIPWRECK.
WELL, IT'S THAT OR WAIT TO READ IT IN THE PAPERS, ISN'T IT?
AND I'VE A FEELING THE HEADLINES WILL SPOIL ALL OF OUR FUCKING BREAKFASTS.

WILL THE REAL TOMMY TAYLOR™ PLEASE RAISE HIS WAND?

Fantasy author's son "a fake, a liar and a con man."

By PETRA CARMICHAELS

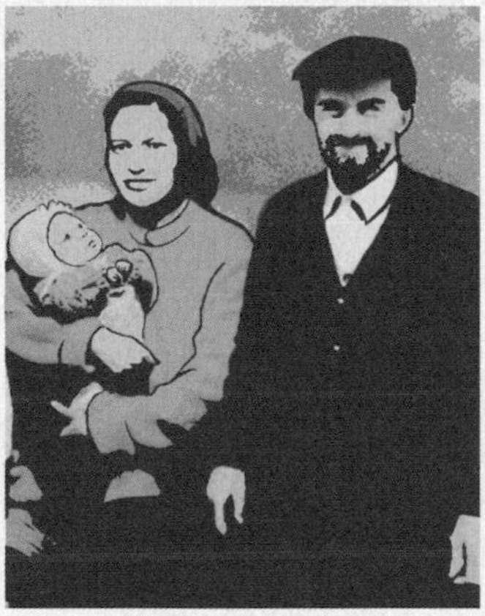

Nikhal and Irina Drasic
Tom Taylor's real parents?

In front of a packed audience at London's thirtieth annual fantasy convention yesterday, Tom "Little Tommy" Taylor was accused of being an identity thief posing as Wilson Taylor's son. Tom stood spellbound like a character in one of his father's books as an unnamed member of the audience revealed that photos and other documents from his childhood had been forged.

Those initial revelations brought an avalanche of further claims, with public officials and trustees of Wilson Taylor's estate alleging that the best-selling author – missing now for more than a decade – had never even had a son in the first place.

"It's fascinating how little documentation there is on Tom Taylor," said Magnus Bethell, the CEO of Redgate Films, who produce the big screen adaptations of the beloved novels. "Wilson always had this child in tow, and he always introduced him as his son. But I never met anyone who knew who his mother was or where or when he'd been born."

Meanwhile, a Bosnian refugee family living in Walsall have come forward to claim that "Tom Taylor" is their own son, Thomas Drasic. The Drasics' claim is that they "loaned" their son to Wilson Taylor via an intermediary so that he could be used as Wilson's own child in photo shoots, but that the author later reneged on the agreement and refused to allow the family visiting rights.

"Why would somebody pretend to be something they're not?" asked Sue Morganstern, an old friend of the Taylor family, when she was approached for comment yesterday. "Obviously, when there's money involved, it's easy to try to stake a claim. But Tommy Taylor belongs to the world. I feel terribly sad this morning: I'd even say bereaved. It's as though something wonderful has been stolen from me. From all of us."

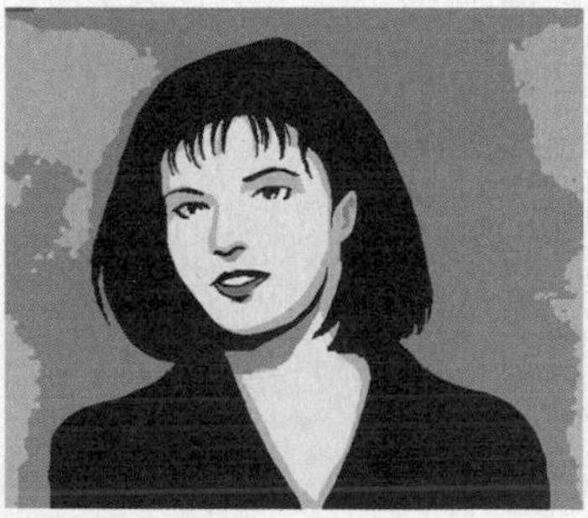

Sue Morganstern

Tom Taylor was unavailable for comment today. His agent, Rupert Swope said his client was "exhausted and overwhelmed" after a busy day at the convention. But already the intensity of the public response is astonishing the authorities, who fear for Taylor's safety if his complicity in a hoax relating to the much-loved books is proved.

day's Stories

nmy Taylor™ and the
n of Salt theatrical
ller

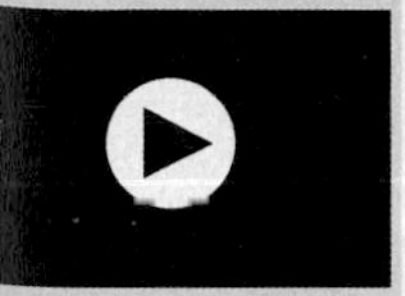

-res) - (low-res)

ere's Wilson? Tommy
ylor™ and the
spiracy theorists

ir top ten Tommy
ylor™ moments

ntoro™ Craze sweeps
an

ecificHut Books
eases Tommy Taylor™
lecters Wheel

vie Props up for
rity Auction

hard Pinder
rds Culled in Cow-
uth Outbreak

phen Leeson
igious Terrorism:
tasy Book Burnings

Celaeno
y Tall Man Discovers
th Chakra

n Palmer
ard Gizzard:
kbook Review

bara G
adly Vestments: A
tory of Inept Magical
ture

Ever
me-Traveling Crime
elist was Jack the
per" Claims Painter

n Strange
History and Practice
English Magic

cent Fiore
ery Voted off Dancing
h the Music of Time

Huxes
ctical Instructions for
a-Store Wizards

bsite of the Day
Taylor™verse Wiki

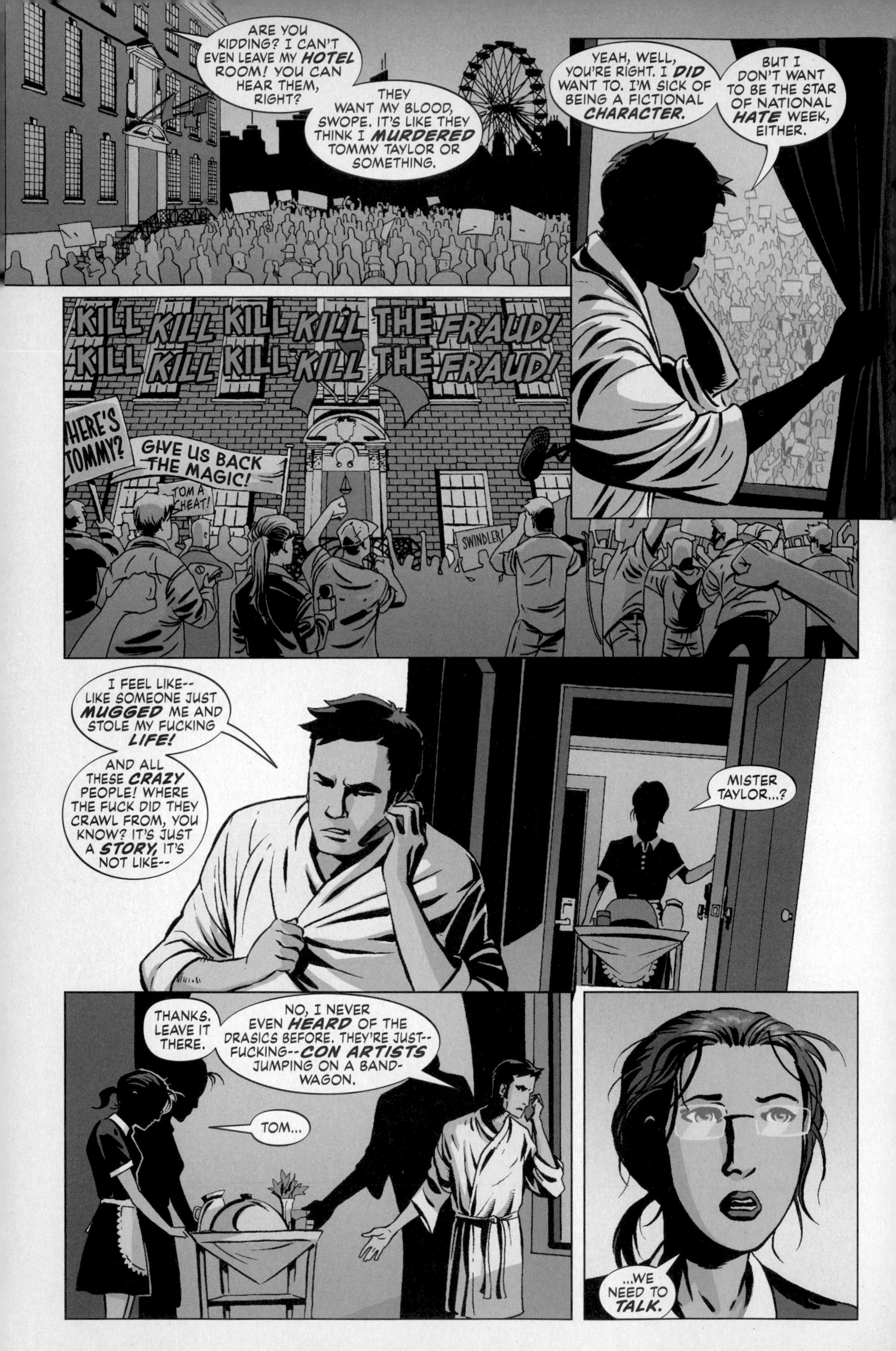
ARE YOU KIDDING? I CAN'T EVEN LEAVE MY HOTEL ROOM! YOU CAN HEAR THEM, RIGHT?
THEY WANT MY BLOOD, SWOPE. IT'S LIKE THEY THINK I MURDERED TOMMY TAYLOR OR SOMETHING.
YEAH, WELL, YOU'RE RIGHT. I DID WANT TO. I'M SICK OF BEING A FICTIONAL CHARACTER.
BUT I DON'T WANT TO BE THE STAR OF NATIONAL HATE WEEK, EITHER.
KILL KILL KILL KILL THE FRAUD!
KILL KILL KILL KILL THE FRAUD!
WHERE'S TOMMY?
GIVE US BACK THE MAGIC!
TOM A CHEAT!
SWINDLER!
I FEEL LIKE-- LIKE SOMEONE JUST MUGGED ME AND STOLE MY FUCKING LIFE!
AND ALL THESE CRAZY PEOPLE! WHERE THE FUCK DID THEY CRAWL FROM, YOU KNOW? IT'S JUST A STORY, IT'S NOT LIKE--
MISTER TAYLOR...?
THANKS. LEAVE IT THERE.
NO, I NEVER EVEN HEARD OF THE DRASICS BEFORE. THEY'RE JUST-- FUCKING--CON ARTISTS JUMPING ON A BAND-WAGON.
TOM...
...WE NEED TO TALK.

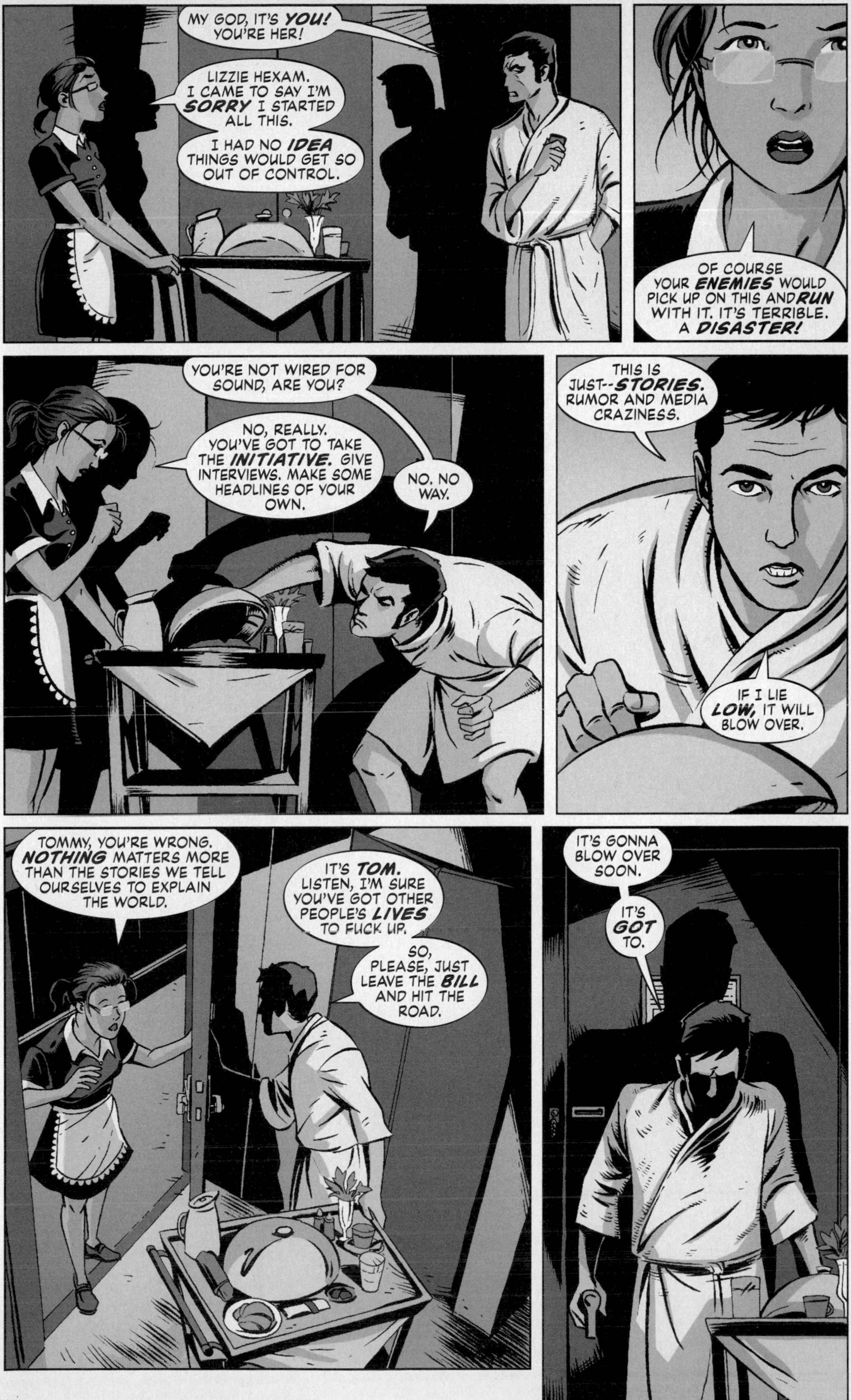

MY GOD, IT'S **YOU!** YOU'RE HER!
LIZZIE HEXAM. I CAME TO SAY I'M **SORRY** I STARTED ALL THIS.
I HAD NO **IDEA** THINGS WOULD GET SO OUT OF CONTROL.
OF COURSE YOUR **ENEMIES** WOULD PICK UP ON THIS AND **RUN** WITH IT. IT'S TERRIBLE. A **DISASTER!**
YOU'RE NOT WIRED FOR SOUND, ARE YOU?
NO, REALLY. YOU'VE GOT TO TAKE THE **INITIATIVE.** GIVE INTERVIEWS. MAKE SOME HEADLINES OF YOUR OWN.
NO. NO WAY.
THIS IS JUST--**STORIES.** RUMOR AND MEDIA CRAZINESS.
IF I LIE **LOW,** IT WILL BLOW OVER.
TOMMY, YOU'RE WRONG. **NOTHING** MATTERS MORE THAN THE STORIES WE TELL OURSELVES TO EXPLAIN THE WORLD.
IT'S **TOM.** LISTEN, I'M SURE YOU'VE GOT OTHER PEOPLE'S **LIVES** TO FUCK UP.
SO, PLEASE, JUST LEAVE THE **BILL** AND HIT THE ROAD.
IT'S GONNA BLOW OVER SOON.
IT'S **GOT** TO.

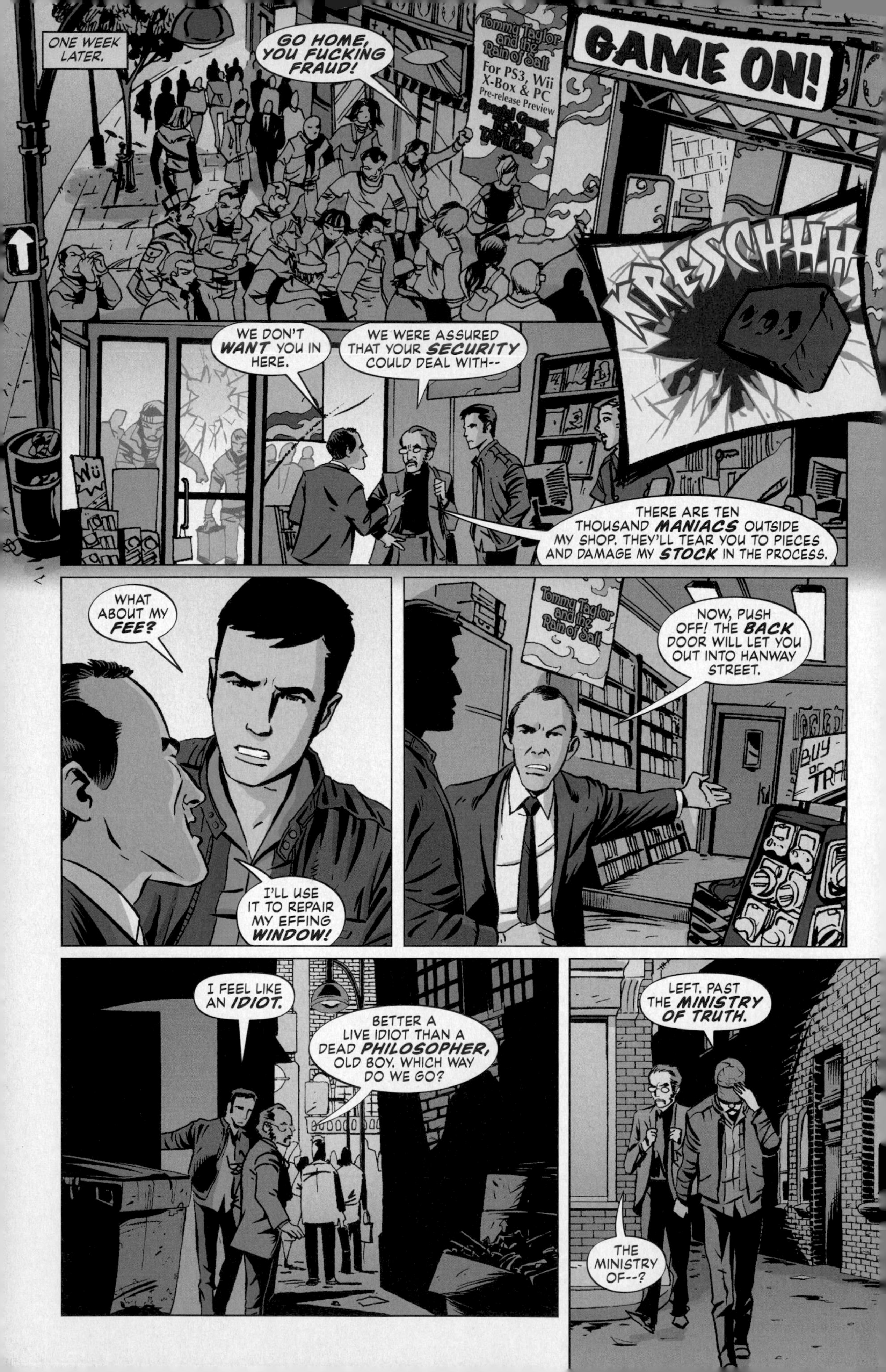
ONE WEEK LATER.
GO HOME, YOU FUCKING FRAUD!
Tommy Taylor and the Rain of Salt
For PS3, Wii X-Box & PC
Pre-release Preview
GAME ON!
KRESCHHH
WE DON'T WANT YOU IN HERE.
WE WERE ASSURED THAT YOUR SECURITY COULD DEAL WITH--
THERE ARE TEN THOUSAND MANIACS OUTSIDE MY SHOP. THEY'LL TEAR YOU TO PIECES AND DAMAGE MY STOCK IN THE PROCESS.
WHAT ABOUT MY FEE?
I'LL USE IT TO REPAIR MY EFFING WINDOW!
Tommy Taylor and the Rain of Salt
NOW, PUSH OFF! THE BACK DOOR WILL LET YOU OUT INTO HANWAY STREET.
I FEEL LIKE AN IDIOT.
BETTER A LIVE IDIOT THAN A DEAD PHILOSOPHER, OLD BOY. WHICH WAY DO WE GO?
LEFT. PAST THE MINISTRY OF TRUTH.
THE MINISTRY OF--?

OH. YOU'RE ABOUT TO DO THAT *THING* AGAIN, AREN'T YOU?

I WISH YOU WOULDN'T

GEORGE ORWELL *WORKED* AT THE SENATE HOUSE LIBRARY FOR YEARS. AND IF YOU READ THE DESCRIPTION IN 1984, IT'S OBVIOUS HE MEANT *THIS* PLACE.

YOU CAN ACTUALLY SEE *ROOM 101*, IF YOU ASK. IT NEVER REALLY HAD A NUMBER, THOUGH. IT'S JUST AN *OFFICE*.

REALLY? YOU AMAZE ME. ENDLESSLY.

OVER THERE IS *CORAM'S FIELDS*. THE FOUNDLING HOSPITAL IN DICKENS' *NO THOROUGHFARE* WAS THERE.

AND IT'S THE MAIN *SETTING* FOR JAMILA GAVIN'S *CORAM BOY.*

I'M SURE IT IS. ≠HEF!≠

THIS IS MY DAD'S *LEGACY* TO ME. LITERARY GEOGRAPHY! HE USED TO DRILL ME ON THIS STUFF LIKE IT REALLY *MATTERED*.

THE ONLY TIME HE EVER *SMILED* AT ME WAS WHEN I PASSED ONE OF HIS STUPID *TRIVIA* QUIZZES.

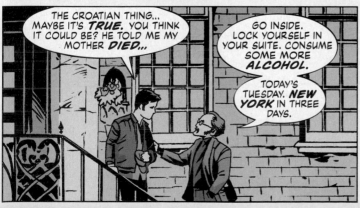

THE CROATIAN THING... MAYBE IT'S *TRUE*. YOU THINK IT COULD BE? HE TOLD ME MY MOTHER *DIED*...

GO INSIDE. LOCK YOURSELF IN YOUR SUITE. CONSUME SOME MORE *ALCOHOL*.

TODAY'S TUESDAY. *NEW YORK* IN THREE DAYS.

THEY *LOVE* YOU IN NEW YORK, TOM. TRUST ME.

IT'LL BE JUST THE PICK-ME-UP YOU *NEED*.

DNN TOMMY IN TROUBLE?

IDDLE EAST "TWELVE HOURS FROM WAR"   DNN   N

AMID SCENES OF PUBLIC OUTRAGE AND NEAR-HYSTERIA, TOM TAYLOR, THE REAL-LIFE *MODEL* FOR THE BELOVED FICTIONAL CREATION TOMMY TAYLOR, ANNOUNCED THE *CANCELLATION* OF HIS NEW YORK SIGNING TOUR TODAY--

DNN MOST FAMOUS BOY ON EARTH
TO BE QUESTIONED?

ELIST DIES IN FIRE TRAGEDY   DNN   SEVEN SHARE

--AS SWISS POLICE REOPEN THEIR INVESTIGATION INTO THE ULTIMATE FATE OF HIS *FATHER.*

DNN TOMMY TAYLOR
AND THE GOLDEN SCAM!

RECORD LOTTERY PAYOUT   DNN   HIMMELKRIEG:

DETRACTORS ARE CLAIMING THAT TOM WAS BORN *THOMAS DRASIC,* OF SERBIAN PARENTAGE. AND THAT HE WAS *USED* BY FAMED AUTHOR WILSON TAYLOR TO GIVE THE TOMMY TAYLOR NOVELS AN EARLY *MARKETING* BOOST.

DNN MISSING AUTHOR THE QUESTIONS REMAIN

RIGHT VICTORY IN GERMAN ELECTION   DNN   MO

THE LITERARY GIANT BEGAN WRITING HIS FANTASY MASTERPIECE LATE IN LIFE, AND NEVER SEEMED COMFORTABLE WITH THE FAME IT BROUGHT HIM.

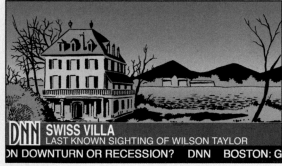

DNN SWISS VILLA
LAST KNOWN SIGHTING OF WILSON TAYLOR

N DOWNTURN OR RECESSION?   DNN   BOSTON: G

ESCAPING PUBLIC LIFE, HE SETTLED HERE, IN SWITZERLAND'S VILLA DIODATI, INTO A RECLUSIVE LIFESTYLE WHICH EARNED HIM COMPARISONS WITH HOWARD HUGHES AND INGMAR BERGMAN.

DNN TOM TAYLOR BACKLASH
THE MAN THEY LOVE TO HATE

Y WEDDING FIRE-BOMBED   DNN   SENATE DEBATES

NOW SON TOM TAYLOR IS AVOIDING THE LIMELIGHT, TOO, AS OUTRAGED FANS ARE *BURNING* HIM IN EFFIGY ACROSS THE GLOBE, AND SUGGESTIONS ARE SURFACING THAT TOM'S *WHEREABOUTS* ON THE NIGHT OF WILSON TAYLOR'S DISAPPEARANCE MAY BE IN QUESTION.

DNN

O² CUTS   DNN   MADONNA TO WRITE OPERA LIBRE

IT SEEMS YOU *CAN* FOOL ALL THE PEOPLE, GARY-- BUT ONLY FOR *SOME* OF THE TIME.

THANK YOU, SARAH.

DNN

RECOVERY HALTED   DNN   DOUBLE BOMBING IN IN

BUT SOME PEOPLE ARE REACTING TO THIS SITUATION VERY *DIFFERENTLY.*

CAROL? ARE YOU WITH US?

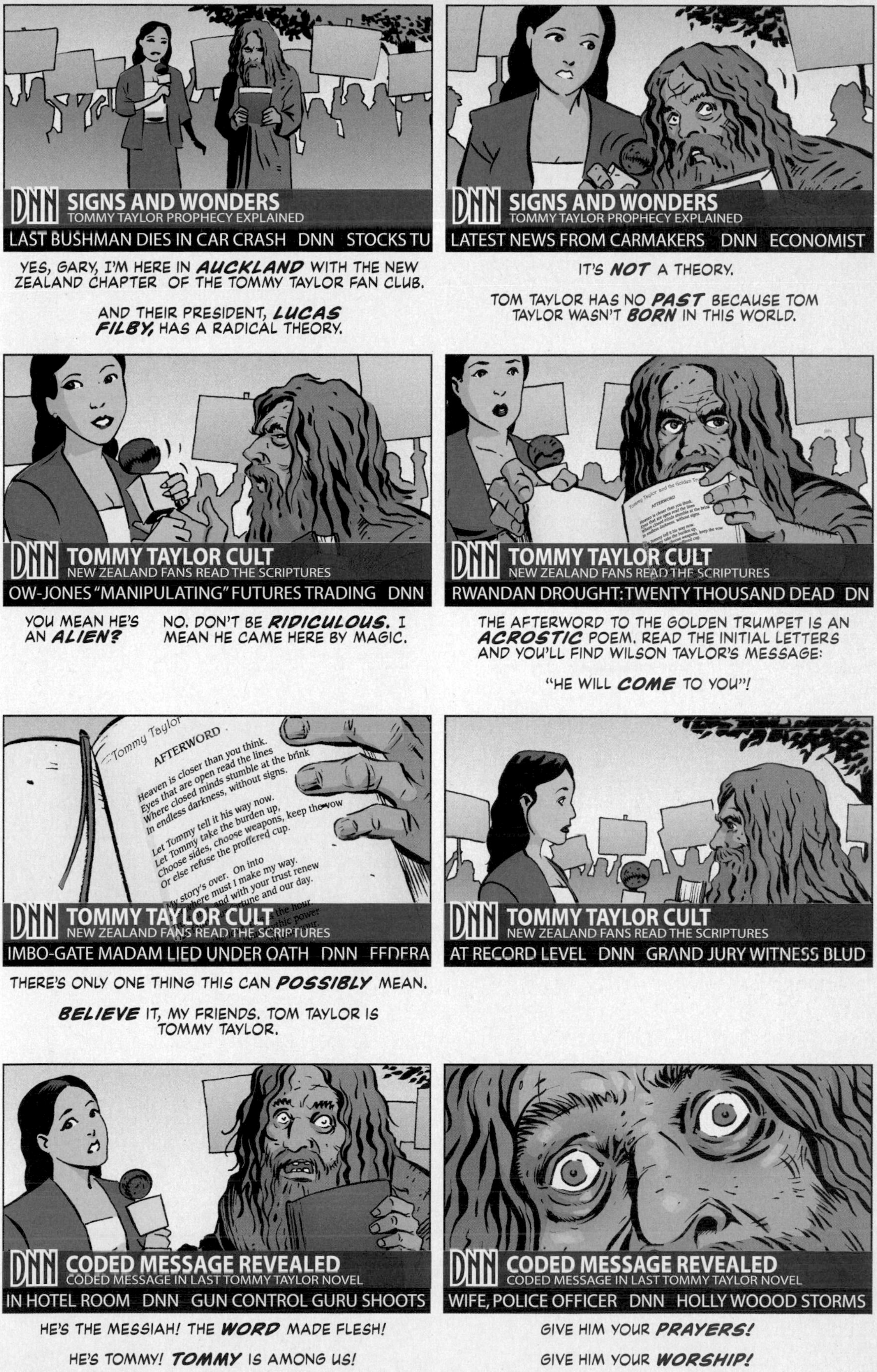
DNN SIGNS AND WONDERS
TOMMY TAYLOR PROPHECY EXPLAINED
LAST BUSHMAN DIES IN CAR CRASH DNN STOCKS TU
YES, GARY, I'M HERE IN AUCKLAND WITH THE NEW ZEALAND CHAPTER OF THE TOMMY TAYLOR FAN CLUB.
AND THEIR PRESIDENT, LUCAS FILBY, HAS A RADICAL THEORY.
DNN SIGNS AND WONDERS
TOMMY TAYLOR PROPHECY EXPLAINED
LATEST NEWS FROM CARMAKERS DNN ECONOMIST
IT'S NOT A THEORY.
TOM TAYLOR HAS NO PAST BECAUSE TOM TAYLOR WASN'T BORN IN THIS WORLD.
DNN TOMMY TAYLOR CULT
NEW ZEALAND FANS READ THE SCRIPTURES
OW-JONES "MANIPULATING" FUTURES TRADING DNN
YOU MEAN HE'S AN ALIEN?
NO. DON'T BE RIDICULOUS. I MEAN HE CAME HERE BY MAGIC.
DNN TOMMY TAYLOR CULT
NEW ZEALAND FANS READ THE SCRIPTURES
RWANDAN DROUGHT: TWENTY THOUSAND DEAD DN
THE AFTERWORD TO THE GOLDEN TRUMPET IS AN ACROSTIC POEM. READ THE INITIAL LETTERS AND YOU'LL FIND WILSON TAYLOR'S MESSAGE:
"HE WILL COME TO YOU"!
Tommy Taylor
AFTERWORD
Heaven is closer than you think.
Eyes that are open read the lines
Where closed minds stumble at the brink
In endless darkness, without signs.
Let Tommy tell it his way now.
Let Tommy take the burden up,
Choose sides, choose weapons, keep the vow
Or else refuse the proffered cup.
My story's over. On into
where must I make my way.
and with your trust renew
fortune and our day.
DNN TOMMY TAYLOR CULT
NEW ZEALAND FANS READ THE SCRIPTURES
IMBO-GATE MADAM LIED UNDER OATH DNN FEDERA
THERE'S ONLY ONE THING THIS CAN POSSIBLY MEAN.
BELIEVE IT, MY FRIENDS. TOM TAYLOR IS TOMMY TAYLOR.
DNN TOMMY TAYLOR CULT
NEW ZEALAND FANS READ THE SCRIPTURES
AT RECORD LEVEL DNN GRAND JURY WITNESS BLUD
DNN CODED MESSAGE REVEALED
CODED MESSAGE IN LAST TOMMY TAYLOR NOVEL
IN HOTEL ROOM DNN GUN CONTROL GURU SHOOTS
HE'S THE MESSIAH! THE WORD MADE FLESH!
HE'S TOMMY! TOMMY IS AMONG US!
DNN CODED MESSAGE REVEALED
CODED MESSAGE IN LAST TOMMY TAYLOR NOVEL
WIFE, POLICE OFFICER DNN HOLLYWOOD STORMS
GIVE HIM YOUR PRAYERS!
GIVE HIM YOUR WORSHIP!

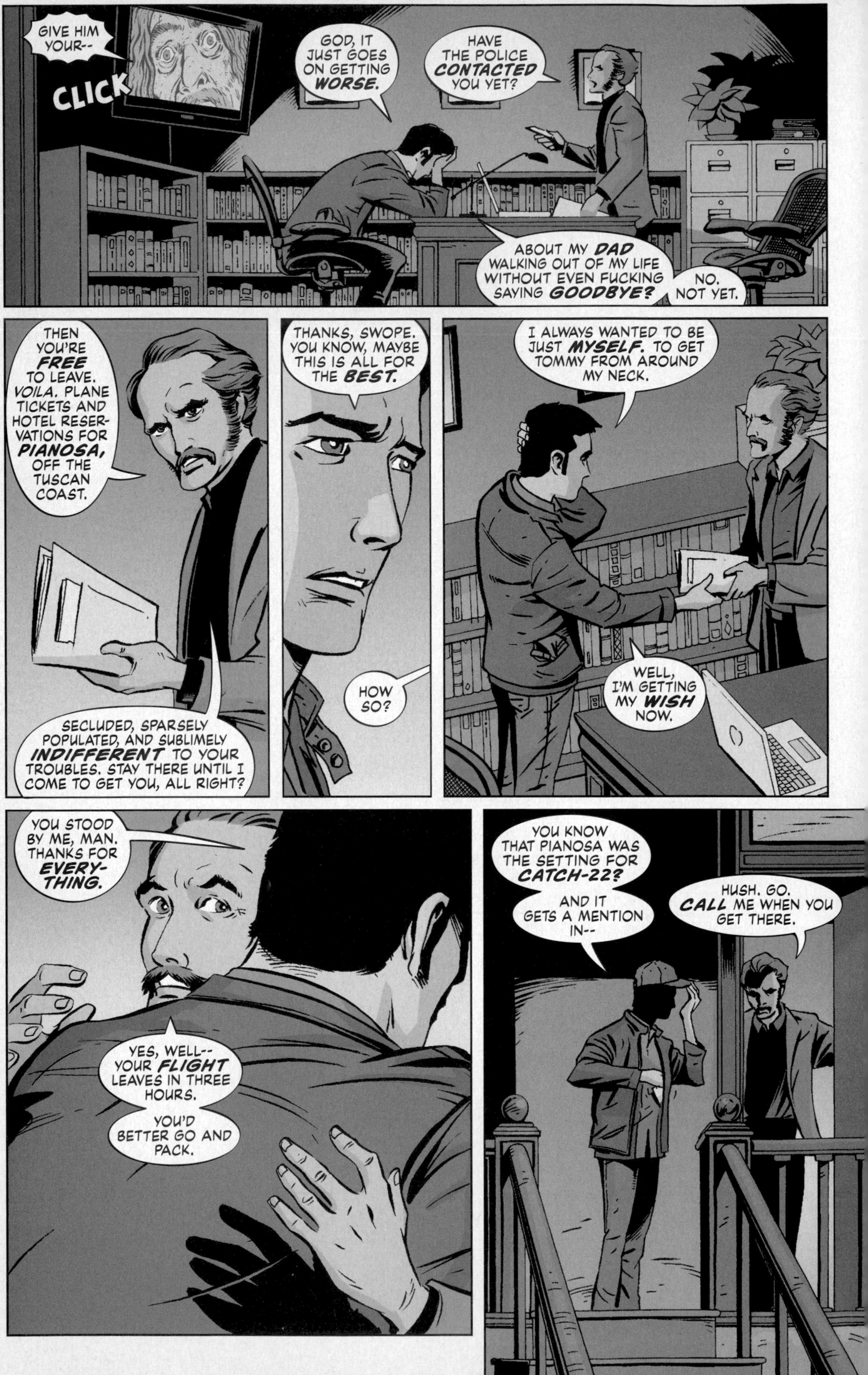
GIVE HIM YOUR--
CLICK
GOD, IT JUST GOES ON GETTING WORSE.
HAVE THE POLICE CONTACTED YOU YET?
ABOUT MY DAD WALKING OUT OF MY LIFE WITHOUT EVEN FUCKING SAYING GOODBYE?
NO. NOT YET.
THEN YOU'RE FREE TO LEAVE. VOILA. PLANE TICKETS AND HOTEL RESERVATIONS FOR PIANOSA, OFF THE TUSCAN COAST.
SECLUDED, SPARSELY POPULATED, AND SUBLIMELY INDIFFERENT TO YOUR TROUBLES. STAY THERE UNTIL I COME TO GET YOU, ALL RIGHT?
THANKS, SWOPE. YOU KNOW, MAYBE THIS IS ALL FOR THE BEST.
HOW SO?
I ALWAYS WANTED TO BE JUST MYSELF. TO GET TOMMY FROM AROUND MY NECK.
WELL, I'M GETTING MY WISH NOW.
YOU STOOD BY ME, MAN. THANKS FOR EVERYTHING.
YES, WELL-- YOUR FLIGHT LEAVES IN THREE HOURS.
YOU'D BETTER GO AND PACK.
YOU KNOW THAT PIANOSA WAS THE SETTING FOR CATCH-22?
AND IT GETS A MENTION IN--
HUSH. GO. CALL ME WHEN YOU GET THERE.

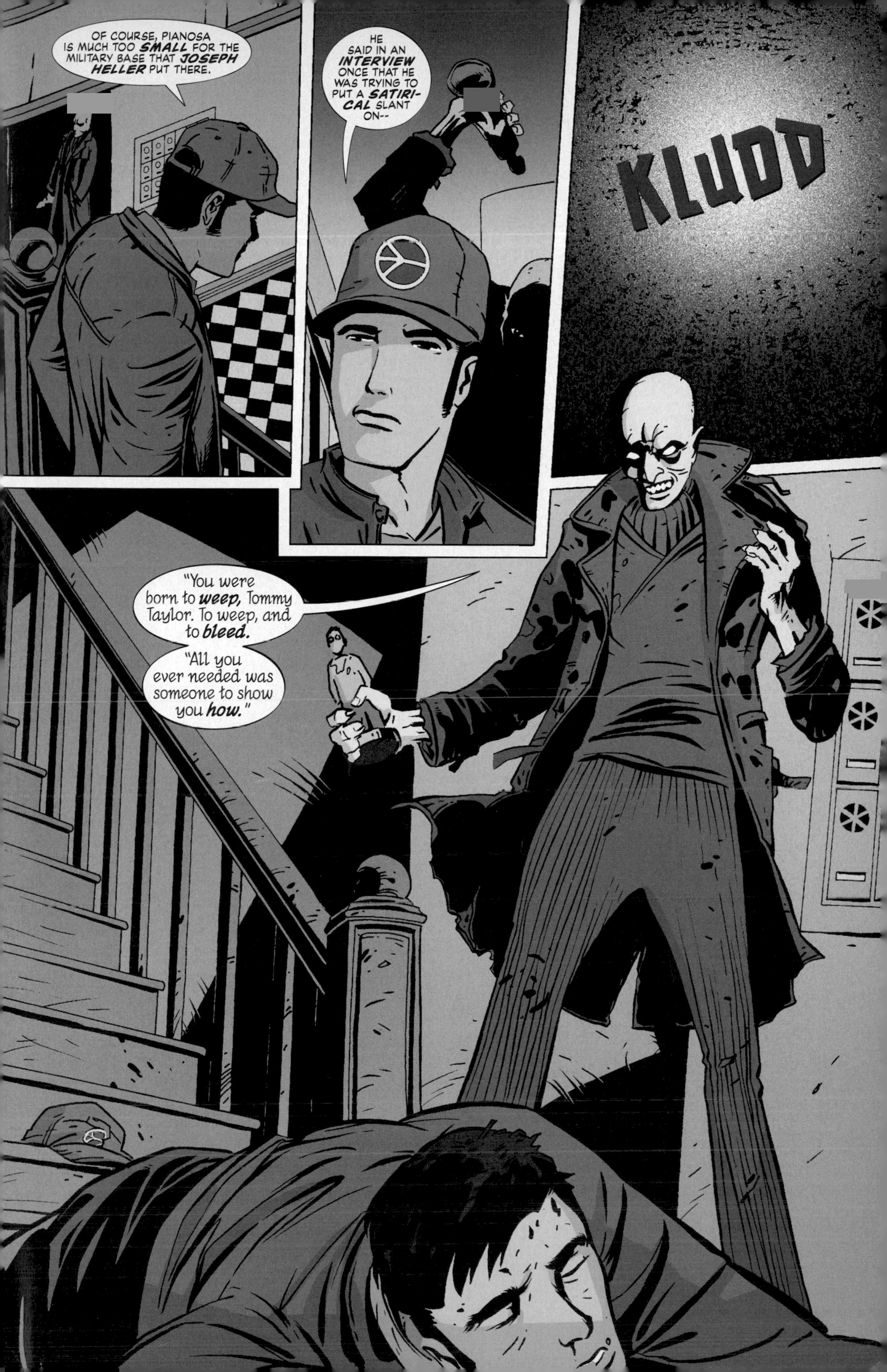

OF COURSE, PIANOSA IS MUCH TOO SMALL FOR THE MILITARY BASE THAT JOSEPH HELLER PUT THERE.
HE SAID IN AN INTERVIEW ONCE THAT HE WAS TRYING TO PUT A SATIRICAL SLANT ON--
KLUDD
"You were born to weep, Tommy Taylor. To weep, and to bleed.
"All you ever needed was someone to show you how."

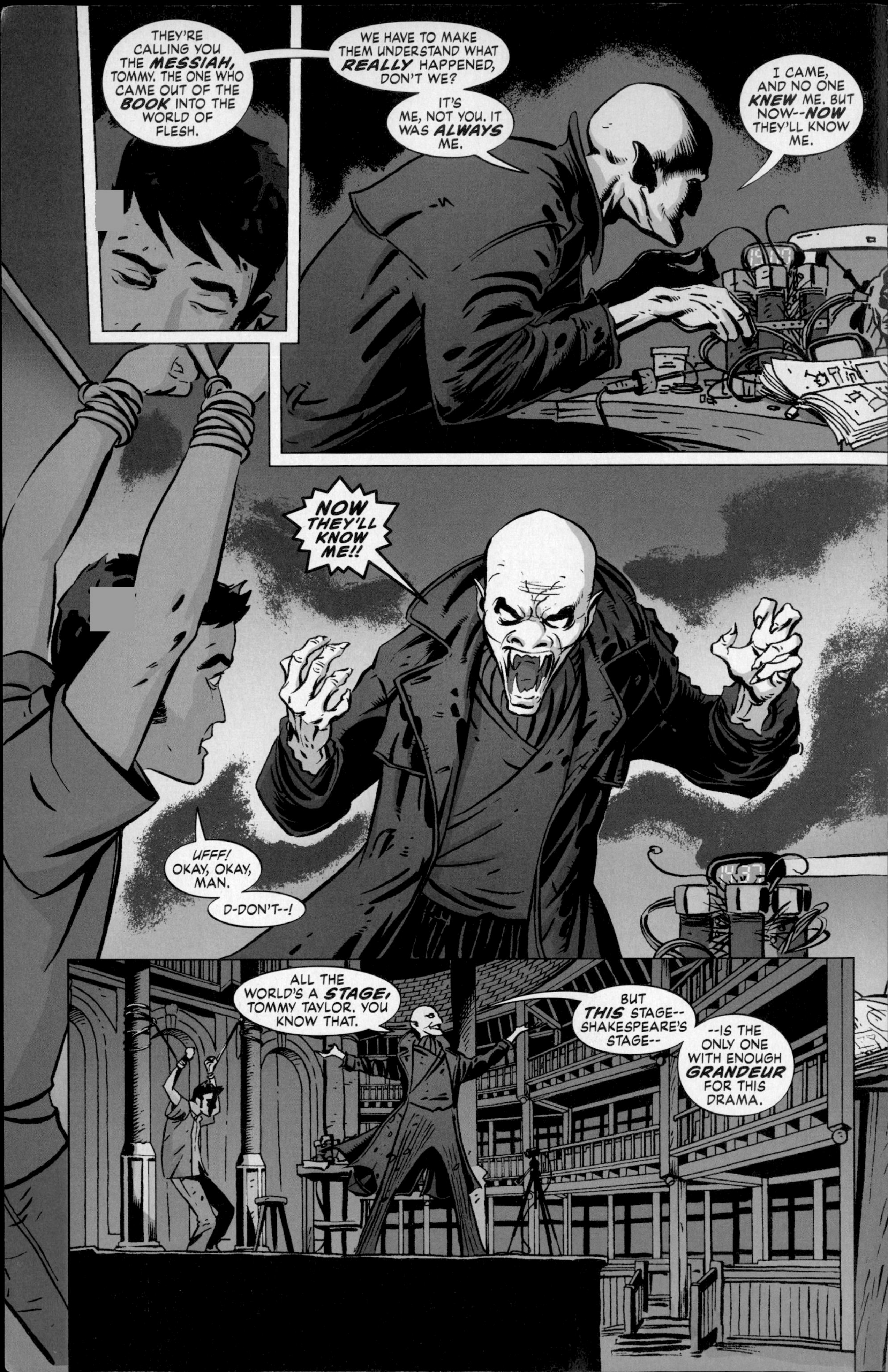
THEY'RE CALLING YOU THE MESSIAH, TOMMY. THE ONE WHO CAME OUT OF THE BOOK INTO THE WORLD OF FLESH.
WE HAVE TO MAKE THEM UNDERSTAND WHAT REALLY HAPPENED, DON'T WE?
IT'S ME, NOT YOU. IT WAS ALWAYS ME.
I CAME, AND NO ONE KNEW ME. BUT NOW--NOW THEY'LL KNOW ME.
NOW THEY'LL KNOW ME!!
UFFF! OKAY, OKAY, MAN.
D-DON'T--!
ALL THE WORLD'S A STAGE, TOMMY TAYLOR. YOU KNOW THAT.
BUT THIS STAGE-- SHAKESPEARE'S STAGE--
--IS THE ONLY ONE WITH ENOUGH GRANDEUR FOR THIS DRAMA.

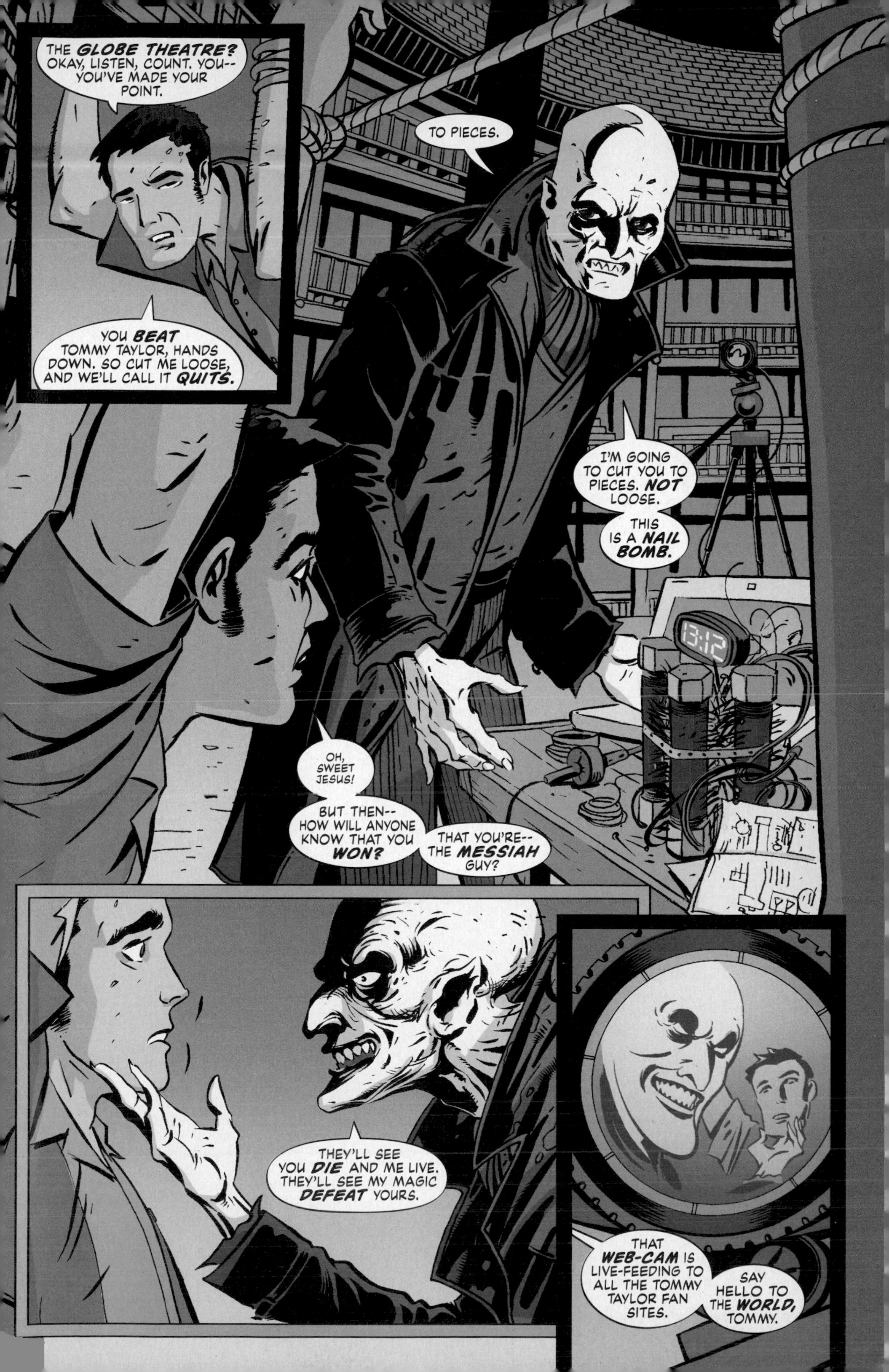
THE GLOBE THEATRE? OKAY, LISTEN, COUNT. YOU-- YOU'VE MADE YOUR POINT.
YOU BEAT TOMMY TAYLOR, HANDS DOWN. SO CUT ME LOOSE, AND WE'LL CALL IT QUITS.
TO PIECES.
I'M GOING TO CUT YOU TO PIECES. NOT LOOSE.
THIS IS A NAIL BOMB.
13:12
OH, SWEET JESUS!
BUT THEN-- HOW WILL ANYONE KNOW THAT YOU WON?
THAT YOU'RE-- THE MESSIAH GUY?
THEY'LL SEE YOU DIE AND ME LIVE. THEY'LL SEE MY MAGIC DEFEAT YOURS.
THAT WEB-CAM IS LIVE-FEEDING TO ALL THE TOMMY TAYLOR FAN SITES.
SAY HELLO TO THE WORLD, TOMMY.

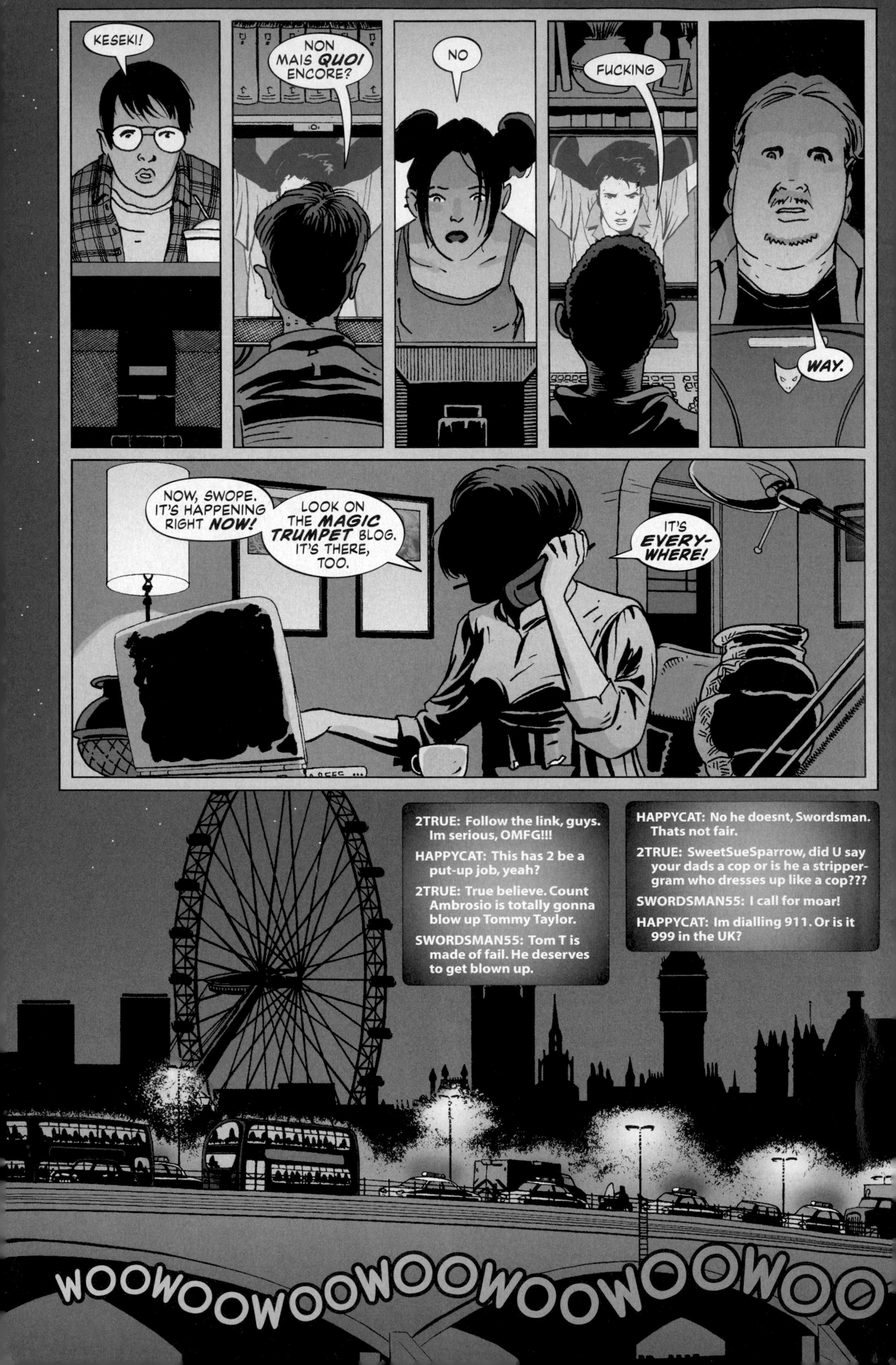
KESEKI!
NON MAIS QUOI ENCORE?
NO
FUCKING
WAY.
NOW, SWOPE. IT'S HAPPENING RIGHT NOW!
LOOK ON THE MAGIC TRUMPET BLOG. IT'S THERE, TOO.
IT'S EVERY-WHERE!
2TRUE: Follow the link, guys. Im serious, OMFG!!!
HAPPYCAT: This has 2 be a put-up job, yeah?
2TRUE: True believe. Count Ambrosio is totally gonna blow up Tommy Taylor.
SWORDSMAN55: Tom T is made of fail. He deserves to get blown up.
HAPPYCAT: No he doesnt, Swordsman. Thats not fair.
2TRUE: SweetSueSparrow, did U say your dads a cop or is he a stripper-gram who dresses up like a cop???
SWORDSMAN55: I call for moar!
HAPPYCAT: Im dialling 911. Or is it 999 in the UK?
WOOWOOWOOWOOWOOWOOWOOWOO

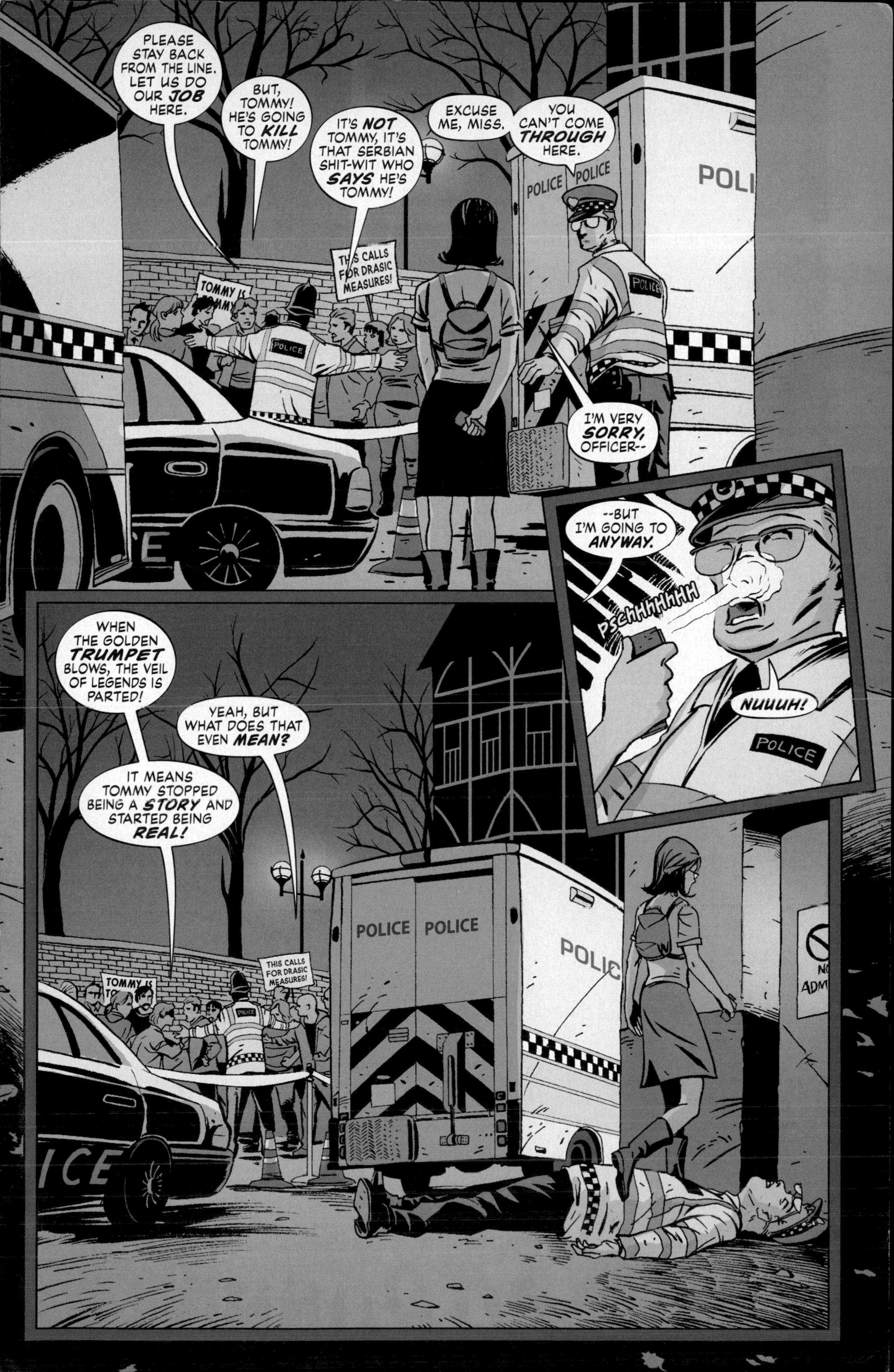
PLEASE STAY BACK FROM THE LINE. LET US DO OUR JOB HERE.
BUT, TOMMY! HE'S GOING TO KILL TOMMY!
IT'S NOT TOMMY, IT'S THAT SERBIAN SHIT-WIT WHO SAYS HE'S TOMMY!
EXCUSE ME, MISS.
YOU CAN'T COME THROUGH HERE.
POLICE POLICE
POLI
THIS CALLS FOR DRASIC MEASURES!
TOMMY IS
POLICE
POLICE
I'M VERY SORRY, OFFICER--
--BUT I'M GOING TO ANYWAY.
PSCHHHHHHH
NUUUH!
POLICE
WHEN THE GOLDEN TRUMPET BLOWS, THE VEIL OF LEGENDS IS PARTED!
YEAH, BUT WHAT DOES THAT EVEN MEAN?
IT MEANS TOMMY STOPPED BEING A STORY AND STARTED BEING REAL!
POLICE POLICE
POLIC
THIS CALLS FOR DRASIC MEASURES!
TOMMY IS
POLICE
ICE

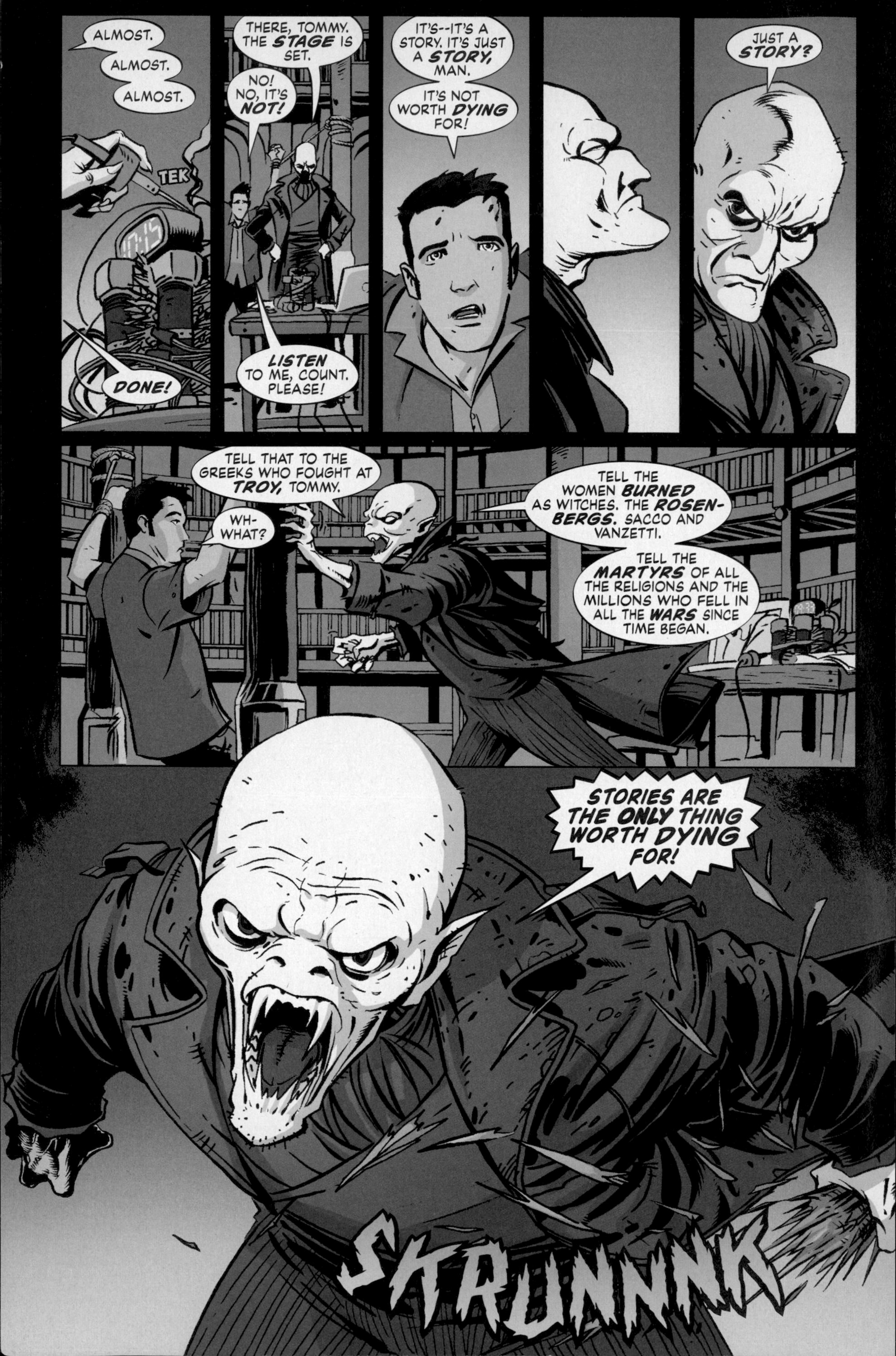
ALMOST.
ALMOST.
ALMOST.
TEK
DONE!
THERE, TOMMY. THE STAGE IS SET.
NO! NO, IT'S NOT!
LISTEN TO ME, COUNT. PLEASE!
IT'S--IT'S A STORY. IT'S JUST A STORY, MAN.
IT'S NOT WORTH DYING FOR!
JUST A STORY?
TELL THAT TO THE GREEKS WHO FOUGHT AT TROY, TOMMY.
WH-WHAT?
TELL THE WOMEN BURNED AS WITCHES. THE ROSEN-BERGS. SACCO AND VANZETTI.
TELL THE MARTYRS OF ALL THE RELIGIONS AND THE MILLIONS WHO FELL IN ALL THE WARS SINCE TIME BEGAN.
STORIES ARE THE ONLY THING WORTH DYING FOR!
SKRUNNNK!

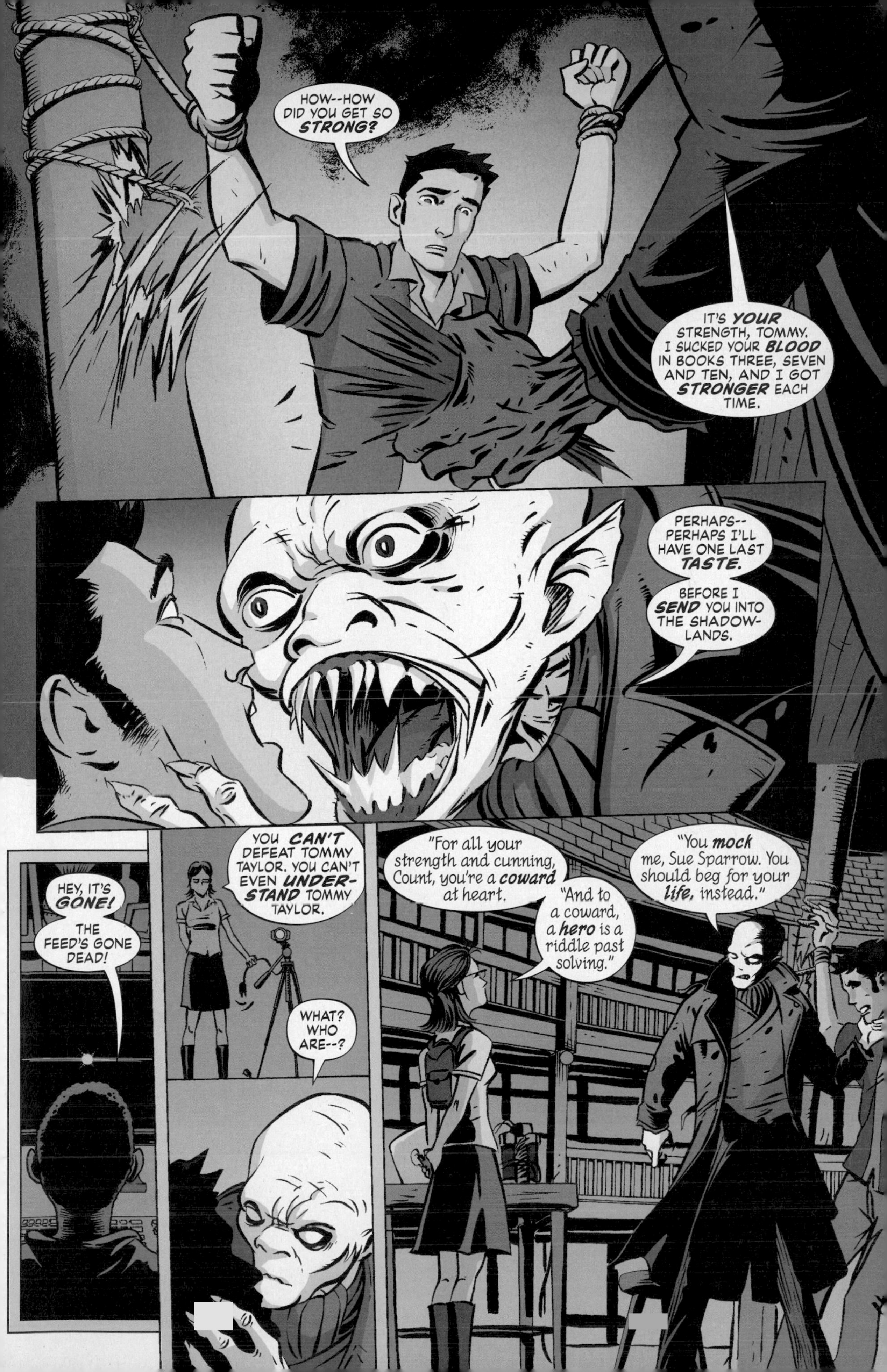
HOW--HOW DID YOU GET SO STRONG?
IT'S YOUR STRENGTH, TOMMY. I SUCKED YOUR BLOOD IN BOOKS THREE, SEVEN AND TEN, AND I GOT STRONGER EACH TIME.
PERHAPS--PERHAPS I'LL HAVE ONE LAST TASTE.
BEFORE I SEND YOU INTO THE SHADOW-LANDS.
HEY, IT'S GONE!
THE FEED'S GONE DEAD!
YOU CAN'T DEFEAT TOMMY TAYLOR. YOU CAN'T EVEN UNDER-STAND TOMMY TAYLOR.
WHAT? WHO ARE--?
"For all your strength and cunning, Count, you're a coward at heart.
"And to a coward, a hero is a riddle past solving."
"You mock me, Sue Sparrow. You should beg for your life, instead."

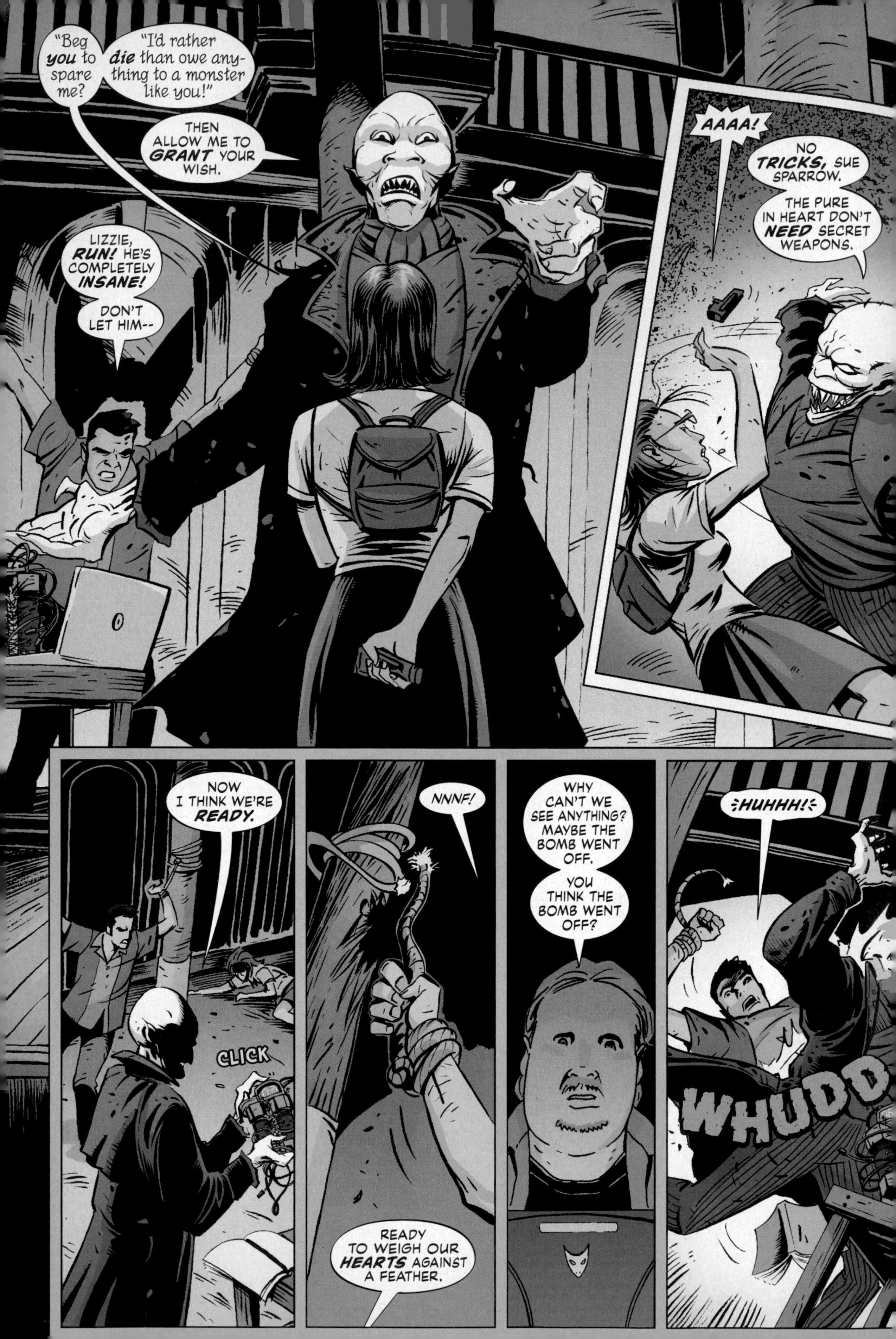

"Beg **you** to spare me?
"I'd rather **die** than owe anything to a monster like you!"
THEN ALLOW ME TO **GRANT** YOUR WISH.
LIZZIE, **RUN!** HE'S COMPLETELY **INSANE!**
DON'T LET HIM--
AAAA!
NO **TRICKS,** SUE SPARROW.
THE PURE IN HEART DON'T **NEED** SECRET WEAPONS.
NOW I THINK WE'RE **READY.**
CLICK
NNNF!
READY TO WEIGH OUR **HEARTS** AGAINST A FEATHER.
WHY CAN'T WE SEE ANYTHING? MAYBE THE BOMB WENT OFF.
YOU THINK THE BOMB WENT OFF?
HUHHH!
WHUDD

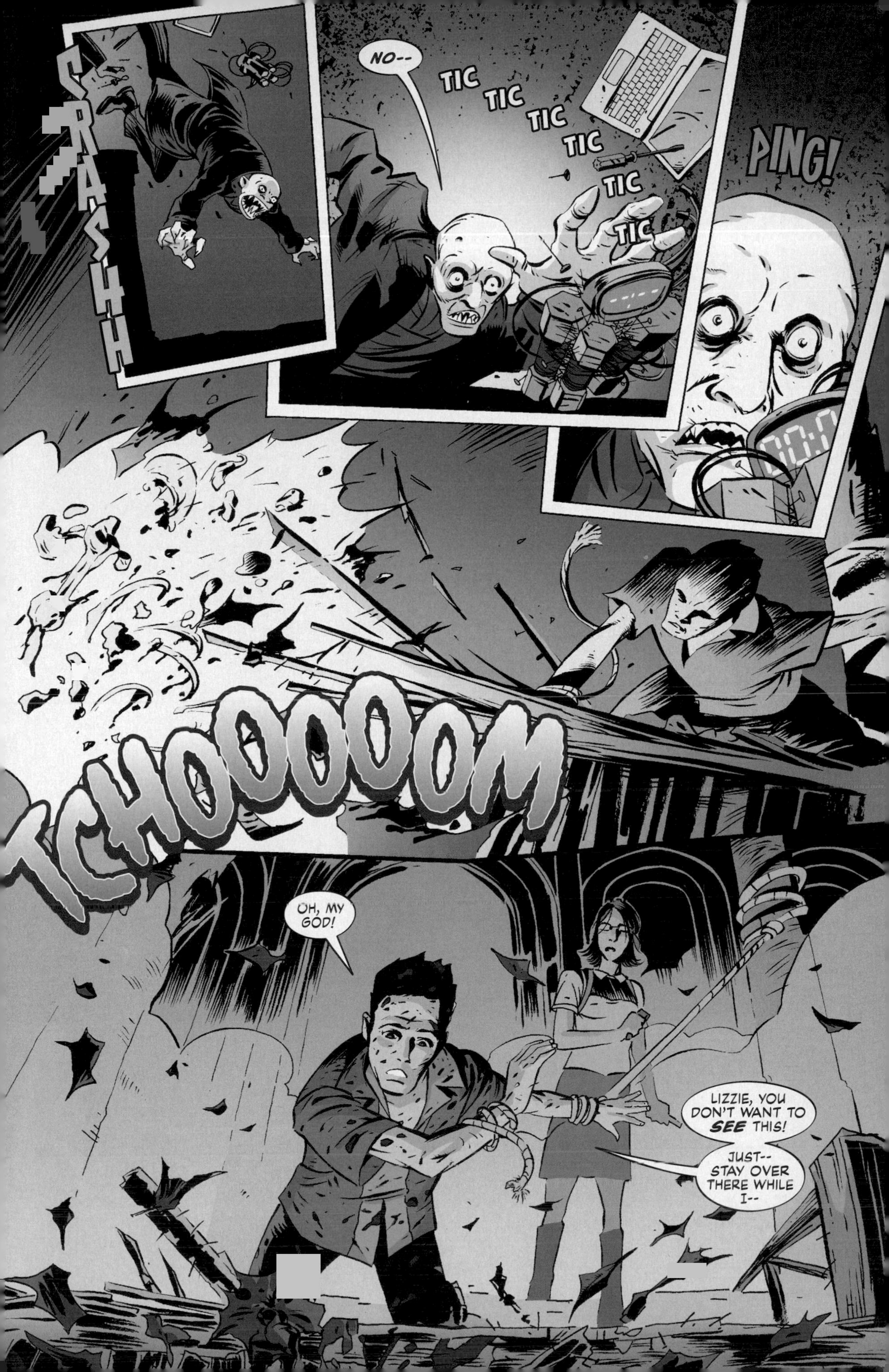
CRASHH
NO--
TIC
TIC
TIC
TIC
TIC
TIC
PING!
TCHOOOOOM
OH, MY GOD!
LIZZIE, YOU DON'T WANT TO *SEE* THIS!
JUST-- STAY OVER THERE WHILE I--

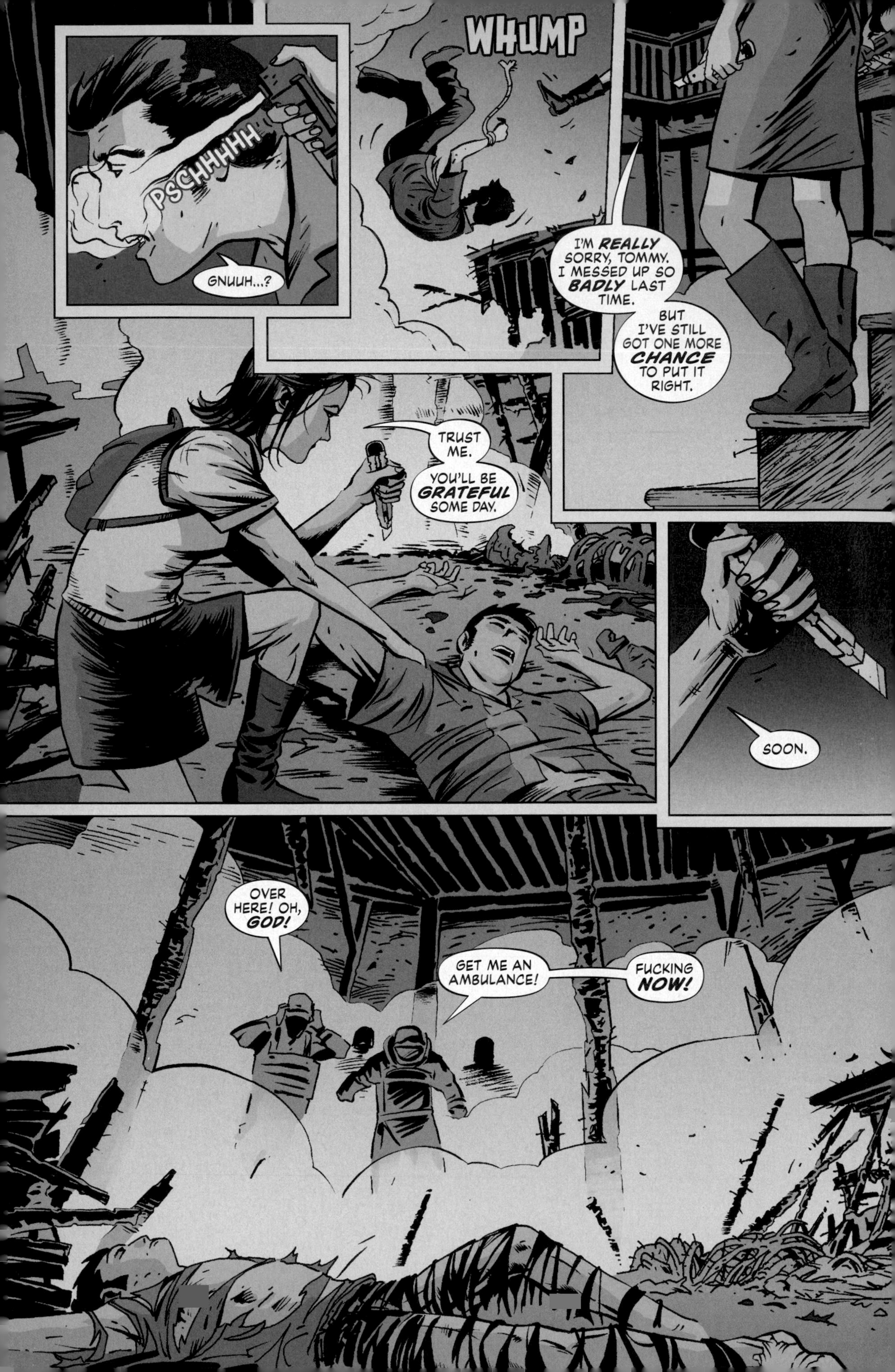
PSCHHHHH
GNUUH...?
WHUMP
I'M REALLY SORRY, TOMMY. I MESSED UP SO BADLY LAST TIME.
BUT I'VE STILL GOT ONE MORE CHANCE TO PUT IT RIGHT.
TRUST ME.
YOU'LL BE GRATEFUL SOME DAY.
SOON.
OVER HERE! OH, GOD!
GET ME AN AMBULANCE!
FUCKING NOW!

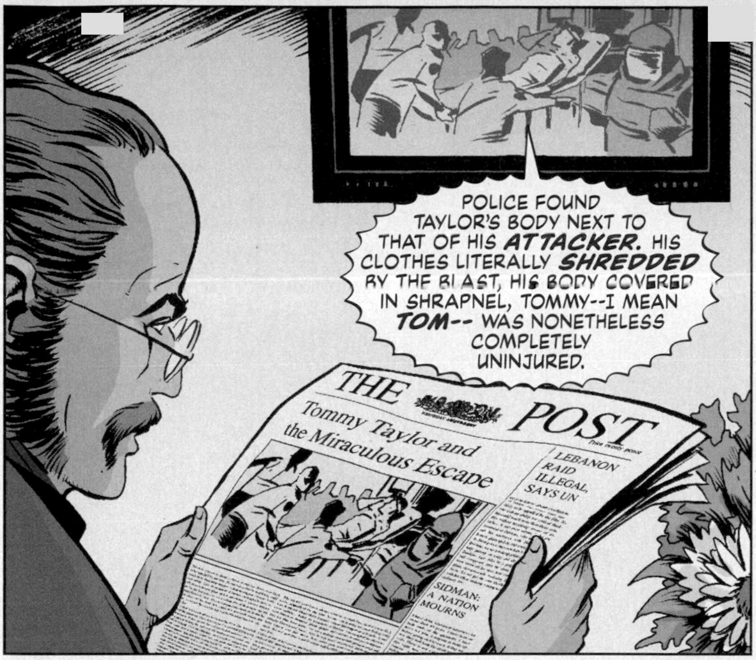
POLICE FOUND TAYLOR'S BODY NEXT TO THAT OF HIS ATTACKER. HIS CLOTHES LITERALLY SHREDDED BY THE BLAST, HIS BODY COVERED IN SHRAPNEL, TOMMY--I MEAN TOM-- WAS NONETHELESS COMPLETELY UNINJURED.
THE POST
Tommy Taylor and the Miraculous Escape
LEBANON RAID ILLEGAL, SAYS UN
SIDMAN: A NATION MOURNS

2TRUE: I tell U man I didnt believe it but now I do.

SweetSueSparrow: Camera didnt show anything, 2TRUE. They were out of sight the whole time.

2TRUE: But the Count got turned into runny chuck steak, SSS, and Tom walked away without a scratch. How can he not be the real deal?

SWORDSMAN55: I agree. Tom is Tommy is Tom is Tommy is Tom is Tommy is Tom is Tommy is Tom is Tommy is Tom is Tommy is Tom is Tommy is Tom

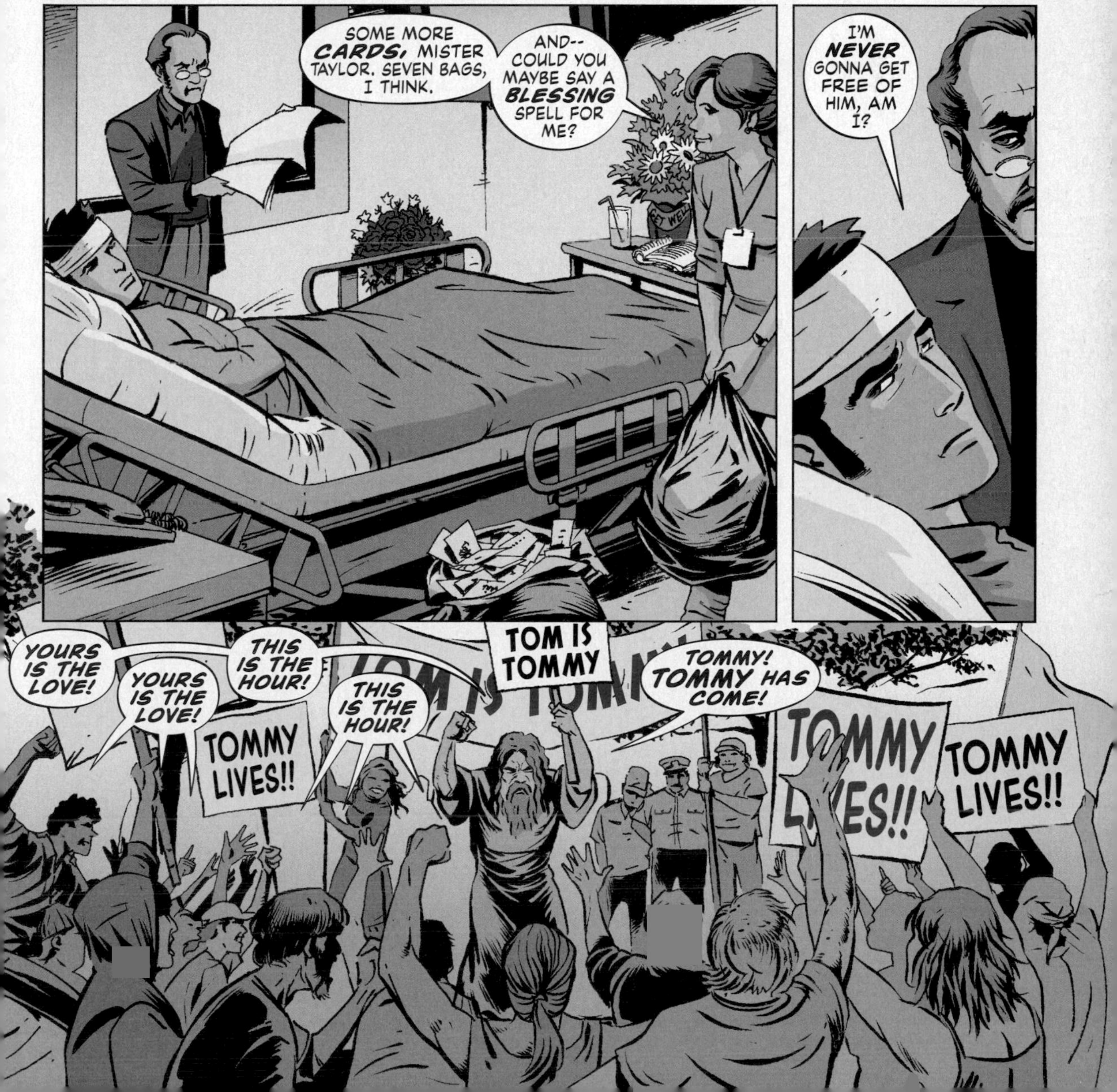
SOME MORE CARDS, MISTER TAYLOR. SEVEN BAGS, I THINK.
AND-- COULD YOU MAYBE SAY A BLESSING SPELL FOR ME?
GET WELL
I'M NEVER GONNA GET FREE OF HIM, AM I?
YOURS IS THE LOVE!
YOURS IS THE LOVE!
THIS IS THE HOUR!
THIS IS THE HOUR!
TOM IS TOMMY
TOM IS TOMMY
TOMMY! TOMMY HAS COME!
TOMMY LIVES!!
TOMMY LIVES!!
TOMMY LIVES!!

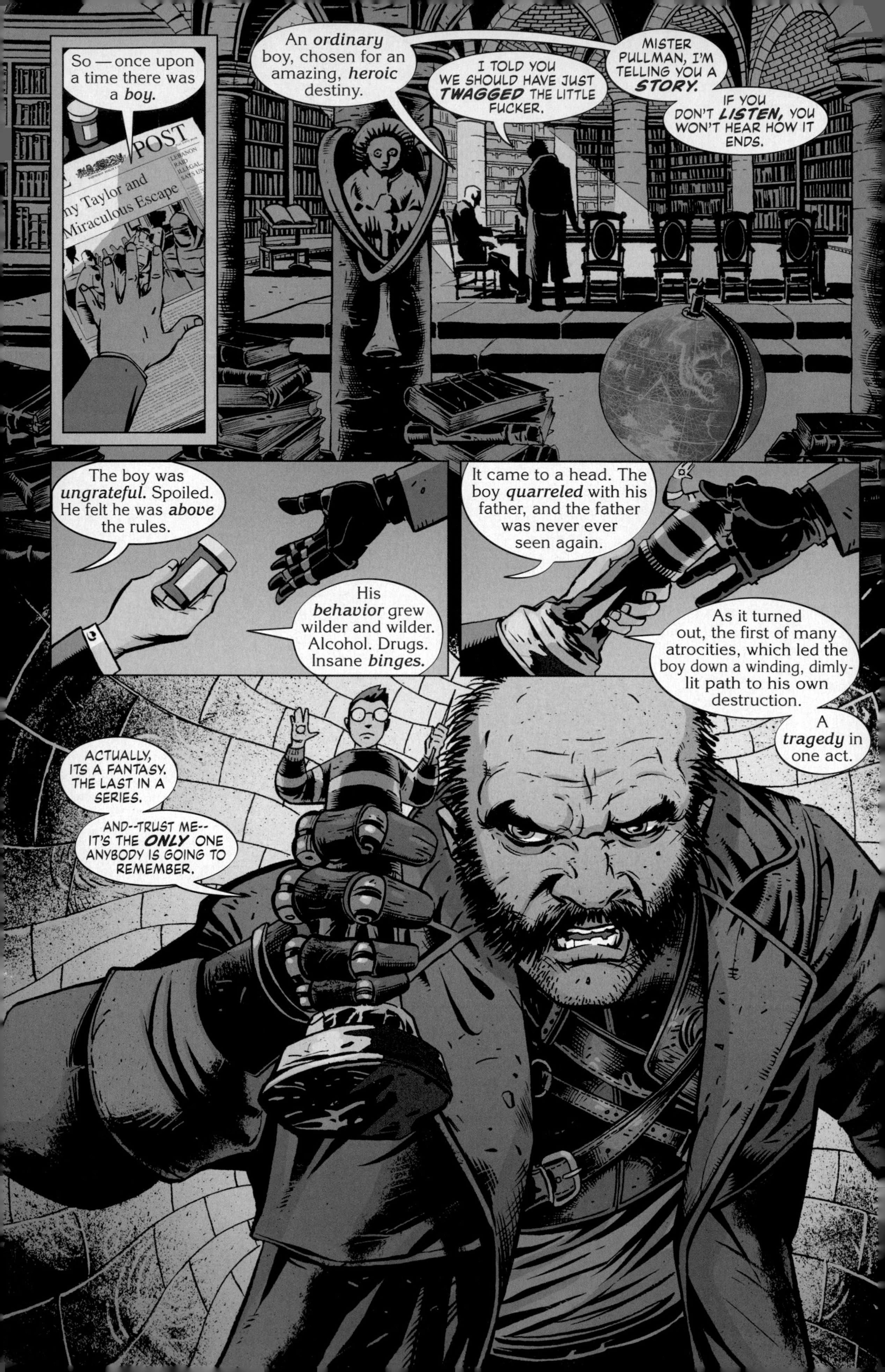

So — once upon a time there was a *boy.*
POST
my Taylor and Miraculous Escape
An *ordinary* boy, chosen for an amazing, *heroic* destiny.
I TOLD YOU WE SHOULD HAVE JUST ***TWAGGED*** THE LITTLE FUCKER.
MISTER PULLMAN, I'M TELLING YOU A ***STORY.***
IF YOU DON'T ***LISTEN,*** YOU WON'T HEAR HOW IT ENDS.
The boy was *ungrateful.* Spoiled. He felt he was *above* the rules.
His *behavior* grew wilder and wilder. Alcohol. Drugs. Insane *binges.*
It came to a head. The boy *quarreled* with his father, and the father was never ever seen again.
As it turned out, the first of many atrocities, which led the boy down a winding, dimly-lit path to his own destruction.
A *tragedy* in one act.
ACTUALLY, ITS A FANTASY. THE LAST IN A SERIES.
AND--TRUST ME-- IT'S THE ***ONLY*** ONE ANYBODY IS GOING TO REMEMBER.

Tommy Taylor and the Bogus Identity
Chapter Two

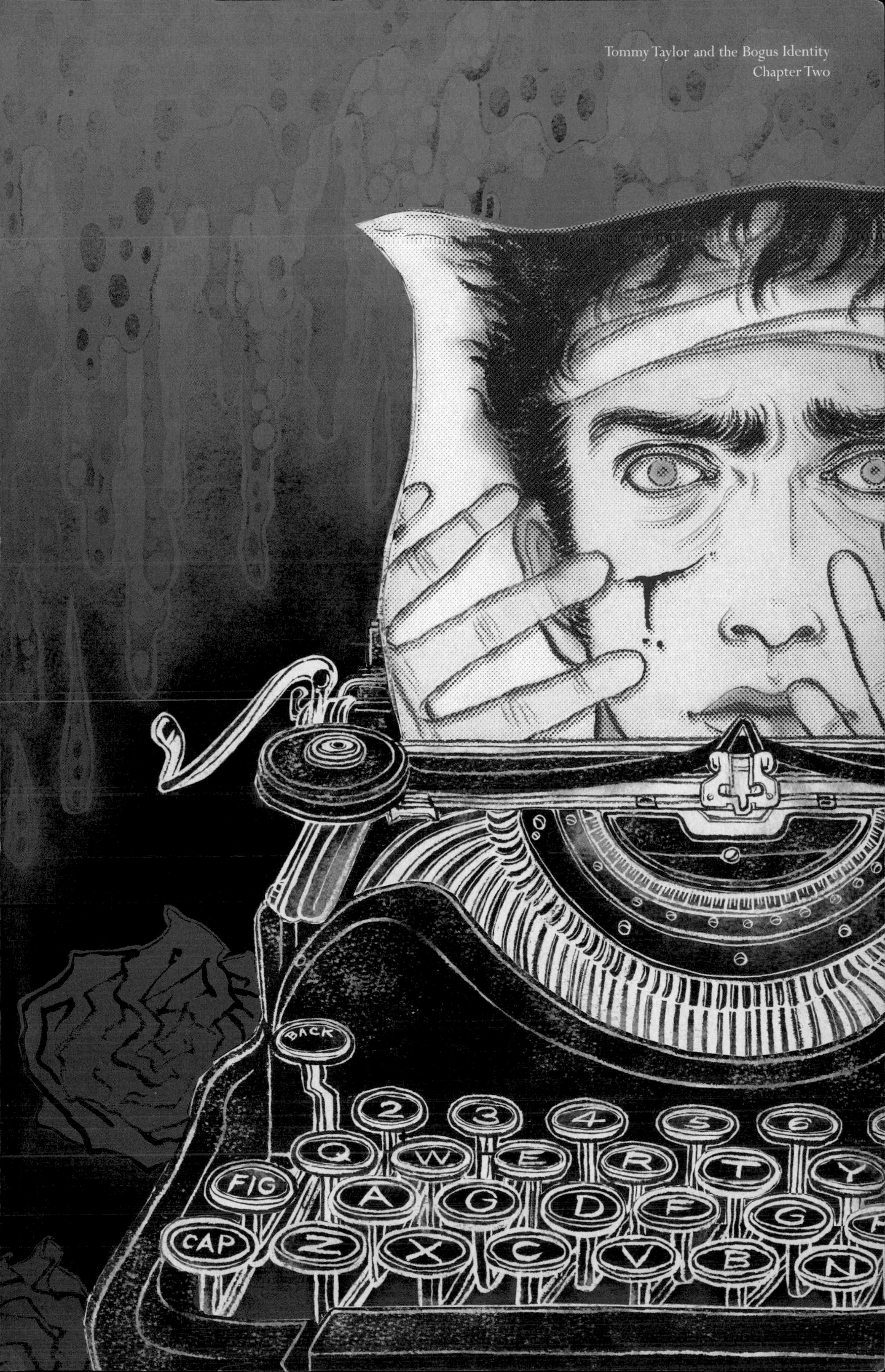
BACK
2 3 4 5 6
Q W E R T Y
FIG A G D F G
CAP Z X C V B N

Sketch by Yuko Shimizu

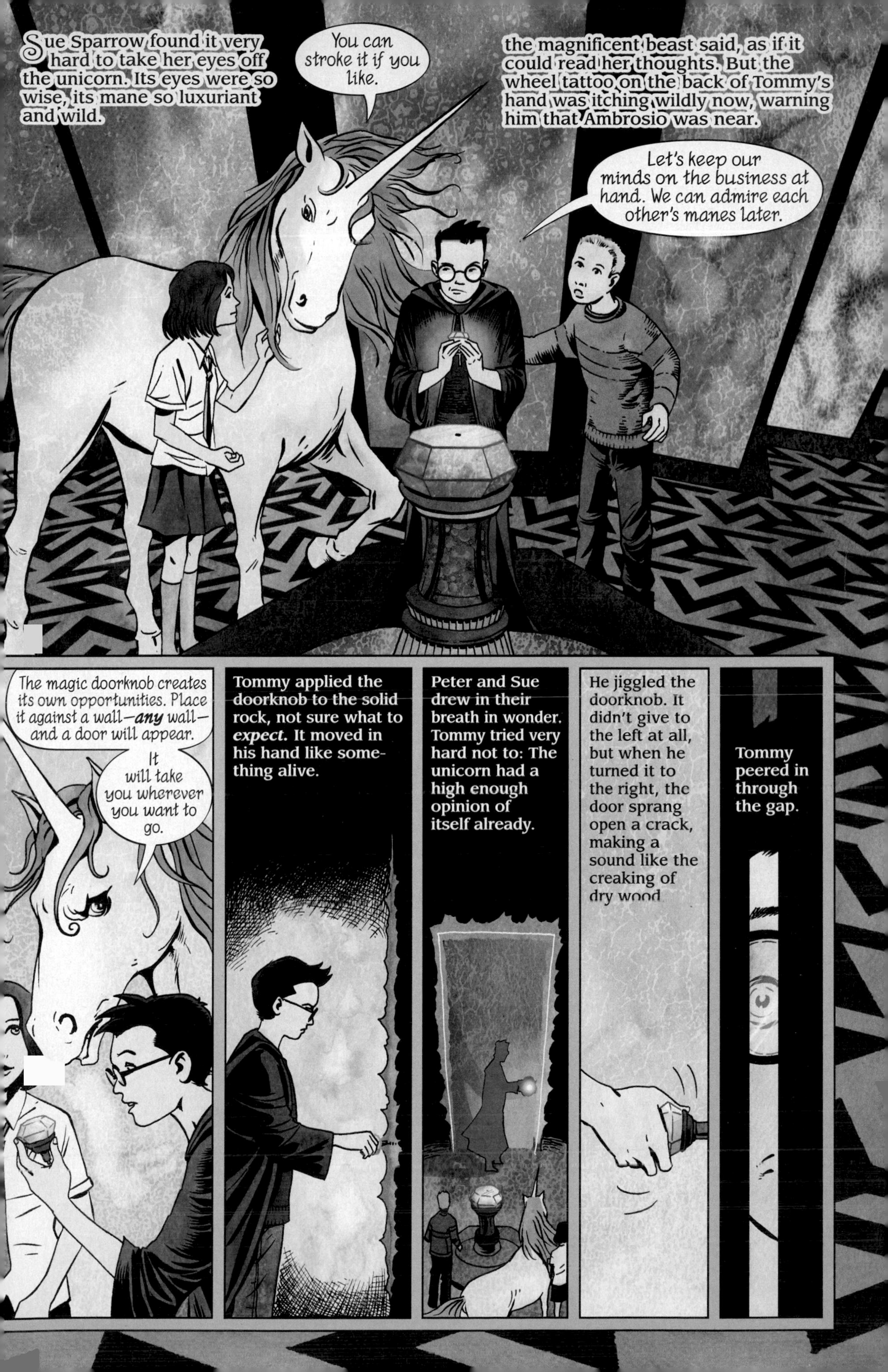
Sue Sparrow found it very hard to take her eyes off the unicorn. Its eyes were so wise, its mane so luxuriant and wild.
You can stroke it if you like.
the magnificent beast said, as if it could read her thoughts. But the wheel tattoo on the back of Tommy's hand was itching wildly now, warning him that Ambrosio was near.
Let's keep our minds on the business at hand. We can admire each other's manes later.
The magic doorknob creates its own opportunities. Place it against a wall—*any* wall—and a door will appear.
It will take you wherever you want to go.
Tommy applied the doorknob to the solid rock, not sure what to *expect.* It moved in his hand like something alive.
Peter and Sue drew in their breath in wonder. Tommy tried very hard not to: The unicorn had a high enough opinion of itself already.
He jiggled the doorknob. It didn't give to the left at all, but when he turned it to the right, the door sprang open a crack, making a sound like the creaking of dry wood.
Tommy peered in through the gap.

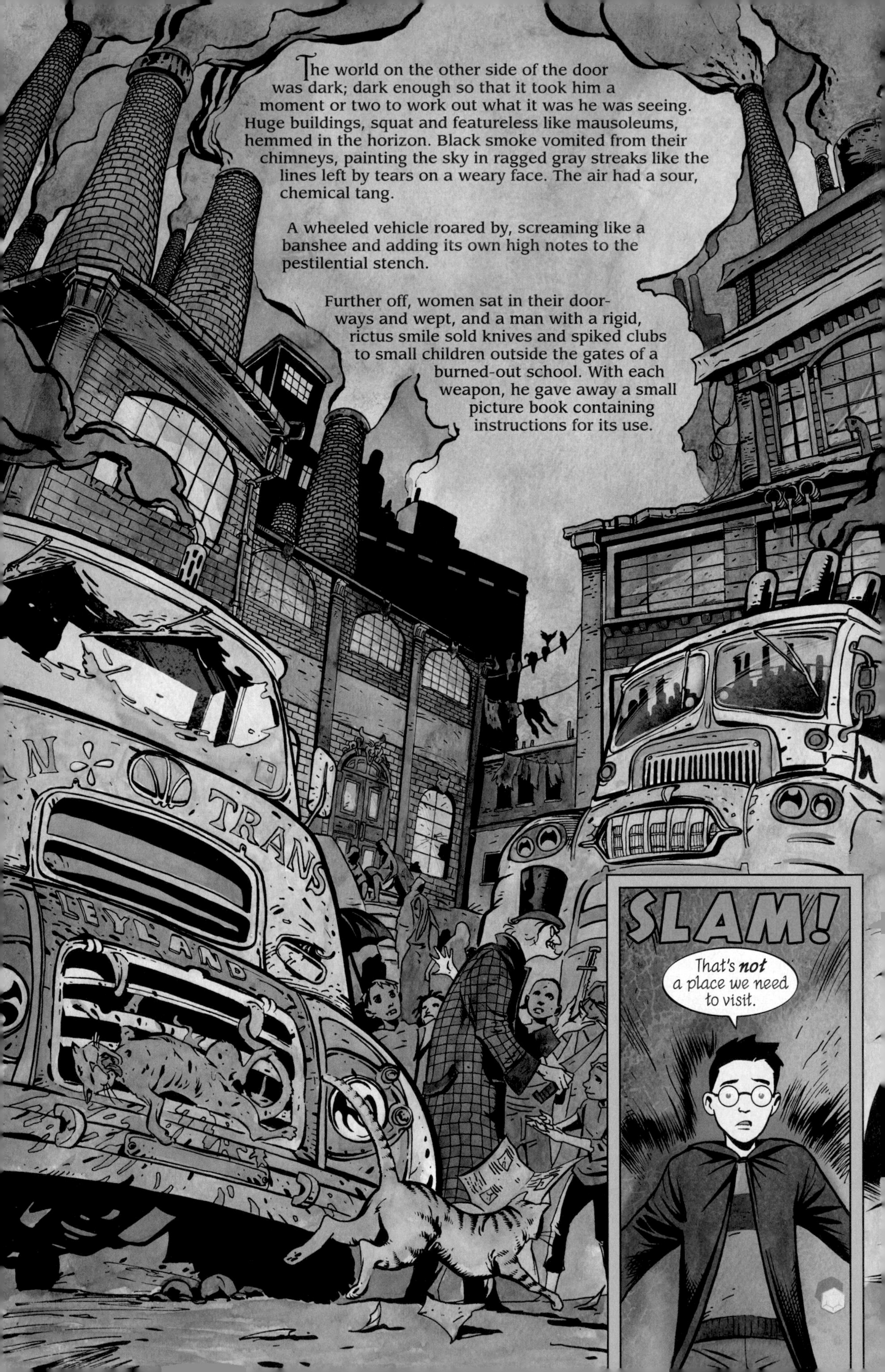
The world on the other side of the door was dark; dark enough so that it took him a moment or two to work out what it was he was seeing. Huge buildings, squat and featureless like mausoleums, hemmed in the horizon. Black smoke vomited from their chimneys, painting the sky in ragged gray streaks like the lines left by tears on a weary face. The air had a sour, chemical tang.
A wheeled vehicle roared by, screaming like a banshee and adding its own high notes to the pestilential stench.
Further off, women sat in their doorways and wept, and a man with a rigid, rictus smile sold knives and spiked clubs to small children outside the gates of a burned-out school. With each weapon, he gave away a small picture book containing instructions for its use.
TRANS
LEYLAND
SLAM!
That's **not** a place we need to visit.

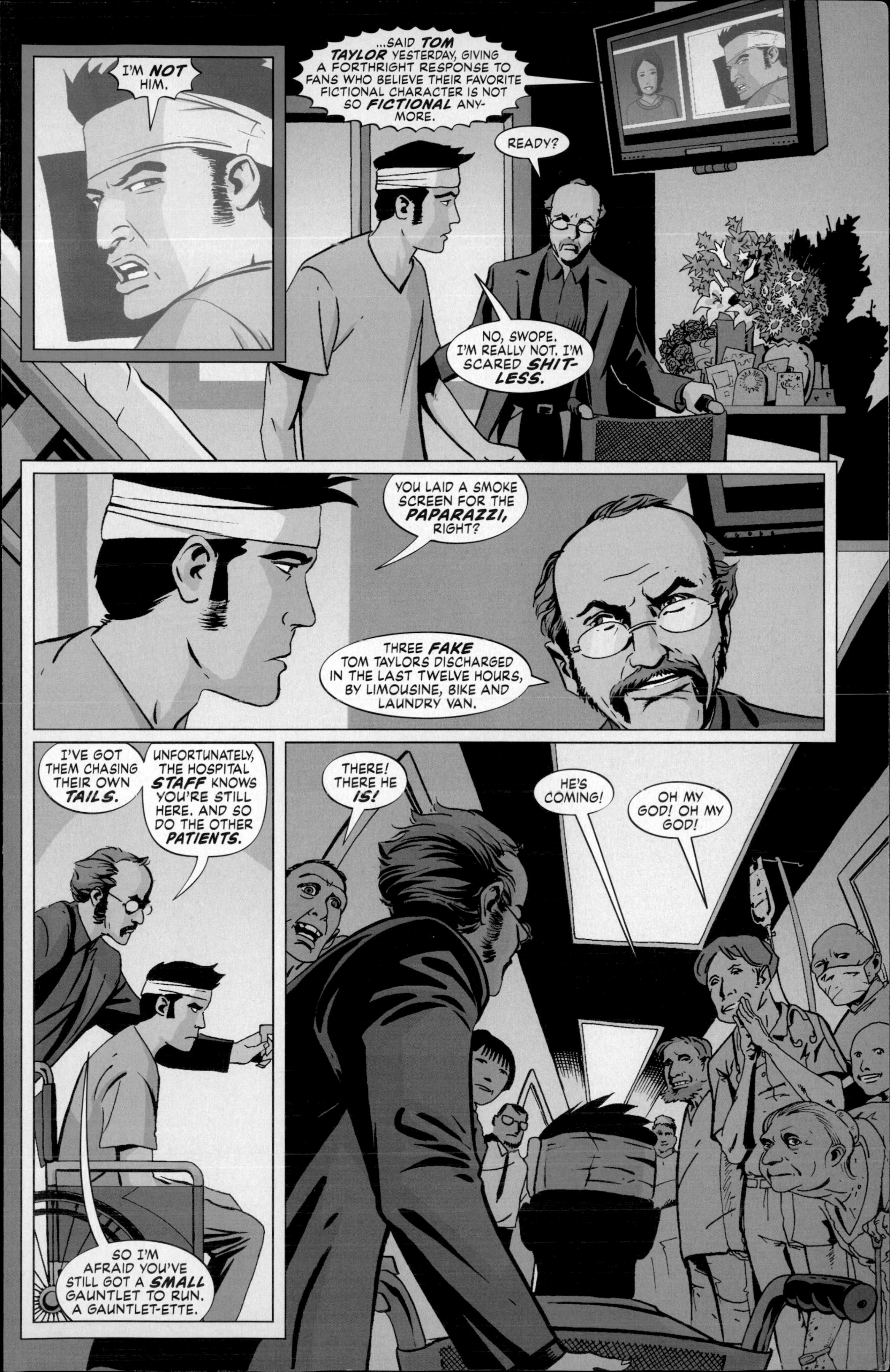
I'M NOT HIM.
...SAID TOM TAYLOR YESTERDAY, GIVING A FORTHRIGHT RESPONSE TO FANS WHO BELIEVE THEIR FAVORITE FICTIONAL CHARACTER IS NOT SO FICTIONAL ANY-MORE.
READY?
NO, SWOPE. I'M REALLY NOT. I'M SCARED SHIT-LESS.
YOU LAID A SMOKE SCREEN FOR THE PAPARAZZI, RIGHT?
THREE FAKE TOM TAYLORS DISCHARGED IN THE LAST TWELVE HOURS, BY LIMOUSINE, BIKE AND LAUNDRY VAN.
I'VE GOT THEM CHASING THEIR OWN TAILS.
UNFORTUNATELY, THE HOSPITAL STAFF KNOWS YOU'RE STILL HERE. AND SO DO THE OTHER PATIENTS.
SO I'M AFRAID YOU'VE STILL GOT A SMALL GAUNTLET TO RUN. A GAUNTLET-ETTE.
THERE! THERE HE IS!
HE'S COMING!
OH MY GOD! OH MY GOD!

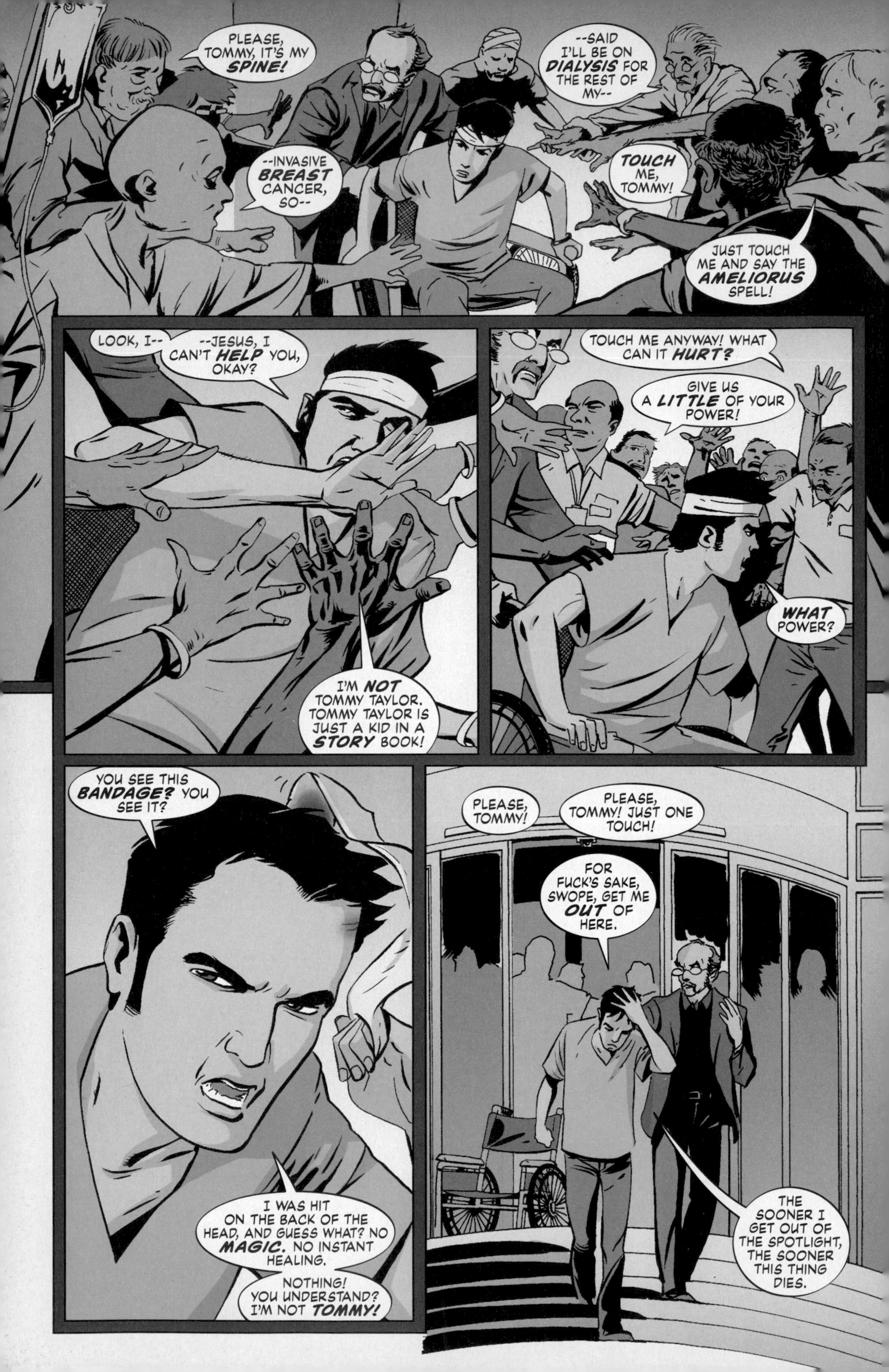
PLEASE, TOMMY, IT'S MY SPINE!
--SAID I'LL BE ON DIALYSIS FOR THE REST OF MY--
--INVASIVE BREAST CANCER, SO--
TOUCH ME, TOMMY!
JUST TOUCH ME AND SAY THE AMELIORUS SPELL!
LOOK, I--
--JESUS, I CAN'T HELP YOU, OKAY?
I'M NOT TOMMY TAYLOR. TOMMY TAYLOR IS JUST A KID IN A STORY BOOK!
TOUCH ME ANYWAY! WHAT CAN IT HURT?
GIVE US A LITTLE OF YOUR POWER!
WHAT POWER?
YOU SEE THIS BANDAGE? YOU SEE IT?
I WAS HIT ON THE BACK OF THE HEAD, AND GUESS WHAT? NO MAGIC. NO INSTANT HEALING.
NOTHING! YOU UNDERSTAND? I'M NOT TOMMY!
PLEASE, TOMMY!
PLEASE, TOMMY! JUST ONE TOUCH!
FOR FUCK'S SAKE, SWOPE, GET ME OUT OF HERE.
THE SOONER I GET OUT OF THE SPOTLIGHT, THE SOONER THIS THING DIES.

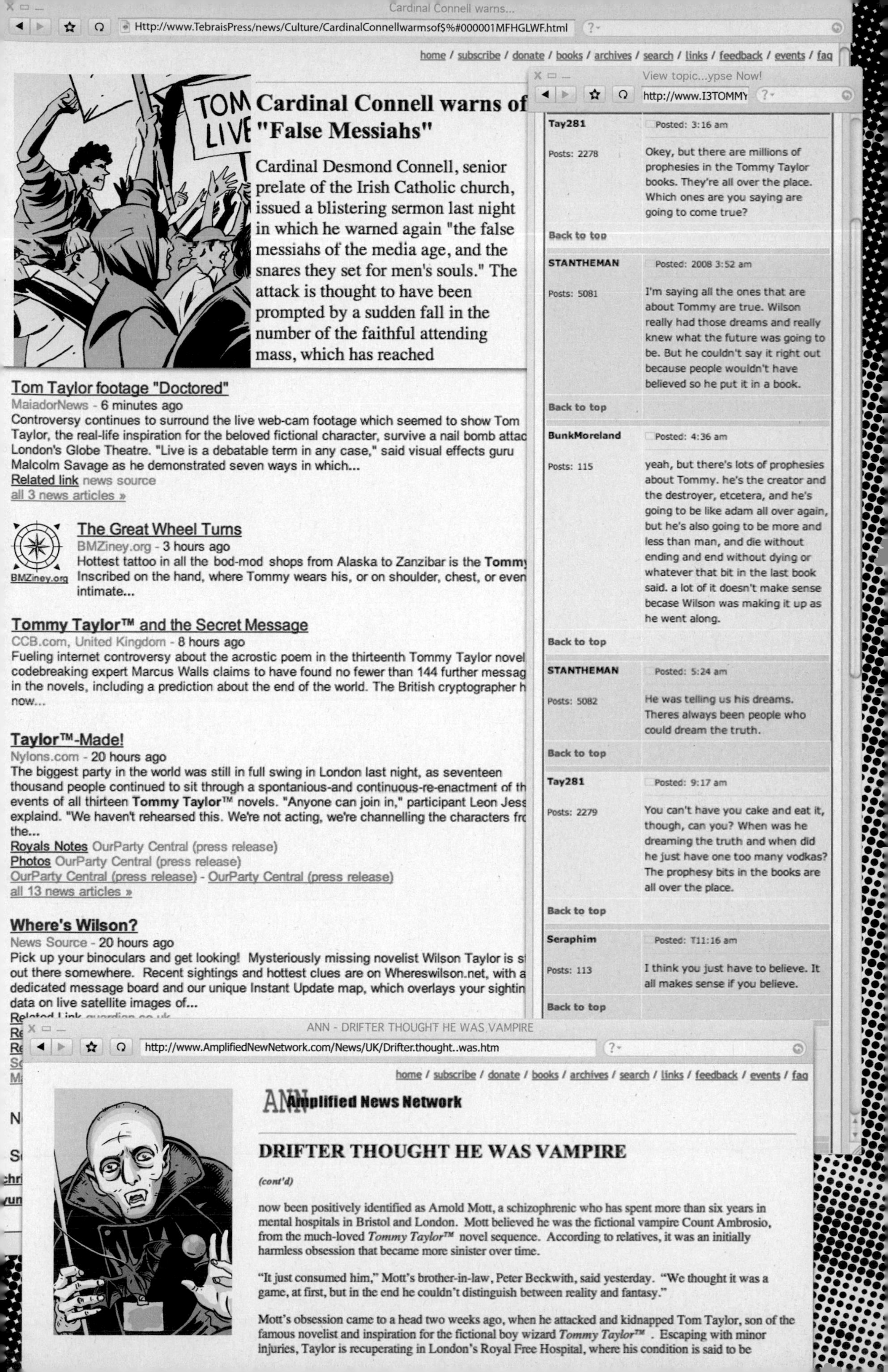
Cardinal Connell warns...
Http://www.TebraisPress/news/Culture/CardinalConnellwarmsof$%#000001MFHGLWF.html
home / subscribe / donate / books / archives / search / links / feedback / events / faq
TOM LIVE
Cardinal Connell warns of "False Messiahs"
Cardinal Desmond Connell, senior prelate of the Irish Catholic church, issued a blistering sermon last night in which he warned again "the false messiahs of the media age, and the snares they set for men's souls." The attack is thought to have been prompted by a sudden fall in the number of the faithful attending mass, which has reached
Tom Taylor footage "Doctored"
MaiadorNews - 6 minutes ago
Controversy continues to surround the live web-cam footage which seemed to show Tom Taylor, the real-life inspiration for the beloved fictional character, survive a nail bomb attac London's Globe Theatre. "Live is a debatable term in any case," said visual effects guru Malcolm Savage as he demonstrated seven ways in which...
Related link news source
all 3 news articles »
The Great Wheel Turns
BMZiney.org - 3 hours ago
Hottest tattoo in all the bod-mod shops from Alaska to Zanzibar is the Tommy Inscribed on the hand, where Tommy wears his, or on shoulder, chest, or even intimate...
BMZiney.org
Tommy Taylor™ and the Secret Message
CCB.com, United Kingdom - 8 hours ago
Fueling internet controversy about the acrostic poem in the thirteenth Tommy Taylor novel codebreaking expert Marcus Walls claims to have found no fewer than 144 further messag in the novels, including a prediction about the end of the world. The British cryptographer h now...
Taylor™-Made!
Nylons.com - 20 hours ago
The biggest party in the world was still in full swing in London last night, as seventeen thousand people continued to sit through a spontanious-and continuous-re-enactment of th events of all thirteen Tommy Taylor™ novels. "Anyone can join in," participant Leon Jess explaind. "We haven't rehearsed this. We're not acting, we're channelling the characters fro the...
Royals Notes OurParty Central (press release)
Photos OurParty Central (press release)
OurParty Central (press release) - OurParty Central (press release)
all 13 news articles »
Where's Wilson?
News Source - 20 hours ago
Pick up your binoculars and get looking! Mysteriously missing novelist Wilson Taylor is st out there somewhere. Recent sightings and hottest clues are on Whereswilson.net, with a dedicated message board and our unique Instant Update map, which overlays your sightin data on live satellite images of...
View topic...ypse Now!
http://www.I3TOMMY
Tay281
Posted: 3:16 am
Posts: 2278
Okey, but there are millions of prophesies in the Tommy Taylor books. They're all over the place. Which ones are you saying are going to come true?
Back to top
STANTHEMAN
Posted: 2008 3:52 am
Posts: 5081
I'm saying all the ones that are about Tommy are true. Wilson really had those dreams and really knew what the future was going to be. But he couldn't say it right out because people wouldn't have believed so he put it in a book.
Back to top
BunkMoreland
Posted: 4:36 am
Posts: 115
yeah, but there's lots of prophesies about Tommy. he's the creator and the destroyer, etcetera, and he's going to be like adam all over again, but he's also going to be more and less than man, and die without ending and end without dying or whatever that bit in the last book said. a lot of it doesn't make sense becase Wilson was making it up as he went along.
Back to top
STANTHEMAN
Posted: 5:24 am
Posts: 5082
He was telling us his dreams. Theres always been people who could dream the truth.
Back to top
Tay281
Posted: 9:17 am
Posts: 2279
You can't have you cake and eat it, though, can you? When was he dreaming the truth and when did he just have one too many vodkas? The prophesy bits in the books are all over the place.
Back to top
Seraphim
Posted: T11:16 am
Posts: 113
I think you just have to believe. It all makes sense if you believe.
Back to top
ANN - DRIFTER THOUGHT HE WAS VAMPIRE
http://www.AmplifiedNewNetwork.com/News/UK/Drifter.thought..was.htm
home / subscribe / donate / books / archives / search / links / feedback / events / faq
ANN Amplified News Network
DRIFTER THOUGHT HE WAS VAMPIRE
(cont'd)
now been positively identified as Arnold Mott, a schizophrenic who has spent more than six years in mental hospitals in Bristol and London. Mott believed he was the fictional vampire Count Ambrosio, from the much-loved Tommy Taylor™ novel sequence. According to relatives, it was an initially harmless obsession that became more sinister over time.
"It just consumed him," Mott's brother-in-law, Peter Beckwith, said yesterday. "We thought it was a game, at first, but in the end he couldn't distinguish between reality and fantasy."
Mott's obsession came to a head two weeks ago, when he attacked and kidnapped Tom Taylor, son of the famous novelist and inspiration for the fictional boy wizard Tommy Taylor™ . Escaping with minor injuries, Taylor is recuperating in London's Royal Free Hospital, where his condition is said to be

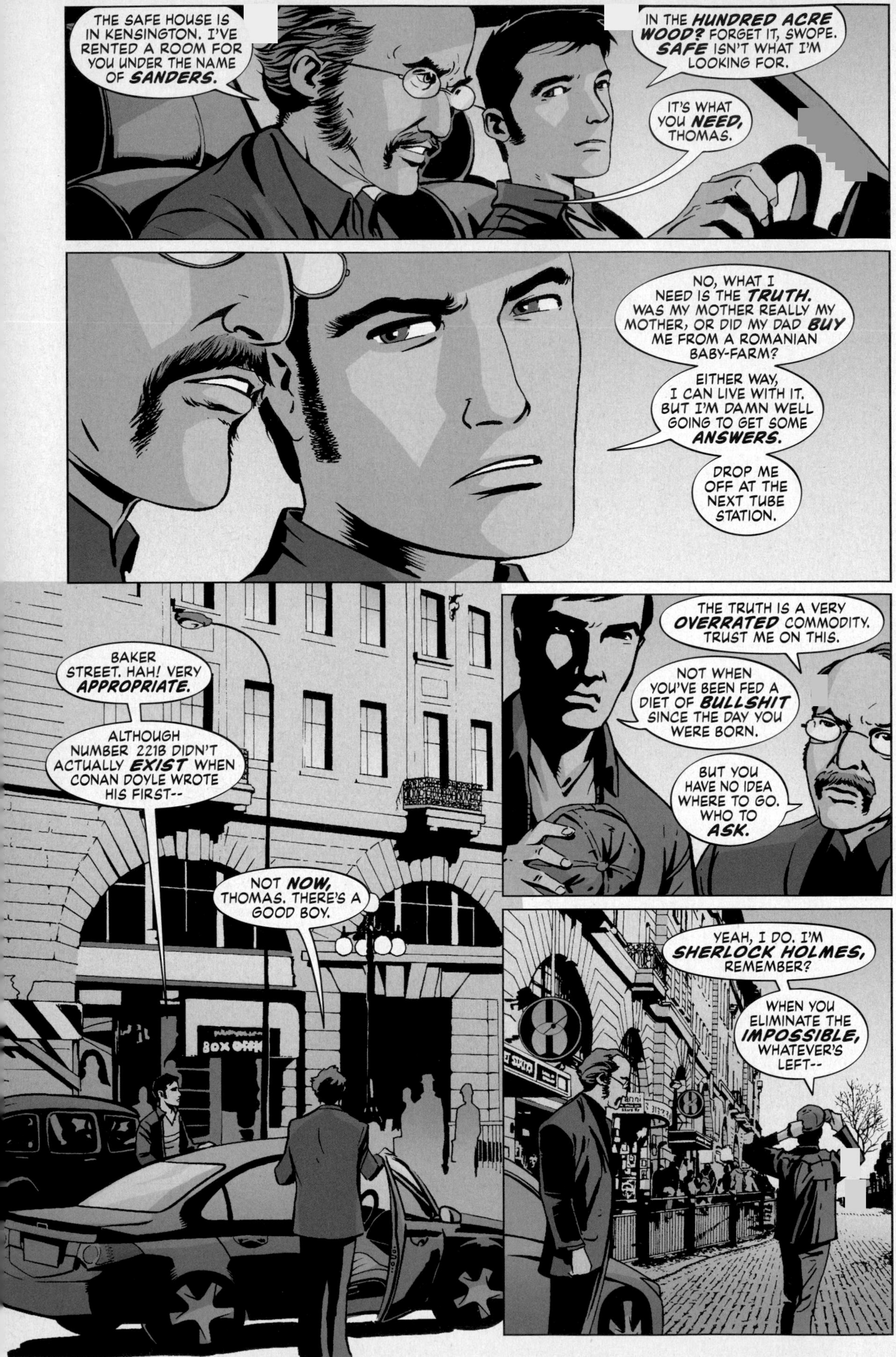
THE SAFE HOUSE IS IN KENSINGTON. I'VE RENTED A ROOM FOR YOU UNDER THE NAME OF SANDERS.
IN THE HUNDRED ACRE WOOD? FORGET IT, SWOPE. SAFE ISN'T WHAT I'M LOOKING FOR.
IT'S WHAT YOU NEED, THOMAS.
NO, WHAT I NEED IS THE TRUTH. WAS MY MOTHER REALLY MY MOTHER, OR DID MY DAD BUY ME FROM A ROMANIAN BABY-FARM?
EITHER WAY, I CAN LIVE WITH IT. BUT I'M DAMN WELL GOING TO GET SOME ANSWERS.
DROP ME OFF AT THE NEXT TUBE STATION.
THE TRUTH IS A VERY OVERRATED COMMODITY. TRUST ME ON THIS.
NOT WHEN YOU'VE BEEN FED A DIET OF BULLSHIT SINCE THE DAY YOU WERE BORN.
BUT YOU HAVE NO IDEA WHERE TO GO. WHO TO ASK.
BAKER STREET. HAH! VERY APPROPRIATE.
ALTHOUGH NUMBER 221B DIDN'T ACTUALLY EXIST WHEN CONAN DOYLE WROTE HIS FIRST--
NOT NOW, THOMAS. THERE'S A GOOD BOY.
BOX OFFI
YEAH, I DO. I'M SHERLOCK HOLMES, REMEMBER?
WHEN YOU ELIMINATE THE IMPOSSIBLE, WHATEVER'S LEFT--

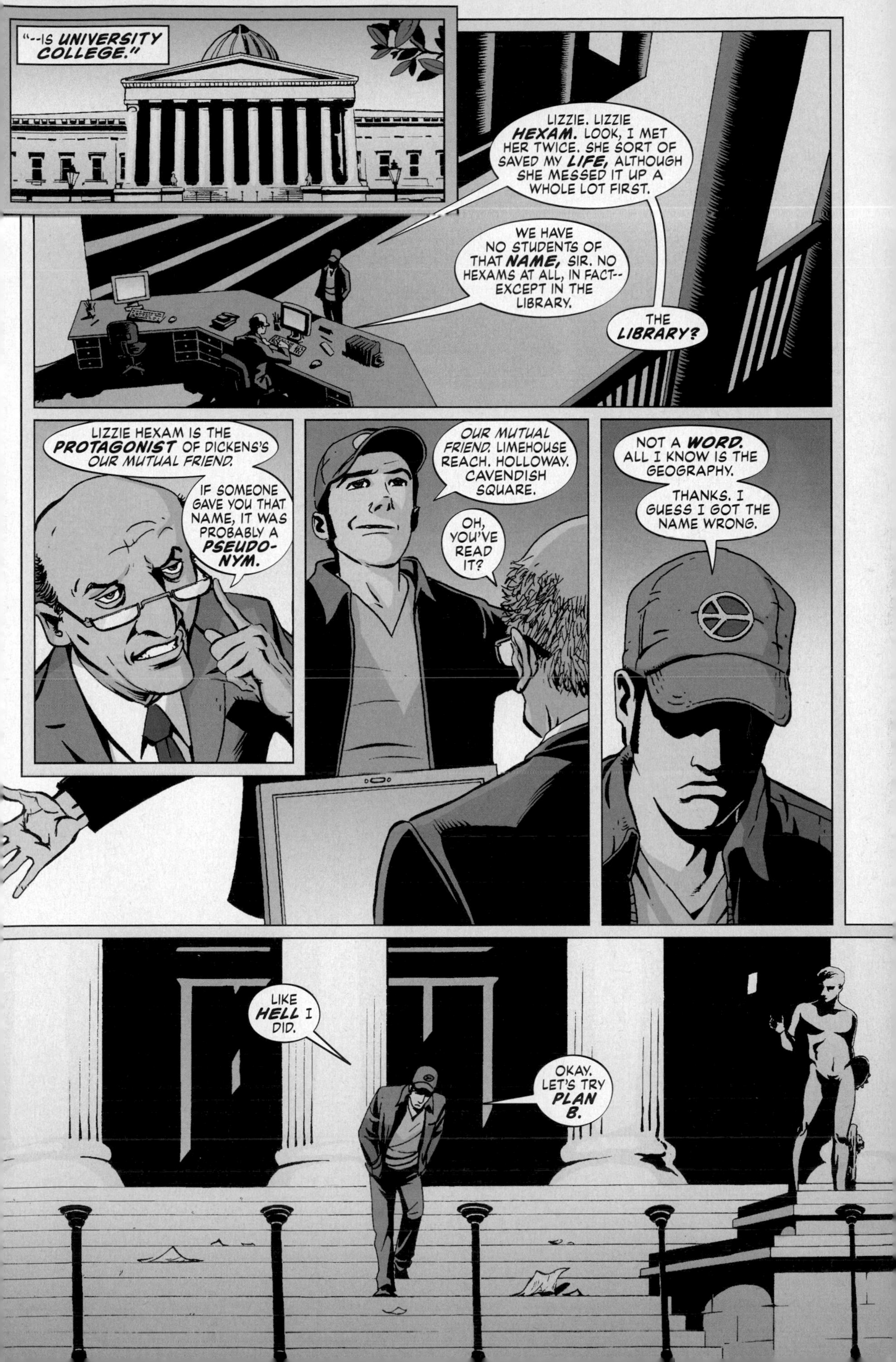
"--IS UNIVERSITY COLLEGE."
LIZZIE. LIZZIE HEXAM. LOOK, I MET HER TWICE. SHE SORT OF SAVED MY LIFE, ALTHOUGH SHE MESSED IT UP A WHOLE LOT FIRST.
WE HAVE NO STUDENTS OF THAT NAME, SIR. NO HEXAMS AT ALL, IN FACT--EXCEPT IN THE LIBRARY.
THE LIBRARY?
LIZZIE HEXAM IS THE PROTAGONIST OF DICKENS'S OUR MUTUAL FRIEND.
IF SOMEONE GAVE YOU THAT NAME, IT WAS PROBABLY A PSEUDO-NYM.
OUR MUTUAL FRIEND. LIMEHOUSE REACH. HOLLOWAY. CAVENDISH SQUARE.
OH, YOU'VE READ IT?
NOT A WORD. ALL I KNOW IS THE GEOGRAPHY.
THANKS. I GUESS I GOT THE NAME WRONG.
LIKE HELL I DID.
OKAY. LET'S TRY PLAN B.

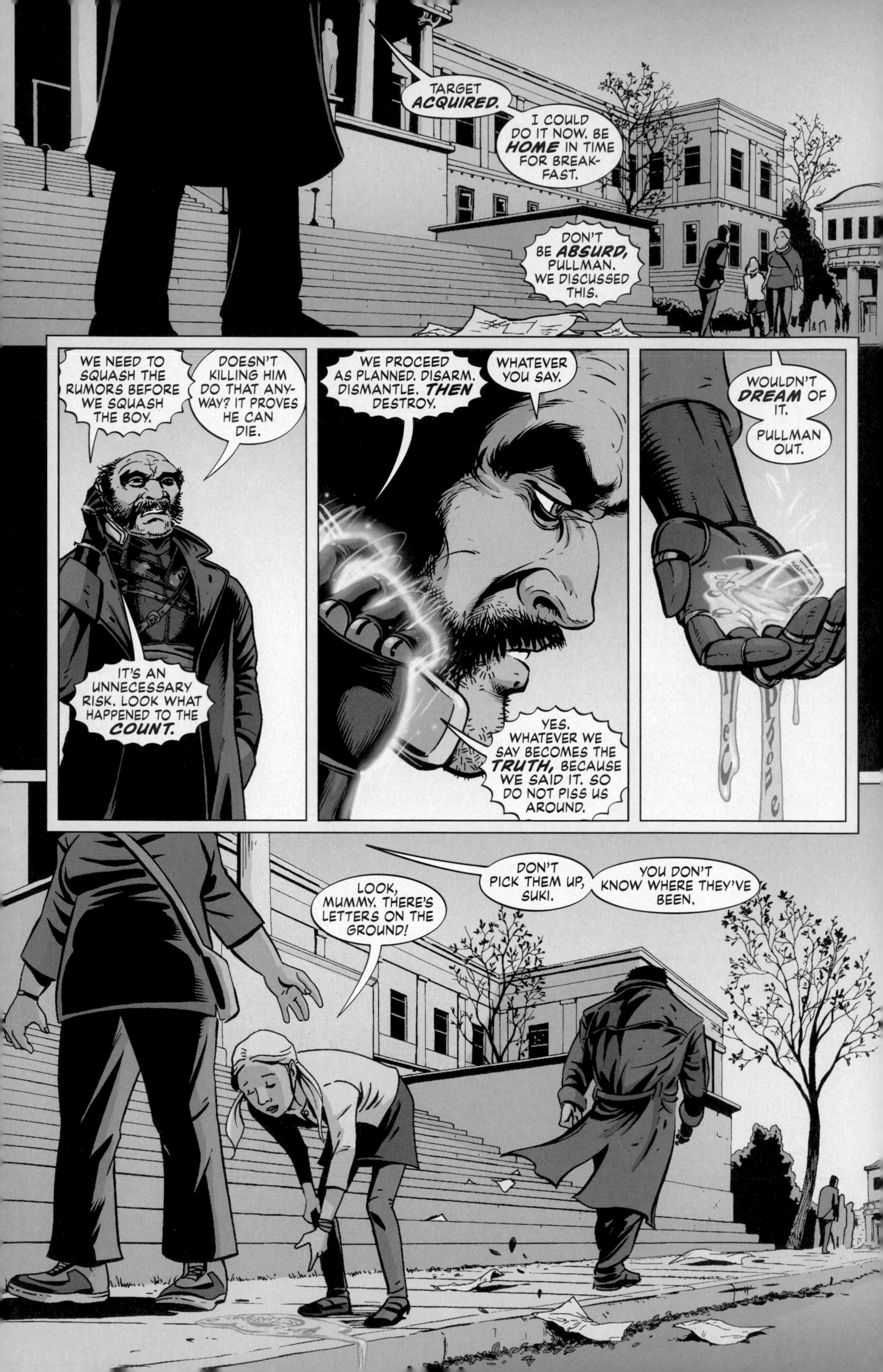
TARGET ACQUIRED.
I COULD DO IT NOW. BE HOME IN TIME FOR BREAK-FAST.
DON'T BE ABSURD, PULLMAN. WE DISCUSSED THIS.
WE NEED TO SQUASH THE RUMORS BEFORE WE SQUASH THE BOY.
DOESN'T KILLING HIM DO THAT ANY-WAY? IT PROVES HE CAN DIE.
IT'S AN UNNECESSARY RISK. LOOK WHAT HAPPENED TO THE COUNT.
WE PROCEED AS PLANNED. DISARM. DISMANTLE. THEN DESTROY.
WHATEVER YOU SAY.
YES. WHATEVER WE SAY BECOMES THE TRUTH, BECAUSE WE SAID IT. SO DO NOT PISS US AROUND.
WOULDN'T DREAM OF IT.
PULLMAN OUT.
LOOK, MUMMY. THERE'S LETTERS ON THE GROUND!
DON'T PICK THEM UP, SUKI.
YOU DON'T KNOW WHERE THEY'VE BEEN.

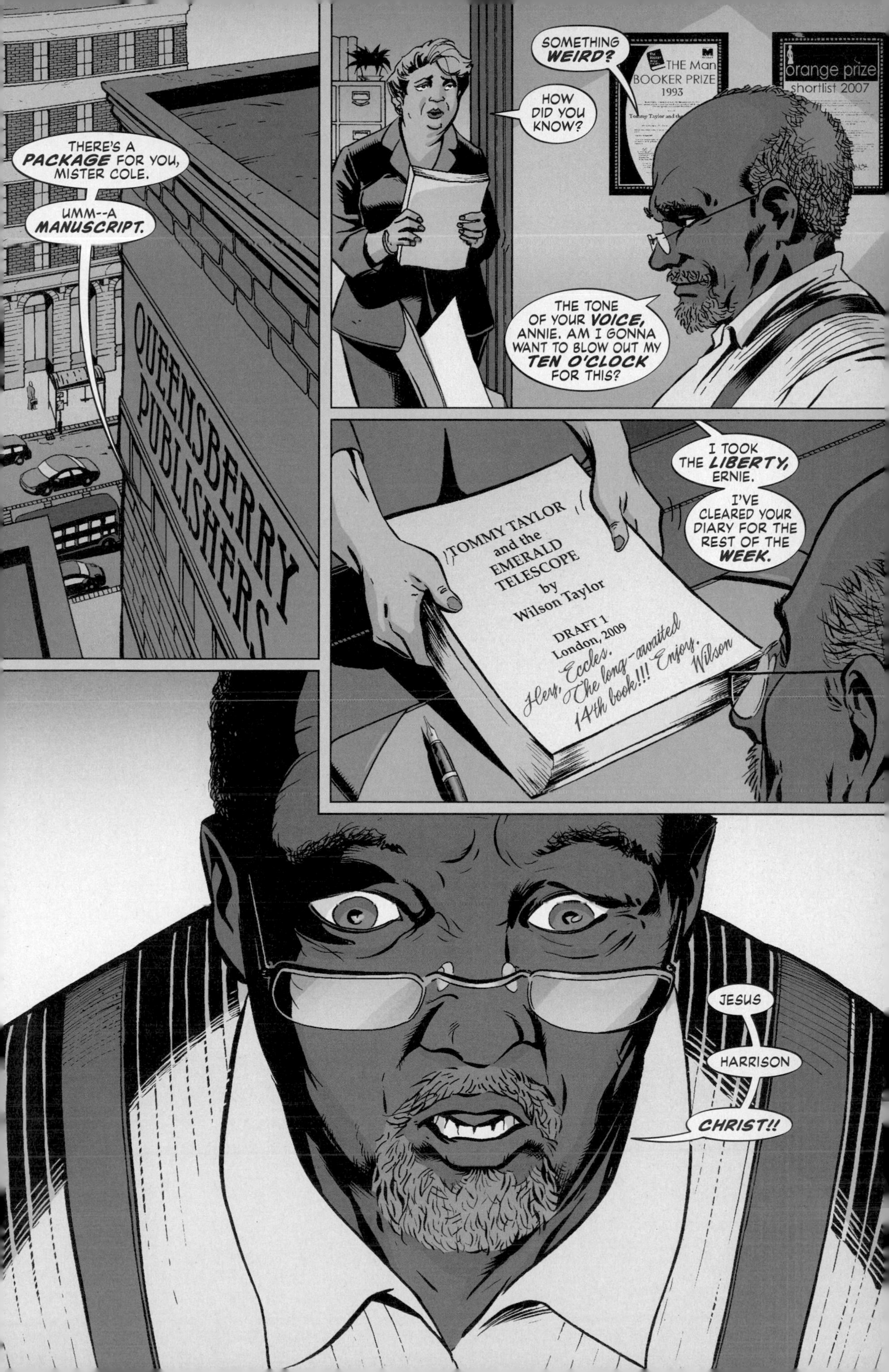
QUEENSBERRY PUBLISHERS
THERE'S A PACKAGE FOR YOU, MISTER COLE.
UMM--A MANUSCRIPT.
SOMETHING WEIRD?
HOW DID YOU KNOW?
THE Man BOOKER PRIZE 1993
Tommy Taylor and the
orange prize shortlist 2007
THE TONE OF YOUR VOICE, ANNIE. AM I GONNA WANT TO BLOW OUT MY TEN O'CLOCK FOR THIS?
I TOOK THE LIBERTY, ERNIE.
I'VE CLEARED YOUR DIARY FOR THE REST OF THE WEEK.
TOMMY TAYLOR and the EMERALD TELESCOPE by Wilson Taylor
DRAFT 1 London, 2009
Hey, Eccles. The long-awaited 14th book!!! Enjoy. Wilson
JESUS
HARRISON
CHRIST!!

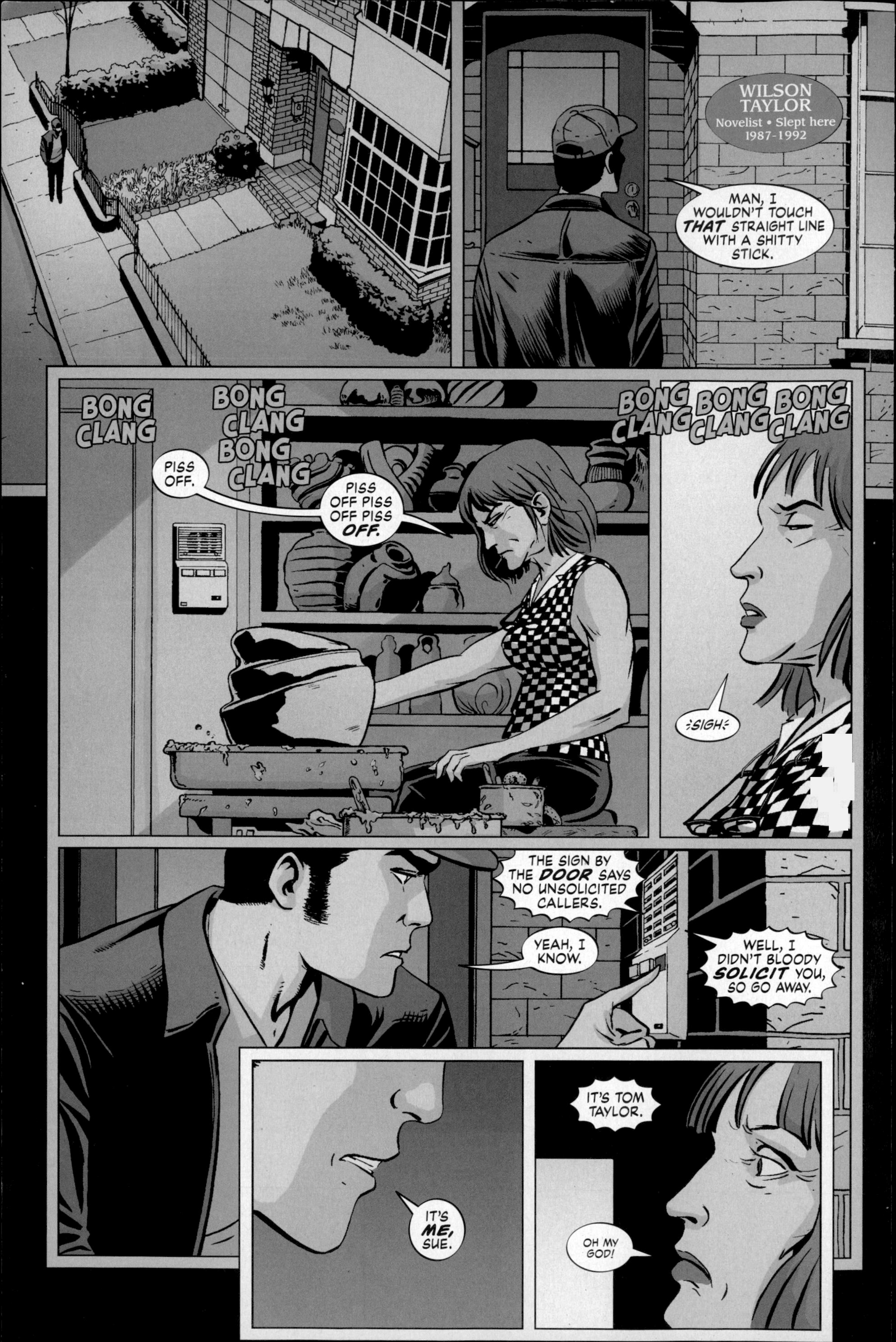
WILSON TAYLOR
Novelist • Slept here
1987-1992
MAN, I WOULDN'T TOUCH THAT STRAIGHT LINE WITH A SHITTY STICK.
BONG CLANG
BONG CLANG BONG CLANG
PISS OFF.
PISS OFF PISS OFF PISS OFF.
BONG CLANG BONG CLANG BONG CLANG
SIGH
THE SIGN BY THE DOOR SAYS NO UNSOLICITED CALLERS.
YEAH, I KNOW.
WELL, I DIDN'T BLOODY SOLICIT YOU, SO GO AWAY.
IT'S ME, SUE.
IT'S TOM TAYLOR.
OH MY GOD!

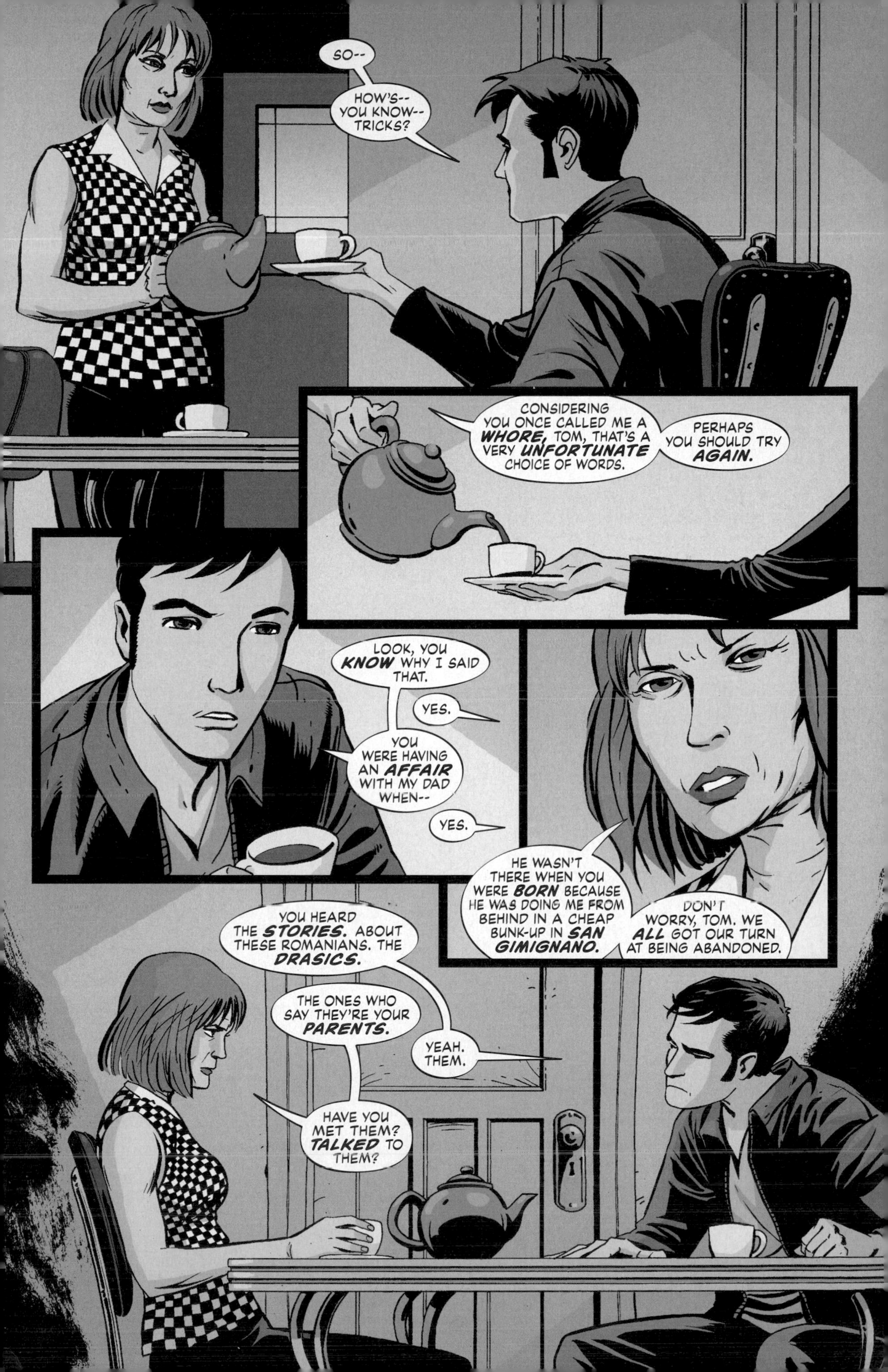
SO--
HOW'S-- YOU KNOW-- TRICKS?
CONSIDERING YOU ONCE CALLED ME A WHORE, TOM, THAT'S A VERY UNFORTUNATE CHOICE OF WORDS.
PERHAPS YOU SHOULD TRY AGAIN.
LOOK, YOU KNOW WHY I SAID THAT.
YES.
YOU WERE HAVING AN AFFAIR WITH MY DAD WHEN--
YES.
HE WASN'T THERE WHEN YOU WERE BORN BECAUSE HE WAS DOING ME FROM BEHIND IN A CHEAP BUNK-UP IN SAN GIMIGNANO.
DON'T WORRY, TOM. WE ALL GOT OUR TURN AT BEING ABANDONED.
YOU HEARD THE STORIES. ABOUT THESE ROMANIANS. THE DRASICS.
THE ONES WHO SAY THEY'RE YOUR PARENTS.
YEAH. THEM.
HAVE YOU MET THEM? TALKED TO THEM?

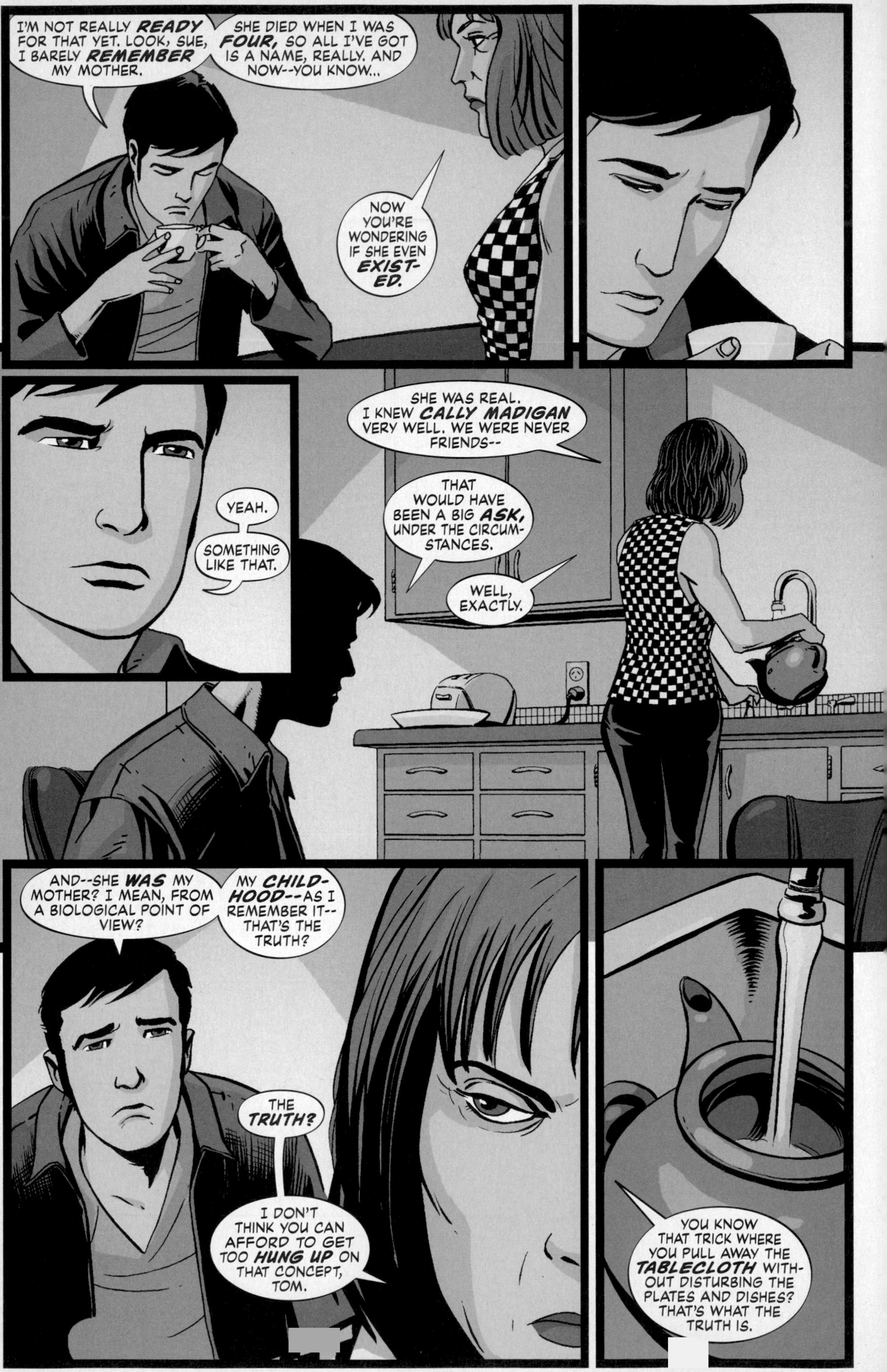
I'M NOT REALLY READY FOR THAT YET. LOOK, SUE, I BARELY REMEMBER MY MOTHER.
SHE DIED WHEN I WAS FOUR, SO ALL I'VE GOT IS A NAME, REALLY. AND NOW--YOU KNOW...
NOW YOU'RE WONDERING IF SHE EVEN EXIST-ED.
YEAH.
SOMETHING LIKE THAT.
SHE WAS REAL. I KNEW CALLY MADIGAN VERY WELL. WE WERE NEVER FRIENDS--
THAT WOULD HAVE BEEN A BIG ASK, UNDER THE CIRCUM-STANCES.
WELL, EXACTLY.
AND--SHE WAS MY MOTHER? I MEAN, FROM A BIOLOGICAL POINT OF VIEW?
MY CHILD-HOOD--AS I REMEMBER IT--THAT'S THE TRUTH?
THE TRUTH?
I DON'T THINK YOU CAN AFFORD TO GET TOO HUNG UP ON THAT CONCEPT, TOM.
YOU KNOW THAT TRICK WHERE YOU PULL AWAY THE TABLECLOTH WITH-OUT DISTURBING THE PLATES AND DISHES? THAT'S WHAT THE TRUTH IS.

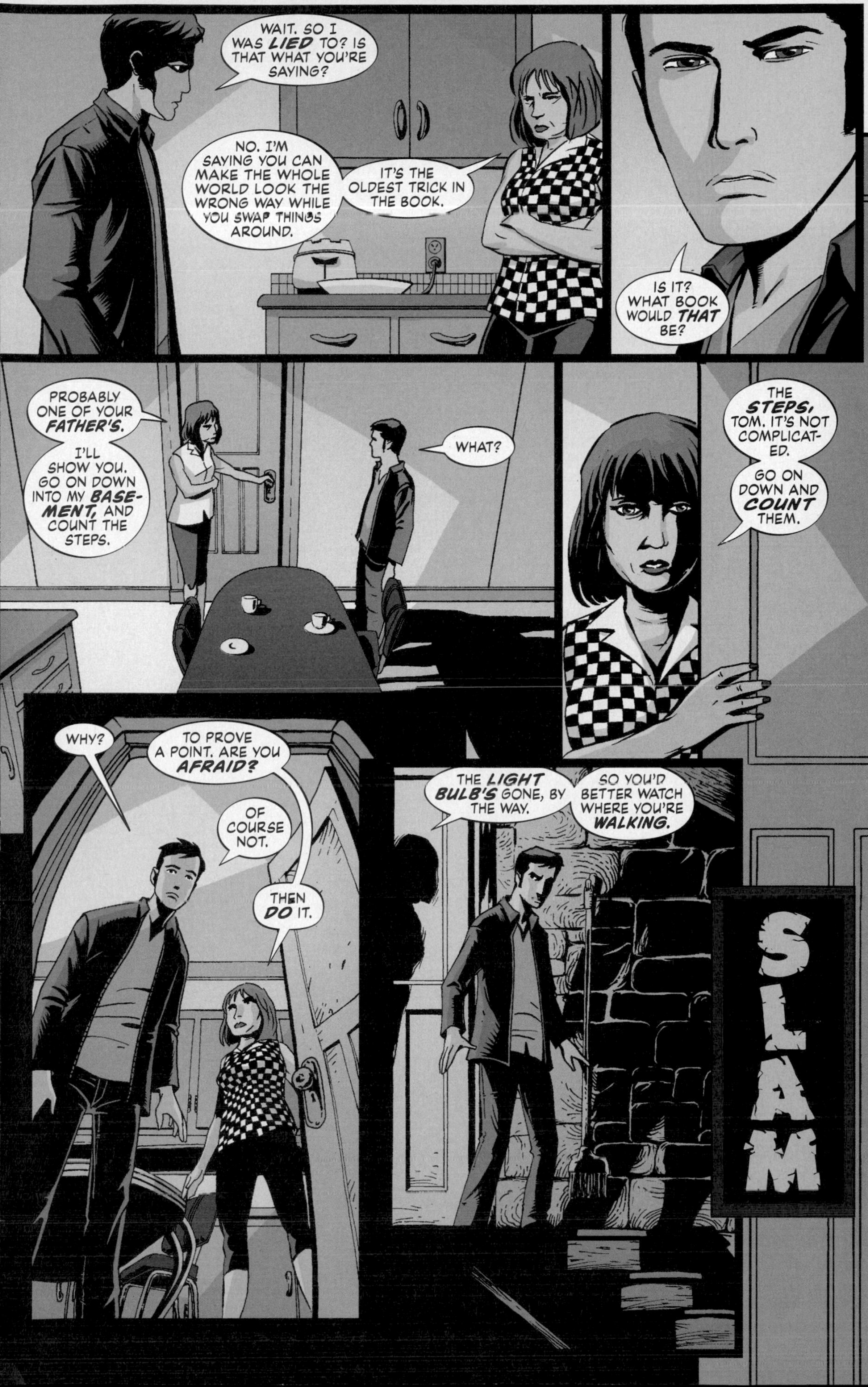
WAIT. SO I WAS LIED TO? IS THAT WHAT YOU'RE SAYING?
NO. I'M SAYING YOU CAN MAKE THE WHOLE WORLD LOOK THE WRONG WAY WHILE YOU SWAP THINGS AROUND.
IT'S THE OLDEST TRICK IN THE BOOK.
IS IT? WHAT BOOK WOULD THAT BE?
PROBABLY ONE OF YOUR FATHER'S.
I'LL SHOW YOU. GO ON DOWN INTO MY BASEMENT, AND COUNT THE STEPS.
WHAT?
THE STEPS, TOM. IT'S NOT COMPLICATED.
GO ON DOWN AND COUNT THEM.
WHY?
TO PROVE A POINT. ARE YOU AFRAID?
OF COURSE NOT.
THEN DO IT.
THE LIGHT BULB'S GONE, BY THE WAY.
SO YOU'D BETTER WATCH WHERE YOU'RE WALKING.
SLAM

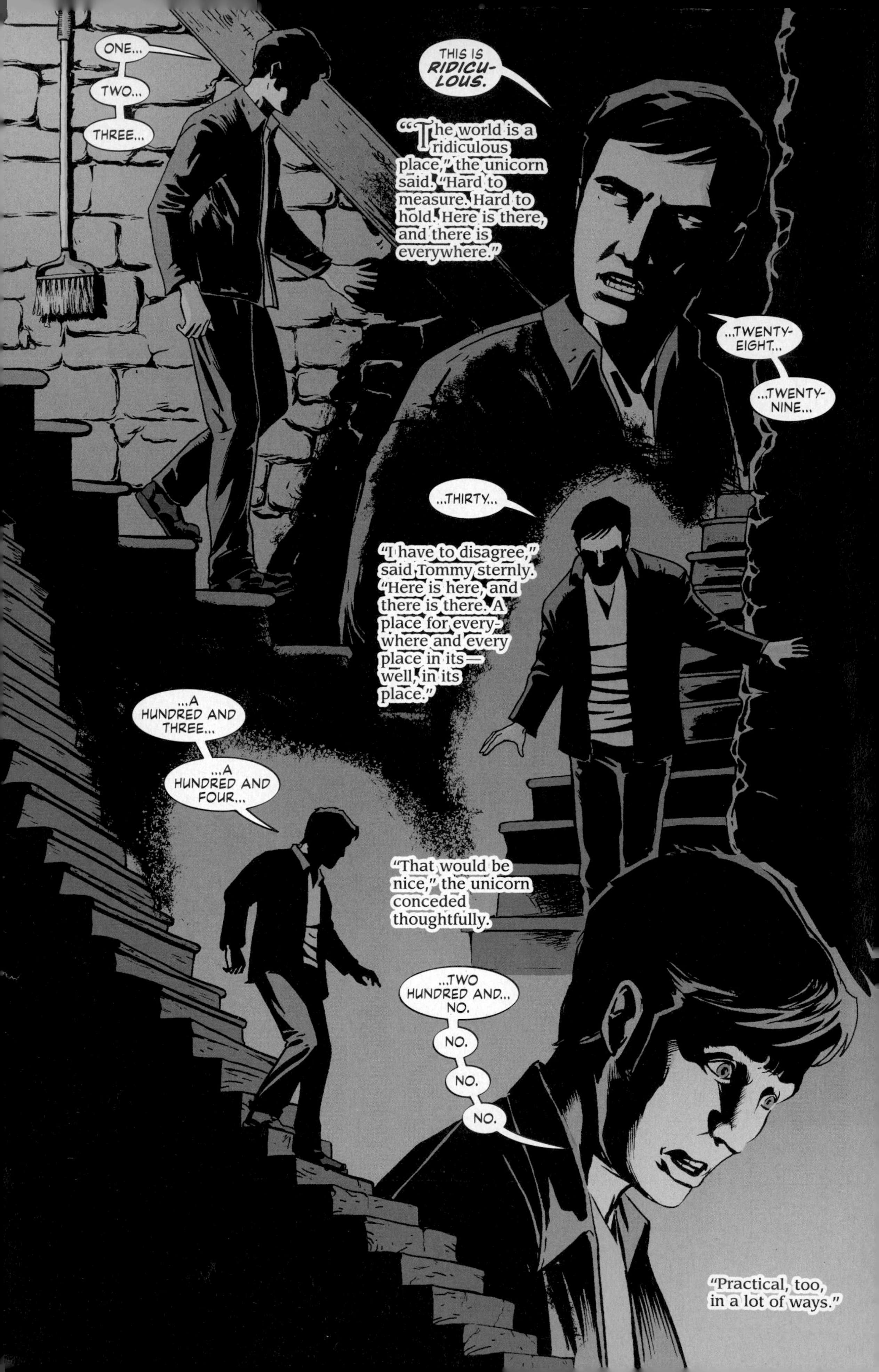
ONE...
TWO...
THREE...
THIS IS RIDICULOUS.
"The world is a ridiculous place," the unicorn said. "Hard to measure. Hard to hold. Here is there, and there is everywhere."
...TWENTY-EIGHT...
...TWENTY-NINE...
...THIRTY...
"I have to disagree," said Tommy sternly. "Here is here, and there is there. A place for every-where and every place in its— well, in its place."
...A HUNDRED AND THREE...
...A HUNDRED AND FOUR...
"That would be nice," the unicorn conceded thoughtfully.
...TWO HUNDRED AND... NO.
NO.
NO.
NO.
"Practical, too, in a lot of ways."

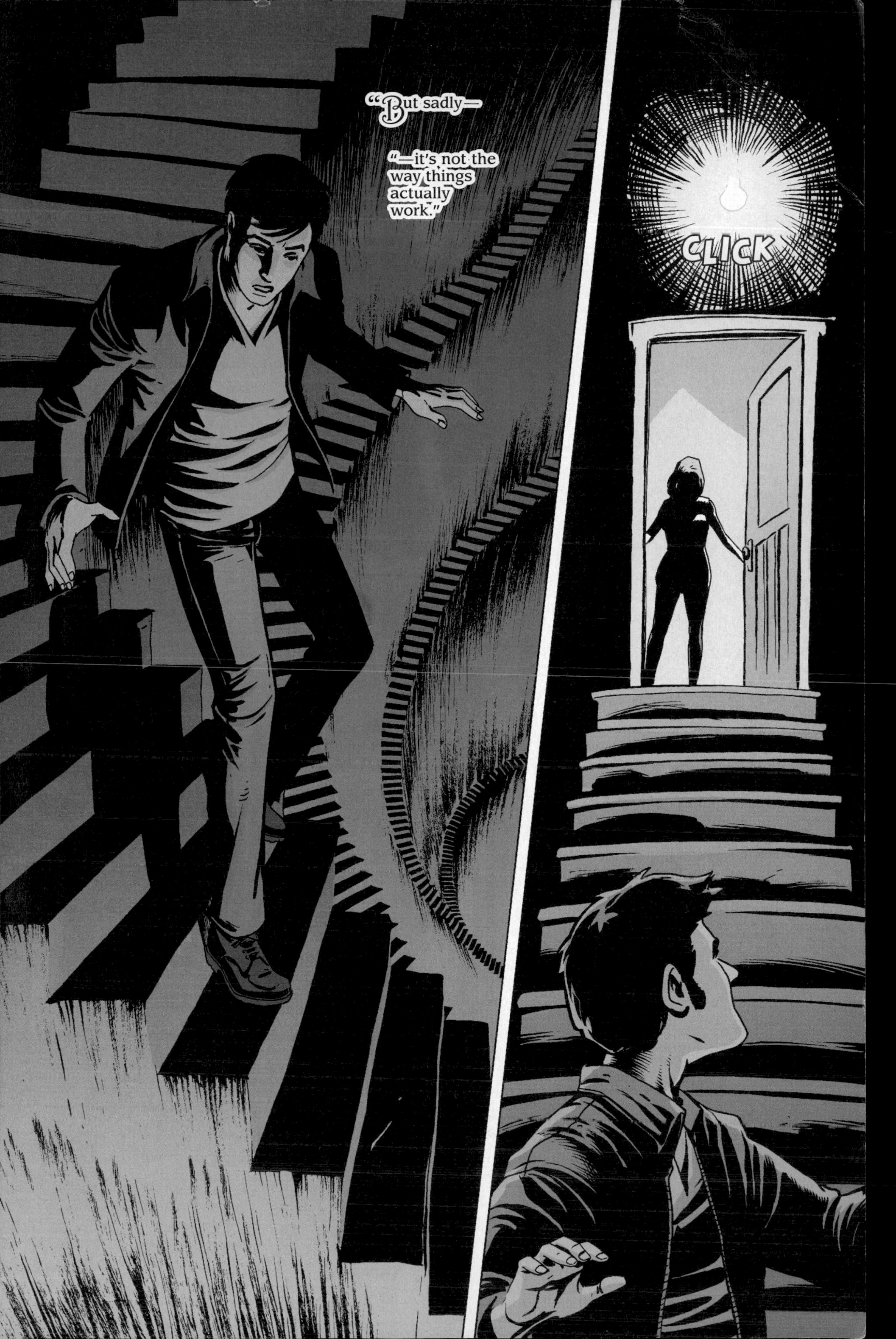
"But sadly—
"—it's not the way things actually work."
CLICK

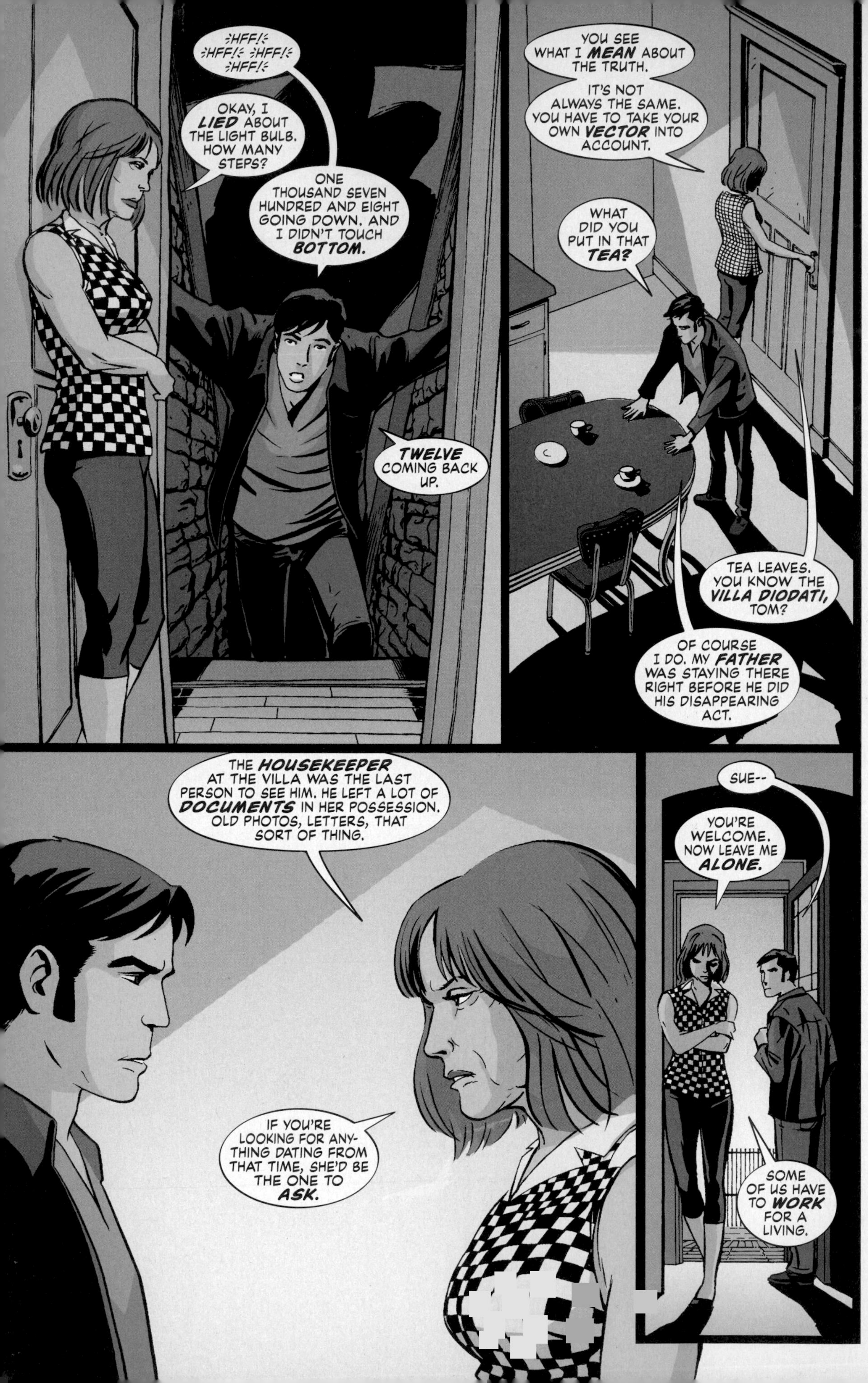
HFF! HFF! HFF! HFF!
OKAY, I LIED ABOUT THE LIGHT BULB. HOW MANY STEPS?
ONE THOUSAND SEVEN HUNDRED AND EIGHT GOING DOWN. AND I DIDN'T TOUCH BOTTOM.
TWELVE COMING BACK UP.
YOU SEE WHAT I MEAN ABOUT THE TRUTH.
IT'S NOT ALWAYS THE SAME. YOU HAVE TO TAKE YOUR OWN VECTOR INTO ACCOUNT.
WHAT DID YOU PUT IN THAT TEA?
TEA LEAVES. YOU KNOW THE VILLA DIODATI, TOM?
OF COURSE I DO. MY FATHER WAS STAYING THERE RIGHT BEFORE HE DID HIS DISAPPEARING ACT.
THE HOUSEKEEPER AT THE VILLA WAS THE LAST PERSON TO SEE HIM. HE LEFT A LOT OF DOCUMENTS IN HER POSSESSION. OLD PHOTOS, LETTERS, THAT SORT OF THING.
IF YOU'RE LOOKING FOR ANY-THING DATING FROM THAT TIME, SHE'D BE THE ONE TO ASK.
SUE--
YOU'RE WELCOME. NOW LEAVE ME ALONE.
SOME OF US HAVE TO WORK FOR A LIVING.

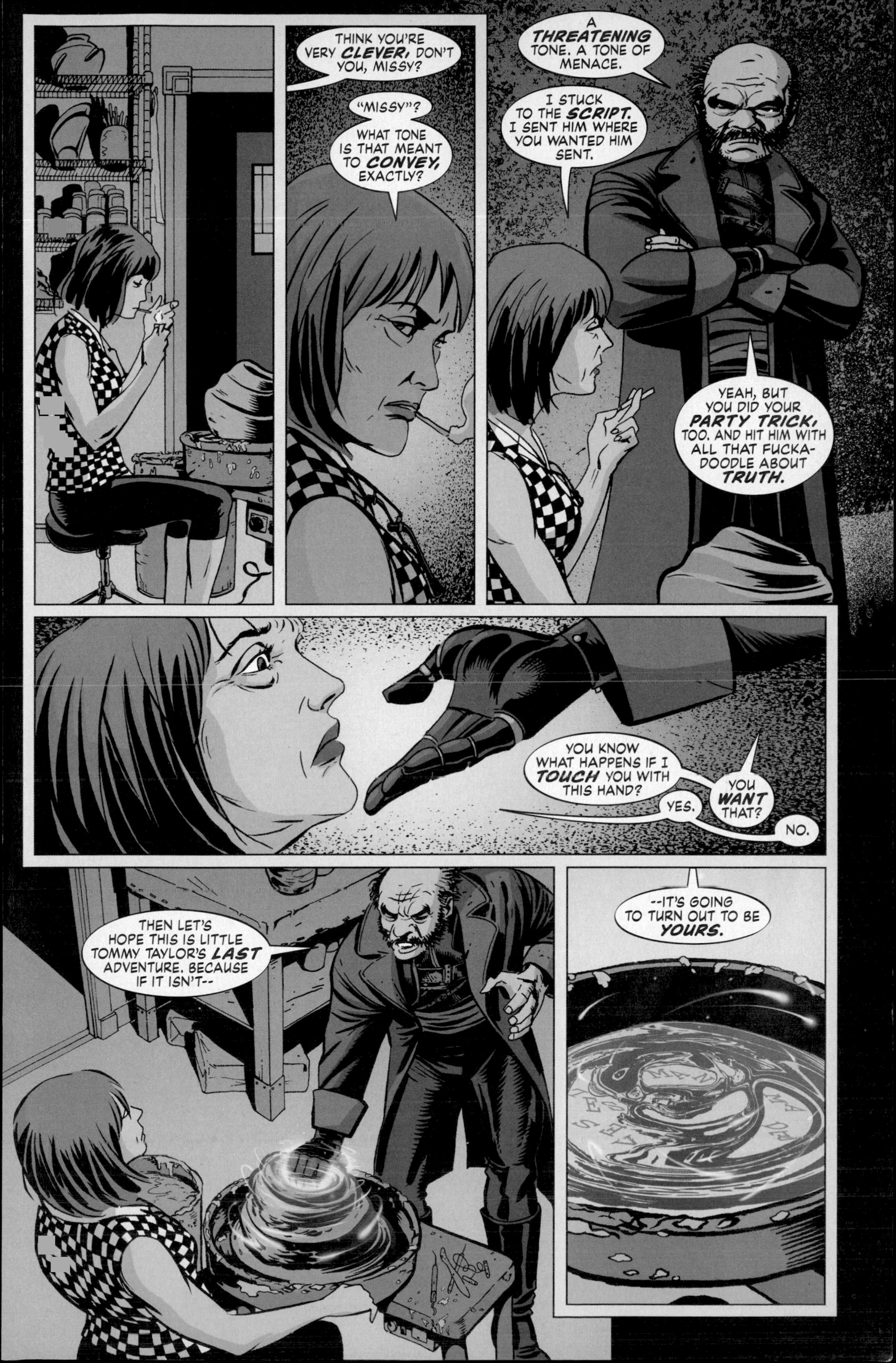
THINK YOU'RE VERY CLEVER, DON'T YOU, MISSY?
"MISSY"? WHAT TONE IS THAT MEANT TO CONVEY, EXACTLY?
A THREATENING TONE. A TONE OF MENACE.
I STUCK TO THE SCRIPT. I SENT HIM WHERE YOU WANTED HIM SENT.
YEAH, BUT YOU DID YOUR PARTY TRICK, TOO. AND HIT HIM WITH ALL THAT FUCKA-DOODLE ABOUT TRUTH.
YOU KNOW WHAT HAPPENS IF I TOUCH YOU WITH THIS HAND?
YES.
YOU WANT THAT?
NO.
THEN LET'S HOPE THIS IS LITTLE TOMMY TAYLOR'S LAST ADVENTURE. BECAUSE IF IT ISN'T--
--IT'S GOING TO TURN OUT TO BE YOURS.

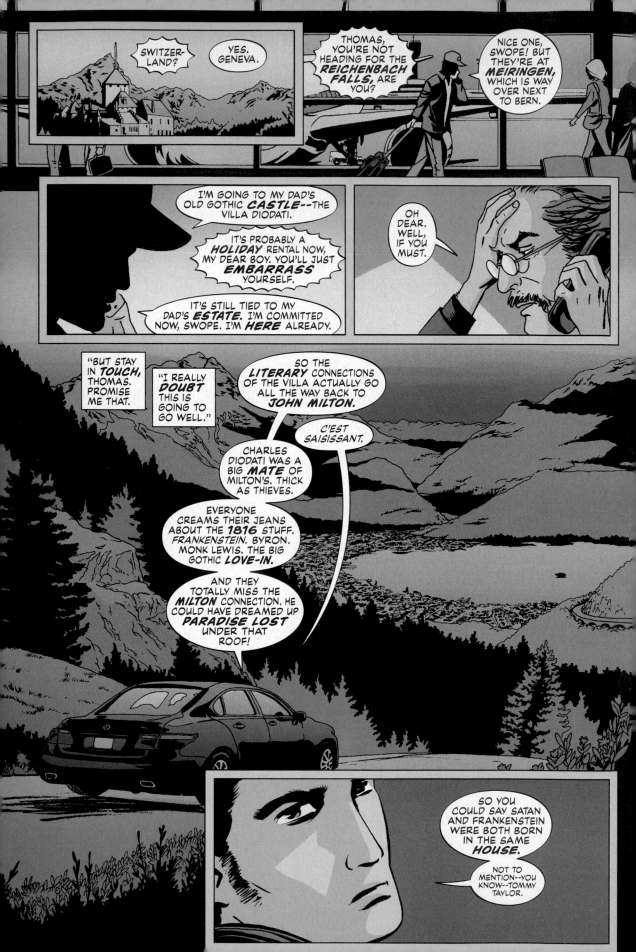

SWITZER-LAND?

YES. GENEVA.

THOMAS, YOU'RE NOT HEADING FOR THE *REICHENBACH FALLS*, ARE YOU?

NICE ONE, SWOPE! BUT THEY'RE AT *MEIRINGEN*, WHICH IS WAY OVER NEXT TO BERN.

I'M GOING TO MY DAD'S OLD GOTHIC *CASTLE*--THE VILLA DIODATI.

IT'S PROBABLY A *HOLIDAY* RENTAL NOW, MY DEAR BOY. YOU'LL JUST *EMBARRASS* YOURSELF.

IT'S STILL TIED TO MY DAD'S *ESTATE*. I'M COMMITTED NOW, SWOPE. I'M *HERE* ALREADY.

OH DEAR. WELL, IF YOU MUST.

"BUT STAY IN *TOUCH*, THOMAS. PROMISE ME THAT."

"I REALLY *DOUBT* THIS IS GOING TO GO WELL."

SO THE *LITERARY* CONNECTIONS OF THE VILLA ACTUALLY GO ALL THE WAY BACK TO *JOHN MILTON*.

C'EST SAISISSANT.

CHARLES DIODATI WAS A BIG *MATE* OF MILTON'S. THICK AS THIEVES.

EVERYONE CREAMS THEIR JEANS ABOUT THE *1816* STUFF. FRANKENSTEIN. BYRON. MONK LEWIS. THE BIG GOTHIC *LOVE-IN*.

AND THEY TOTALLY MISS THE *MILTON* CONNECTION. HE COULD HAVE DREAMED UP *PARADISE LOST* UNDER THAT ROOF!

SO YOU COULD SAY SATAN AND FRANKENSTEIN WERE BOTH BORN IN THE SAME *HOUSE*.

NOT TO MENTION--YOU KNOW--TOMMY TAYLOR.

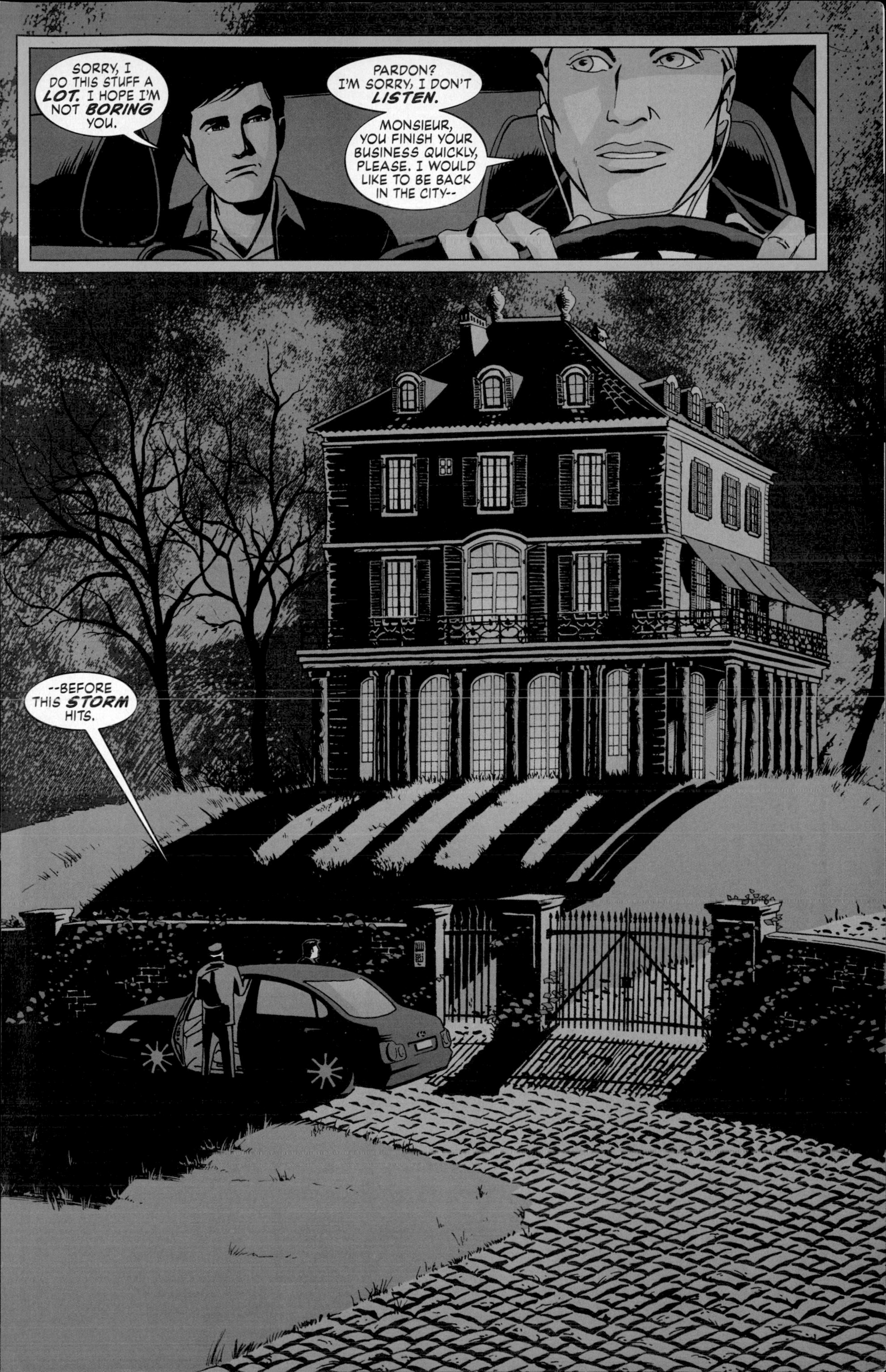

SORRY, I DO THIS STUFF A LOT. I HOPE I'M NOT BORING YOU.
PARDON? I'M SORRY, I DON'T LISTEN.
MONSIEUR, YOU FINISH YOUR BUSINESS QUICKLY, PLEASE. I WOULD LIKE TO BE BACK IN THE CITY--
--BEFORE THIS STORM HITS.

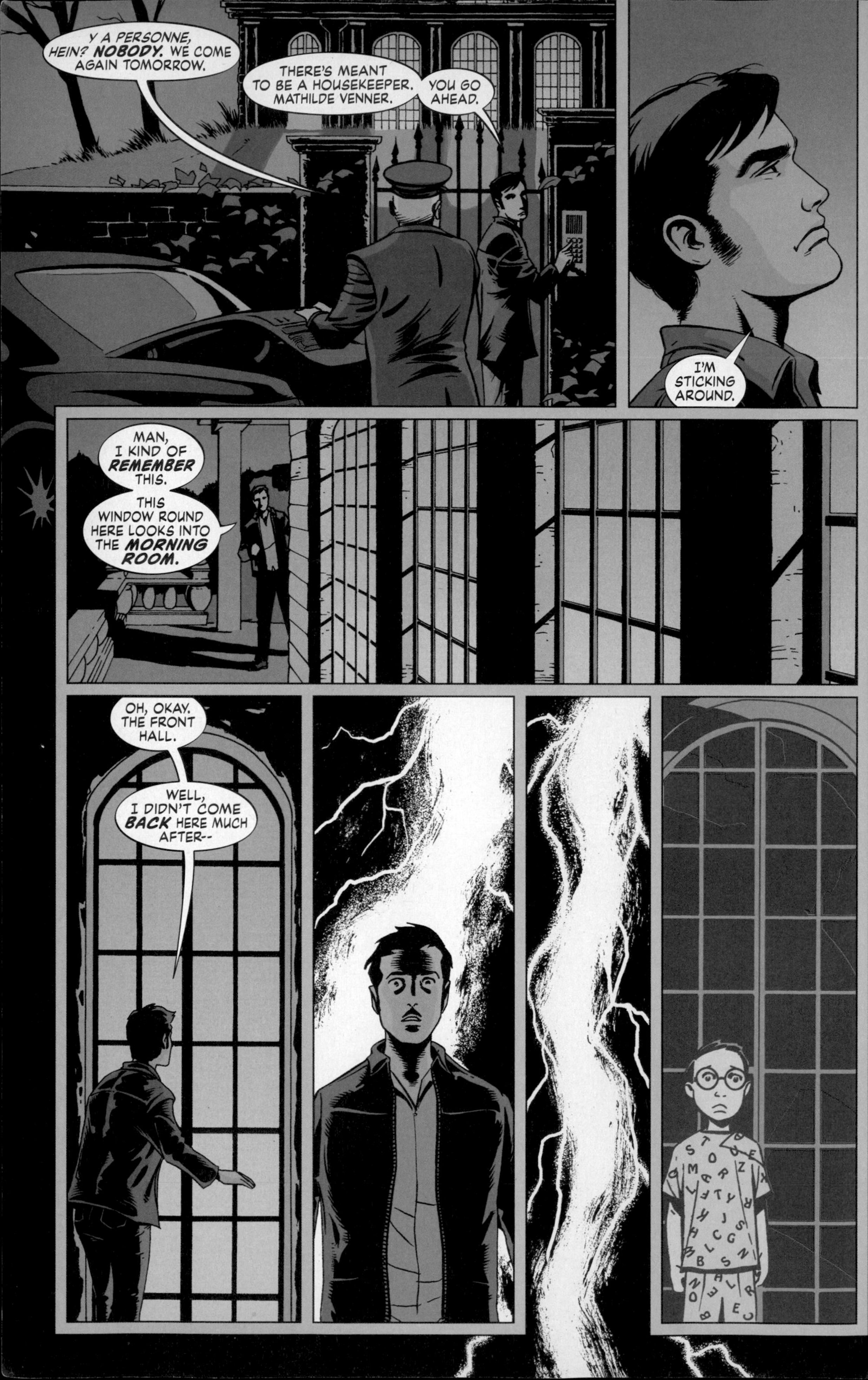
Y A PERSONNE, HEIN? NOBODY. WE COME AGAIN TOMORROW.
THERE'S MEANT TO BE A HOUSEKEEPER. MATHILDE VENNER.
YOU GO AHEAD.
I'M STICKING AROUND.
MAN, I KIND OF REMEMBER THIS.
THIS WINDOW ROUND HERE LOOKS INTO THE MORNING ROOM.
OH, OKAY. THE FRONT HALL.
WELL, I DIDN'T COME BACK HERE MUCH AFTER--

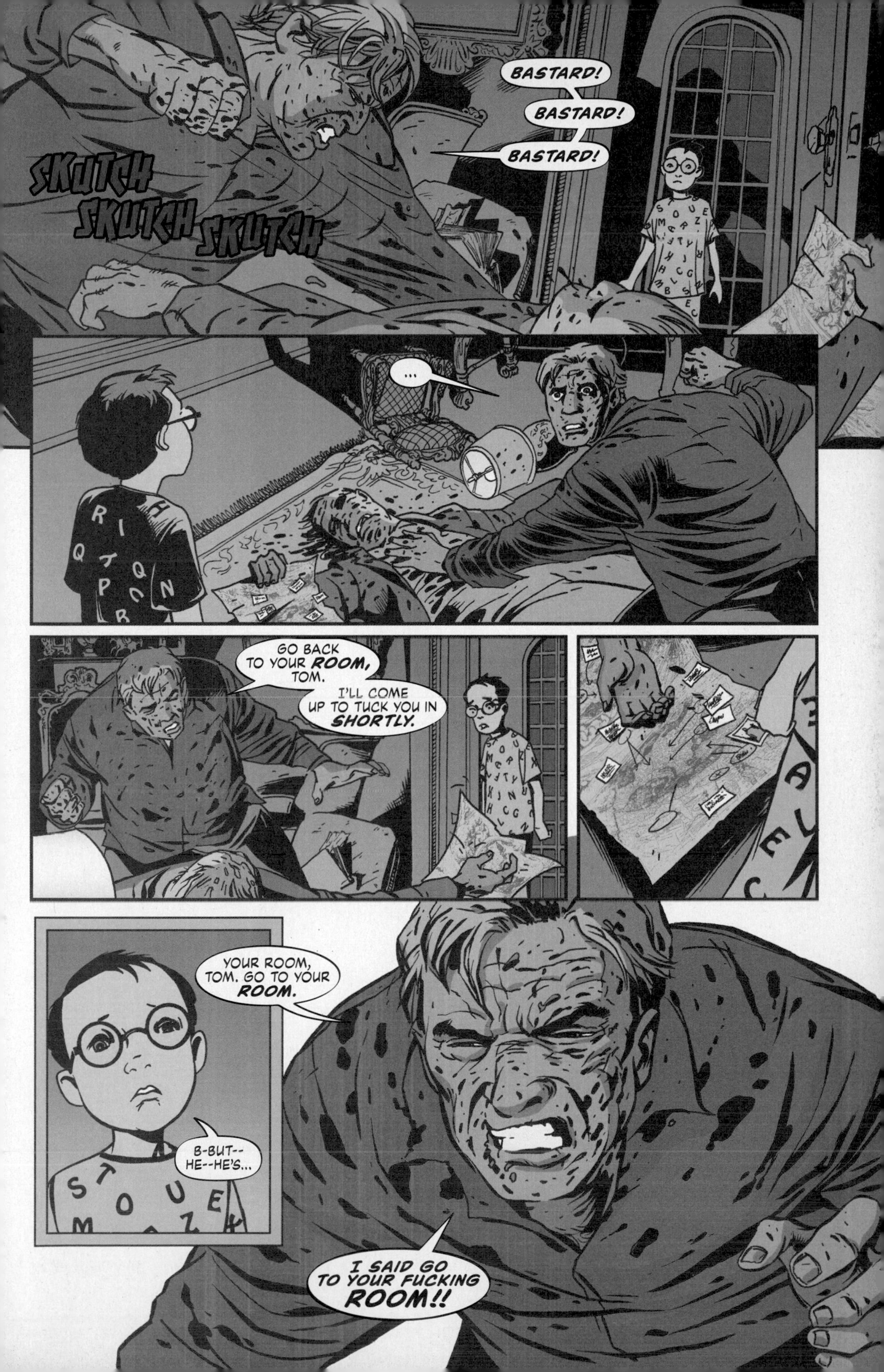
BASTARD!
BASTARD!
BASTARD!
SKUTCH
SKUTCH
SKUTCH
...
GO BACK TO YOUR ROOM, TOM.
I'LL COME UP TO TUCK YOU IN SHORTLY.
YOUR ROOM, TOM. GO TO YOUR ROOM.
B-BUT-- HE--HE'S...
I SAID GO TO YOUR FUCKING ROOM!!

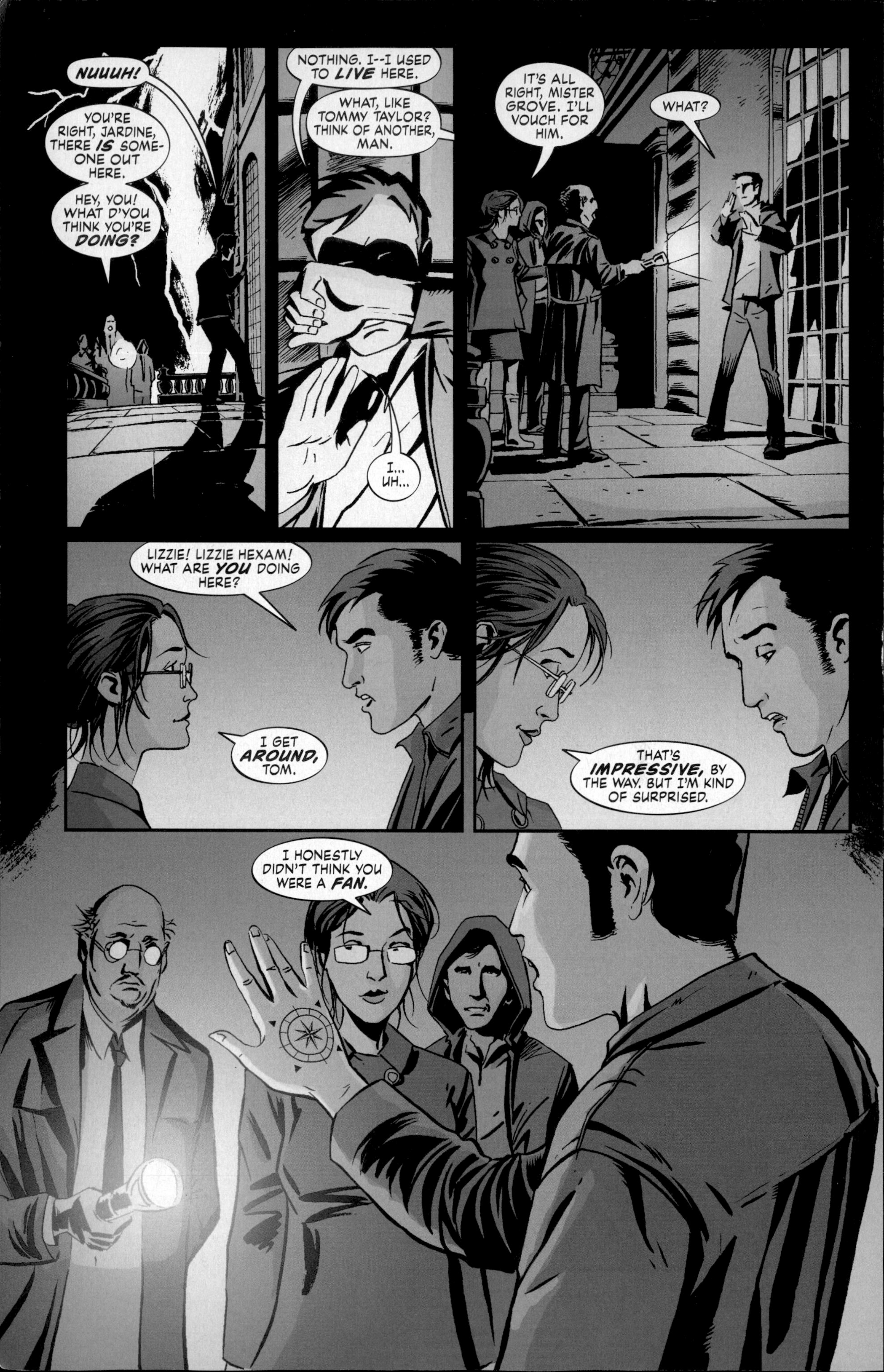
NUUUH!
YOU'RE RIGHT, JARDINE, THERE IS SOME-ONE OUT HERE.
HEY, YOU! WHAT D'YOU THINK YOU'RE DOING?
NOTHING. I--I USED TO LIVE HERE.
WHAT, LIKE TOMMY TAYLOR? THINK OF ANOTHER, MAN.
I... UH...
IT'S ALL RIGHT, MISTER GROVE. I'LL VOUCH FOR HIM.
WHAT?
LIZZIE! LIZZIE HEXAM! WHAT ARE YOU DOING HERE?
I GET AROUND, TOM.
THAT'S IMPRESSIVE, BY THE WAY. BUT I'M KIND OF SURPRISED.
I HONESTLY DIDN'T THINK YOU WERE A FAN.

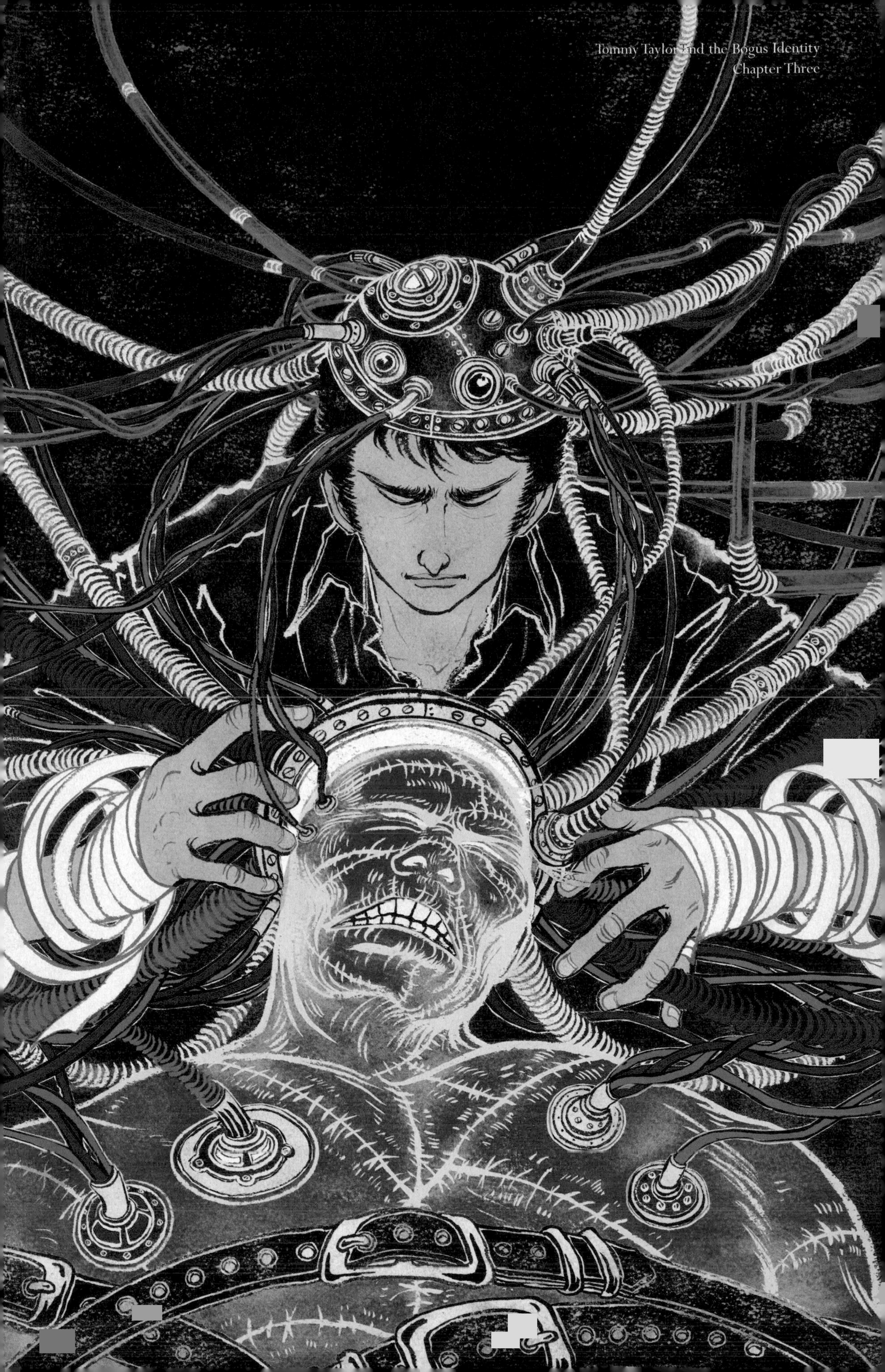
Tommy Taylor and the Bogus Identity
Chapter Three

Sketch by Yuko Shimizu

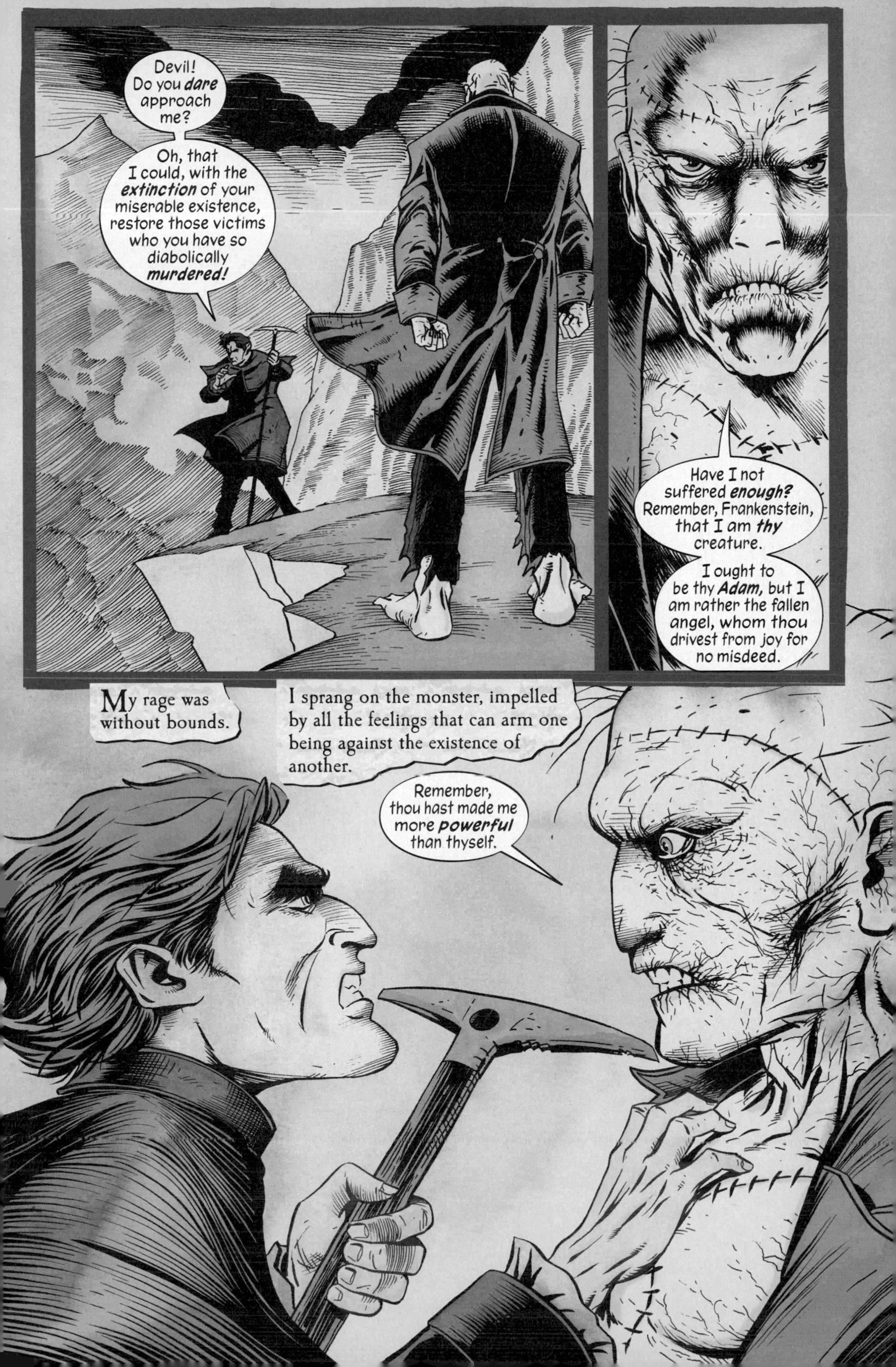
Devil! Do you *dare* approach me?
Oh, that I could, with the *extinction* of your miserable existence, restore those victims who you have so diabolically *murdered!*
Have I not suffered *enough?* Remember, Frankenstein, that I am *thy* creature.
I ought to be thy *Adam,* but I am rather the fallen angel, whom thou drivest from joy for no misdeed.
My rage was without bounds.
I sprang on the monster, impelled by all the feelings that can arm one being against the existence of another.
Remember, thou hast made me more *powerful* than thyself.

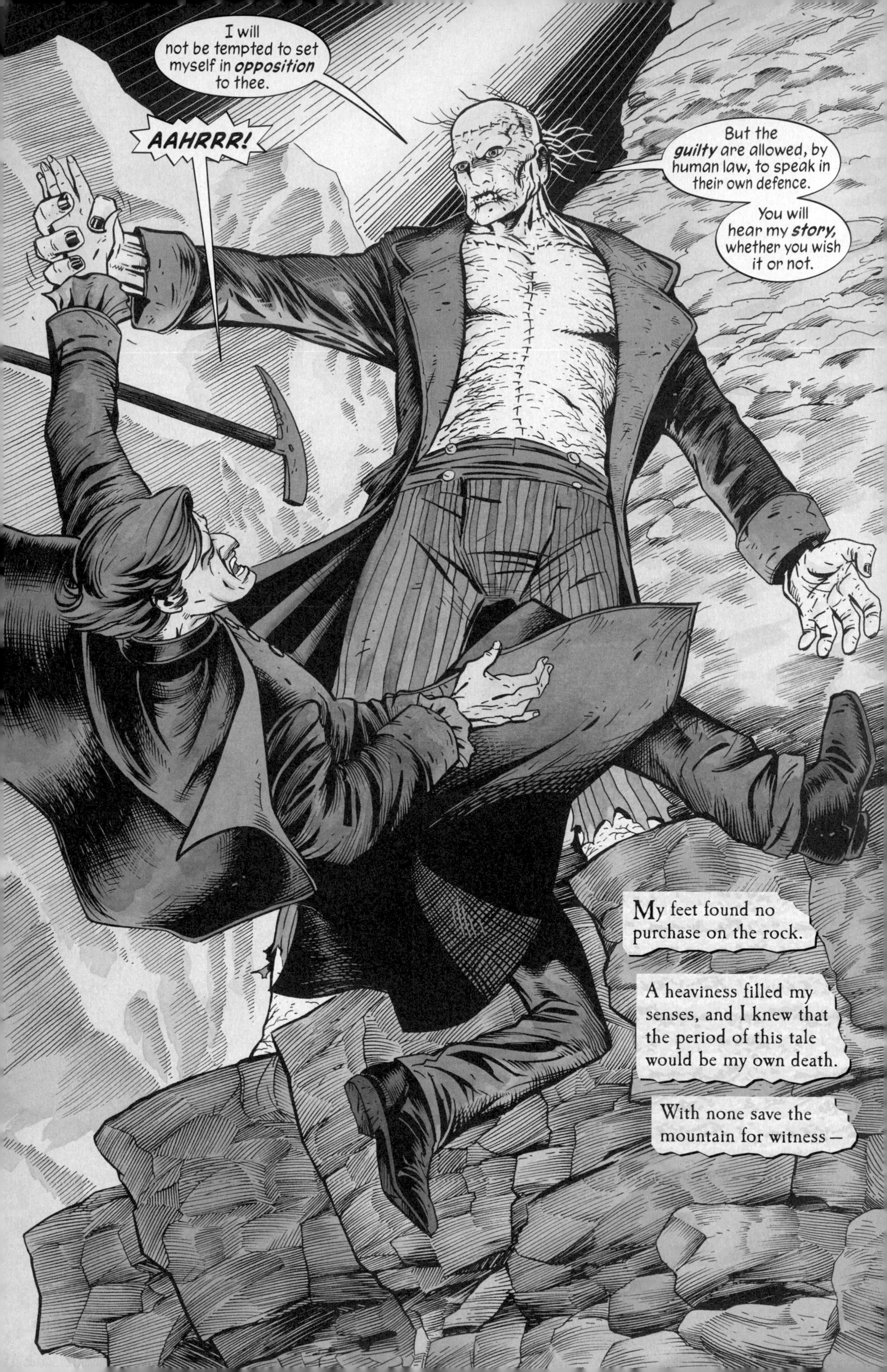
I will not be tempted to set myself in *opposition* to thee.
AAHRRR!
But the *guilty* are allowed, by human law, to speak in their own defence.
You will hear my *story,* whether you wish it or not.
My feet found no purchase on the rock.
A heaviness filled my senses, and I knew that the period of this tale would be my own death.
With none save the mountain for witness —

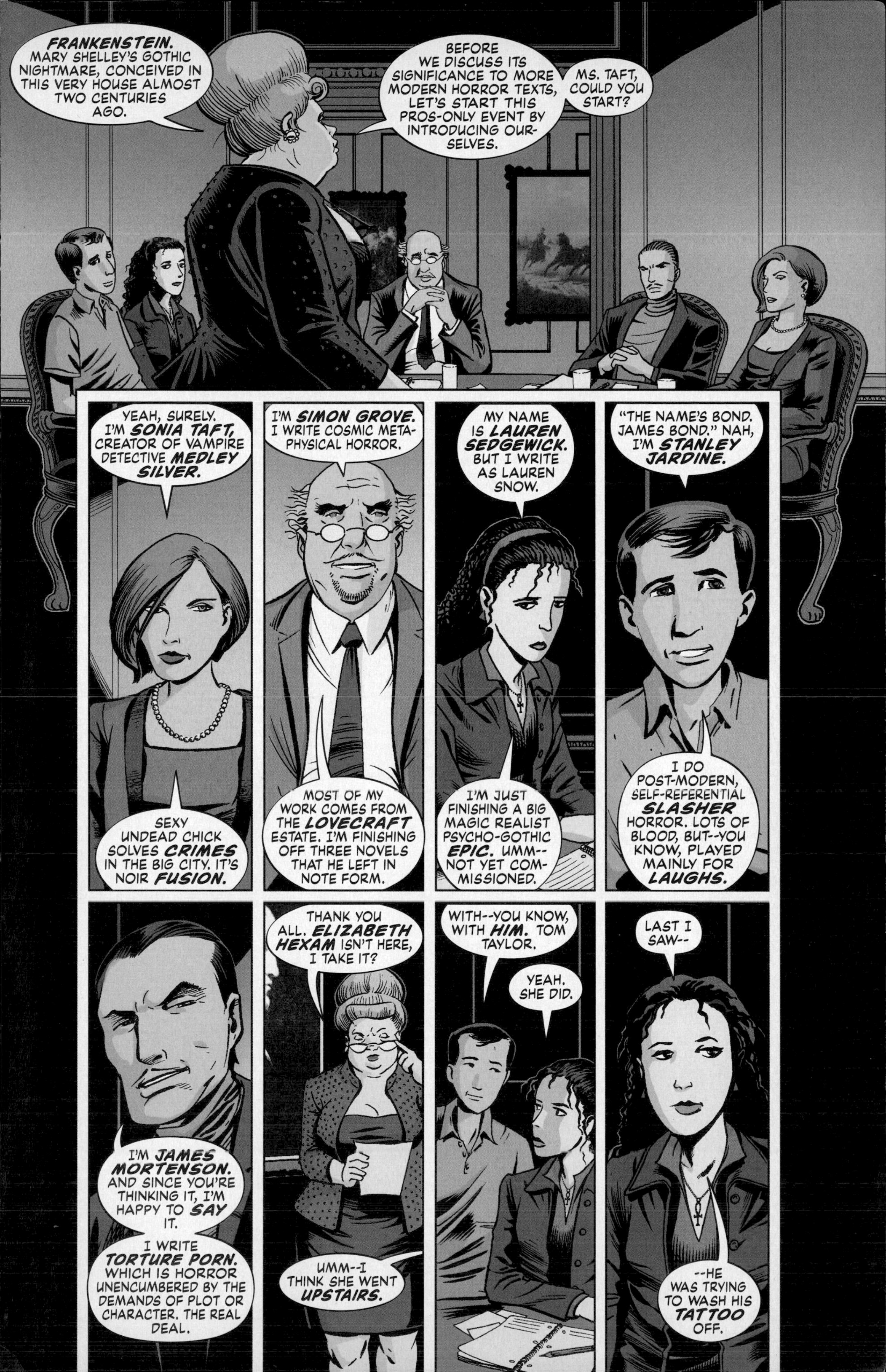
FRANKENSTEIN. MARY SHELLEY'S GOTHIC NIGHTMARE, CONCEIVED IN THIS VERY HOUSE ALMOST TWO CENTURIES AGO.
BEFORE WE DISCUSS ITS SIGNIFICANCE TO MORE MODERN HORROR TEXTS, LET'S START THIS PROS-ONLY EVENT BY INTRODUCING OURSELVES.
MS. TAFT, COULD YOU START?
YEAH, SURELY. I'M SONIA TAFT, CREATOR OF VAMPIRE DETECTIVE MEDLEY SILVER.
SEXY UNDEAD CHICK SOLVES CRIMES IN THE BIG CITY. IT'S NOIR FUSION.
I'M SIMON GROVE. I WRITE COSMIC METAPHYSICAL HORROR.
MOST OF MY WORK COMES FROM THE LOVECRAFT ESTATE. I'M FINISHING OFF THREE NOVELS THAT HE LEFT IN NOTE FORM.
MY NAME IS LAUREN SEDGEWICK. BUT I WRITE AS LAUREN SNOW.
I'M JUST FINISHING A BIG MAGIC REALIST PSYCHO-GOTHIC EPIC. UMM--NOT YET COMMISSIONED.
"THE NAME'S BOND. JAMES BOND." NAH, I'M STANLEY JARDINE.
I DO POST-MODERN, SELF-REFERENTIAL SLASHER HORROR. LOTS OF BLOOD, BUT--YOU KNOW, PLAYED MAINLY FOR LAUGHS.
I'M JAMES MORTENSON. AND SINCE YOU'RE THINKING IT, I'M HAPPY TO SAY IT.
I WRITE TORTURE PORN. WHICH IS HORROR UNENCUMBERED BY THE DEMANDS OF PLOT OR CHARACTER. THE REAL DEAL.
THANK YOU ALL. ELIZABETH HEXAM ISN'T HERE, I TAKE IT?
UMM--I THINK SHE WENT UPSTAIRS.
WITH--YOU KNOW, WITH HIM. TOM TAYLOR.
YEAH. SHE DID.
LAST I SAW--
--HE WAS TRYING TO WASH HIS TATTOO OFF.

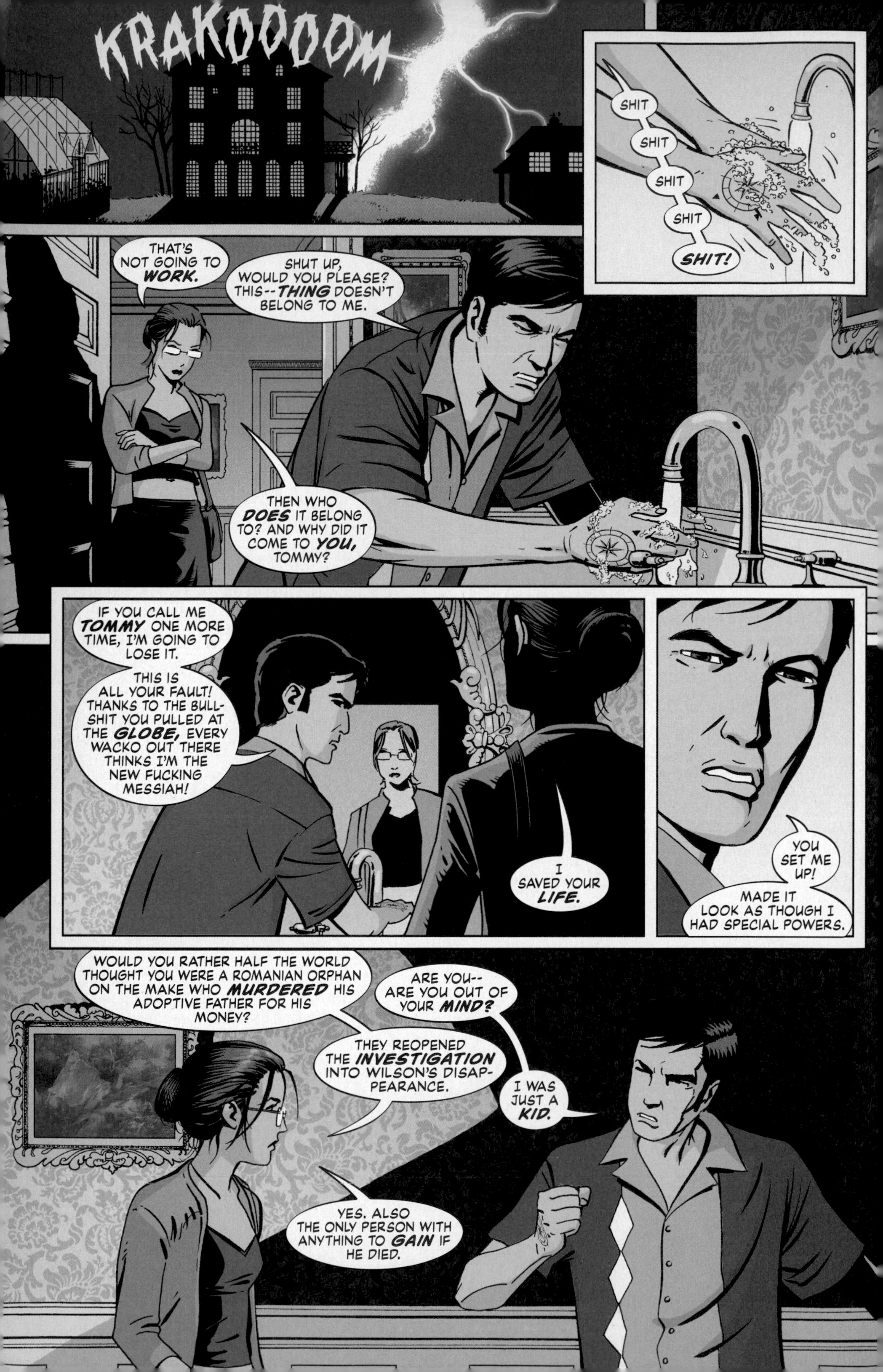
KRAKOOOOM
SHIT
SHIT
SHIT
SHIT
SHIT!
THAT'S NOT GOING TO WORK.
SHUT UP, WOULD YOU PLEASE? THIS--THING DOESN'T BELONG TO ME.
THEN WHO DOES IT BELONG TO? AND WHY DID IT COME TO YOU, TOMMY?
IF YOU CALL ME TOMMY ONE MORE TIME, I'M GOING TO LOSE IT.
THIS IS ALL YOUR FAULT! THANKS TO THE BULL-SHIT YOU PULLED AT THE GLOBE, EVERY WACKO OUT THERE THINKS I'M THE NEW FUCKING MESSIAH!
I SAVED YOUR LIFE.
YOU SET ME UP!
MADE IT LOOK AS THOUGH I HAD SPECIAL POWERS.
WOULD YOU RATHER HALF THE WORLD THOUGHT YOU WERE A ROMANIAN ORPHAN ON THE MAKE WHO MURDERED HIS ADOPTIVE FATHER FOR HIS MONEY?
ARE YOU-- ARE YOU OUT OF YOUR MIND?
THEY REOPENED THE INVESTIGATION INTO WILSON'S DISAP-PEARANCE.
I WAS JUST A KID.
YES. ALSO THE ONLY PERSON WITH ANYTHING TO GAIN IF HE DIED.

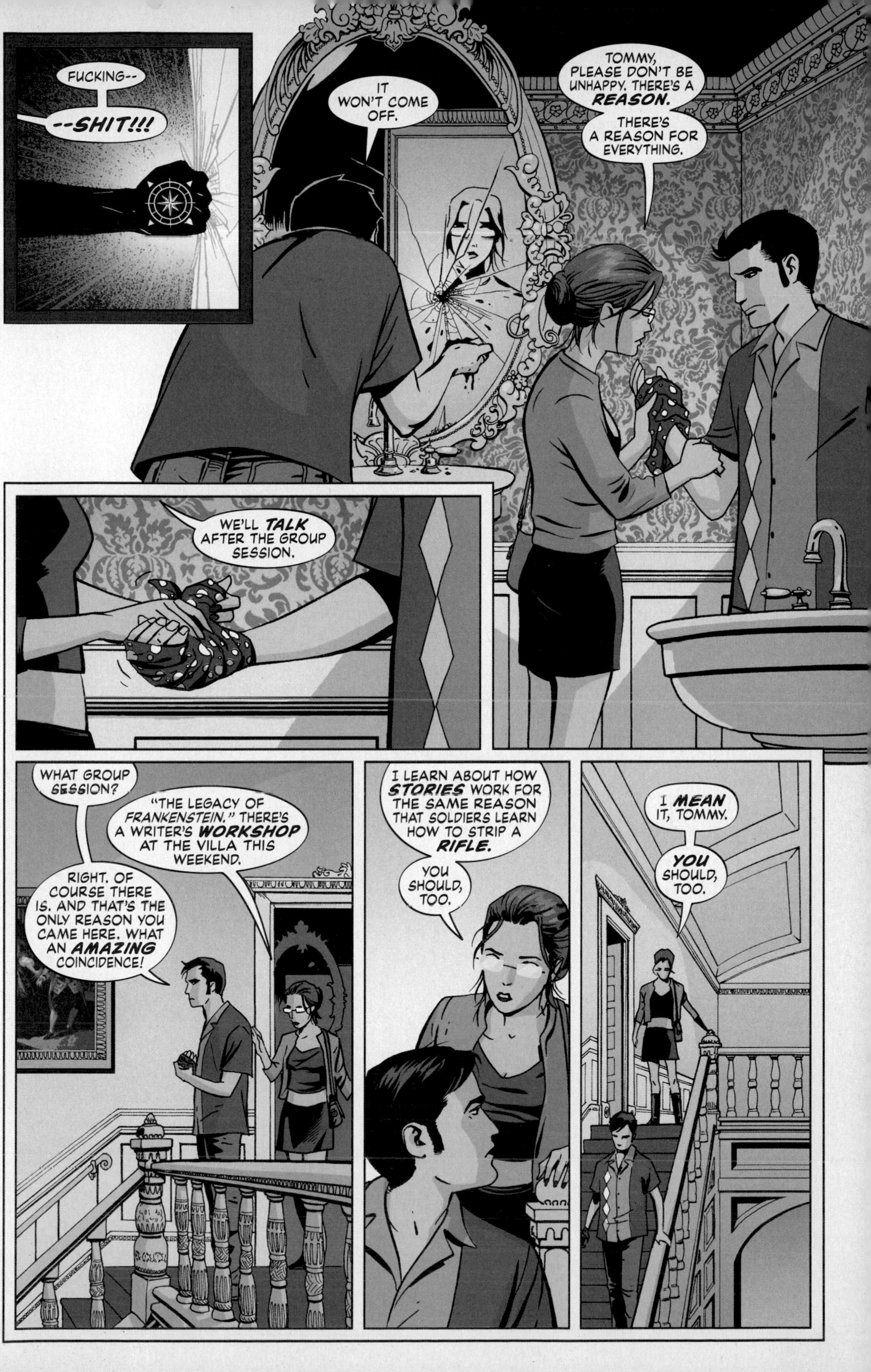
FUCKING--
--SHIT!!!
IT WON'T COME OFF.
TOMMY, PLEASE DON'T BE UNHAPPY. THERE'S A REASON.
THERE'S A REASON FOR EVERYTHING.
WE'LL TALK AFTER THE GROUP SESSION.
WHAT GROUP SESSION?
"THE LEGACY OF FRANKENSTEIN." THERE'S A WRITER'S WORKSHOP AT THE VILLA THIS WEEKEND.
RIGHT. OF COURSE THERE IS. AND THAT'S THE ONLY REASON YOU CAME HERE. WHAT AN AMAZING COINCIDENCE!
I LEARN ABOUT HOW STORIES WORK FOR THE SAME REASON THAT SOLDIERS LEARN HOW TO STRIP A RIFLE.
YOU SHOULD, TOO.
I MEAN IT, TOMMY.
YOU SHOULD, TOO.

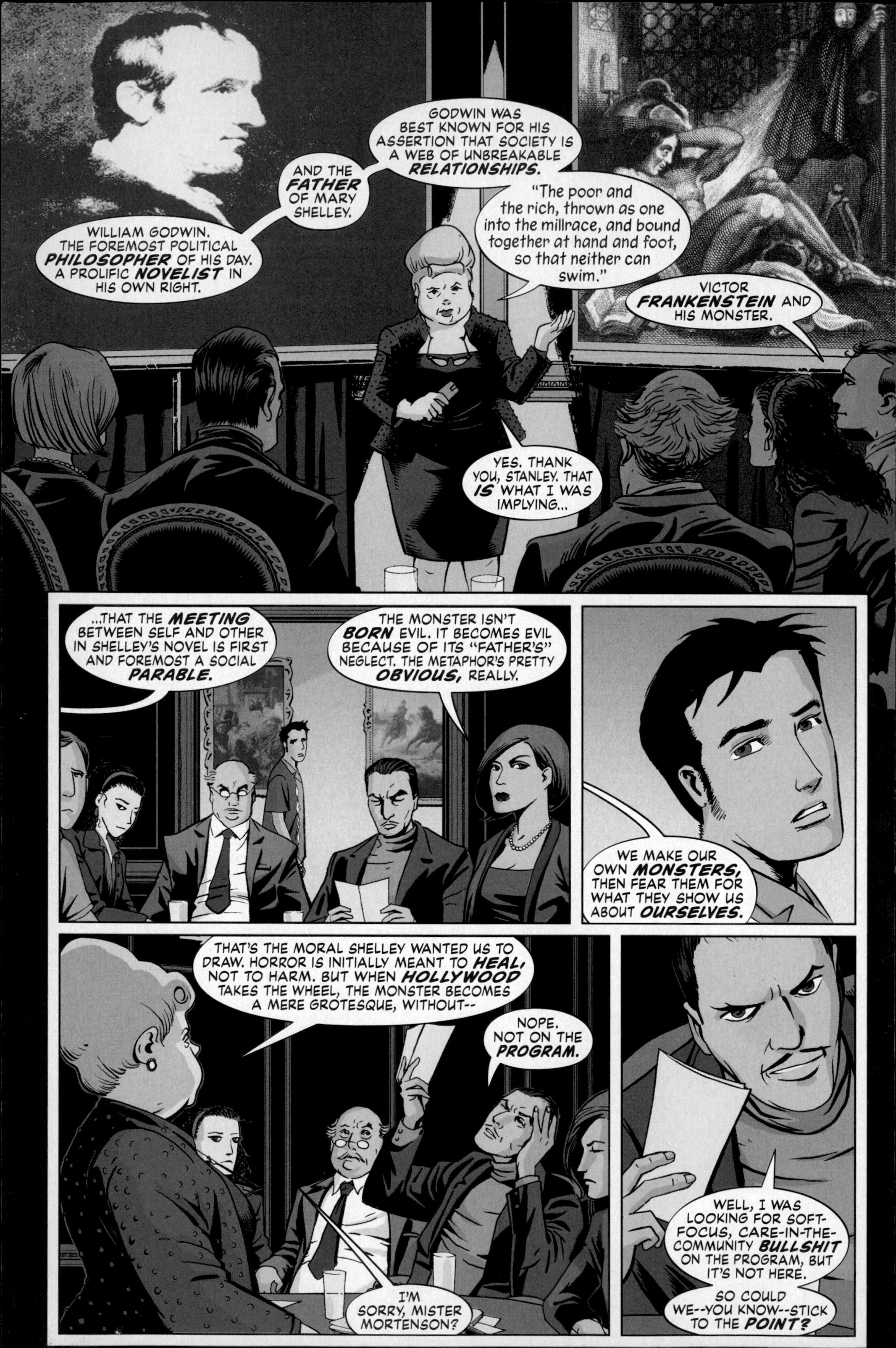
WILLIAM GODWIN. THE FOREMOST POLITICAL PHILOSOPHER OF HIS DAY. A PROLIFIC NOVELIST IN HIS OWN RIGHT.
AND THE FATHER OF MARY SHELLEY.
GODWIN WAS BEST KNOWN FOR HIS ASSERTION THAT SOCIETY IS A WEB OF UNBREAKABLE RELATIONSHIPS.
"The poor and the rich, thrown as one into the millrace, and bound together at hand and foot, so that neither can swim."
VICTOR FRANKENSTEIN AND HIS MONSTER.
YES. THANK YOU, STANLEY. THAT IS WHAT I WAS IMPLYING...
...THAT THE MEETING BETWEEN SELF AND OTHER IN SHELLEY'S NOVEL IS FIRST AND FOREMOST A SOCIAL PARABLE.
THE MONSTER ISN'T BORN EVIL. IT BECOMES EVIL BECAUSE OF ITS "FATHER'S" NEGLECT. THE METAPHOR'S PRETTY OBVIOUS, REALLY.
WE MAKE OUR OWN MONSTERS, THEN FEAR THEM FOR WHAT THEY SHOW US ABOUT OURSELVES.
THAT'S THE MORAL SHELLEY WANTED US TO DRAW. HORROR IS INITIALLY MEANT TO HEAL, NOT TO HARM. BUT WHEN HOLLYWOOD TAKES THE WHEEL, THE MONSTER BECOMES A MERE GROTESQUE, WITHOUT--
NOPE. NOT ON THE PROGRAM.
I'M SORRY, MISTER MORTENSON?
WELL, I WAS LOOKING FOR SOFT-FOCUS, CARE-IN-THE-COMMUNITY BULLSHIT ON THE PROGRAM, BUT IT'S NOT HERE.
SO COULD WE--YOU KNOW--STICK TO THE POINT?

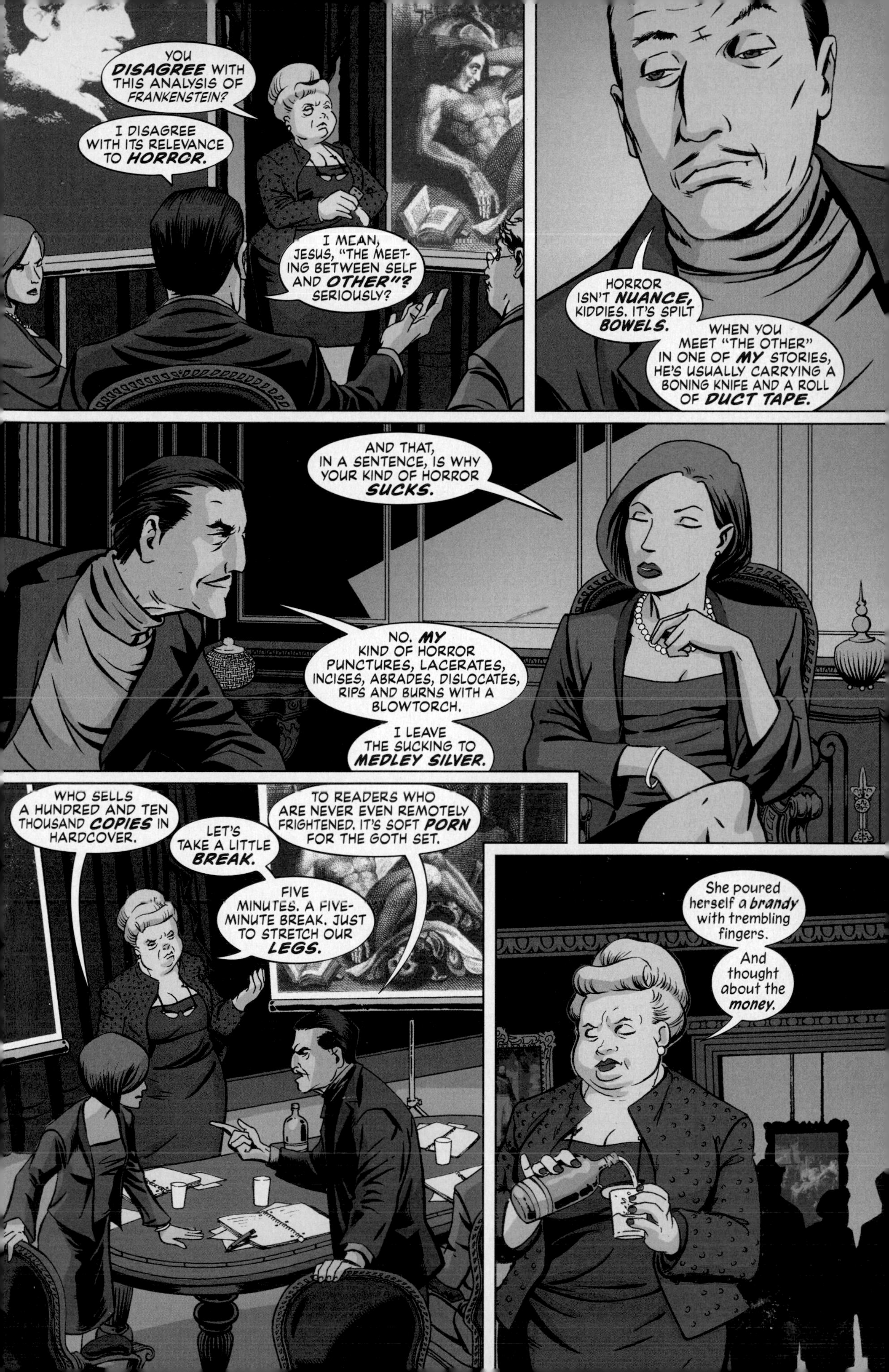
YOU DISAGREE WITH THIS ANALYSIS OF FRANKENSTEIN?
I DISAGREE WITH ITS RELEVANCE TO HORROR.
I MEAN, JESUS, "THE MEETING BETWEEN SELF AND OTHER"? SERIOUSLY?
HORROR ISN'T NUANCE, KIDDIES. IT'S SPILT BOWELS.
WHEN YOU MEET "THE OTHER" IN ONE OF MY STORIES, HE'S USUALLY CARRYING A BONING KNIFE AND A ROLL OF DUCT TAPE.
AND THAT, IN A SENTENCE, IS WHY YOUR KIND OF HORROR SUCKS.
NO. MY KIND OF HORROR PUNCTURES, LACERATES, INCISES, ABRADES, DISLOCATES, RIPS AND BURNS WITH A BLOWTORCH.
I LEAVE THE SUCKING TO MEDLEY SILVER.
WHO SELLS A HUNDRED AND TEN THOUSAND COPIES IN HARDCOVER.
LET'S TAKE A LITTLE BREAK.
TO READERS WHO ARE NEVER EVEN REMOTELY FRIGHTENED. IT'S SOFT PORN FOR THE GOTH SET.
FIVE MINUTES. A FIVE-MINUTE BREAK. JUST TO STRETCH OUR LEGS.
She poured herself a brandy with trembling fingers.
And thought about the money.

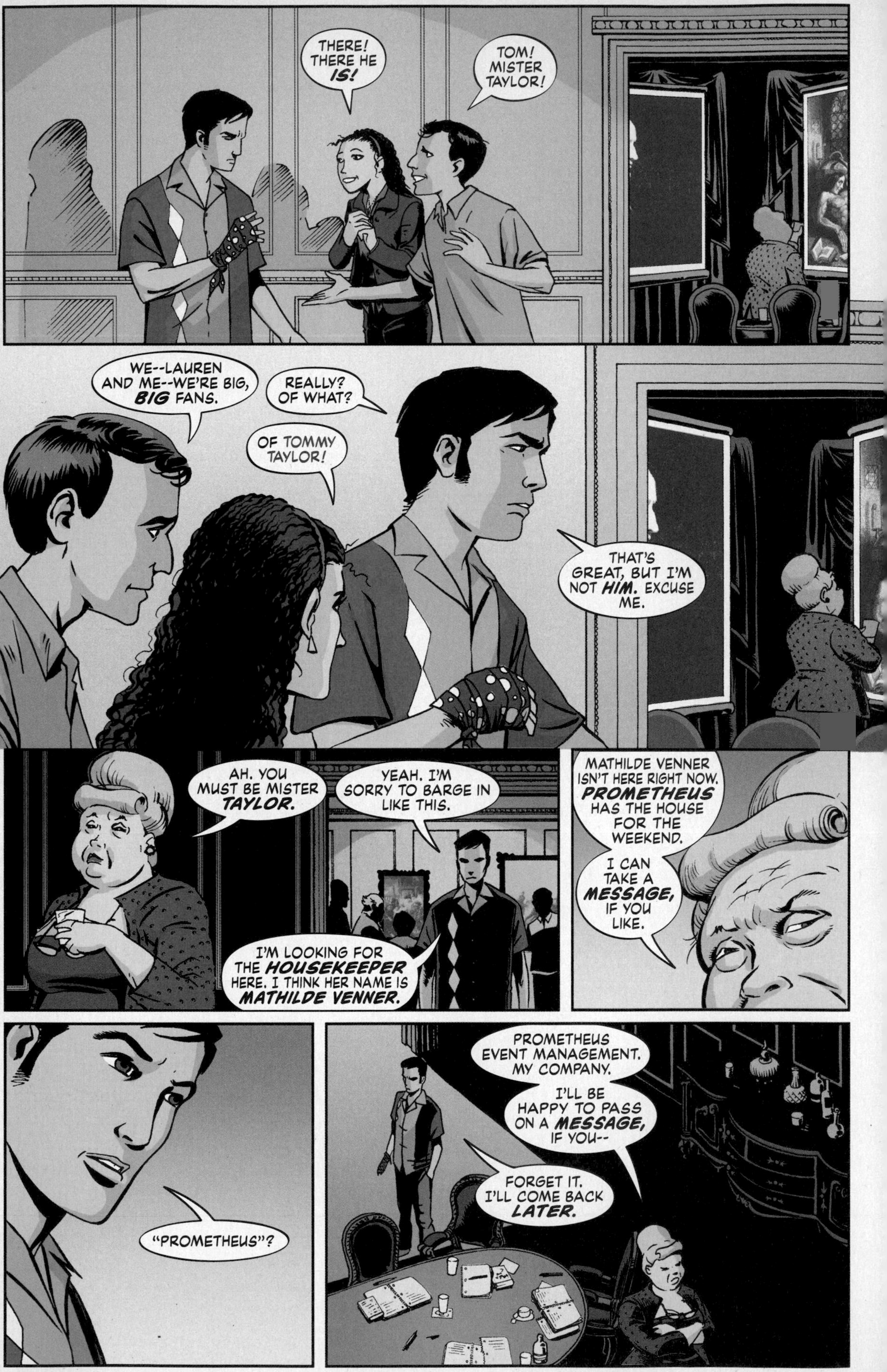
THERE! THERE HE IS!
TOM! MISTER TAYLOR!
WE--LAUREN AND ME--WE'RE BIG, BIG FANS.
REALLY? OF WHAT?
OF TOMMY TAYLOR!
THAT'S GREAT, BUT I'M NOT HIM. EXCUSE ME.
AH. YOU MUST BE MISTER TAYLOR.
YEAH. I'M SORRY TO BARGE IN LIKE THIS.
I'M LOOKING FOR THE HOUSEKEEPER HERE. I THINK HER NAME IS MATHILDE VENNER.
MATHILDE VENNER ISN'T HERE RIGHT NOW. PROMETHEUS HAS THE HOUSE FOR THE WEEKEND.
I CAN TAKE A MESSAGE, IF YOU LIKE.
"PROMETHEUS"?
PROMETHEUS EVENT MANAGEMENT. MY COMPANY.
I'LL BE HAPPY TO PASS ON A MESSAGE, IF YOU--
FORGET IT. I'LL COME BACK LATER.

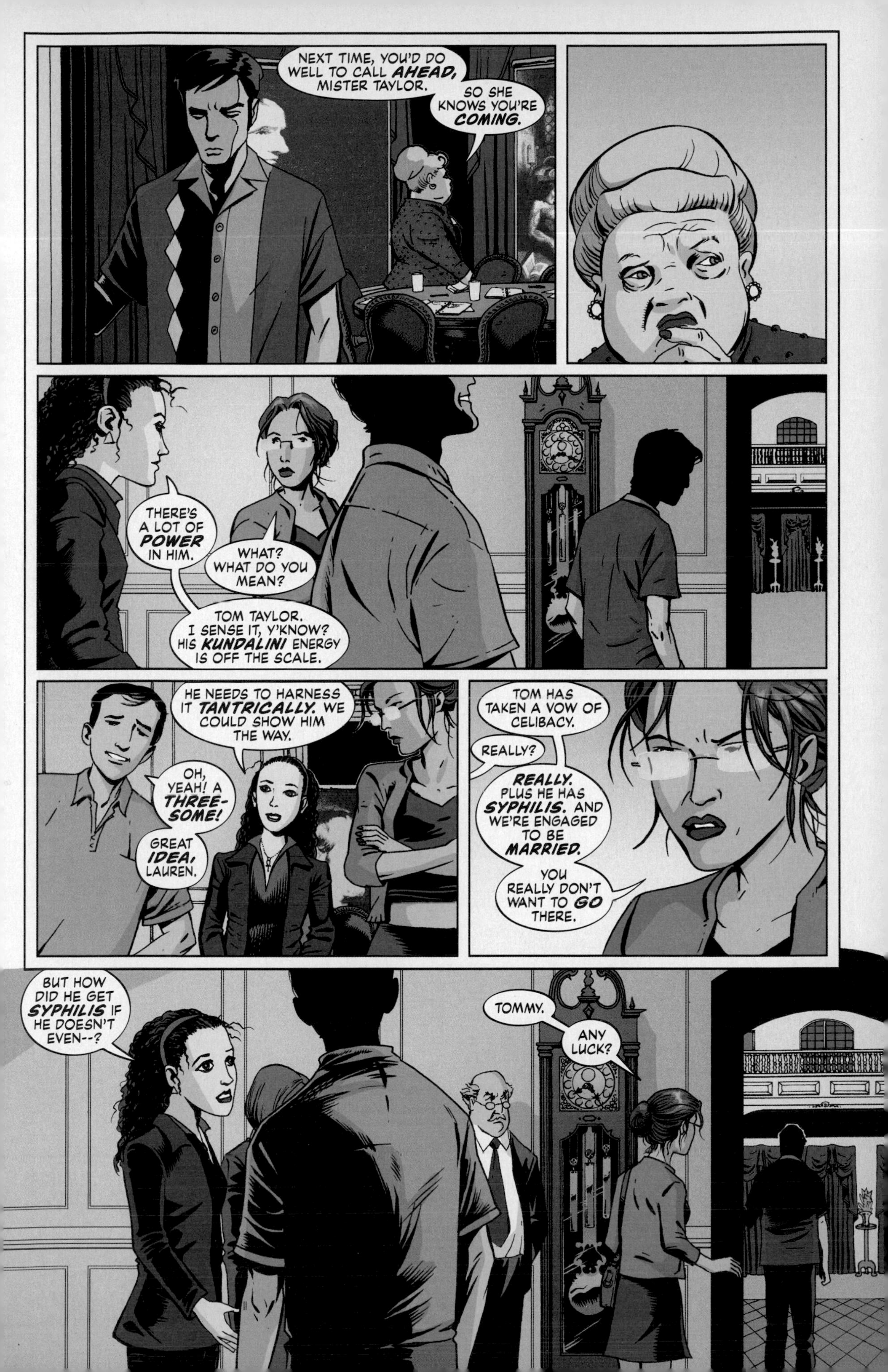
NEXT TIME, YOU'D DO WELL TO CALL AHEAD, MISTER TAYLOR.
SO SHE KNOWS YOU'RE COMING.
THERE'S A LOT OF POWER IN HIM.
WHAT? WHAT DO YOU MEAN?
TOM TAYLOR. I SENSE IT, Y'KNOW? HIS KUNDALINI ENERGY IS OFF THE SCALE.
HE NEEDS TO HARNESS IT TANTRICALLY. WE COULD SHOW HIM THE WAY.
OH, YEAH! A THREE-SOME!
GREAT IDEA, LAUREN.
TOM HAS TAKEN A VOW OF CELIBACY.
REALLY?
REALLY. PLUS HE HAS SYPHILIS. AND WE'RE ENGAGED TO BE MARRIED.
YOU REALLY DON'T WANT TO GO THERE.
BUT HOW DID HE GET SYPHILIS IF HE DOESN'T EVEN--?
TOMMY.
ANY LUCK?

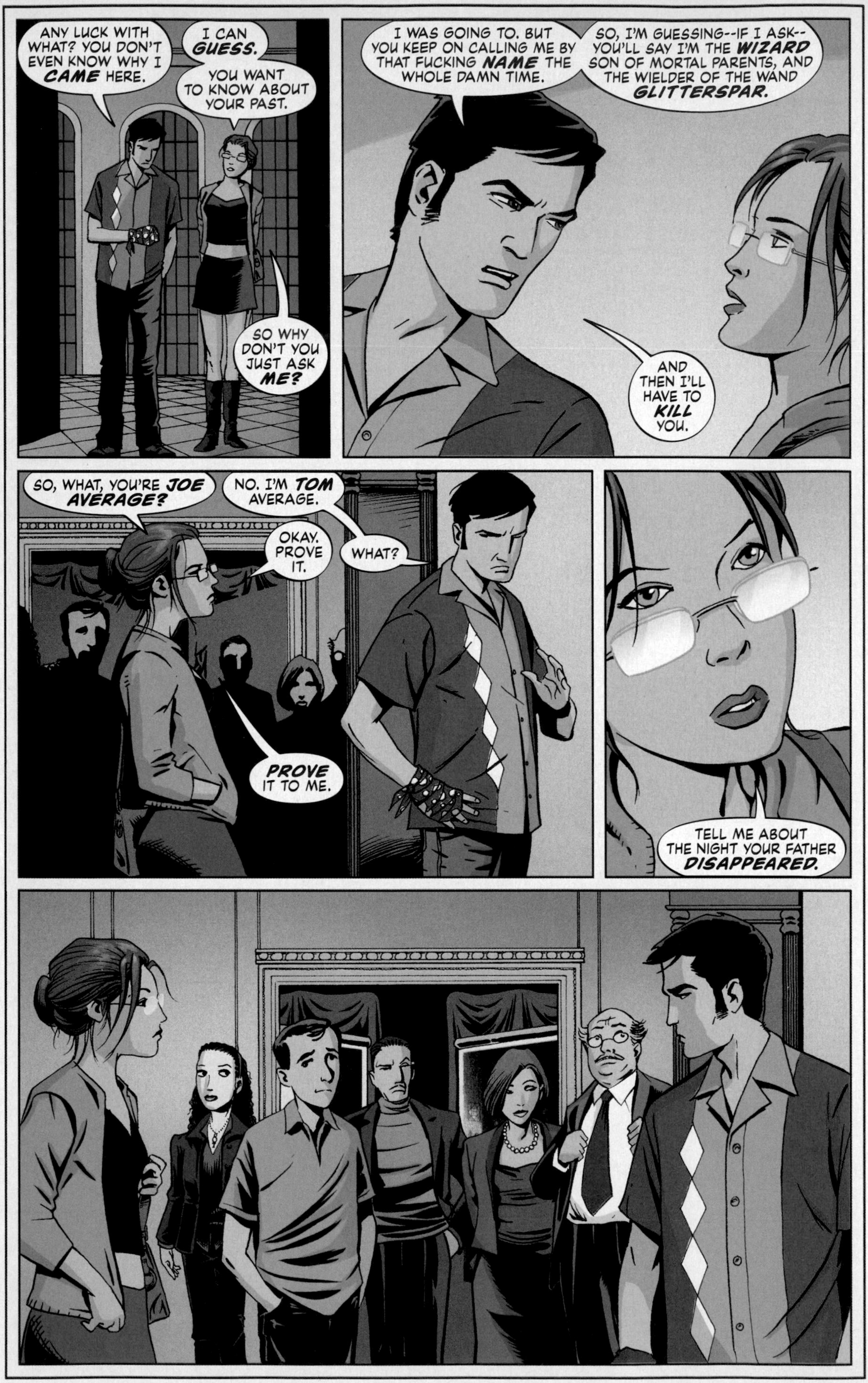
ANY LUCK WITH WHAT? YOU DON'T EVEN KNOW WHY I CAME HERE.
I CAN GUESS.
YOU WANT TO KNOW ABOUT YOUR PAST.
SO WHY DON'T YOU JUST ASK ME?
I WAS GOING TO. BUT YOU KEEP ON CALLING ME BY THAT FUCKING NAME THE WHOLE DAMN TIME.
SO, I'M GUESSING--IF I ASK--YOU'LL SAY I'M THE WIZARD SON OF MORTAL PARENTS, AND THE WIELDER OF THE WAND GLITTERSPAR.
AND THEN I'LL HAVE TO KILL YOU.
SO, WHAT, YOU'RE JOE AVERAGE?
NO. I'M TOM AVERAGE.
OKAY. PROVE IT.
WHAT?
PROVE IT TO ME.
TELL ME ABOUT THE NIGHT YOUR FATHER DISAPPEARED.

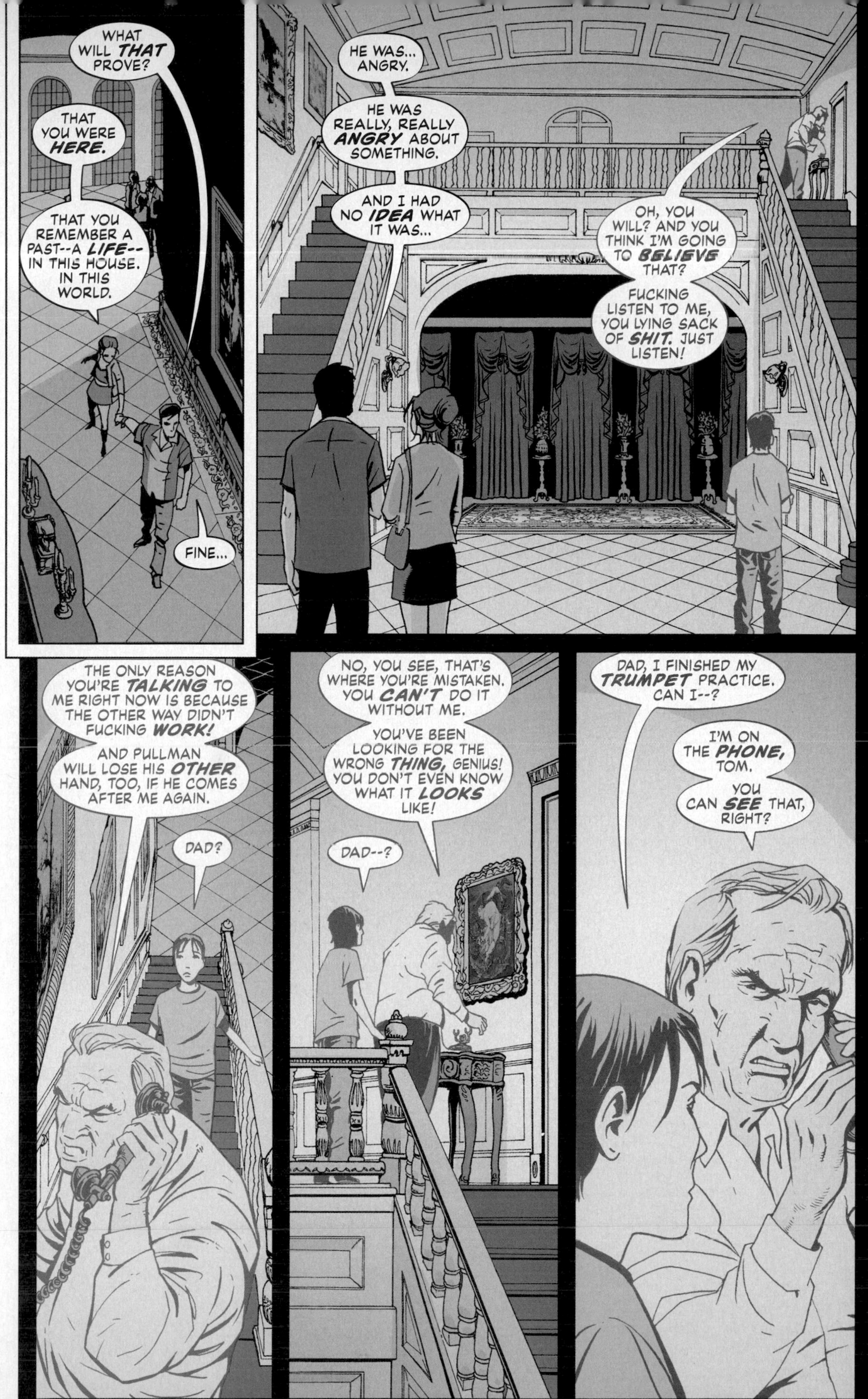
WHAT WILL THAT PROVE?
THAT YOU WERE HERE.
THAT YOU REMEMBER A PAST--A LIFE-- IN THIS HOUSE. IN THIS WORLD.
FINE...
HE WAS... ANGRY.
HE WAS REALLY, REALLY ANGRY ABOUT SOMETHING.
AND I HAD NO IDEA WHAT IT WAS...
OH, YOU WILL? AND YOU THINK I'M GOING TO BELIEVE THAT?
FUCKING LISTEN TO ME, YOU LYING SACK OF SHIT. JUST LISTEN!
THE ONLY REASON YOU'RE TALKING TO ME RIGHT NOW IS BECAUSE THE OTHER WAY DIDN'T FUCKING WORK!
AND PULLMAN WILL LOSE HIS OTHER HAND, TOO, IF HE COMES AFTER ME AGAIN.
DAD?
NO, YOU SEE, THAT'S WHERE YOU'RE MISTAKEN. YOU CAN'T DO IT WITHOUT ME.
YOU'VE BEEN LOOKING FOR THE WRONG THING, GENIUS! YOU DON'T EVEN KNOW WHAT IT LOOKS LIKE!
DAD--?
DAD, I FINISHED MY TRUMPET PRACTICE. CAN I--?
I'M ON THE PHONE, TOM.
YOU CAN SEE THAT, RIGHT?

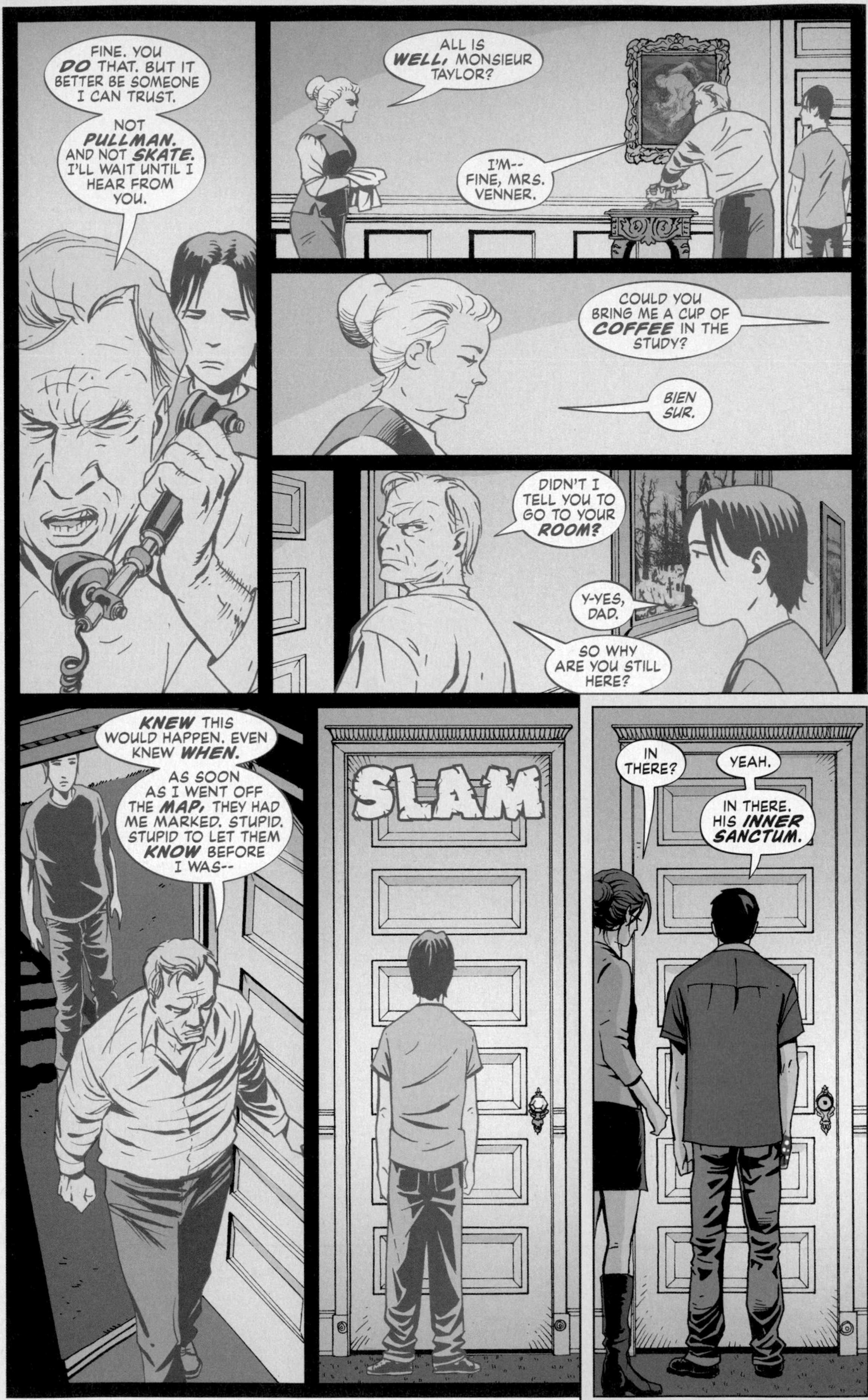
FINE. YOU DO THAT. BUT IT BETTER BE SOMEONE I CAN TRUST.
NOT PULLMAN. AND NOT SKATE. I'LL WAIT UNTIL I HEAR FROM YOU.
ALL IS WELL, MONSIEUR TAYLOR?
I'M-- FINE, MRS. VENNER.
COULD YOU BRING ME A CUP OF COFFEE IN THE STUDY?
BIEN SUR.
DIDN'T I TELL YOU TO GO TO YOUR ROOM?
Y-YES, DAD.
SO WHY ARE YOU STILL HERE?
KNEW THIS WOULD HAPPEN. EVEN KNEW WHEN.
AS SOON AS I WENT OFF THE MAP, THEY HAD ME MARKED. STUPID. STUPID TO LET THEM KNOW BEFORE I WAS--
SLAM
IN THERE?
YEAH.
IN THERE. HIS INNER SANCTUM.

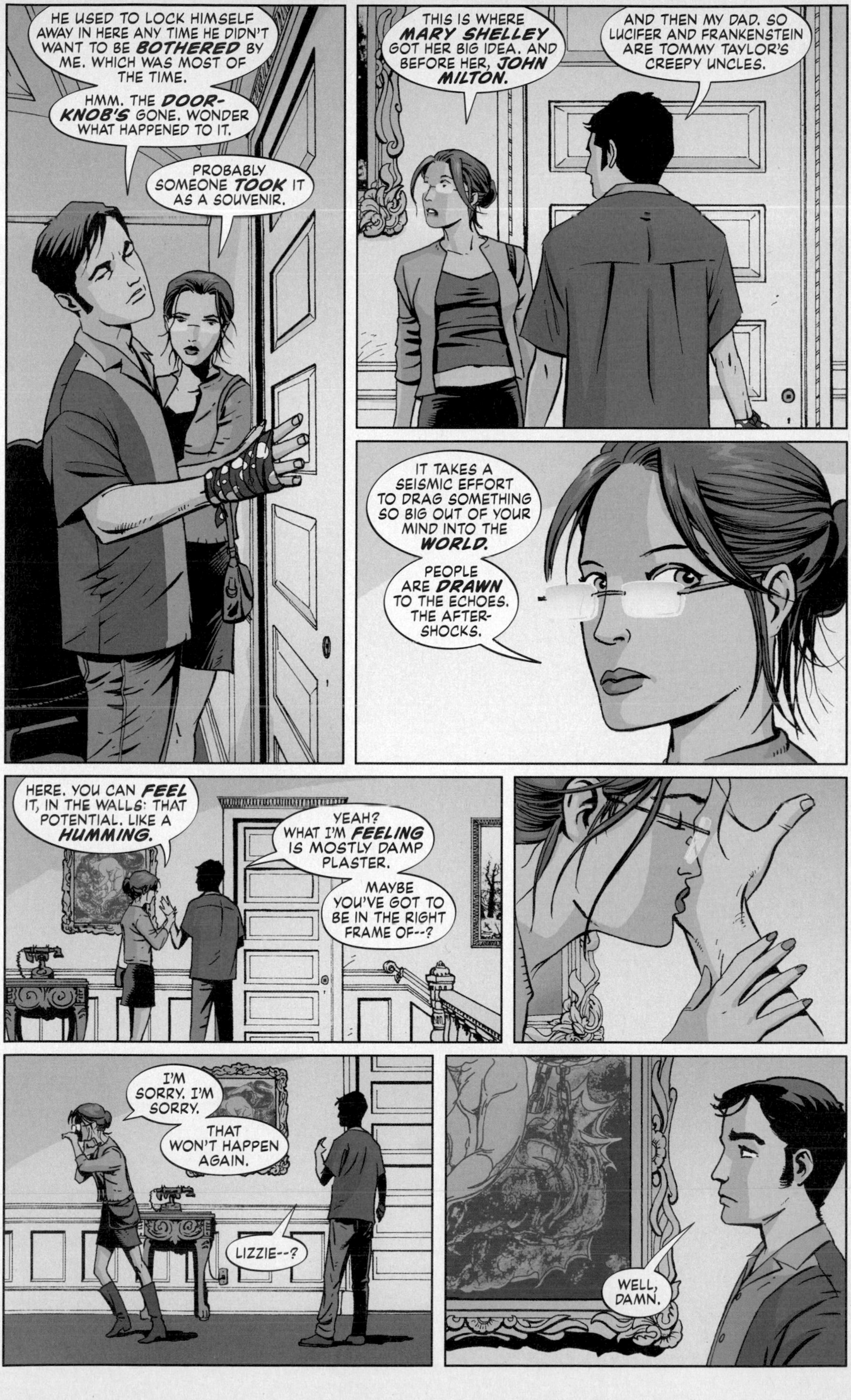
HE USED TO LOCK HIMSELF AWAY IN HERE ANY TIME HE DIDN'T WANT TO BE BOTHERED BY ME. WHICH WAS MOST OF THE TIME.
HMM. THE DOOR-KNOB'S GONE. WONDER WHAT HAPPENED TO IT.
PROBABLY SOMEONE TOOK IT AS A SOUVENIR.
THIS IS WHERE MARY SHELLEY GOT HER BIG IDEA. AND BEFORE HER, JOHN MILTON.
AND THEN MY DAD. SO LUCIFER AND FRANKENSTEIN ARE TOMMY TAYLOR'S CREEPY UNCLES.
IT TAKES A SEISMIC EFFORT TO DRAG SOMETHING SO BIG OUT OF YOUR MIND INTO THE WORLD.
PEOPLE ARE DRAWN TO THE ECHOES. THE AFTER-SHOCKS.
HERE. YOU CAN FEEL IT, IN THE WALLS: THAT POTENTIAL. LIKE A HUMMING.
YEAH? WHAT I'M FEELING IS MOSTLY DAMP PLASTER.
MAYBE YOU'VE GOT TO BE IN THE RIGHT FRAME OF--?
I'M SORRY. I'M SORRY.
THAT WON'T HAPPEN AGAIN.
LIZZIE--?
WELL, DAMN.

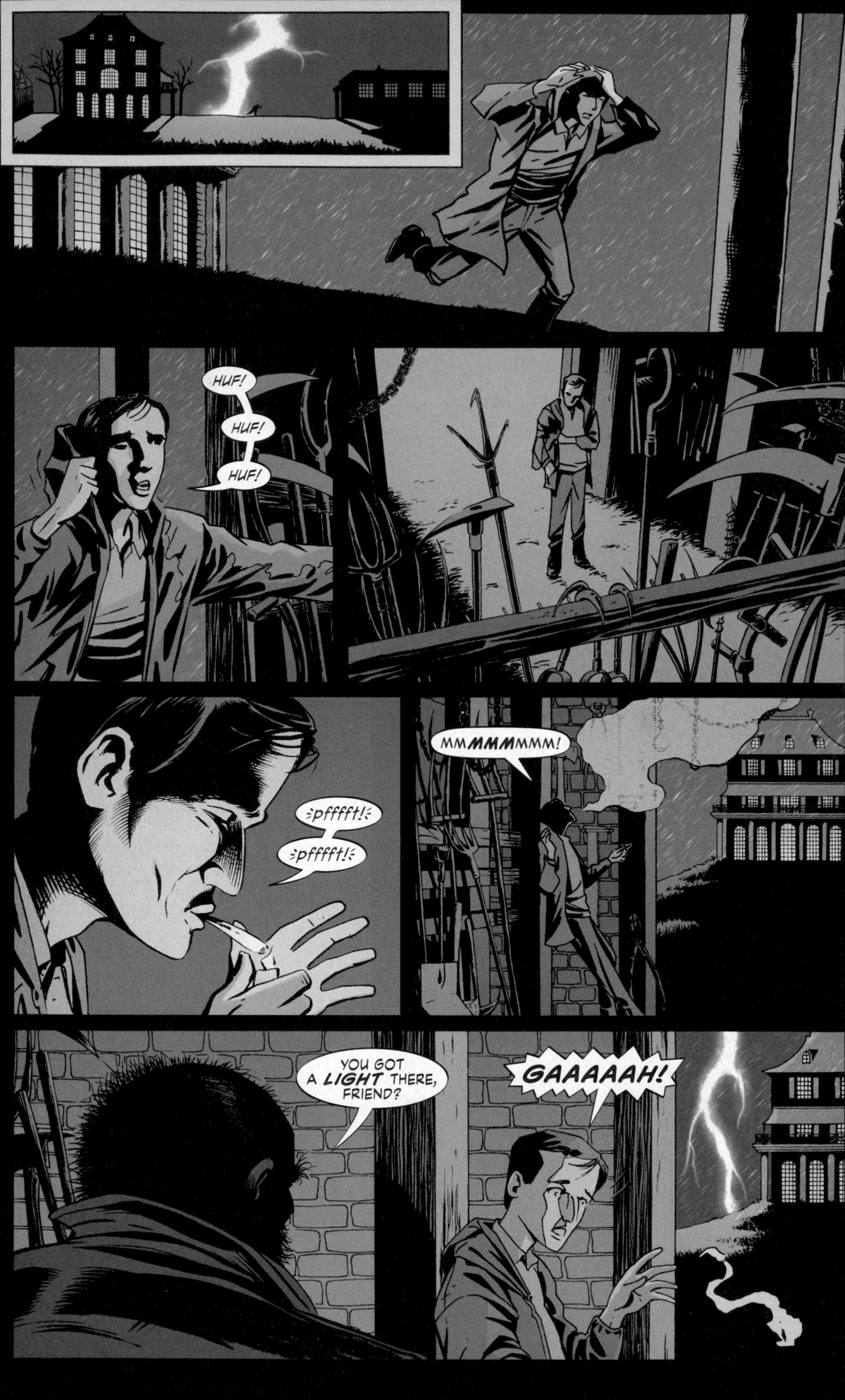
HUF!
HUF!
HUF!
pfffft!
pfffft!
MMMMMMMM!
YOU GOT A LIGHT THERE, FRIEND?
GAAAAAH!

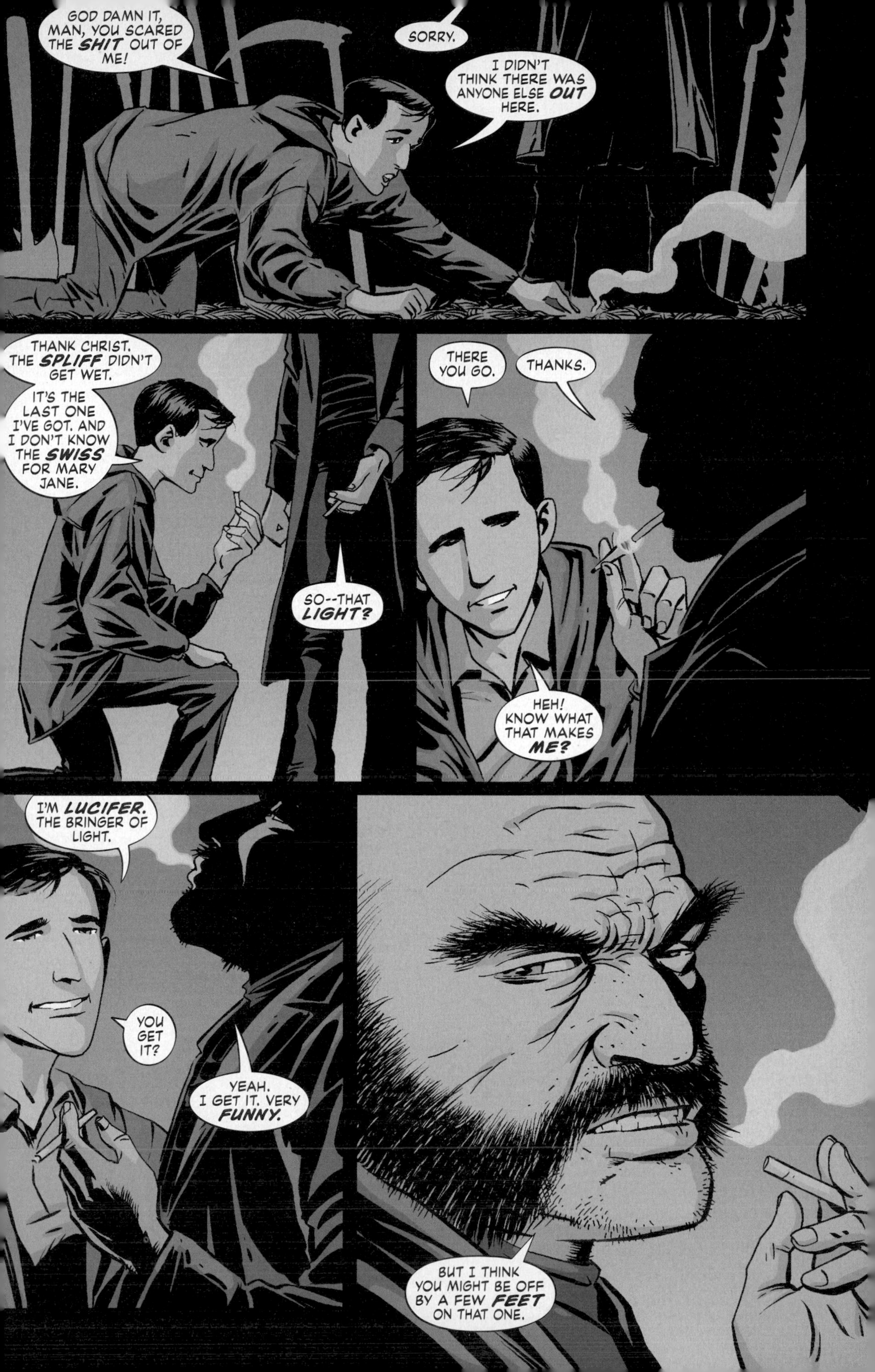
GOD DAMN IT, MAN, YOU SCARED THE SHIT OUT OF ME!
SORRY.
I DIDN'T THINK THERE WAS ANYONE ELSE OUT HERE.
THANK CHRIST. THE SPLIFF DIDN'T GET WET.
IT'S THE LAST ONE I'VE GOT. AND I DON'T KNOW THE SWISS FOR MARY JANE.
SO--THAT LIGHT?
THERE YOU GO.
THANKS.
HEH! KNOW WHAT THAT MAKES ME?
I'M LUCIFER. THE BRINGER OF LIGHT.
YOU GET IT?
YEAH. I GET IT. VERY FUNNY.
BUT I THINK YOU MIGHT BE OFF BY A FEW FEET ON THAT ONE.

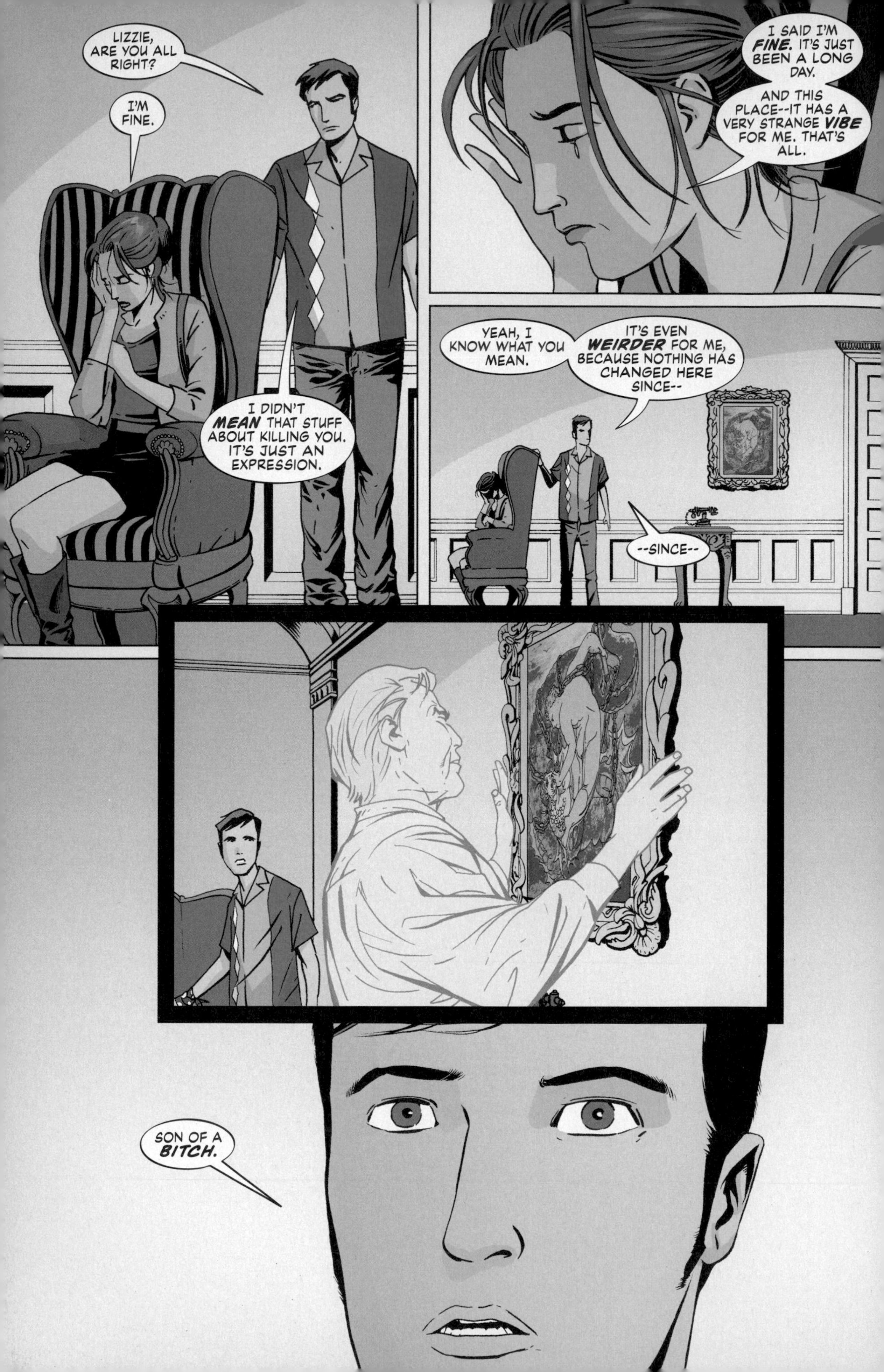

LIZZIE, ARE YOU ALL RIGHT?
I'M FINE.
I DIDN'T MEAN THAT STUFF ABOUT KILLING YOU. IT'S JUST AN EXPRESSION.
I SAID I'M FINE. IT'S JUST BEEN A LONG DAY.
AND THIS PLACE--IT HAS A VERY STRANGE VIBE FOR ME. THAT'S ALL.
YEAH, I KNOW WHAT YOU MEAN.
IT'S EVEN WEIRDER FOR ME, BECAUSE NOTHING HAS CHANGED HERE SINCE--
--SINCE--
SON OF A BITCH.

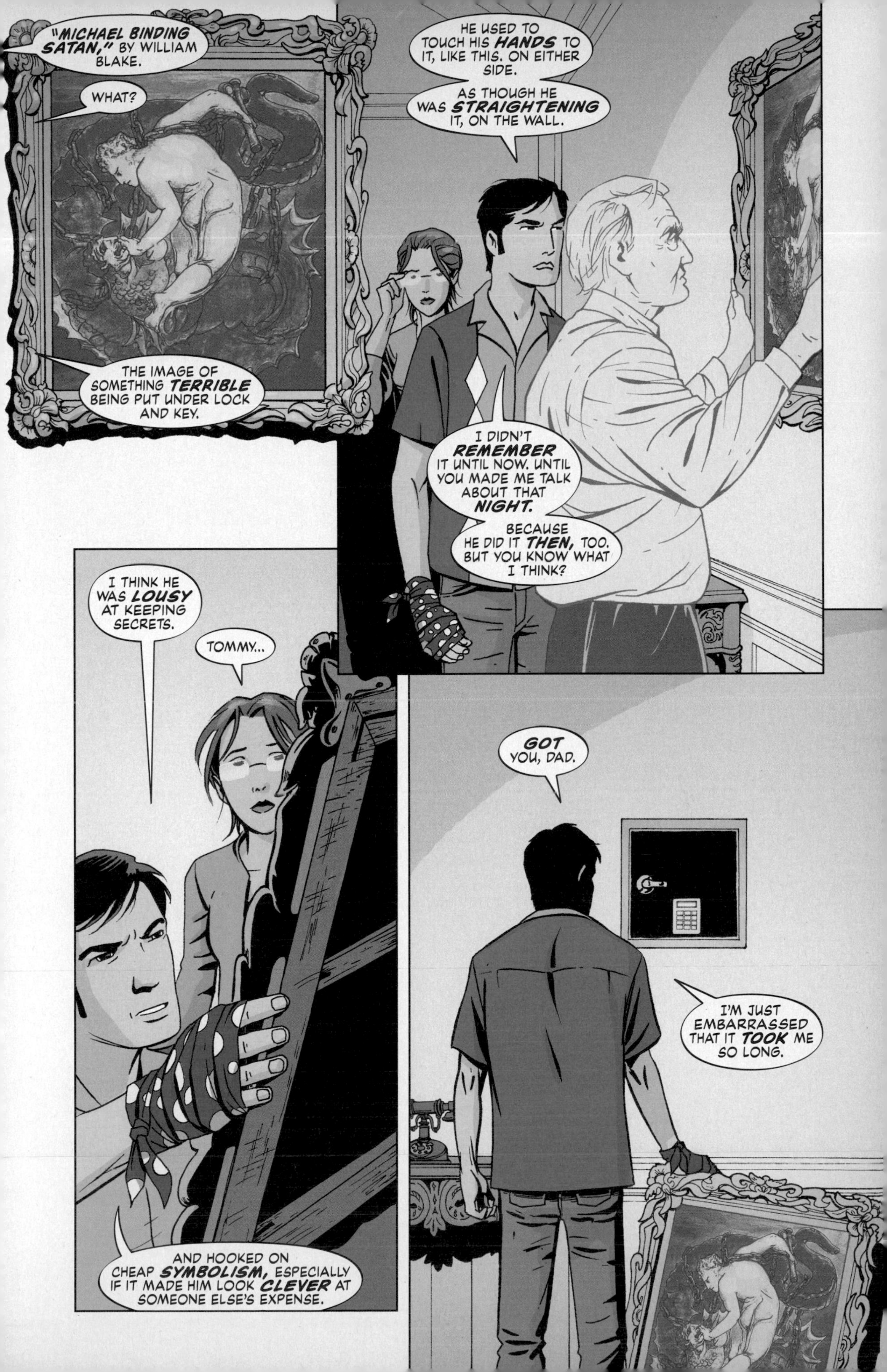
"MICHAEL BINDING SATAN," BY WILLIAM BLAKE.
WHAT?
THE IMAGE OF SOMETHING TERRIBLE BEING PUT UNDER LOCK AND KEY.
HE USED TO TOUCH HIS HANDS TO IT, LIKE THIS. ON EITHER SIDE.
AS THOUGH HE WAS STRAIGHTENING IT, ON THE WALL.
I DIDN'T REMEMBER IT UNTIL NOW. UNTIL YOU MADE ME TALK ABOUT THAT NIGHT.
BECAUSE HE DID IT THEN, TOO. BUT YOU KNOW WHAT I THINK?
I THINK HE WAS LOUSY AT KEEPING SECRETS.
TOMMY...
AND HOOKED ON CHEAP SYMBOLISM, ESPECIALLY IF IT MADE HIM LOOK CLEVER AT SOMEONE ELSE'S EXPENSE.
GOT YOU, DAD.
I'M JUST EMBARRASSED THAT IT TOOK ME SO LONG.

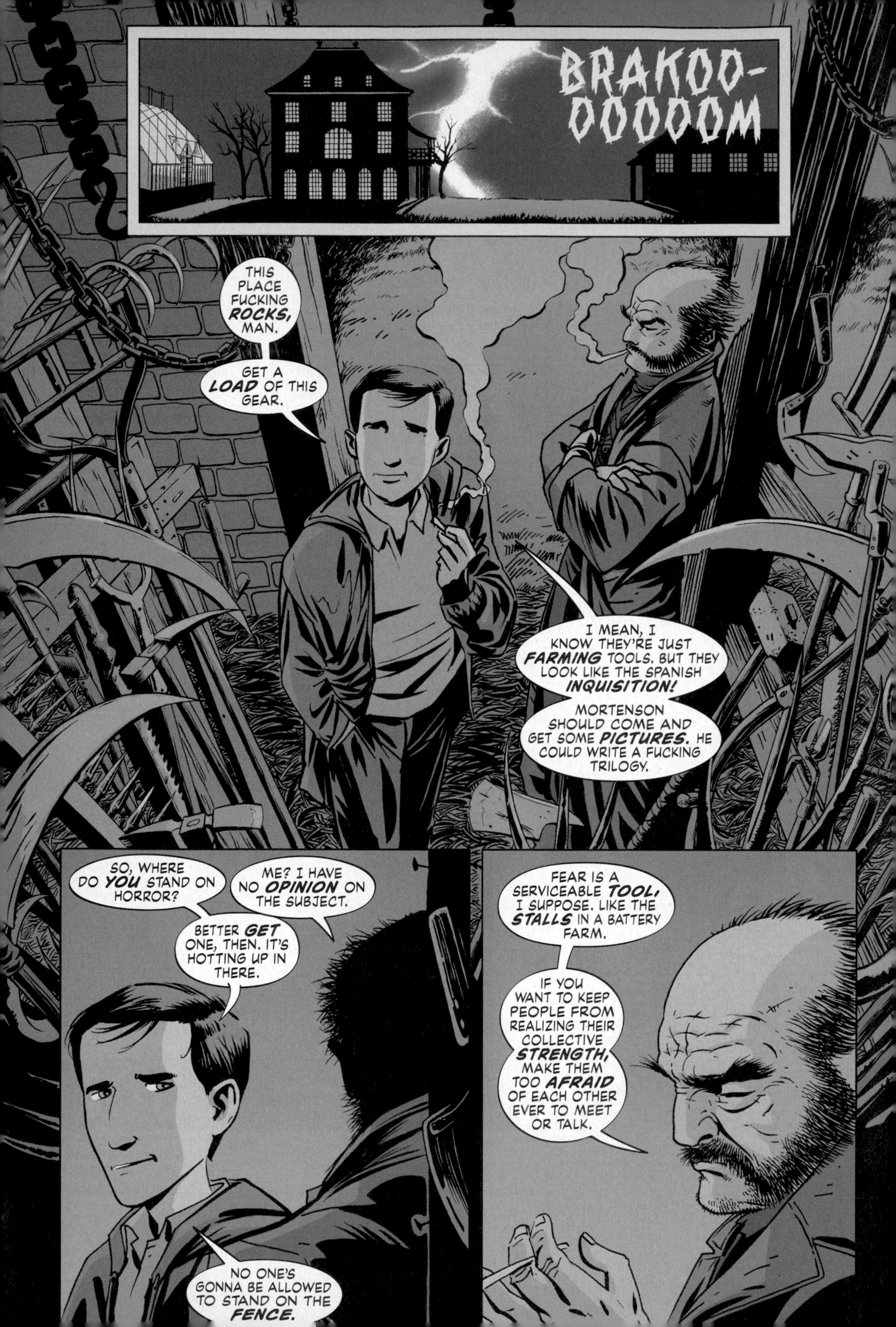
BRAKOO-OOOOOM
THIS PLACE FUCKING ROCKS, MAN.
GET A LOAD OF THIS GEAR.
I MEAN, I KNOW THEY'RE JUST FARMING TOOLS. BUT THEY LOOK LIKE THE SPANISH INQUISITION!
MORTENSON SHOULD COME AND GET SOME PICTURES. HE COULD WRITE A FUCKING TRILOGY.
SO, WHERE DO YOU STAND ON HORROR?
ME? I HAVE NO OPINION ON THE SUBJECT.
BETTER GET ONE, THEN. IT'S HOTTING UP IN THERE.
NO ONE'S GONNA BE ALLOWED TO STAND ON THE FENCE.
FEAR IS A SERVICEABLE TOOL, I SUPPOSE. LIKE THE STALLS IN A BATTERY FARM.
IF YOU WANT TO KEEP PEOPLE FROM REALIZING THEIR COLLECTIVE STRENGTH, MAKE THEM TOO AFRAID OF EACH OTHER EVER TO MEET OR TALK.

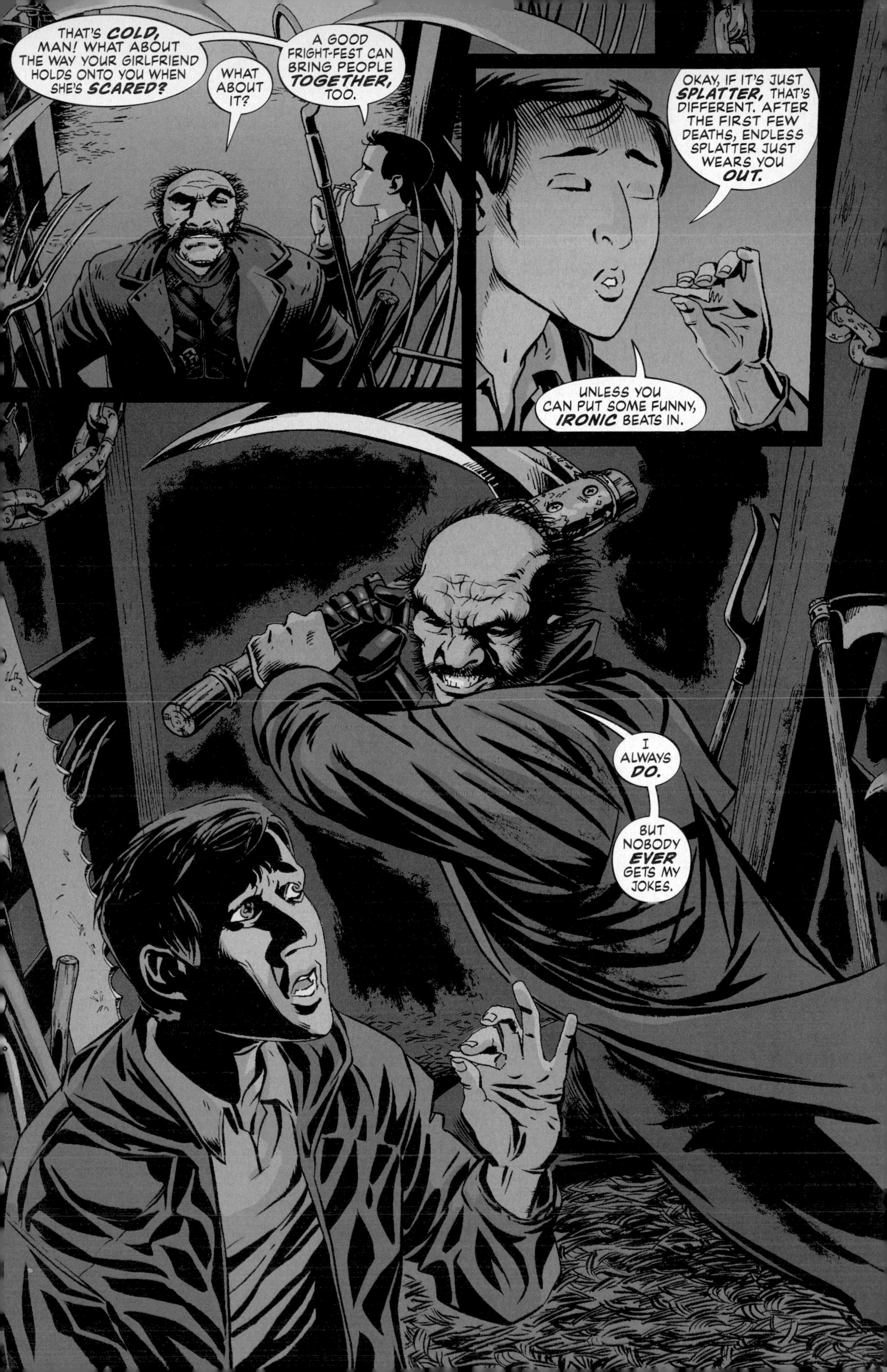
THAT'S COLD, MAN! WHAT ABOUT THE WAY YOUR GIRLFRIEND HOLDS ONTO YOU WHEN SHE'S SCARED?
WHAT ABOUT IT?
A GOOD FRIGHT-FEST CAN BRING PEOPLE TOGETHER, TOO.
OKAY, IF IT'S JUST SPLATTER, THAT'S DIFFERENT. AFTER THE FIRST FEW DEATHS, ENDLESS SPLATTER JUST WEARS YOU OUT.
UNLESS YOU CAN PUT SOME FUNNY, IRONIC BEATS IN.
I ALWAYS DO.
BUT NOBODY EVER GETS MY JOKES.

THE KEYPAD HAS *LETTERS* INSTEAD OF NUMBERS.

TOMMY, NOW MIGHT NOT BE THE BEST *TIME* FOR THIS.

NOW IS THE *ONLY* TIME. AS SOON AS THE RAIN LETS UP, I'M *OUT* OF HERE.

W-I-L-S-O-N-T-A-Y-L-O-R. NO. NOT THAT.

T-O-M-M-Y-T-A-Y-L-O-R. NOT THAT, EITHER.

I GUESS HE'D HAVE TO BE PRETTY *STUPID* TO PICK SOMETHING THAT OBVIOUS.

MAYBE HE DIDN'T EVEN GO FOR A *WORD.*

I WONDER...

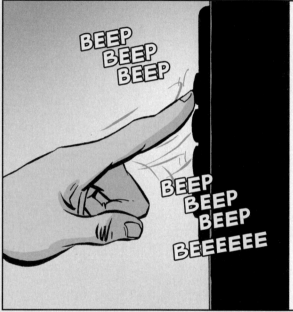

BEEP BEEP BEEP

BEEP BEEP BEEP BEEEEEE

HAH!

SFFFFFFF

THREE'S THE *CHARM.* HOW ABOUT THAT?

SO LET'S *SEE.*

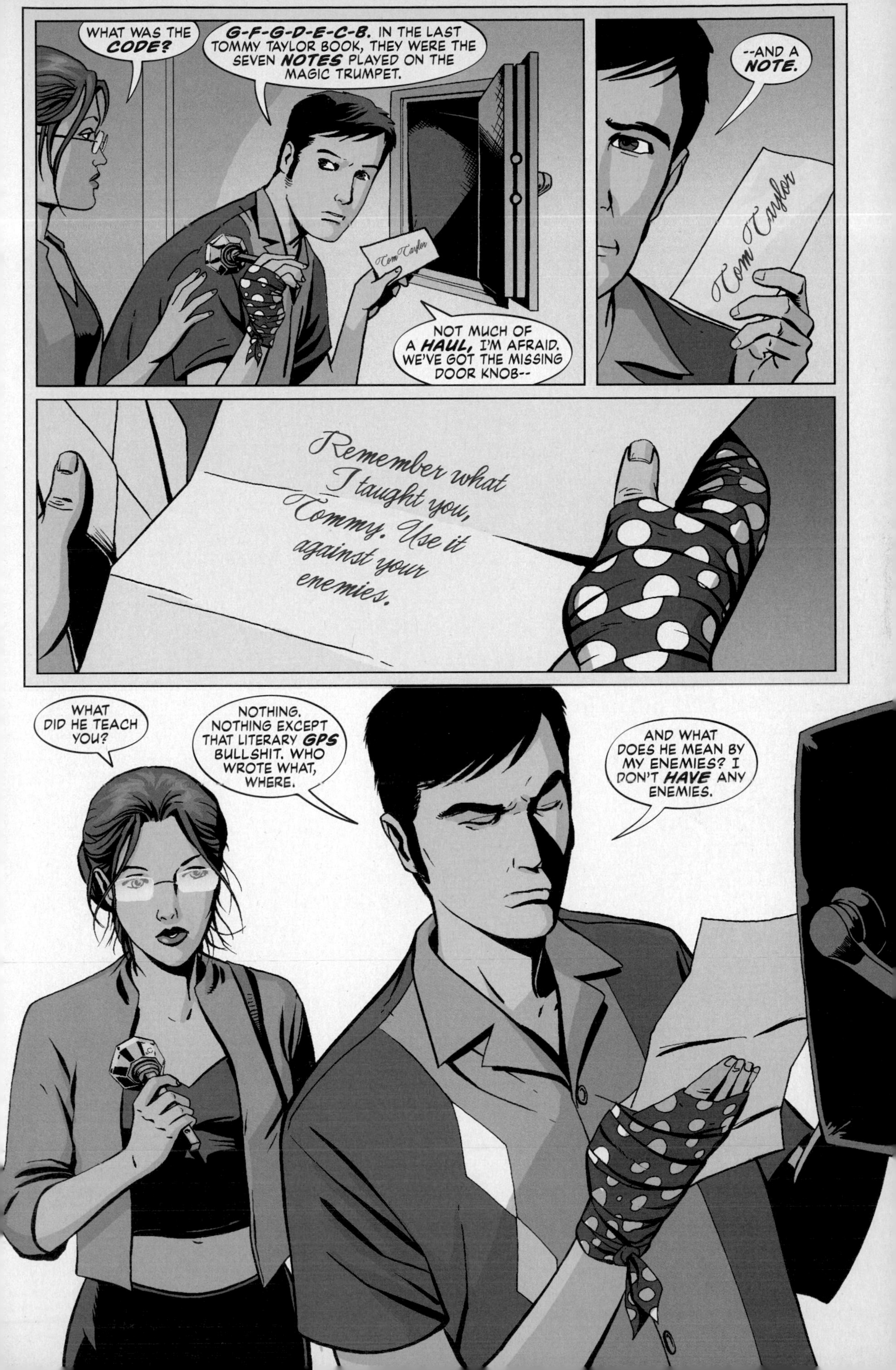
WHAT WAS THE CODE?
G-F-G-D-E-C-B. IN THE LAST TOMMY TAYLOR BOOK, THEY WERE THE SEVEN NOTES PLAYED ON THE MAGIC TRUMPET.
NOT MUCH OF A HAUL, I'M AFRAID. WE'VE GOT THE MISSING DOOR KNOB--
--AND A NOTE.
Tom Taylor
Remember what I taught you, Tommy. Use it against your enemies.
WHAT DID HE TEACH YOU?
NOTHING. NOTHING EXCEPT THAT LITERARY GPS BULLSHIT. WHO WROTE WHAT, WHERE.
AND WHAT DOES HE MEAN BY MY ENEMIES? I DON'T HAVE ANY ENEMIES.

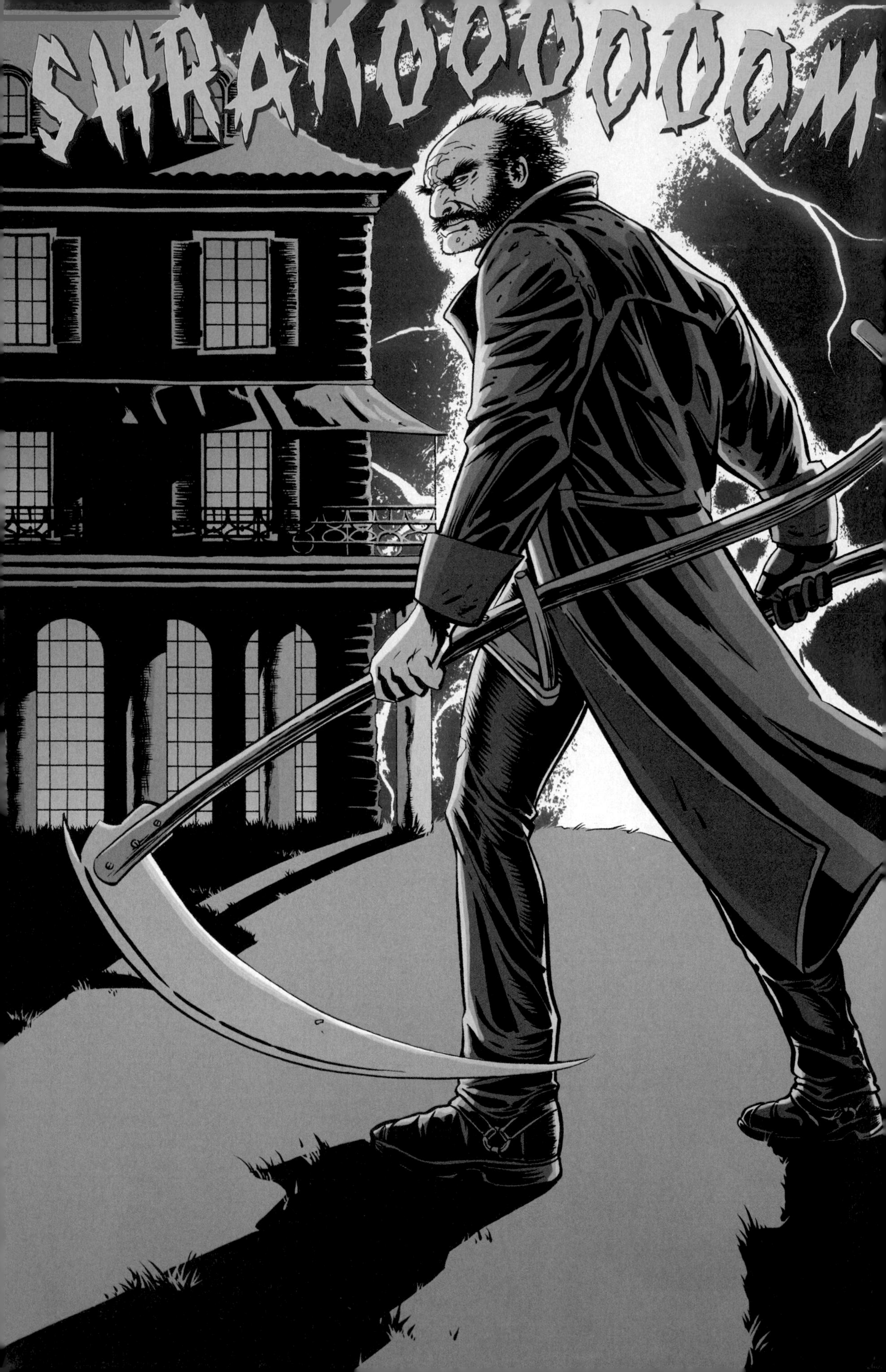
SHRAKOOOOOOM

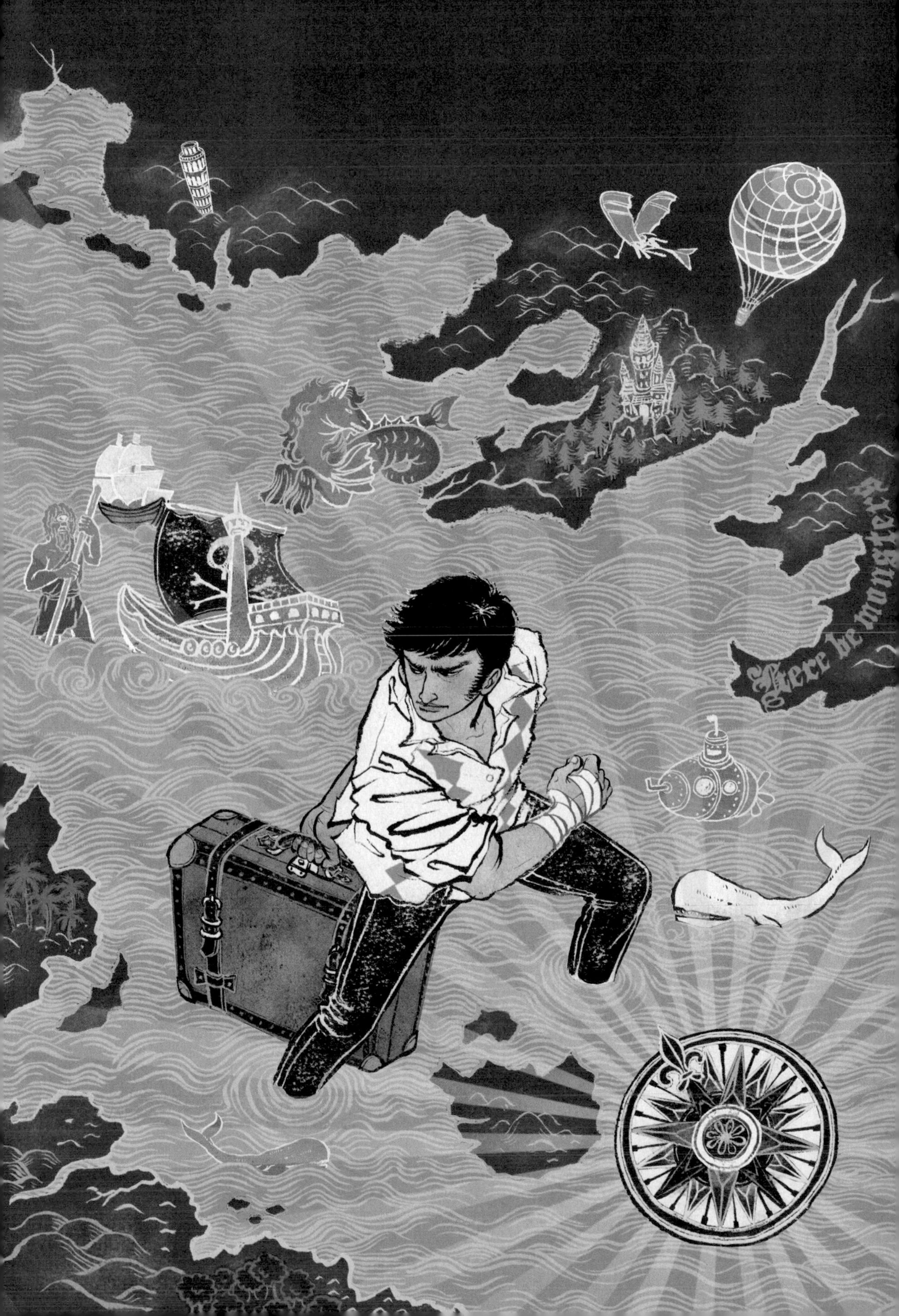
Here be monsters

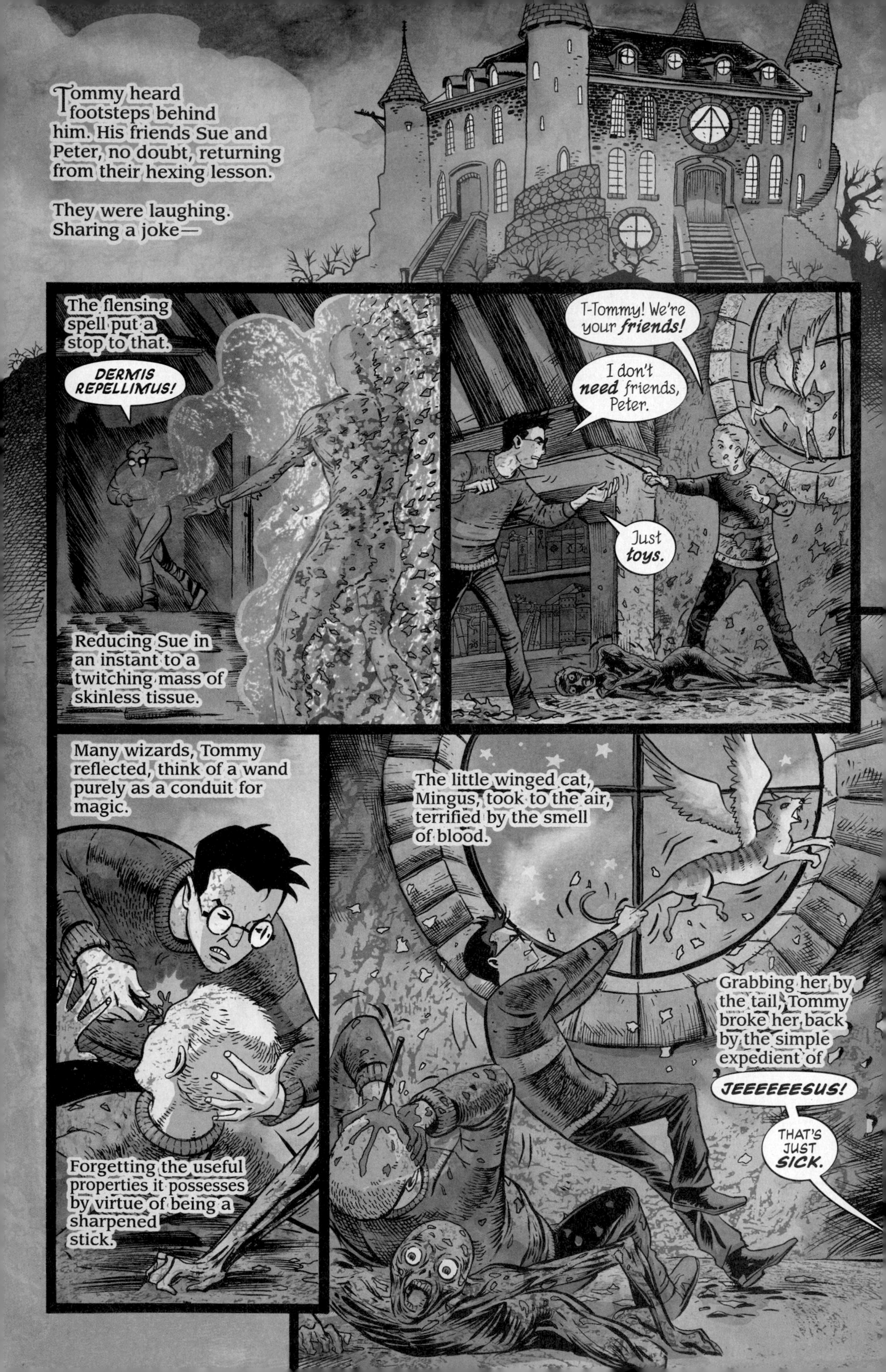
Tommy heard footsteps behind him. His friends Sue and Peter, no doubt, returning from their hexing lesson.
They were laughing. Sharing a joke—
The flensing spell put a stop to that.
DERMIS REPELLIMUS!
Reducing Sue in an instant to a twitching mass of skinless tissue.
T-Tommy! We're your friends!
I don't need friends, Peter.
Just toys.
Many wizards, Tommy reflected, think of a wand purely as a conduit for magic.
Forgetting the useful properties it possesses by virtue of being a sharpened stick.
The little winged cat, Mingus, took to the air, terrified by the smell of blood.
Grabbing her by the tail, Tommy broke her back by the simple expedient of
JEEEEEESUS!
THAT'S JUST SICK.

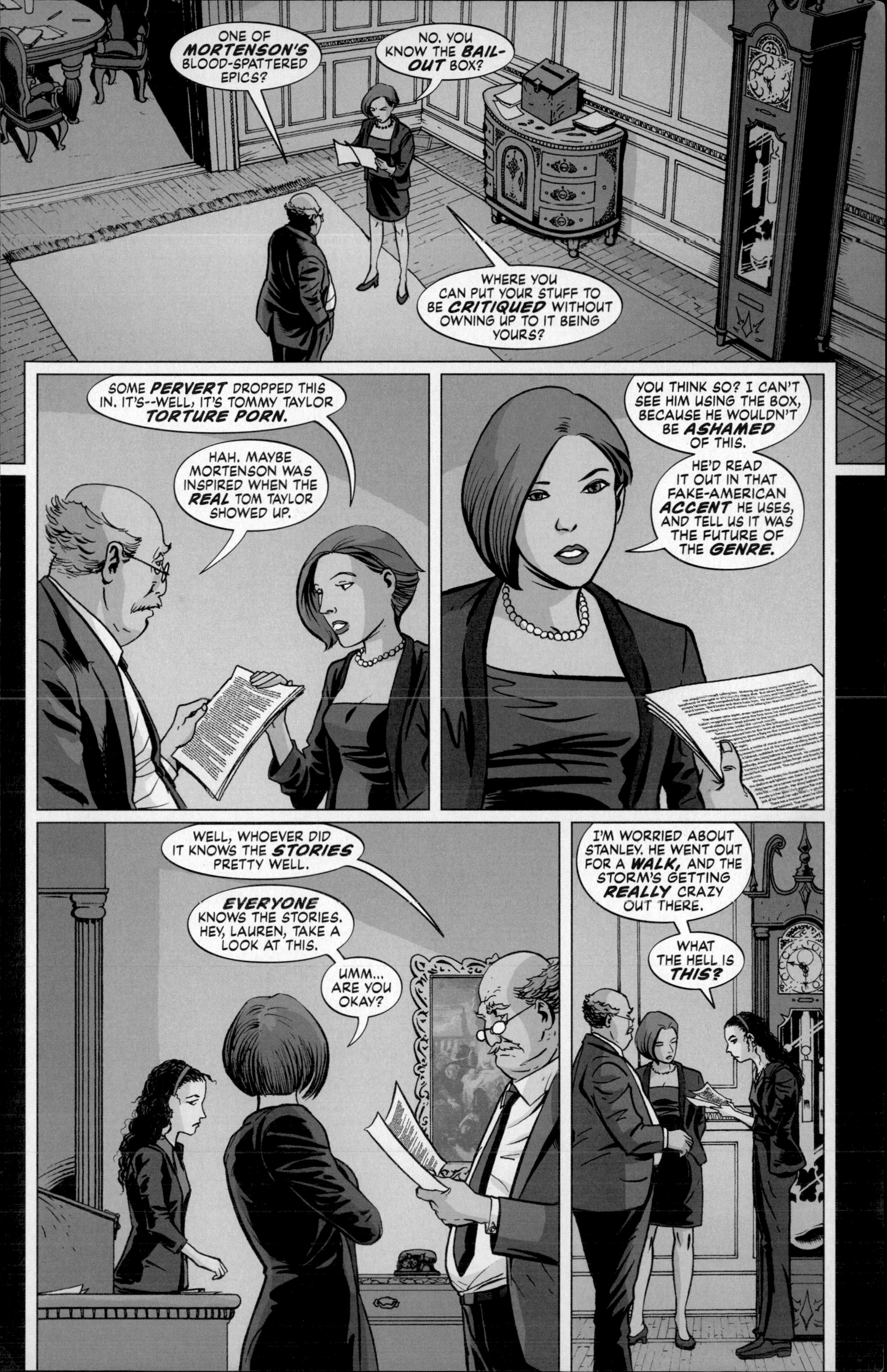

ONE OF MORTENSON'S BLOOD-SPATTERED EPICS?
NO. YOU KNOW THE BAIL-OUT BOX?
WHERE YOU CAN PUT YOUR STUFF TO BE CRITIQUED WITHOUT OWNING UP TO IT BEING YOURS?
SOME PERVERT DROPPED THIS IN. IT'S--WELL, IT'S TOMMY TAYLOR TORTURE PORN.
HAH. MAYBE MORTENSON WAS INSPIRED WHEN THE REAL TOM TAYLOR SHOWED UP.
YOU THINK SO? I CAN'T SEE HIM USING THE BOX, BECAUSE HE WOULDN'T BE ASHAMED OF THIS.
HE'D READ IT OUT IN THAT FAKE-AMERICAN ACCENT HE USES, AND TELL US IT WAS THE FUTURE OF THE GENRE.
WELL, WHOEVER DID IT KNOWS THE STORIES PRETTY WELL.
EVERYONE KNOWS THE STORIES. HEY, LAUREN, TAKE A LOOK AT THIS.
UMM... ARE YOU OKAY?
I'M WORRIED ABOUT STANLEY. HE WENT OUT FOR A WALK, AND THE STORM'S GETTING REALLY CRAZY OUT THERE.
WHAT THE HELL IS THIS?

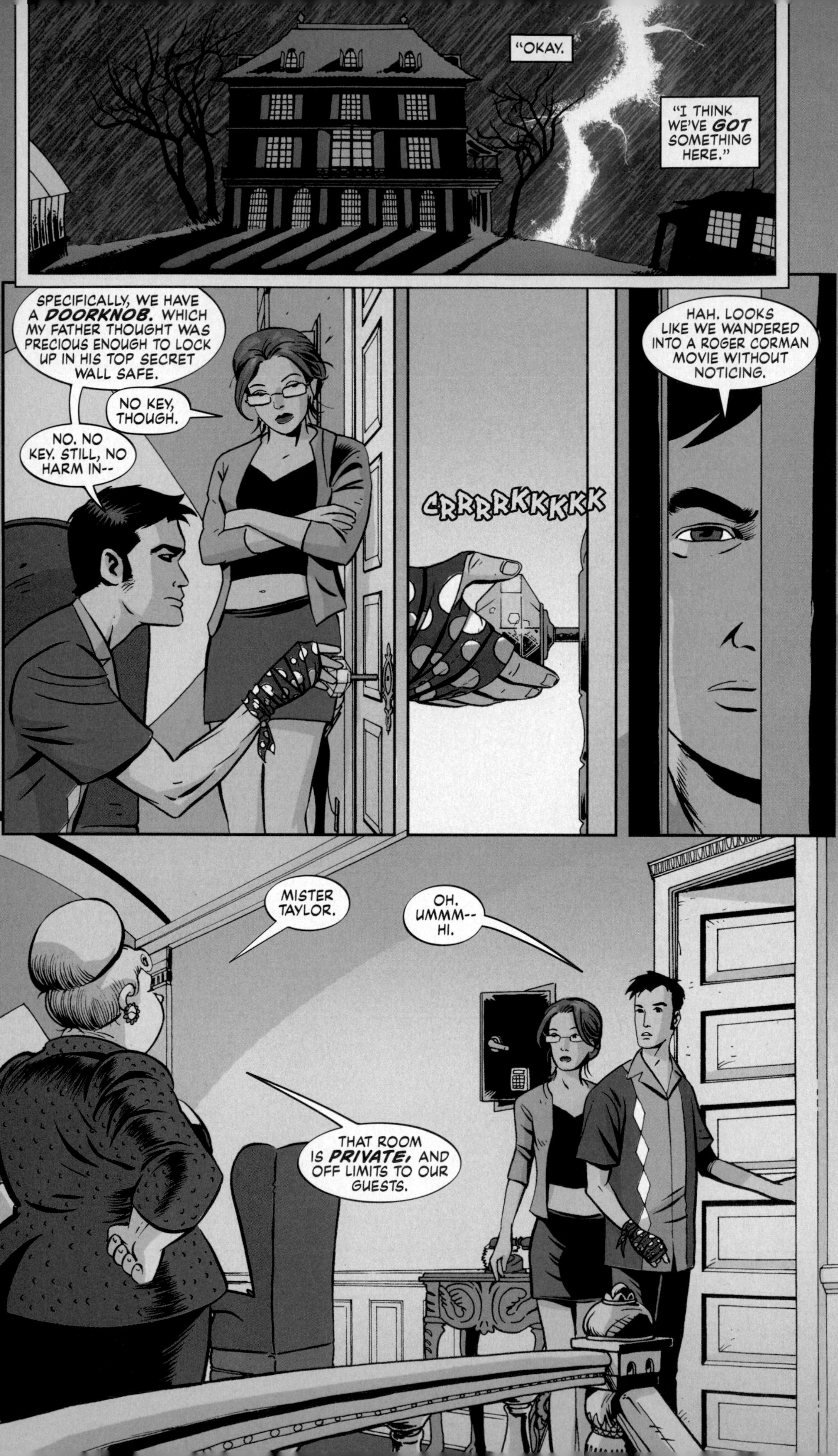
"OKAY.
"I THINK WE'VE GOT SOMETHING HERE."
SPECIFICALLY, WE HAVE A DOORKNOB. WHICH MY FATHER THOUGHT WAS PRECIOUS ENOUGH TO LOCK UP IN HIS TOP SECRET WALL SAFE.
NO KEY, THOUGH.
NO. NO KEY. STILL, NO HARM IN--
CRRRRKKKKK
HAH. LOOKS LIKE WE WANDERED INTO A ROGER CORMAN MOVIE WITHOUT NOTICING.
MISTER TAYLOR.
OH. UMMM-- HI.
THAT ROOM IS PRIVATE, AND OFF LIMITS TO OUR GUESTS.

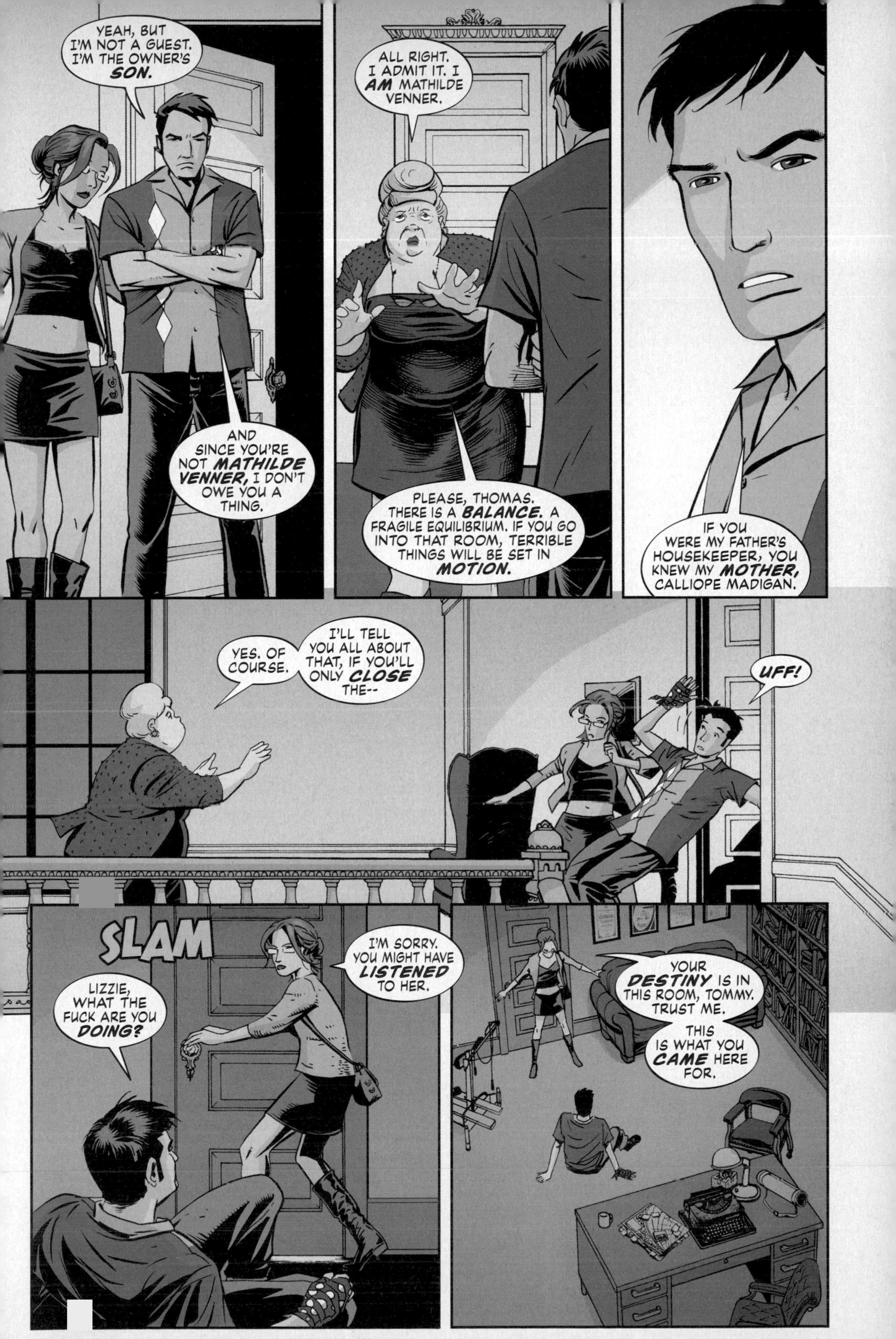
YEAH, BUT I'M NOT A GUEST. I'M THE OWNER'S SON.
AND SINCE YOU'RE NOT MATHILDE VENNER, I DON'T OWE YOU A THING.
ALL RIGHT. I ADMIT IT. I AM MATHILDE VENNER.
PLEASE, THOMAS. THERE IS A BALANCE. A FRAGILE EQUILIBRIUM. IF YOU GO INTO THAT ROOM, TERRIBLE THINGS WILL BE SET IN MOTION.
IF YOU WERE MY FATHER'S HOUSEKEEPER, YOU KNEW MY MOTHER, CALLIOPE MADIGAN.
YES. OF COURSE.
I'LL TELL YOU ALL ABOUT THAT, IF YOU'LL ONLY CLOSE THE--
UFF!
SLAM
LIZZIE, WHAT THE FUCK ARE YOU DOING?
I'M SORRY. YOU MIGHT HAVE LISTENED TO HER.
YOUR DESTINY IS IN THIS ROOM, TOMMY. TRUST ME.
THIS IS WHAT YOU CAME HERE FOR.

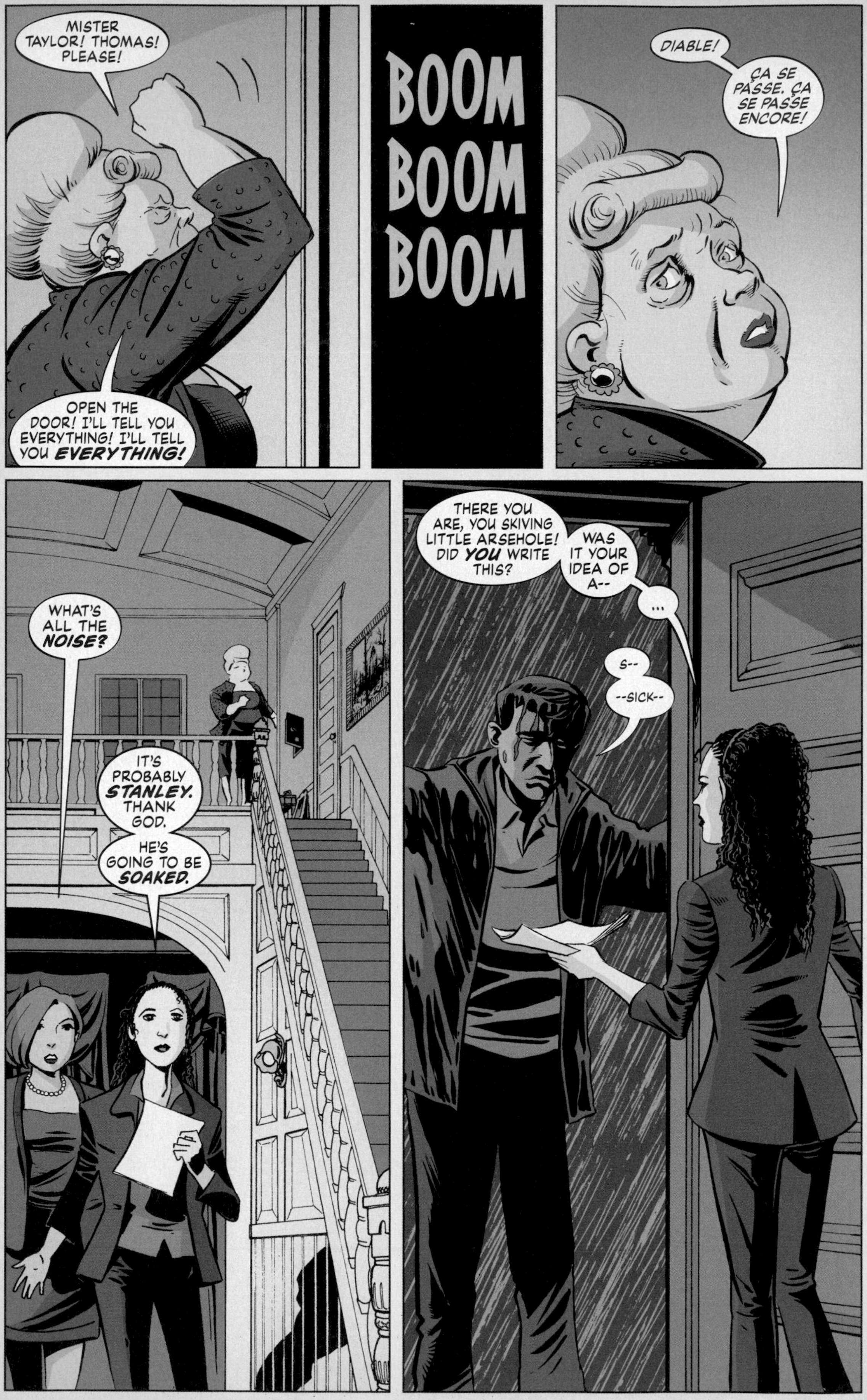
MISTER TAYLOR! THOMAS! PLEASE!
OPEN THE DOOR! I'LL TELL YOU EVERYTHING! I'LL TELL YOU EVERYTHING!
BOOM BOOM BOOM
DIABLE!
ÇA SE PASSE. ÇA SE PASSE ENCORE!
WHAT'S ALL THE NOISE?
IT'S PROBABLY STANLEY. THANK GOD.
HE'S GOING TO BE SOAKED.
THERE YOU ARE, YOU SKIVING LITTLE ARSEHOLE! DID YOU WRITE THIS?
WAS IT YOUR IDEA OF A--
...
S--
--SICK--

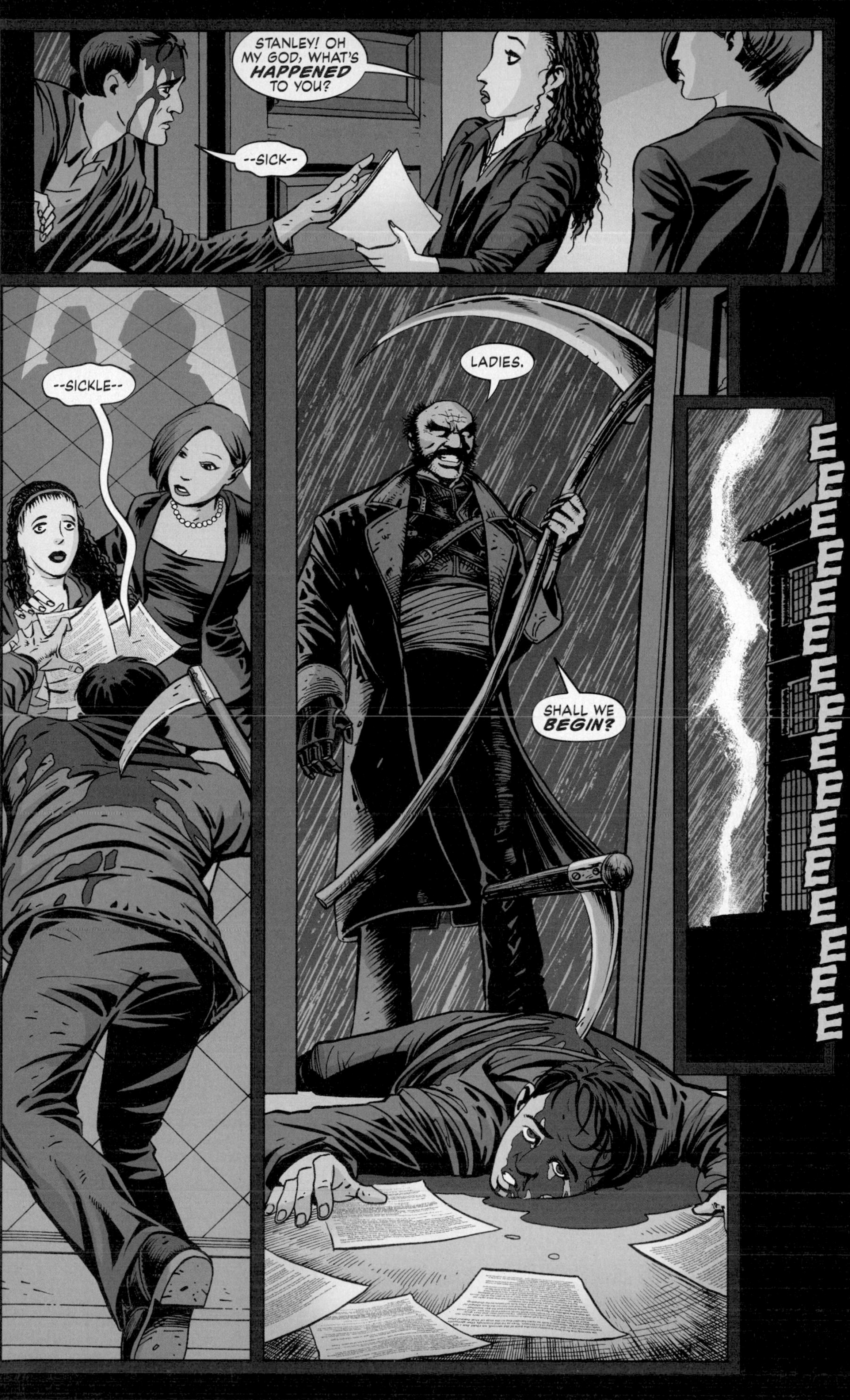
STANLEY! OH MY GOD, WHAT'S **HAPPENED** TO YOU?
--SICK--
--SICKLE--
LADIES.
SHALL WE **BEGIN?**
EEEEEEEEEEEEEEEE

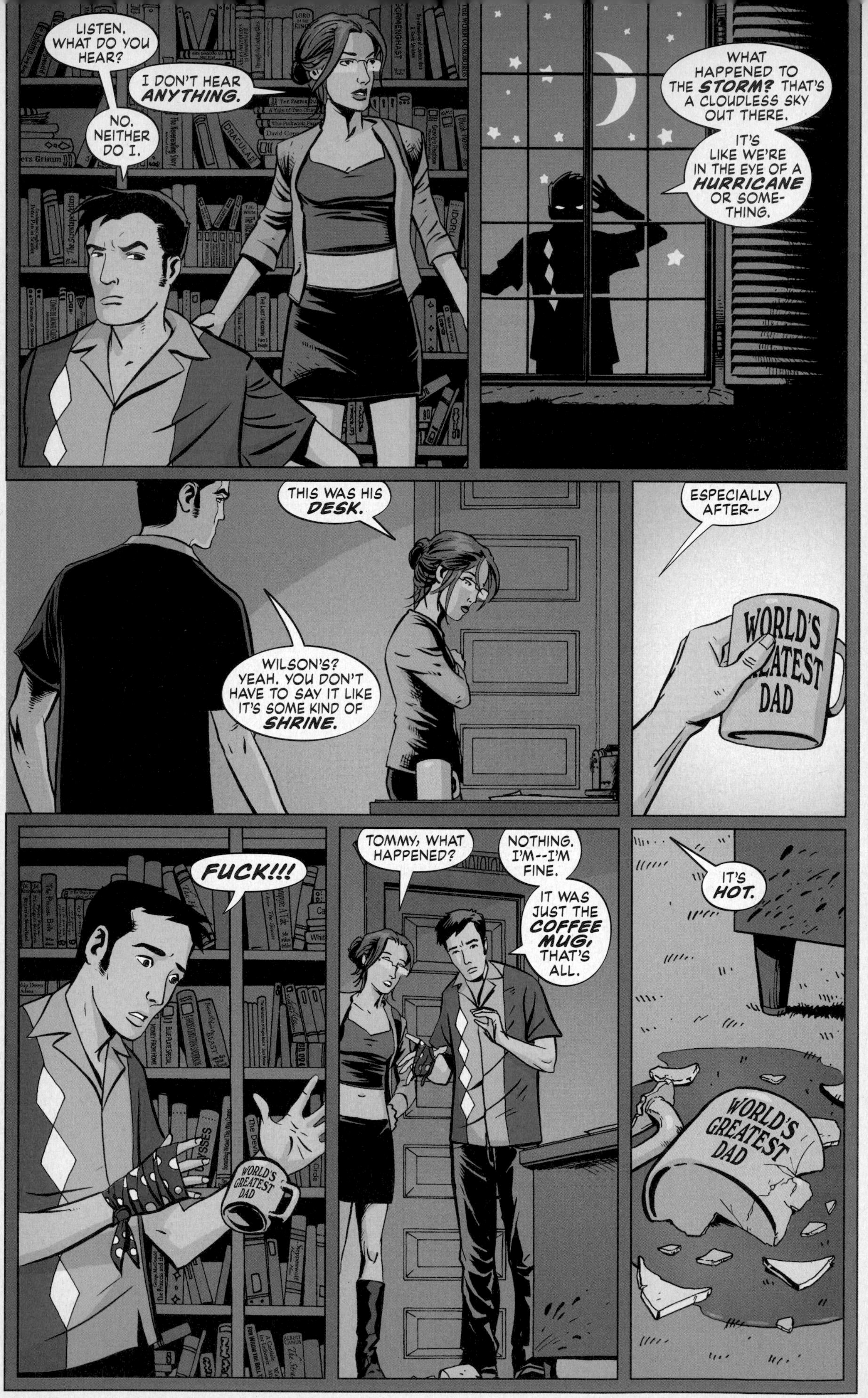
LISTEN. WHAT DO YOU HEAR?
I DON'T HEAR ANYTHING.
NO. NEITHER DO I.
WHAT HAPPENED TO THE STORM? THAT'S A CLOUDLESS SKY OUT THERE.
IT'S LIKE WE'RE IN THE EYE OF A HURRICANE OR SOMETHING.
THIS WAS HIS DESK.
WILSON'S? YEAH. YOU DON'T HAVE TO SAY IT LIKE IT'S SOME KIND OF SHRINE.
ESPECIALLY AFTER--
WORLD'S GREATEST DAD
FUCK!!!
WORLD'S GREATEST DAD
TOMMY, WHAT HAPPENED?
NOTHING. I'M--I'M FINE.
IT WAS JUST THE COFFEE MUG, THAT'S ALL.
IT'S HOT.
WORLD'S GREATEST DAD

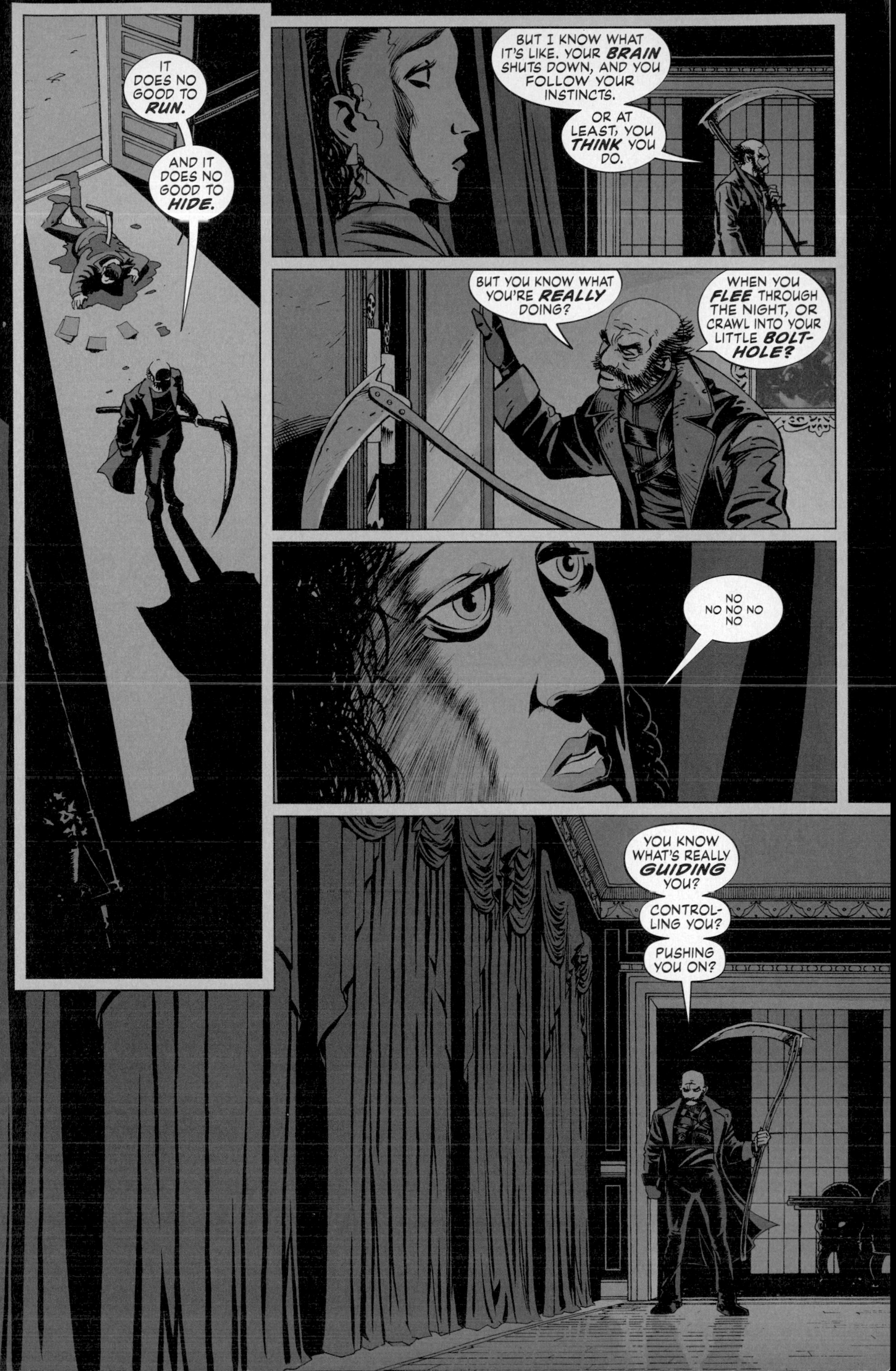
IT DOES NO GOOD TO RUN.
AND IT DOES NO GOOD TO HIDE.
BUT I KNOW WHAT IT'S LIKE. YOUR BRAIN SHUTS DOWN, AND YOU FOLLOW YOUR INSTINCTS.
OR AT LEAST, YOU THINK YOU DO.
BUT YOU KNOW WHAT YOU'RE REALLY DOING?
WHEN YOU FLEE THROUGH THE NIGHT, OR CRAWL INTO YOUR LITTLE BOLT-HOLE?
NO NO NO NO NO
YOU KNOW WHAT'S REALLY GUIDING YOU?
CONTROL-LING YOU?
PUSHING YOU ON?

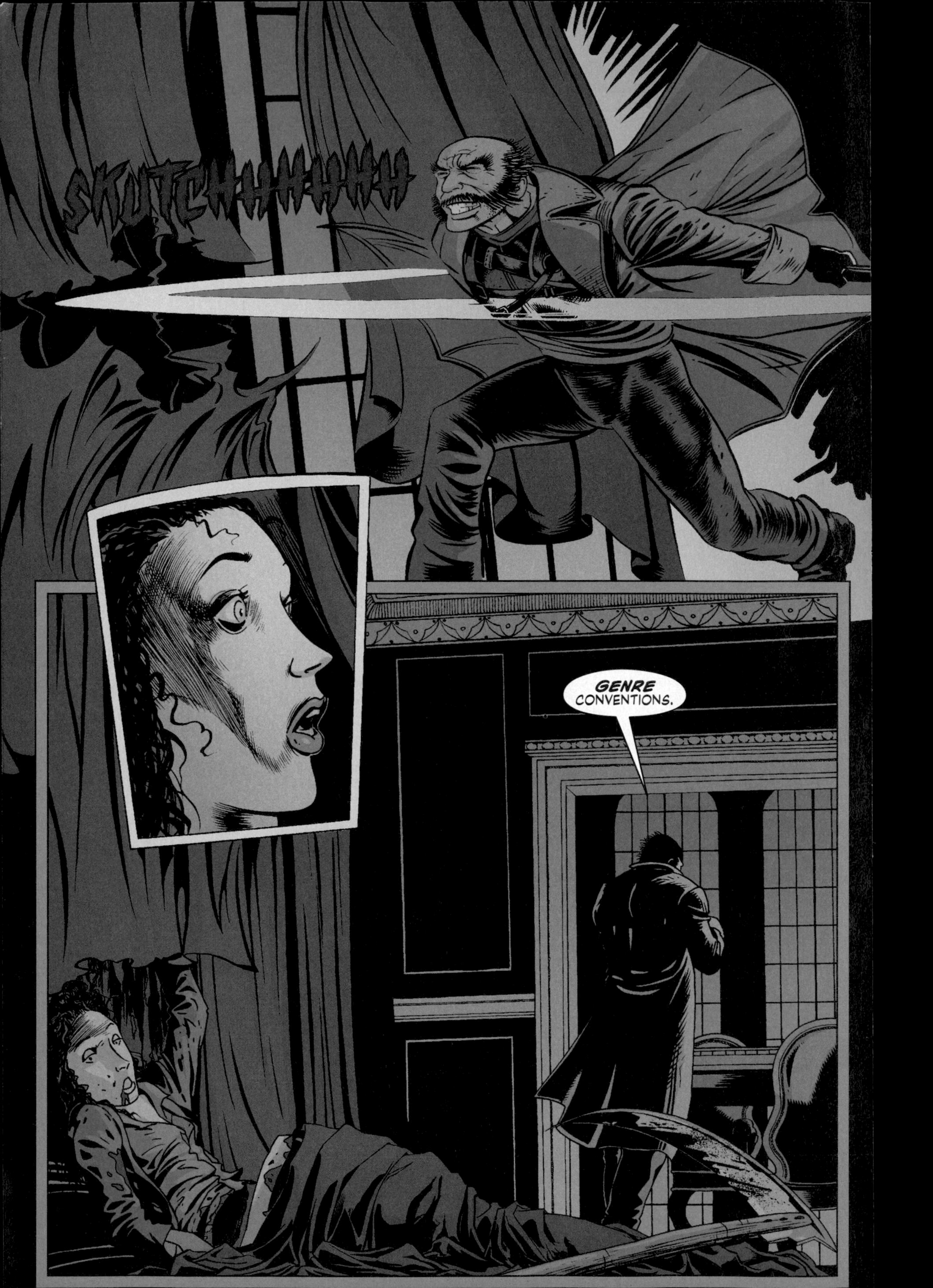
SKUTCHHHHHH
GENRE CONVENTIONS.

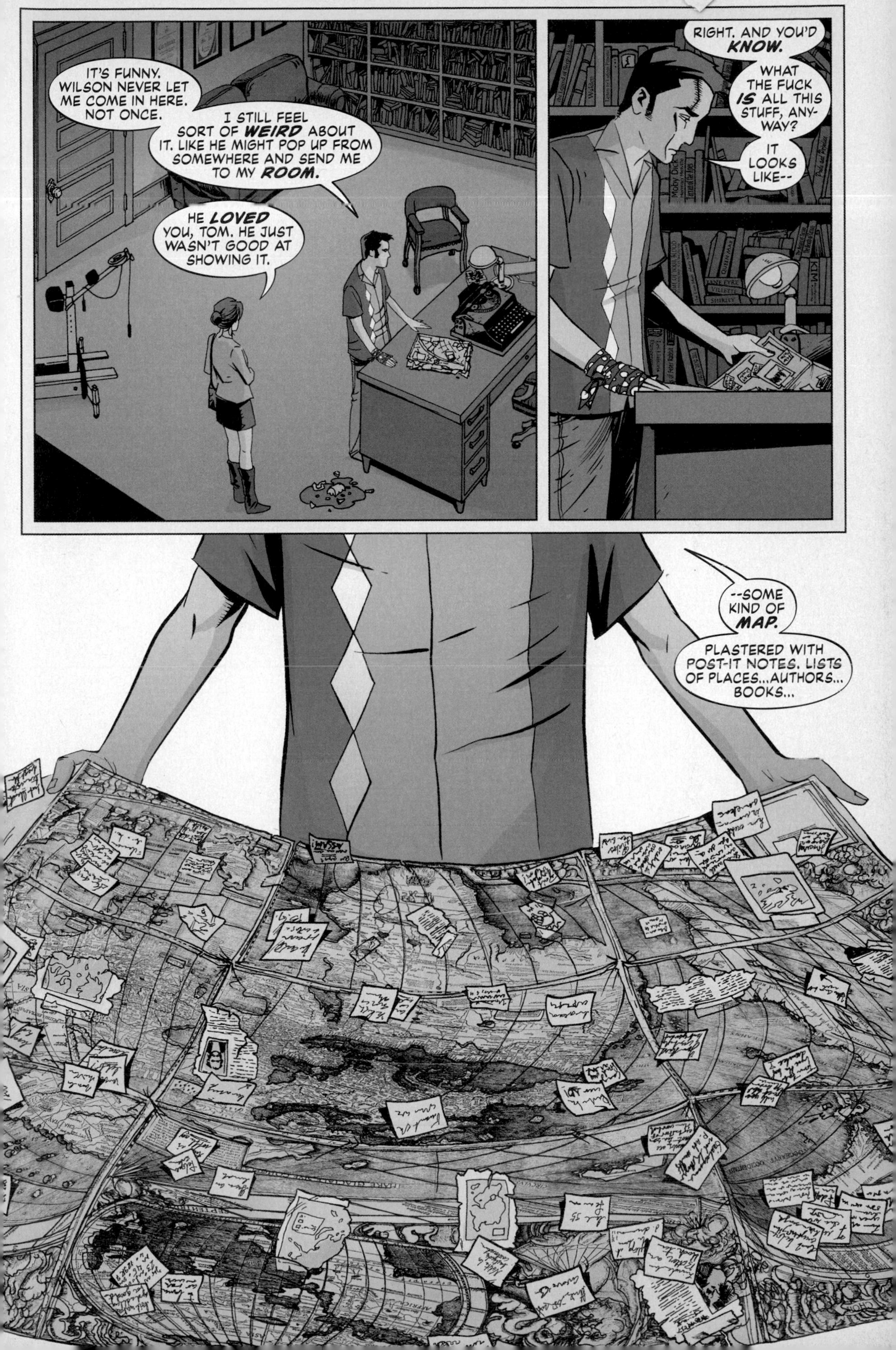
IT'S FUNNY. WILSON NEVER LET ME COME IN HERE. NOT ONCE.
I STILL FEEL SORT OF WEIRD ABOUT IT. LIKE HE MIGHT POP UP FROM SOMEWHERE AND SEND ME TO MY ROOM.
HE LOVED YOU, TOM. HE JUST WASN'T GOOD AT SHOWING IT.
RIGHT. AND YOU'D KNOW.
WHAT THE FUCK IS ALL THIS STUFF, ANYWAY?
IT LOOKS LIKE--
--SOME KIND OF MAP.
PLASTERED WITH POST-IT NOTES. LISTS OF PLACES...AUTHORS... BOOKS...

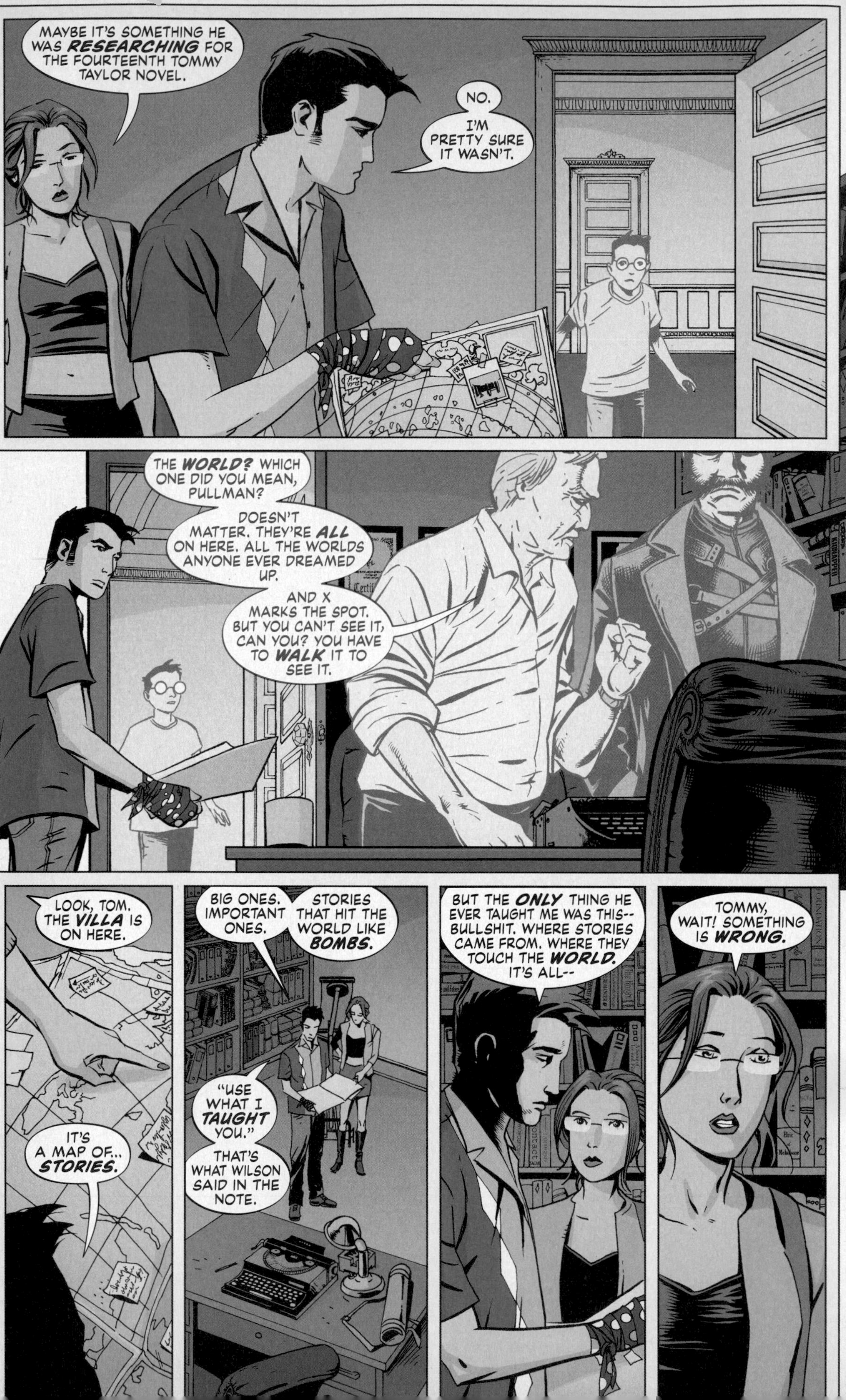
MAYBE IT'S SOMETHING HE WAS RESEARCHING FOR THE FOURTEENTH TOMMY TAYLOR NOVEL.
NO.
I'M PRETTY SURE IT WASN'T.
THE WORLD? WHICH ONE DID YOU MEAN, PULLMAN?
DOESN'T MATTER. THEY'RE ALL ON HERE. ALL THE WORLDS ANYONE EVER DREAMED UP.
AND X MARKS THE SPOT. BUT YOU CAN'T SEE IT, CAN YOU? YOU HAVE TO WALK IT TO SEE IT.
LOOK, TOM. THE VILLA IS ON HERE.
IT'S A MAP OF... STORIES.
BIG ONES. IMPORTANT ONES.
STORIES THAT HIT THE WORLD LIKE BOMBS.
"USE WHAT I TAUGHT YOU."
THAT'S WHAT WILSON SAID IN THE NOTE.
BUT THE ONLY THING HE EVER TAUGHT ME WAS THIS-- BULLSHIT. WHERE STORIES CAME FROM. WHERE THEY TOUCH THE WORLD. IT'S ALL--
TOMMY, WAIT! SOMETHING IS WRONG.

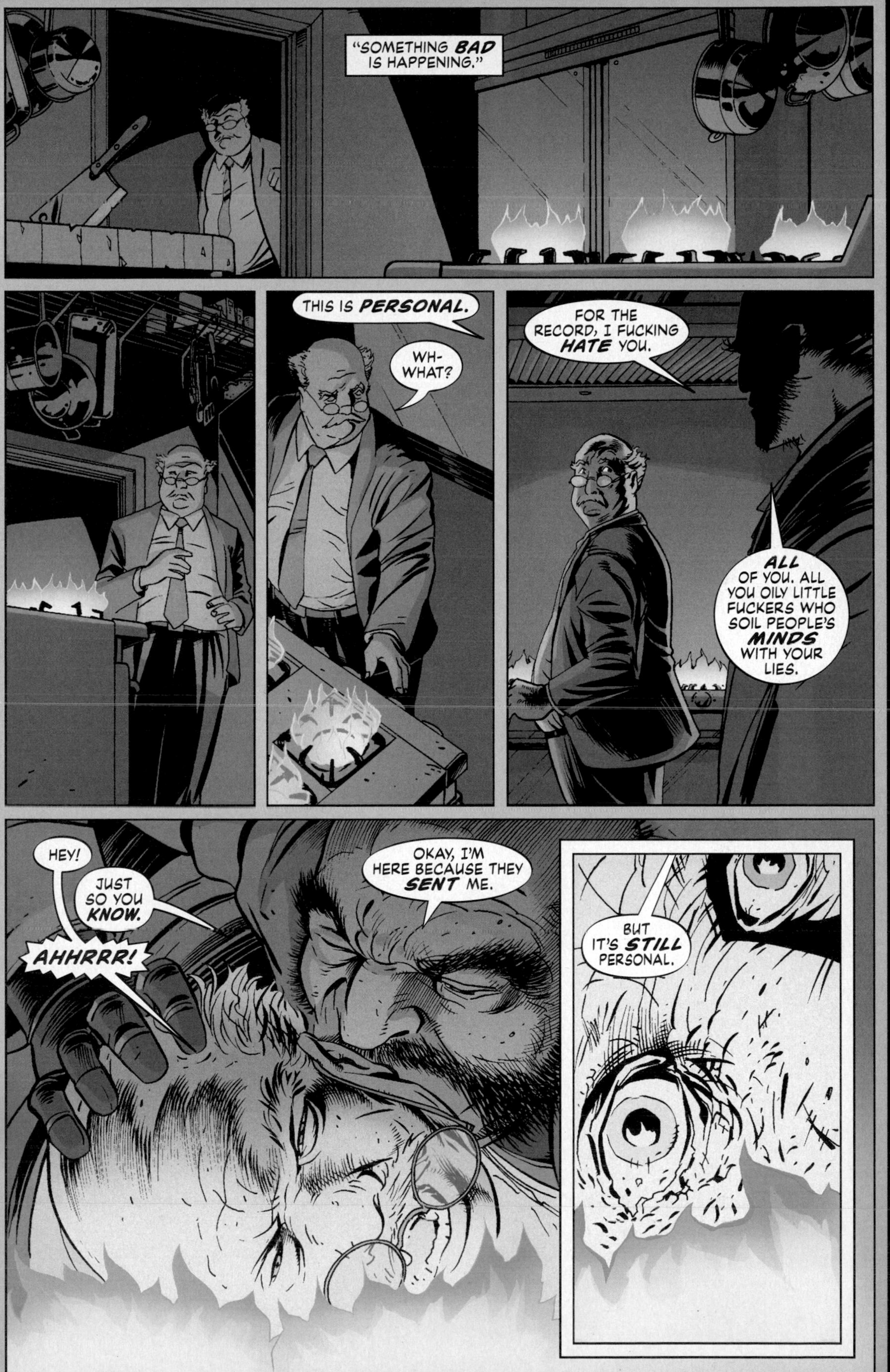
"SOMETHING BAD IS HAPPENING."
THIS IS PERSONAL.
WH- WHAT?
FOR THE RECORD, I FUCKING HATE YOU.
ALL OF YOU. ALL YOU OILY LITTLE FUCKERS WHO SOIL PEOPLE'S MINDS WITH YOUR LIES.
HEY!
JUST SO YOU KNOW.
AHHRRR!
OKAY, I'M HERE BECAUSE THEY SENT ME.
BUT IT'S STILL PERSONAL.

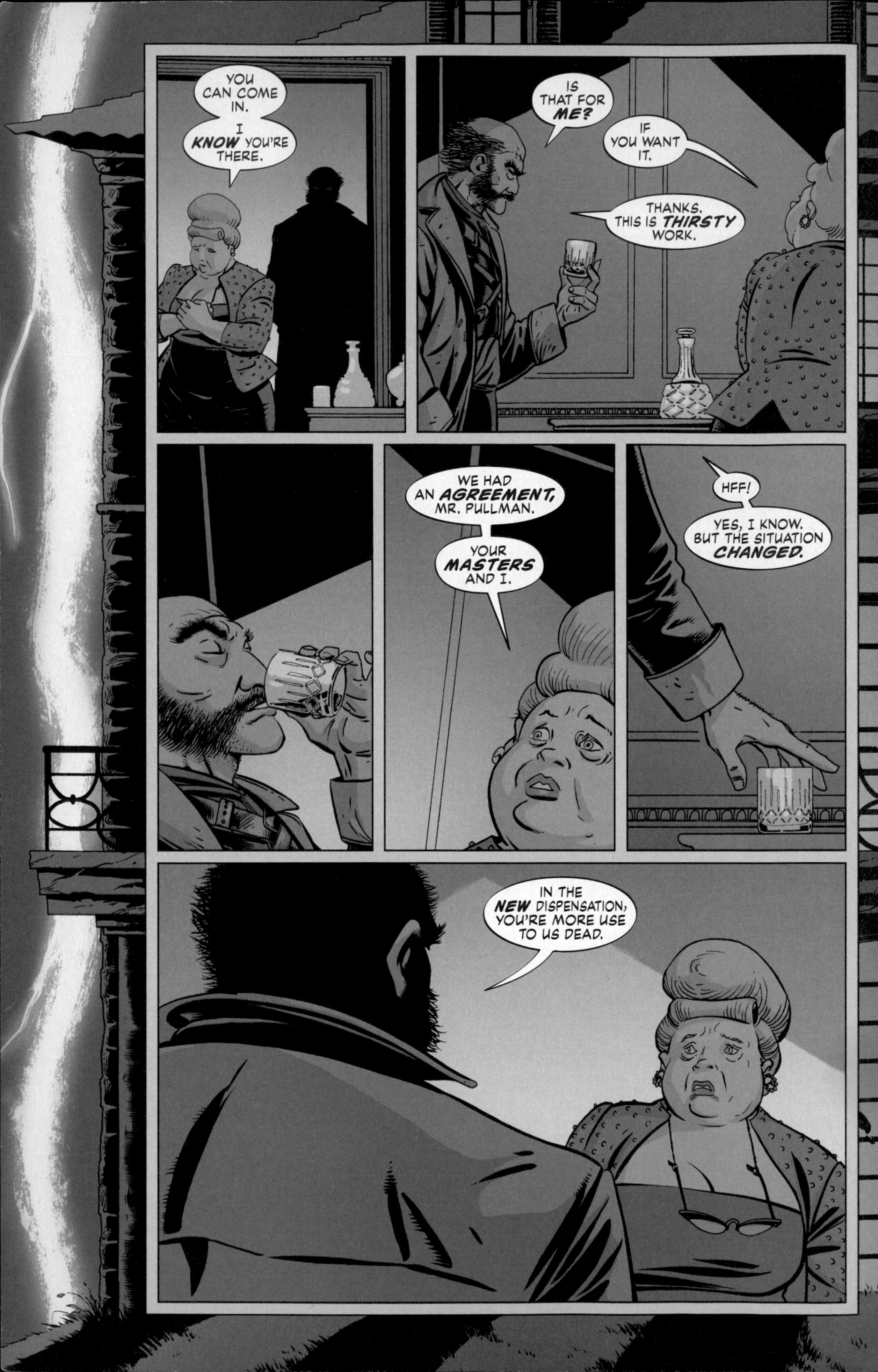
YOU CAN COME IN.
I KNOW YOU'RE THERE.
IS THAT FOR ME?
IF YOU WANT IT.
THANKS. THIS IS THIRSTY WORK.
WE HAD AN AGREEMENT, MR. PULLMAN.
YOUR MASTERS AND I.
HFF!
YES, I KNOW. BUT THE SITUATION CHANGED.
IN THE NEW DISPENSATION, YOU'RE MORE USE TO US DEAD.

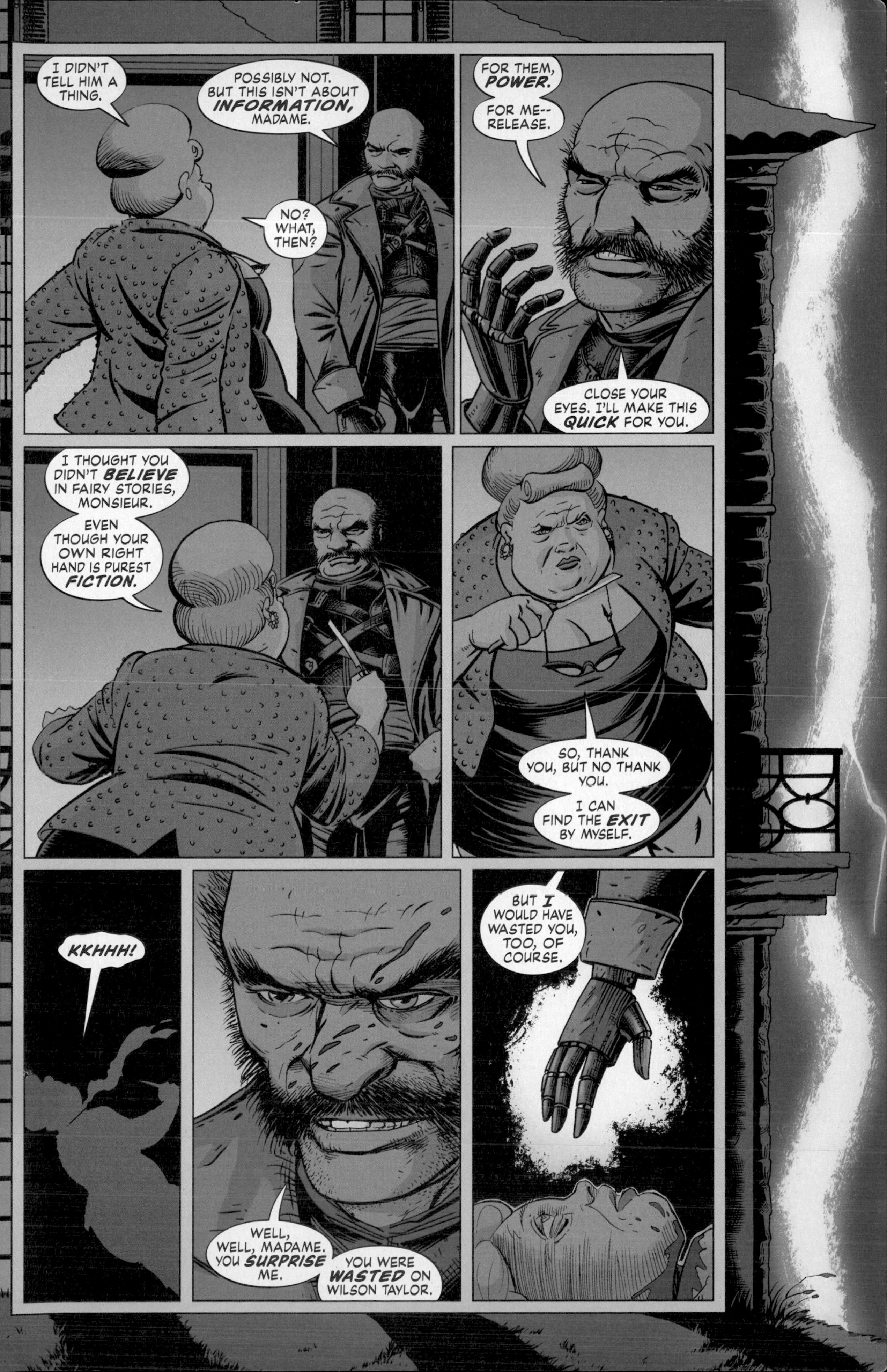
I DIDN'T TELL HIM A THING.
POSSIBLY NOT. BUT THIS ISN'T ABOUT INFORMATION, MADAME.
NO? WHAT, THEN?
FOR THEM, POWER.
FOR ME-- RELEASE.
CLOSE YOUR EYES. I'LL MAKE THIS QUICK FOR YOU.
I THOUGHT YOU DIDN'T BELIEVE IN FAIRY STORIES, MONSIEUR.
EVEN THOUGH YOUR OWN RIGHT HAND IS PUREST FICTION.
SO, THANK YOU, BUT NO THANK YOU.
I CAN FIND THE EXIT BY MYSELF.
KKHHH!
WELL, WELL, MADAME. YOU SURPRISE ME.
YOU WERE WASTED ON WILSON TAYLOR.
BUT I WOULD HAVE WASTED YOU, TOO, OF COURSE.

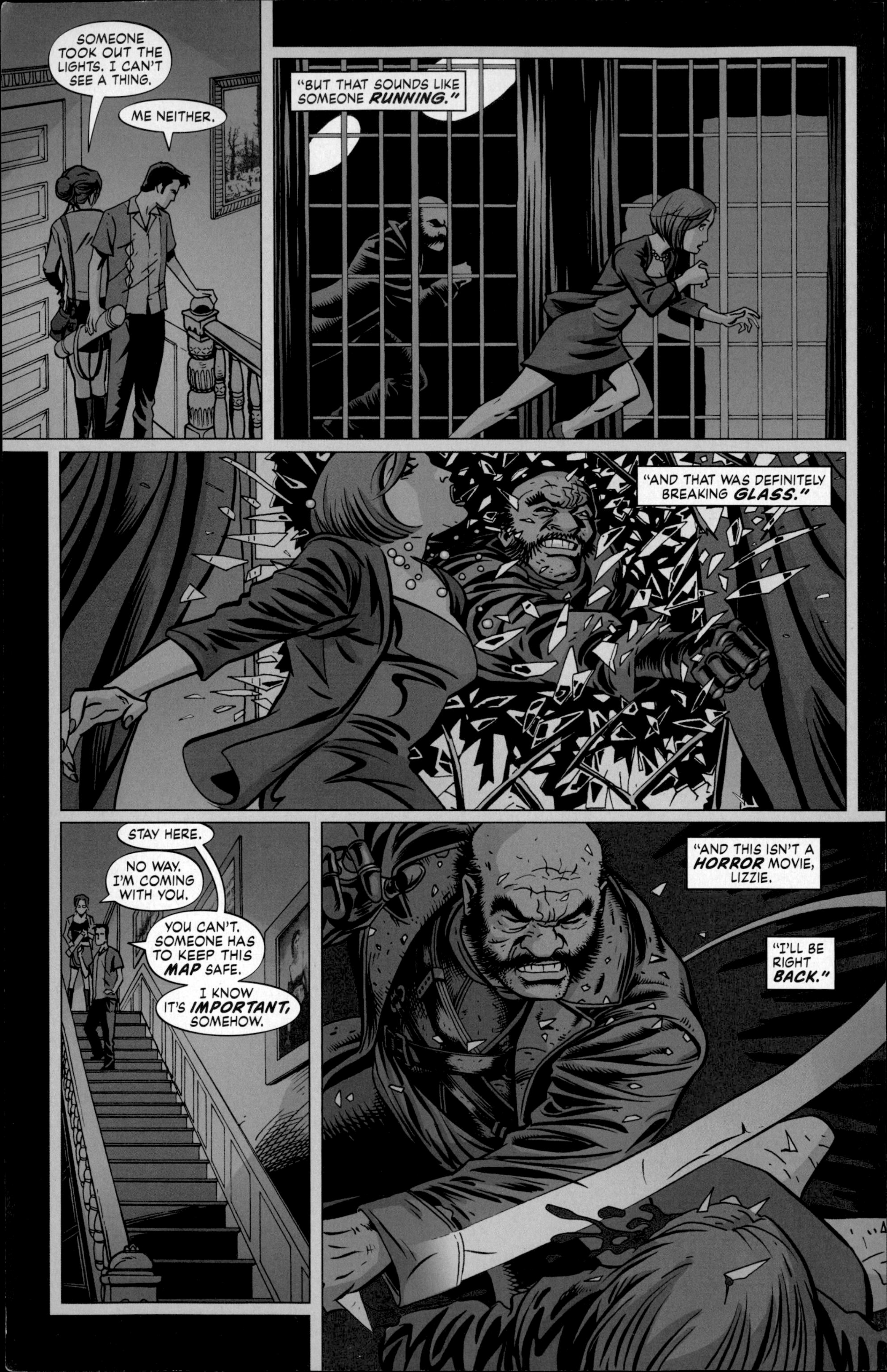
SOMEONE TOOK OUT THE LIGHTS. I CAN'T SEE A THING.
ME NEITHER.
"BUT THAT SOUNDS LIKE SOMEONE RUNNING."
"AND THAT WAS DEFINITELY BREAKING GLASS."
STAY HERE.
NO WAY. I'M COMING WITH YOU.
YOU CAN'T. SOMEONE HAS TO KEEP THIS MAP SAFE.
I KNOW IT'S IMPORTANT, SOMEHOW.
"AND THIS ISN'T A HORROR MOVIE, LIZZIE.
"I'LL BE RIGHT BACK."

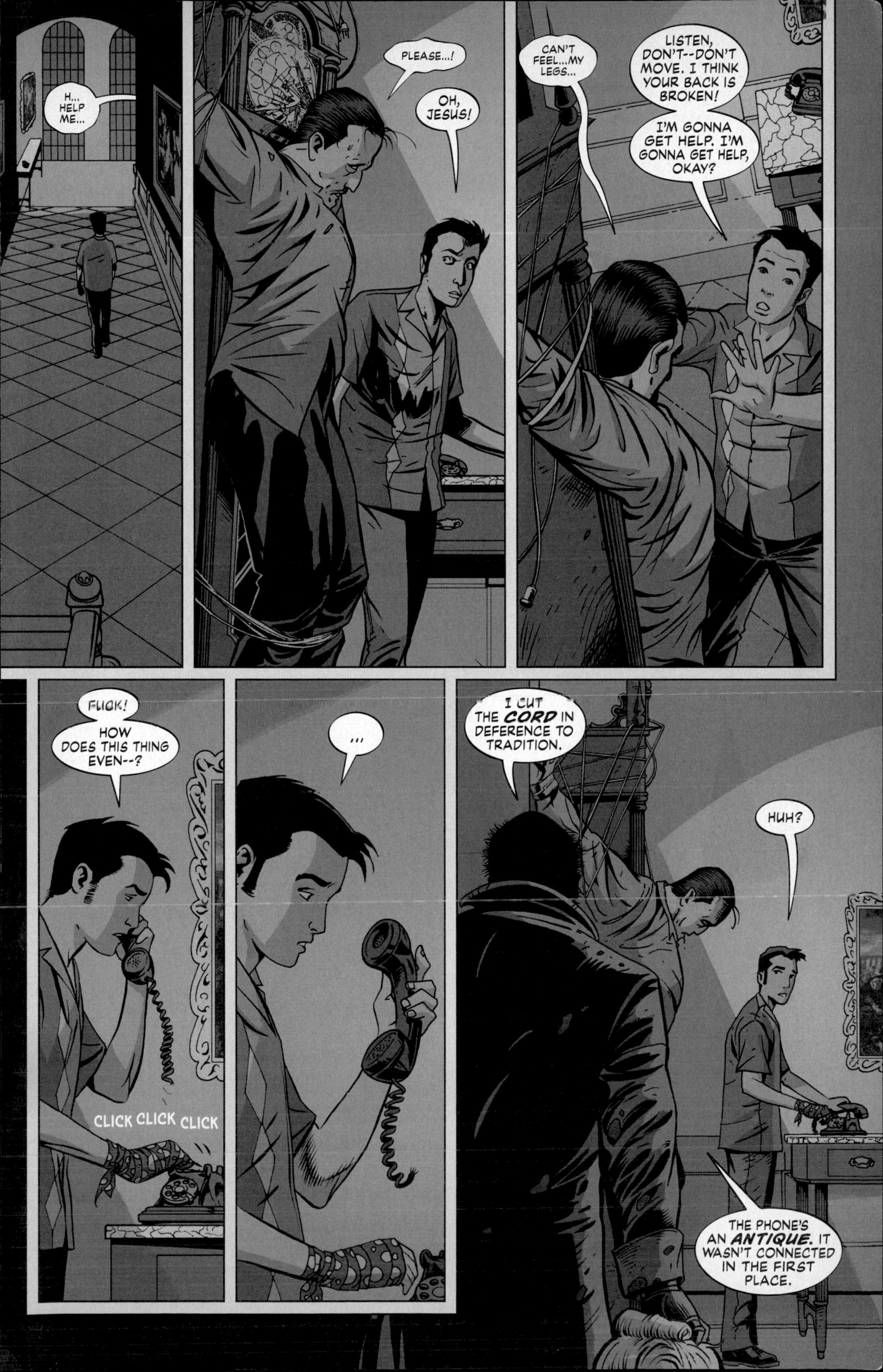
H... HELP ME...
PLEASE...!
OH, JESUS!
CAN'T FEEL...MY LEGS...
LISTEN, DON'T--DON'T MOVE. I THINK YOUR BACK IS BROKEN!
I'M GONNA GET HELP. I'M GONNA GET HELP, OKAY?
FUCK!
HOW DOES THIS THING EVEN--?
CLICK CLICK CLICK
...
I CUT THE CORD IN DEFERENCE TO TRADITION.
HUH?
THE PHONE'S AN ANTIQUE. IT WASN'T CONNECTED IN THE FIRST PLACE.

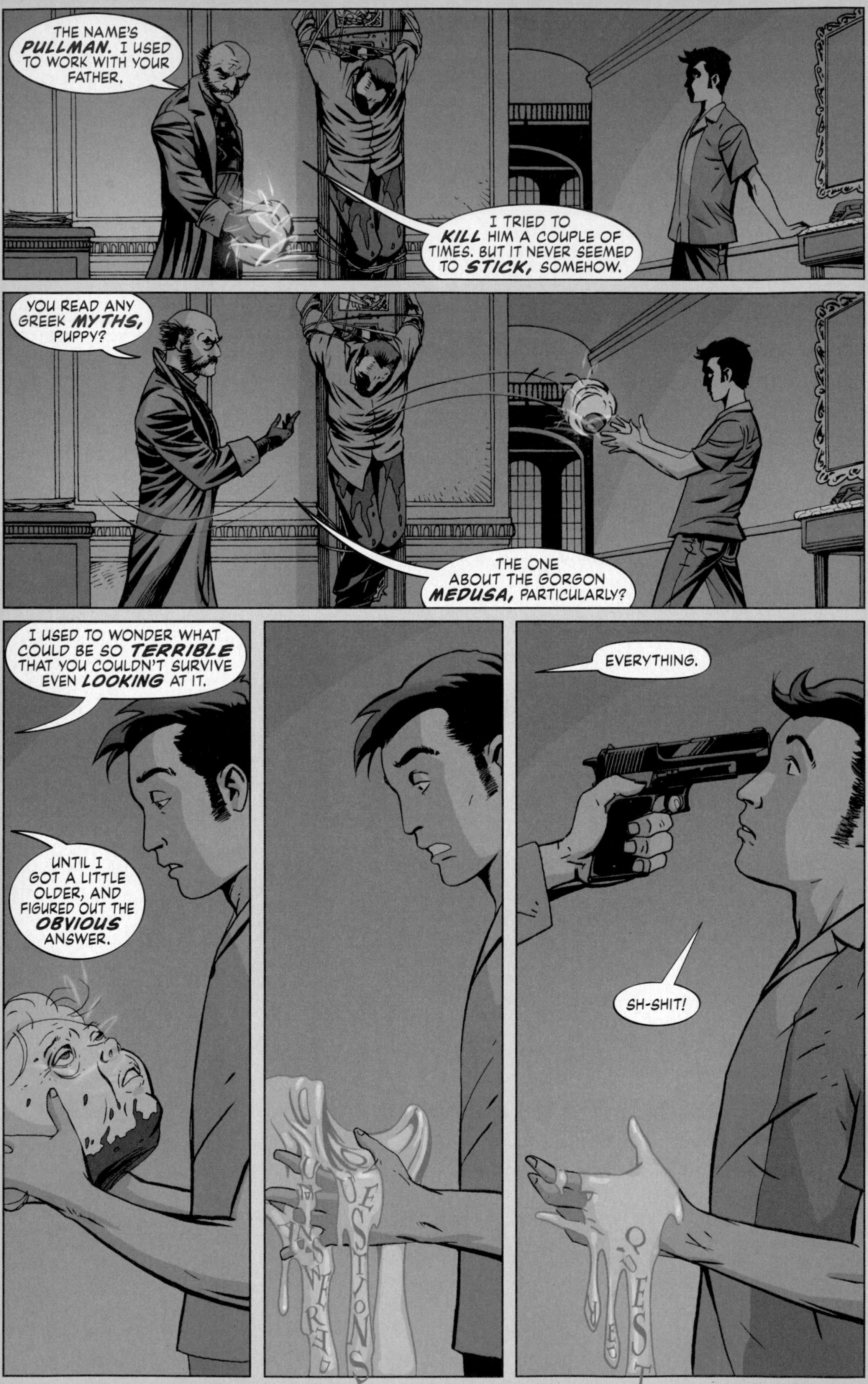
THE NAME'S PULLMAN. I USED TO WORK WITH YOUR FATHER.
I TRIED TO KILL HIM A COUPLE OF TIMES. BUT IT NEVER SEEMED TO STICK, SOMEHOW.
YOU READ ANY GREEK MYTHS, PUPPY?
THE ONE ABOUT THE GORGON MEDUSA, PARTICULARLY?
I USED TO WONDER WHAT COULD BE SO TERRIBLE THAT YOU COULDN'T SURVIVE EVEN LOOKING AT IT.
UNTIL I GOT A LITTLE OLDER, AND FIGURED OUT THE OBVIOUS ANSWER.
EVERYTHING.
SH-SHIT!

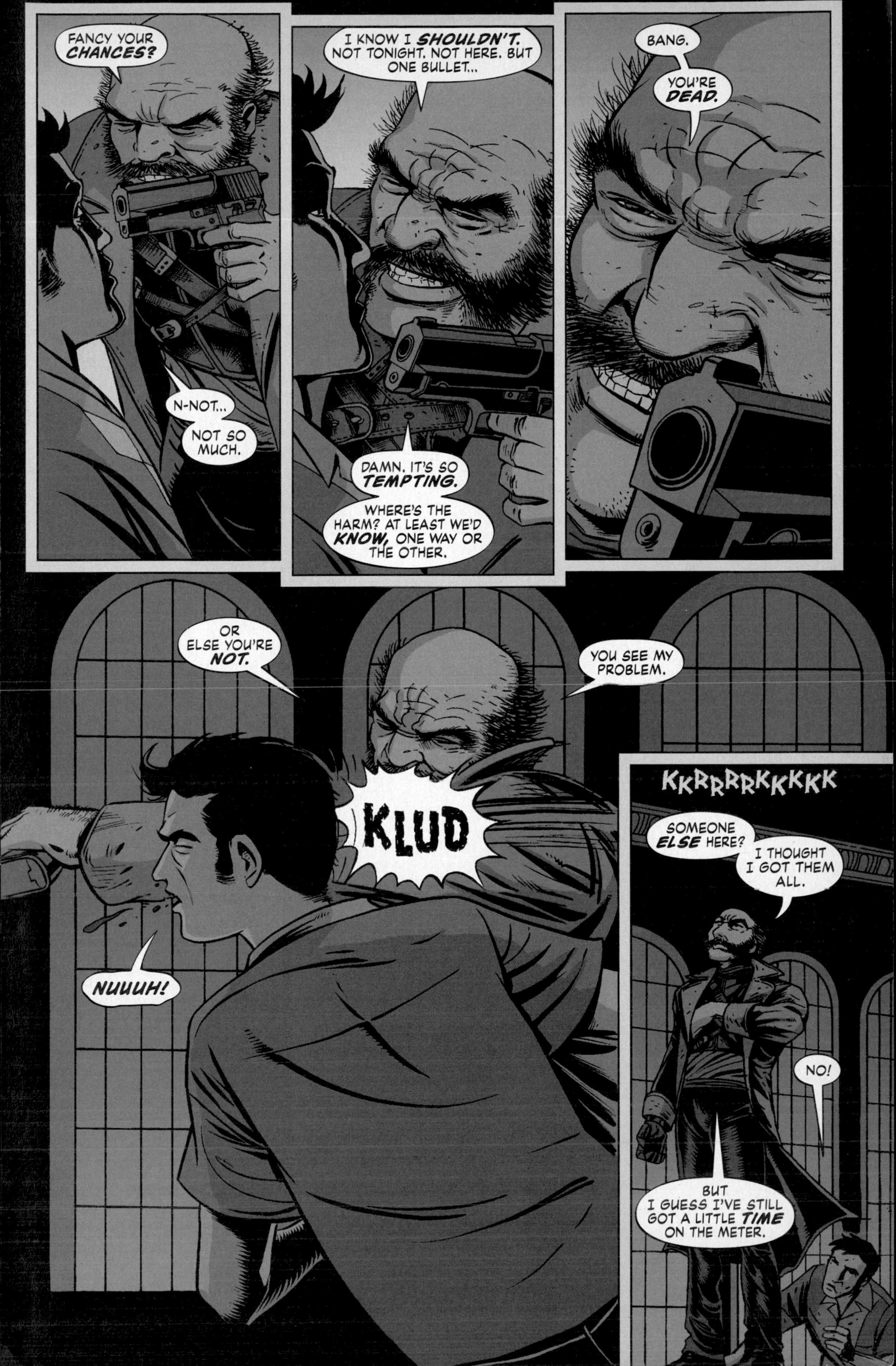
FANCY YOUR CHANCES?
N-NOT...
NOT SO MUCH.
I KNOW I SHOULDN'T. NOT TONIGHT. NOT HERE. BUT ONE BULLET...
DAMN. IT'S SO TEMPTING.
WHERE'S THE HARM? AT LEAST WE'D KNOW, ONE WAY OR THE OTHER.
BANG.
YOU'RE DEAD.
OR ELSE YOU'RE NOT.
YOU SEE MY PROBLEM.
KLUD
NUUUH!
KKRRRRKKKKK
SOMEONE ELSE HERE?
I THOUGHT I GOT THEM ALL.
NO!
BUT I GUESS I'VE STILL GOT A LITTLE TIME ON THE METER.

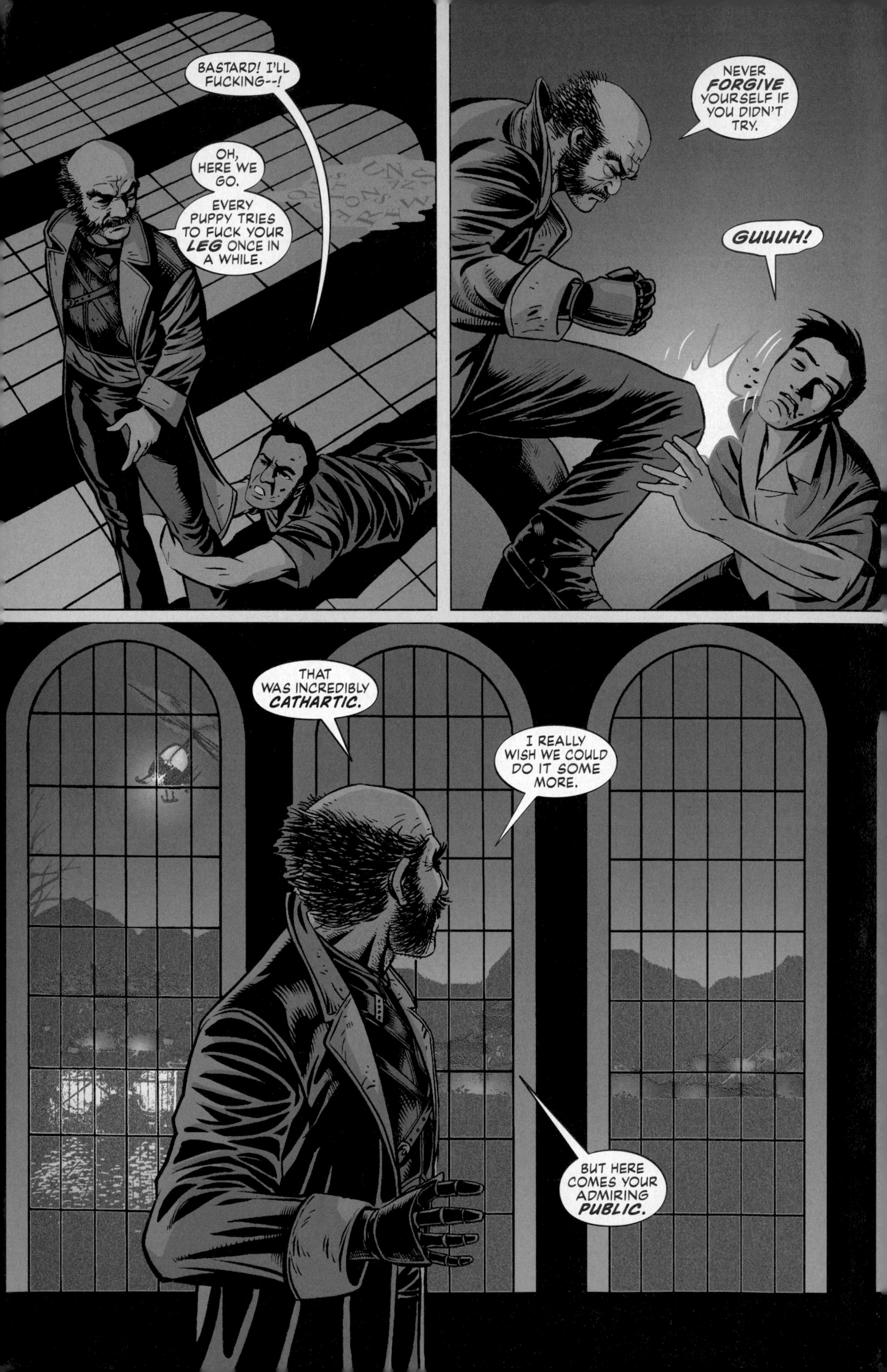
BASTARD! I'LL FUCKING--!
OH, HERE WE GO.
EVERY PUPPY TRIES TO FUCK YOUR LEG ONCE IN A WHILE.
NEVER FORGIVE YOURSELF IF YOU DIDN'T TRY.
GUUUH!
THAT WAS INCREDIBLY CATHARTIC.
I REALLY WISH WE COULD DO IT SOME MORE.
BUT HERE COMES YOUR ADMIRING PUBLIC.

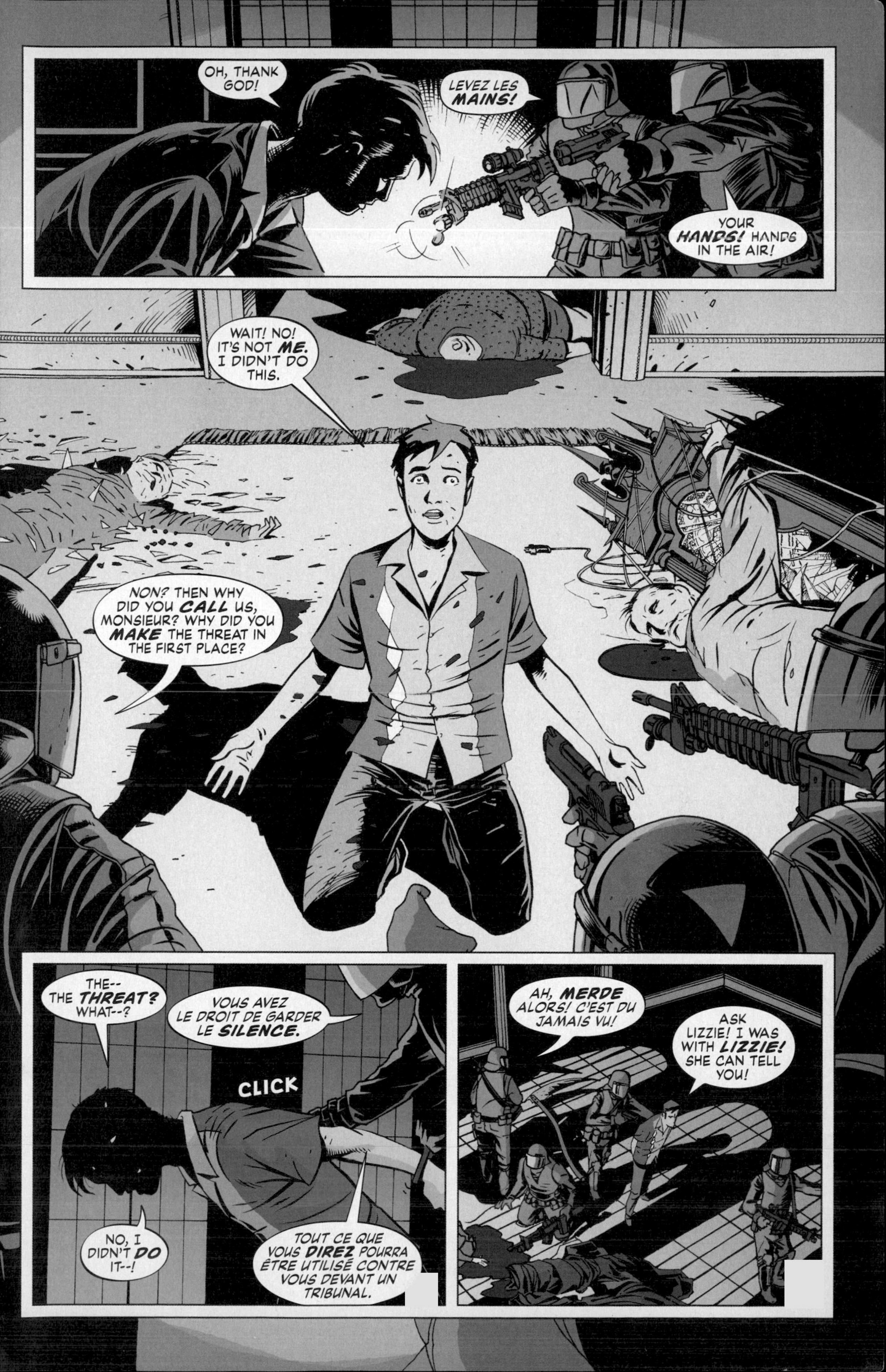
OH, THANK GOD!
LEVEZ LES MAINS!
YOUR HANDS! HANDS IN THE AIR!
WAIT! NO! IT'S NOT ME. I DIDN'T DO THIS.
NON? THEN WHY DID YOU CALL US, MONSIEUR? WHY DID YOU MAKE THE THREAT IN THE FIRST PLACE?
THE-- THE THREAT? WHAT--?
VOUS AVEZ LE DROIT DE GARDER LE SILENCE.
CLICK
NO, I DIDN'T DO IT--!
TOUT CE QUE VOUS DIREZ POURRA ÊTRE UTILISÉ CONTRE VOUS DEVANT UN TRIBUNAL.
AH, MERDE ALORS! C'EST DU JAMAIS VU!
ASK LIZZIE! I WAS WITH LIZZIE! SHE CAN TELL YOU!

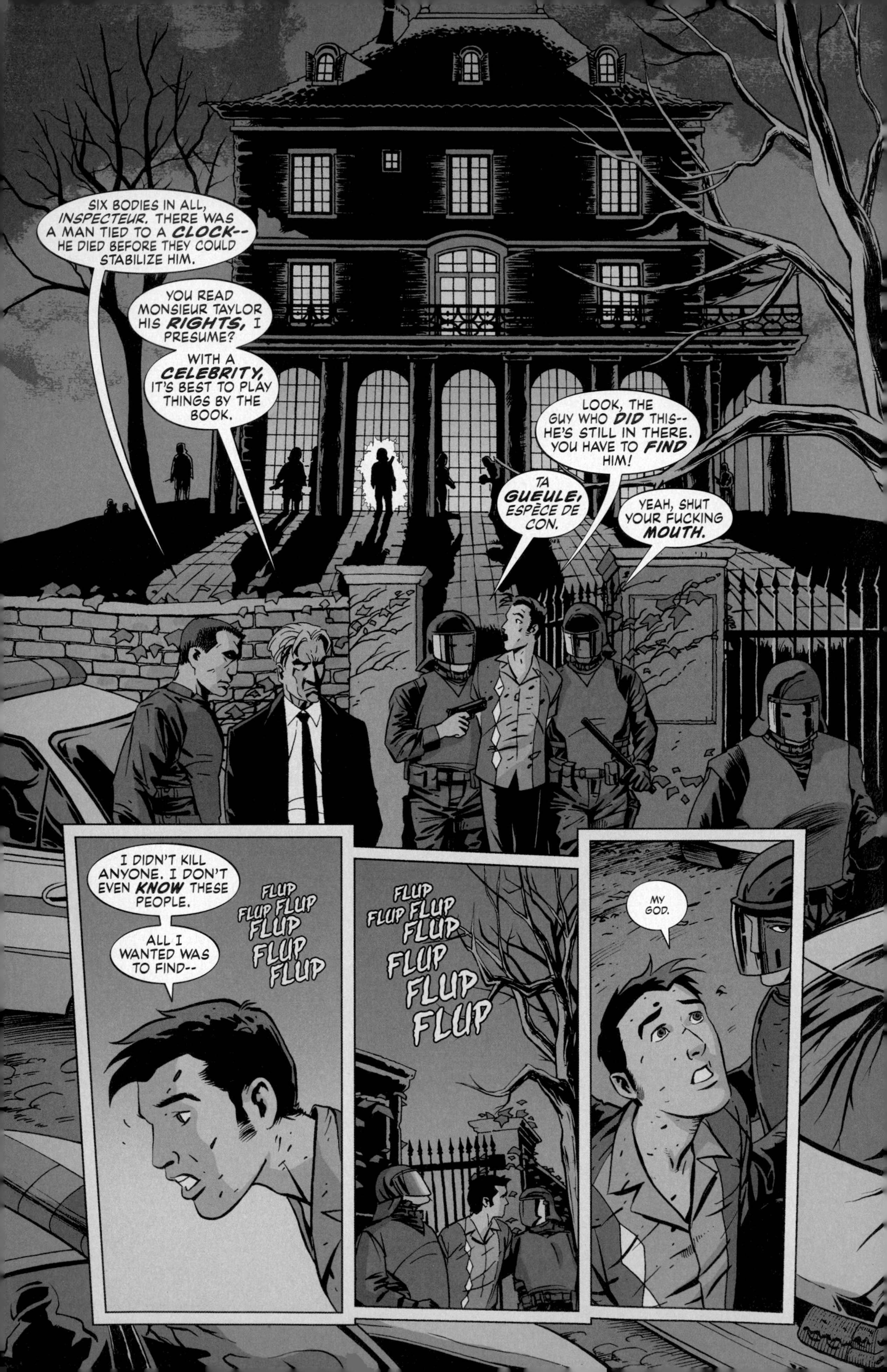
SIX BODIES IN ALL, INSPECTEUR. THERE WAS A MAN TIED TO A CLOCK-- HE DIED BEFORE THEY COULD STABILIZE HIM.
YOU READ MONSIEUR TAYLOR HIS RIGHTS, I PRESUME?
WITH A CELEBRITY, IT'S BEST TO PLAY THINGS BY THE BOOK.
LOOK, THE GUY WHO DID THIS-- HE'S STILL IN THERE. YOU HAVE TO FIND HIM!
TA GUEULE, ESPÈCE DE CON.
YEAH, SHUT YOUR FUCKING MOUTH.
I DIDN'T KILL ANYONE. I DON'T EVEN KNOW THESE PEOPLE.
ALL I WANTED WAS TO FIND--
FLUP FLUP FLUP FLUP FLUP FLUP
FLUP FLUP FLUP FLUP FLUP FLUP FLUP
MY GOD.

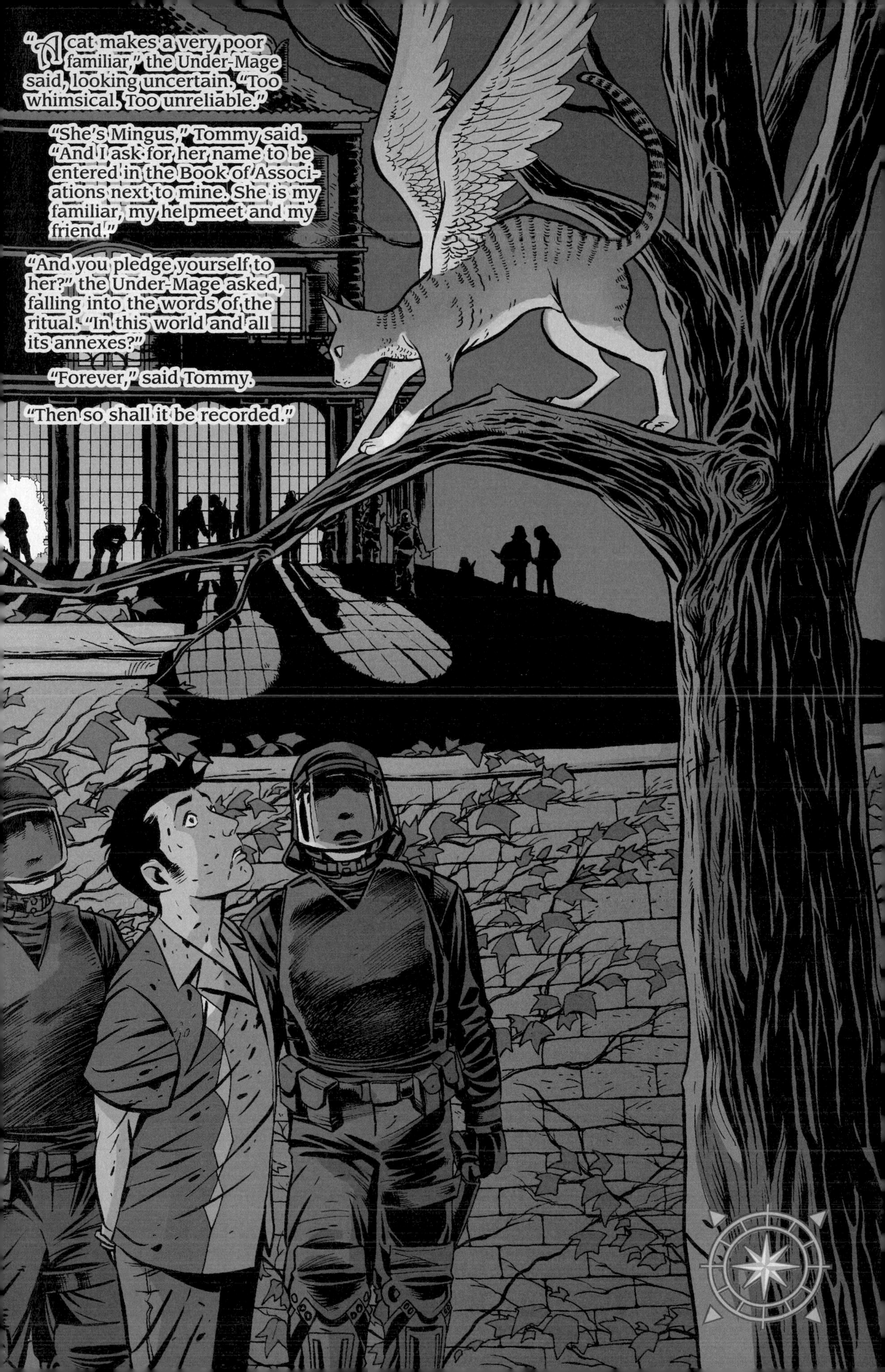
"A cat makes a very poor familiar," the Under-Mage said, looking uncertain. "Too whimsical. Too unreliable."
"She's Mingus," Tommy said. "And I ask for her name to be entered in the Book of Associations next to mine. She is my familiar, my helpmeet and my friend."
"And you pledge yourself to her?" the Under-Mage asked, falling into the words of the ritual. "In this world and all its annexes?"
"Forever," said Tommy.
"Then so shall it be recorded."

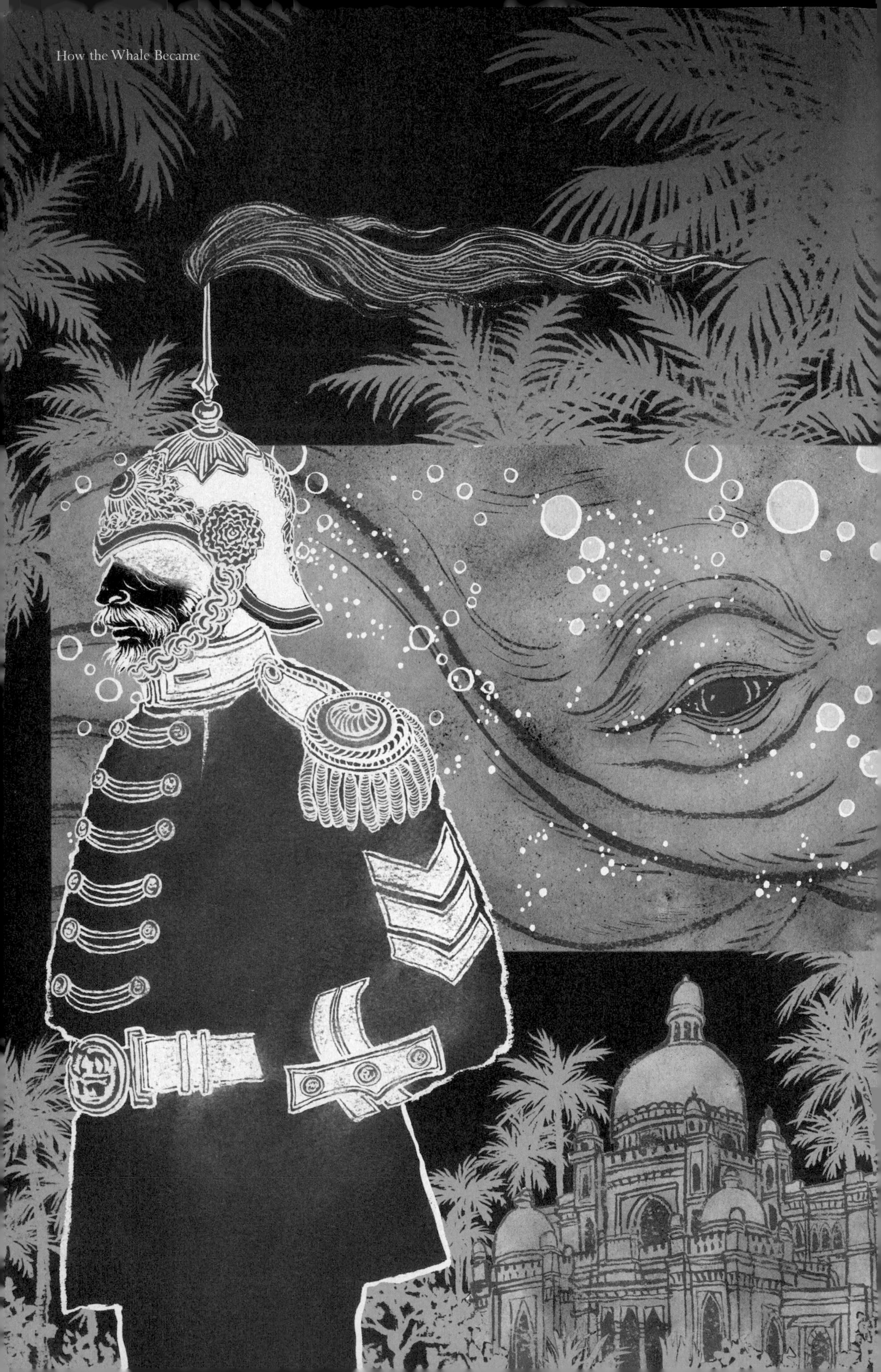

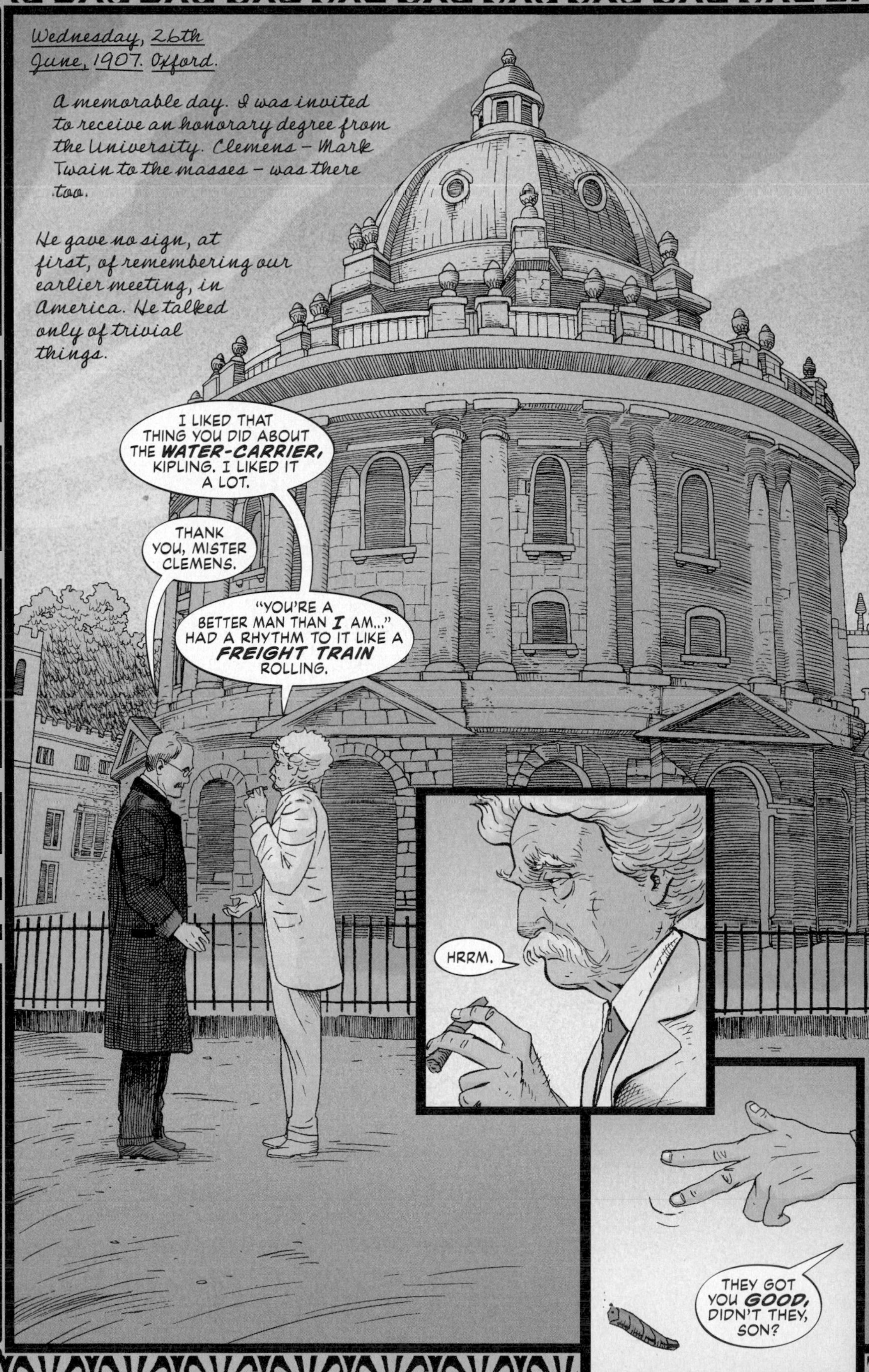
Wednesday, 26th June, 1907. Oxford.
A memorable day. I was invited to receive an honorary degree from the University. Clemens – Mark Twain to the masses – was there too.
He gave no sign, at first, of remembering our earlier meeting, in America. He talked only of trivial things.
I LIKED THAT THING YOU DID ABOUT THE WATER-CARRIER, KIPLING. I LIKED IT A LOT.
THANK YOU, MISTER CLEMENS.
"YOU'RE A BETTER MAN THAN I AM..." HAD A RHYTHM TO IT LIKE A FREIGHT TRAIN ROLLING.
HRRM.
THEY GOT YOU GOOD, DIDN'T THEY, SON?

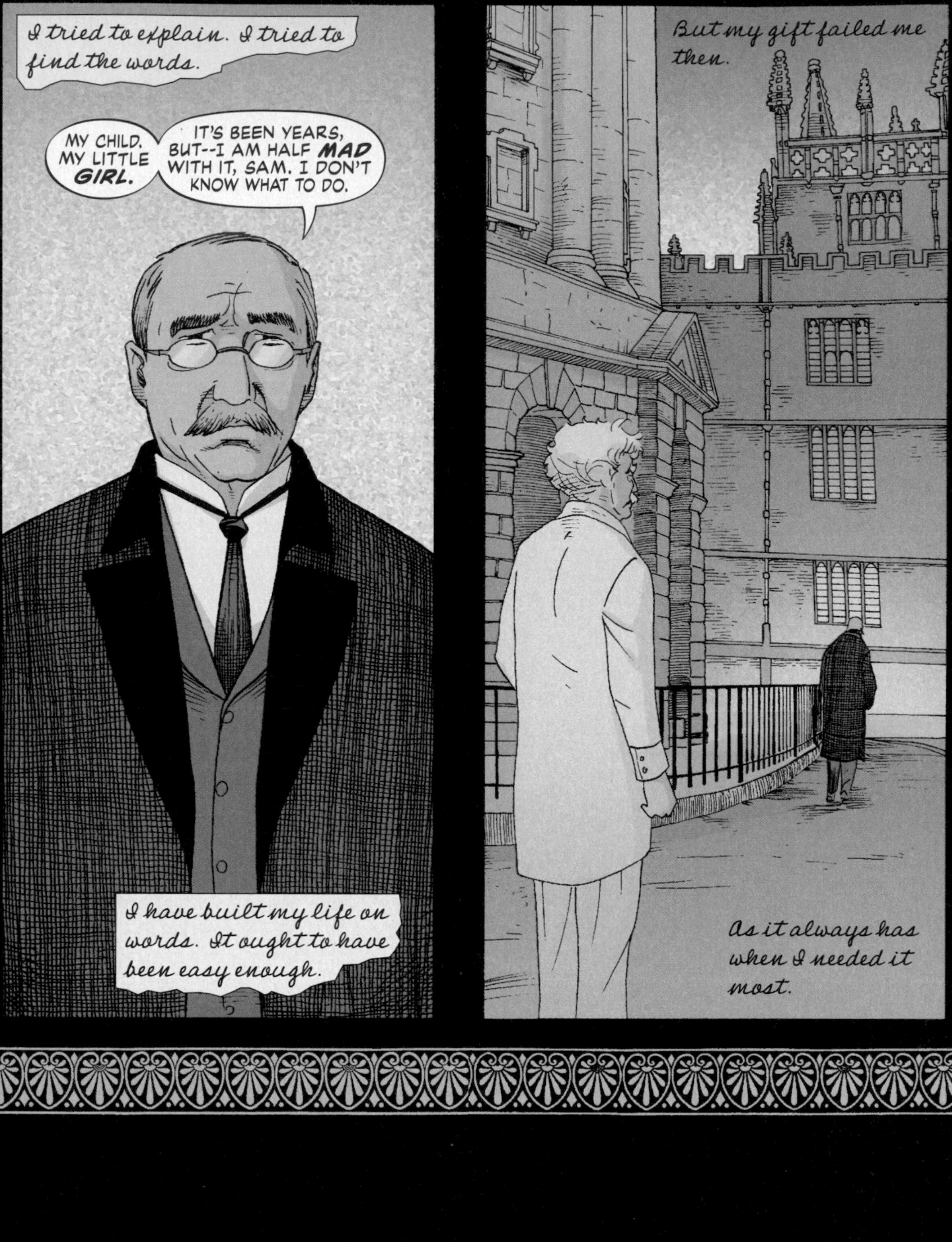
I tried to explain. I tried to find the words.
MY CHILD. MY LITTLE GIRL.
IT'S BEEN YEARS, BUT--I AM HALF MAD WITH IT, SAM. I DON'T KNOW WHAT TO DO.
I have built my life on words. It ought to have been easy enough.
But my gift failed me then.
As it always has when I needed it most.

How The Whale Became

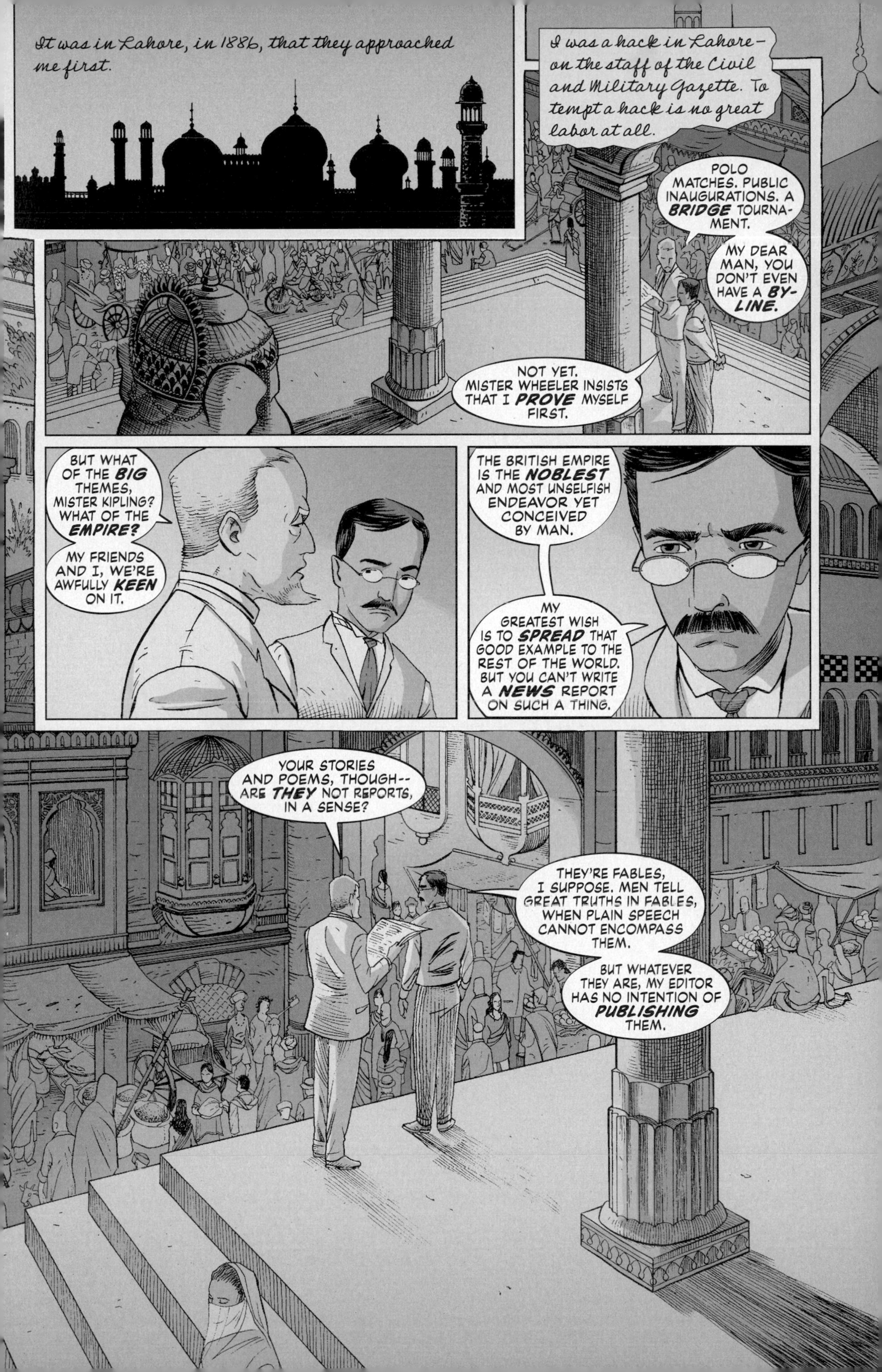
It was in Lahore, in 1886, that they approached me first.
I was a hack in Lahore—on the staff of the Civil and Military Gazette. To tempt a hack is no great labor at all.
POLO MATCHES. PUBLIC INAUGURATIONS. A BRIDGE TOURNAMENT.
MY DEAR MAN, YOU DON'T EVEN HAVE A BY-LINE.
NOT YET. MISTER WHEELER INSISTS THAT I PROVE MYSELF FIRST.
BUT WHAT OF THE BIG THEMES, MISTER KIPLING? WHAT OF THE EMPIRE?
MY FRIENDS AND I, WE'RE AWFULLY KEEN ON IT.
THE BRITISH EMPIRE IS THE NOBLEST AND MOST UNSELFISH ENDEAVOR YET CONCEIVED BY MAN.
MY GREATEST WISH IS TO SPREAD THAT GOOD EXAMPLE TO THE REST OF THE WORLD. BUT YOU CAN'T WRITE A NEWS REPORT ON SUCH A THING.
YOUR STORIES AND POEMS, THOUGH--ARE THEY NOT REPORTS, IN A SENSE?
THEY'RE FABLES, I SUPPOSE. MEN TELL GREAT TRUTHS IN FABLES, WHEN PLAIN SPEECH CANNOT ENCOMPASS THEM.
BUT WHATEVER THEY ARE, MY EDITOR HAS NO INTENTION OF PUBLISHING THEM.

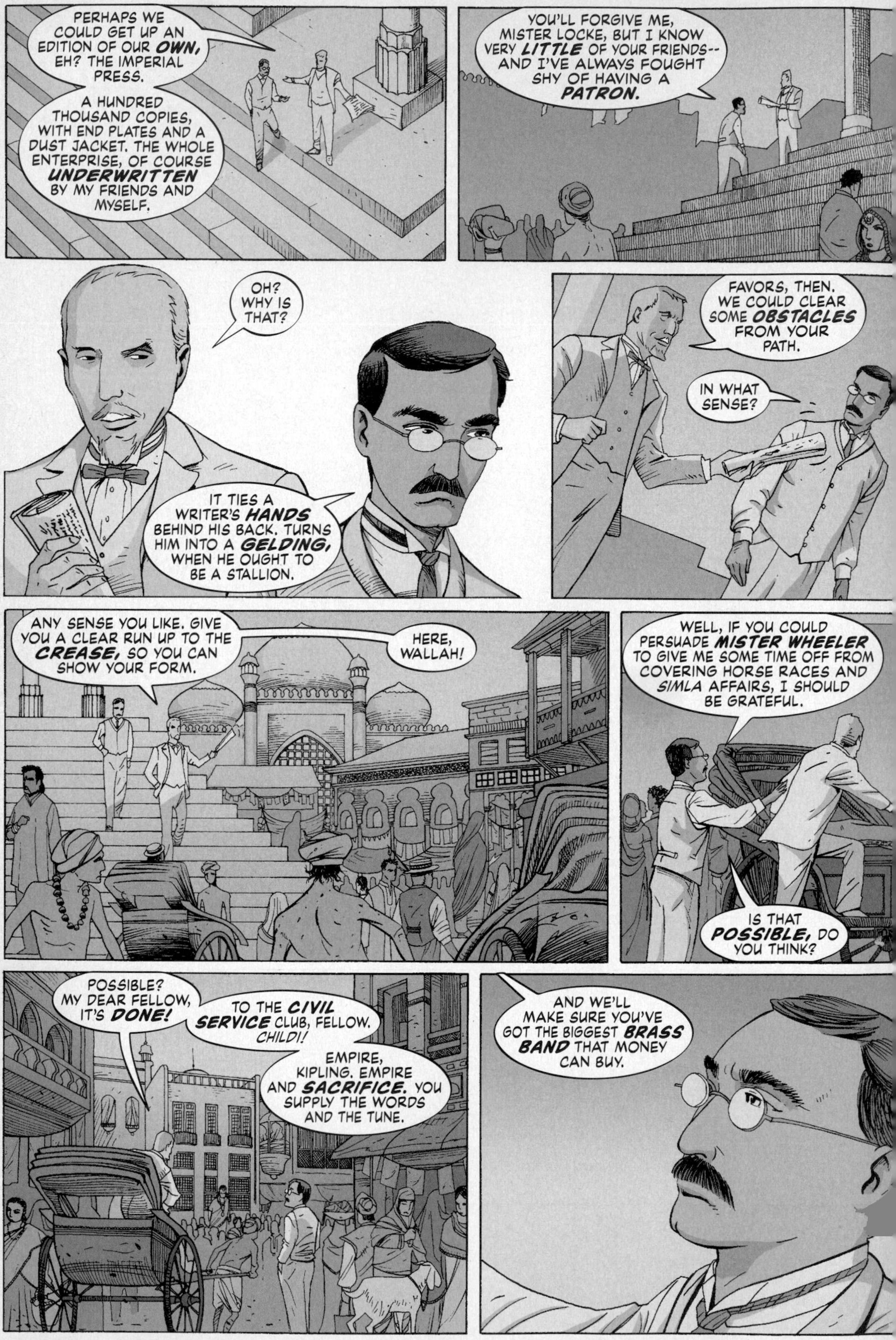
PERHAPS WE COULD GET UP AN EDITION OF OUR OWN, EH? THE IMPERIAL PRESS.
A HUNDRED THOUSAND COPIES, WITH END PLATES AND A DUST JACKET. THE WHOLE ENTERPRISE, OF COURSE UNDERWRITTEN BY MY FRIENDS AND MYSELF.
YOU'LL FORGIVE ME, MISTER LOCKE, BUT I KNOW VERY LITTLE OF YOUR FRIENDS-- AND I'VE ALWAYS FOUGHT SHY OF HAVING A PATRON.
OH? WHY IS THAT?
IT TIES A WRITER'S HANDS BEHIND HIS BACK. TURNS HIM INTO A GELDING, WHEN HE OUGHT TO BE A STALLION.
FAVORS, THEN. WE COULD CLEAR SOME OBSTACLES FROM YOUR PATH.
IN WHAT SENSE?
ANY SENSE YOU LIKE. GIVE YOU A CLEAR RUN UP TO THE CREASE, SO YOU CAN SHOW YOUR FORM.
HERE, WALLAH!
WELL, IF YOU COULD PERSUADE MISTER WHEELER TO GIVE ME SOME TIME OFF FROM COVERING HORSE RACES AND SIMLA AFFAIRS, I SHOULD BE GRATEFUL.
IS THAT POSSIBLE, DO YOU THINK?
POSSIBLE? MY DEAR FELLOW, IT'S DONE!
TO THE CIVIL SERVICE CLUB, FELLOW. CHILDI!
EMPIRE, KIPLING. EMPIRE AND SACRIFICE. YOU SUPPLY THE WORDS AND THE TUNE.
AND WE'LL MAKE SURE YOU'VE GOT THE BIGGEST BRASS BAND THAT MONEY CAN BUY.

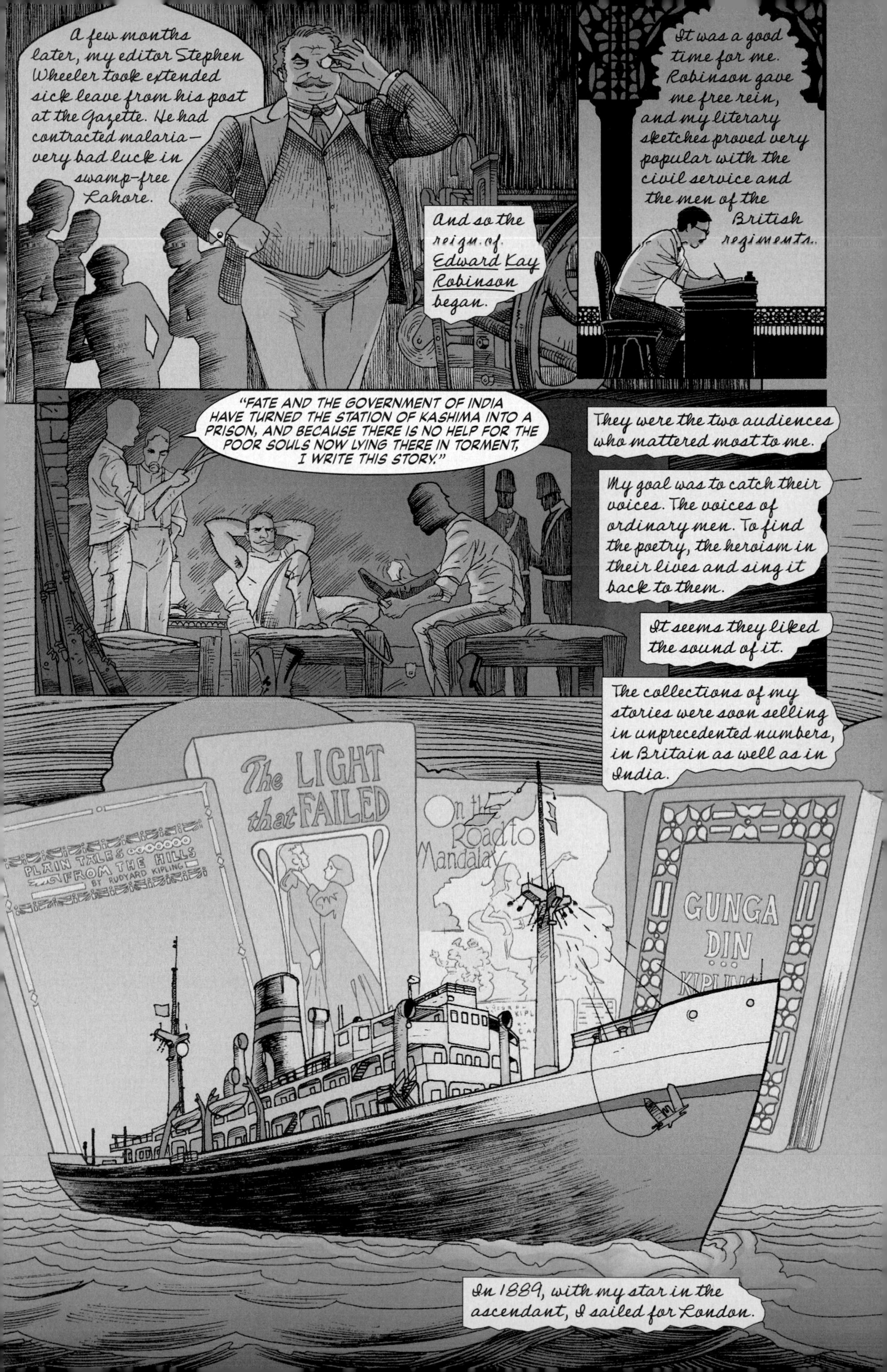
A few months later, my editor Stephen Wheeler took extended sick leave from his post at the Gazette. He had contracted malaria—very bad luck in swamp-free Lahore.
And so the reign of Edward Kay Robinson began.
It was a good time for me. Robinson gave me free rein, and my literary sketches proved very popular with the civil service and the men of the British regiments.
"FATE AND THE GOVERNMENT OF INDIA HAVE TURNED THE STATION OF KASHIMA INTO A PRISON, AND BECAUSE THERE IS NO HELP FOR THE POOR SOULS NOW LYING THERE IN TORMENT, I WRITE THIS STORY."
They were the two audiences who mattered most to me.
My goal was to catch their voices. The voices of ordinary men. To find the poetry, the heroism in their lives and sing it back to them.
It seems they liked the sound of it.
The collections of my stories were soon selling in unprecedented numbers, in Britain as well as in India.
PLAIN TALES FROM THE HILLS
BY RUDYARD KIPLING
The LIGHT that FAILED
On the Road to Mandalay
GUNGA DIN
In 1889, with my star in the ascendant, I sailed for London.

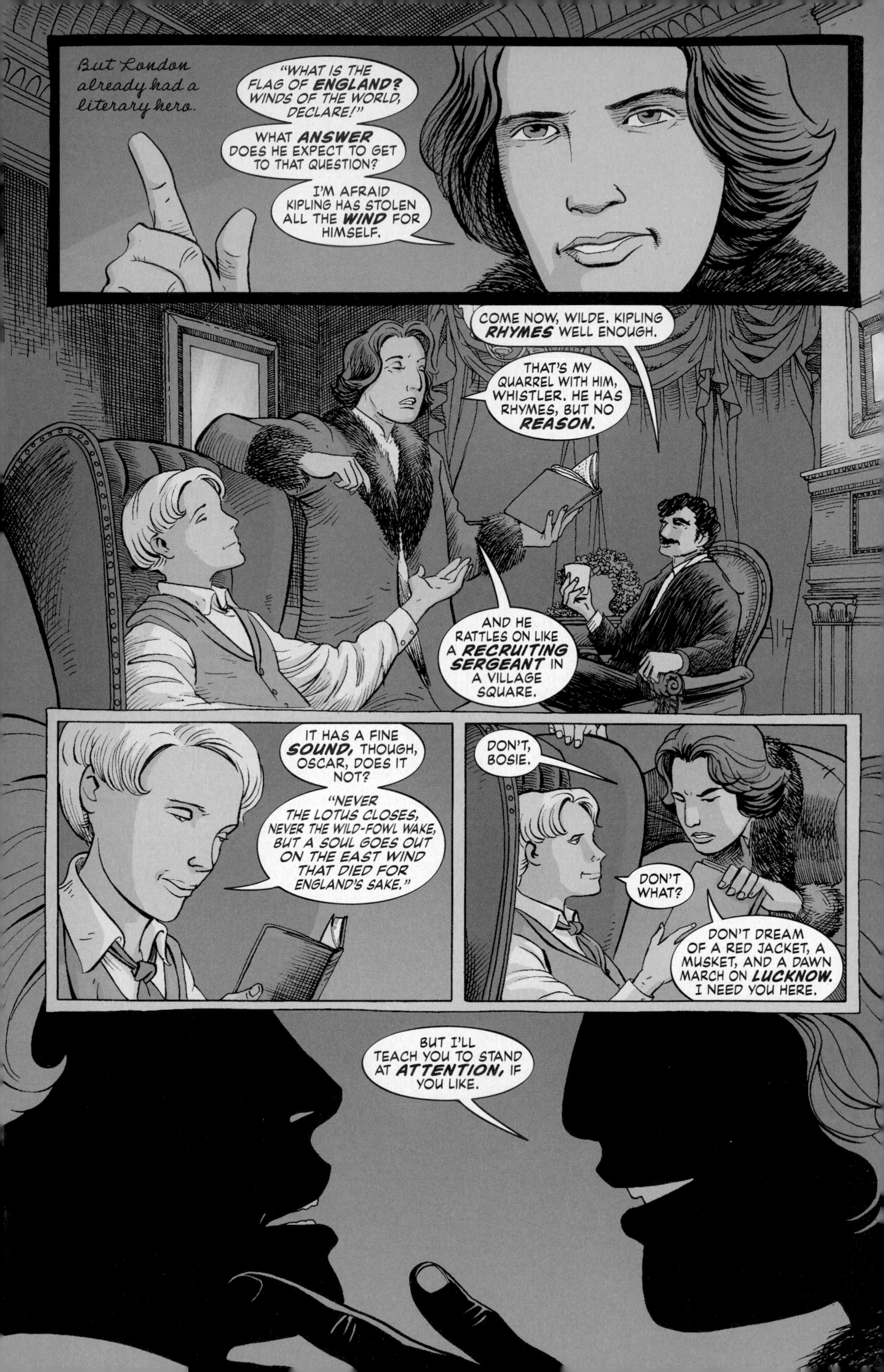
But London already had a literary hero.
"WHAT IS THE FLAG OF ENGLAND? WINDS OF THE WORLD, DECLARE!"
WHAT ANSWER DOES HE EXPECT TO GET TO THAT QUESTION?
I'M AFRAID KIPLING HAS STOLEN ALL THE WIND FOR HIMSELF.
COME NOW, WILDE. KIPLING RHYMES WELL ENOUGH.
THAT'S MY QUARREL WITH HIM, WHISTLER. HE HAS RHYMES, BUT NO REASON.
AND HE RATTLES ON LIKE A RECRUITING SERGEANT IN A VILLAGE SQUARE.
IT HAS A FINE SOUND, THOUGH, OSCAR, DOES IT NOT?
"NEVER THE LOTUS CLOSES, NEVER THE WILD-FOWL WAKE, BUT A SOUL GOES OUT ON THE EAST WIND THAT DIED FOR ENGLAND'S SAKE."
DON'T, BOSIE.
DON'T WHAT?
DON'T DREAM OF A RED JACKET, A MUSKET, AND A DAWN MARCH ON LUCKNOW. I NEED YOU HERE.
BUT I'LL TEACH YOU TO STAND AT ATTENTION, IF YOU LIKE.

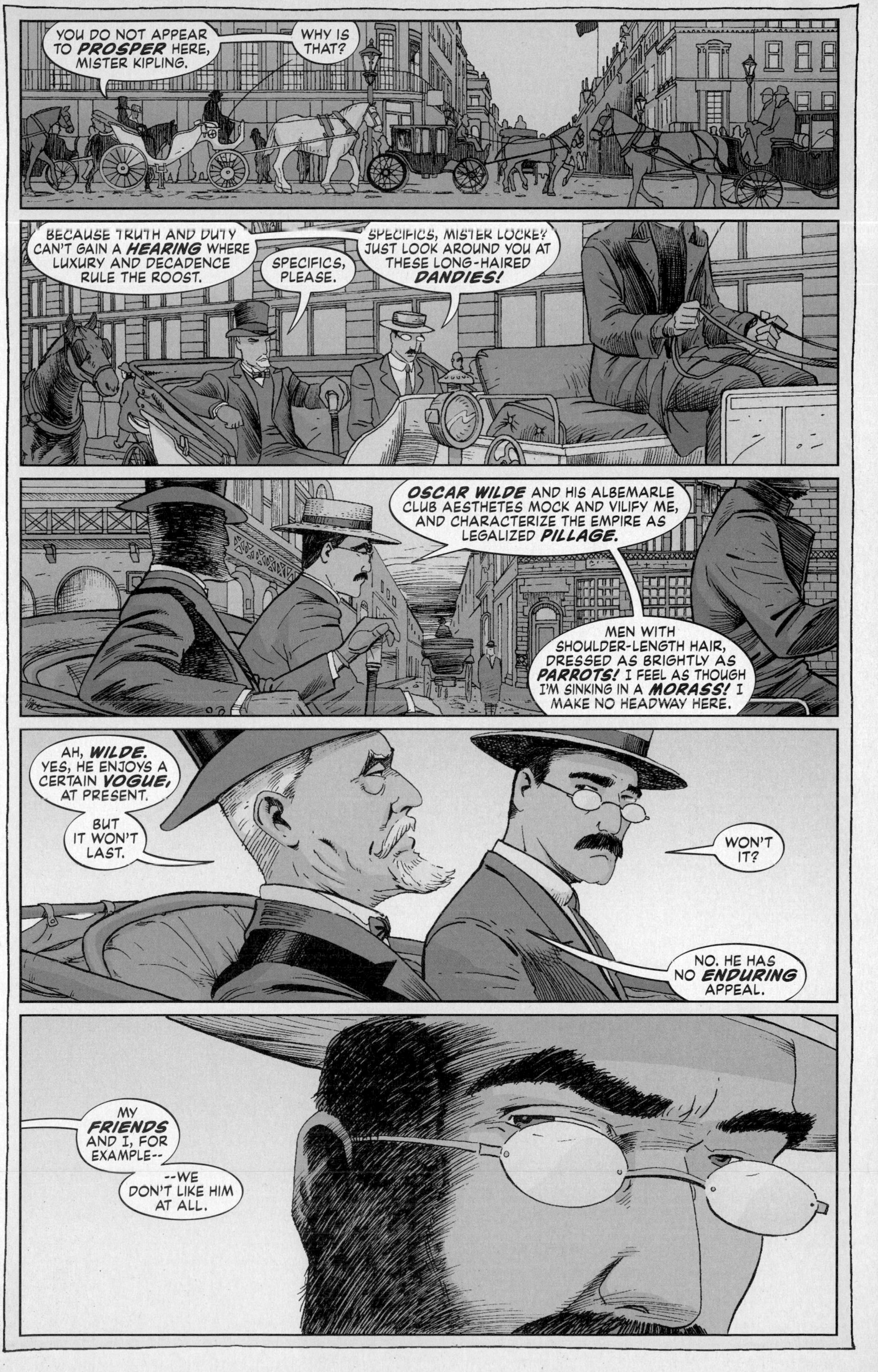
YOU DO NOT APPEAR TO PROSPER HERE, MISTER KIPLING.
WHY IS THAT?
BECAUSE TRUTH AND DUTY CAN'T GAIN A HEARING WHERE LUXURY AND DECADENCE RULE THE ROOST.
SPECIFICS, PLEASE.
SPECIFICS, MISTER LOCKE? JUST LOOK AROUND YOU AT THESE LONG-HAIRED DANDIES!
OSCAR WILDE AND HIS ALBEMARLE CLUB AESTHETES MOCK AND VILIFY ME, AND CHARACTERIZE THE EMPIRE AS LEGALIZED PILLAGE.
MEN WITH SHOULDER-LENGTH HAIR, DRESSED AS BRIGHTLY AS PARROTS! I FEEL AS THOUGH I'M SINKING IN A MORASS! I MAKE NO HEADWAY HERE.
AH, WILDE. YES, HE ENJOYS A CERTAIN VOGUE, AT PRESENT.
BUT IT WON'T LAST.
WON'T IT?
NO. HE HAS NO ENDURING APPEAL.
MY FRIENDS AND I, FOR EXAMPLE--
--WE DON'T LIKE HIM AT ALL.

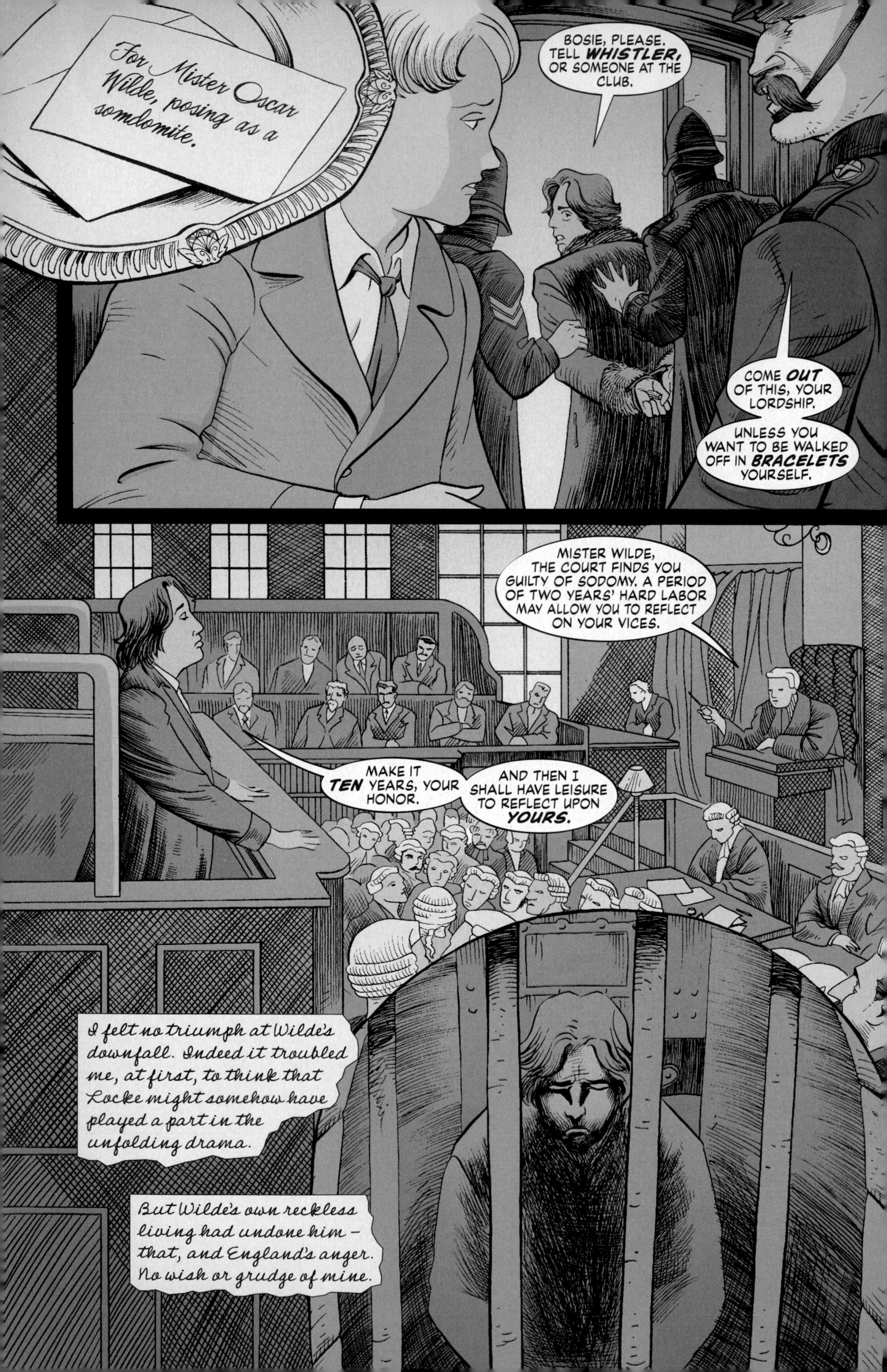
For Mister Oscar Wilde, posing as a somdomite.
BOSIE, PLEASE. TELL WHISTLER, OR SOMEONE AT THE CLUB.
COME OUT OF THIS, YOUR LORDSHIP.
UNLESS YOU WANT TO BE WALKED OFF IN BRACELETS YOURSELF.
MISTER WILDE, THE COURT FINDS YOU GUILTY OF SODOMY. A PERIOD OF TWO YEARS' HARD LABOR MAY ALLOW YOU TO REFLECT ON YOUR VICES.
MAKE IT TEN YEARS, YOUR HONOR.
AND THEN I SHALL HAVE LEISURE TO REFLECT UPON YOURS.
I felt no triumph at Wilde's downfall. Indeed it troubled me, at first, to think that Locke might somehow have played a part in the unfolding drama.
But Wilde's own reckless living had undone him – that, and England's anger. No wish or grudge of mine.

And so I forgot my scruples, or at any rate stowed them out of sight.

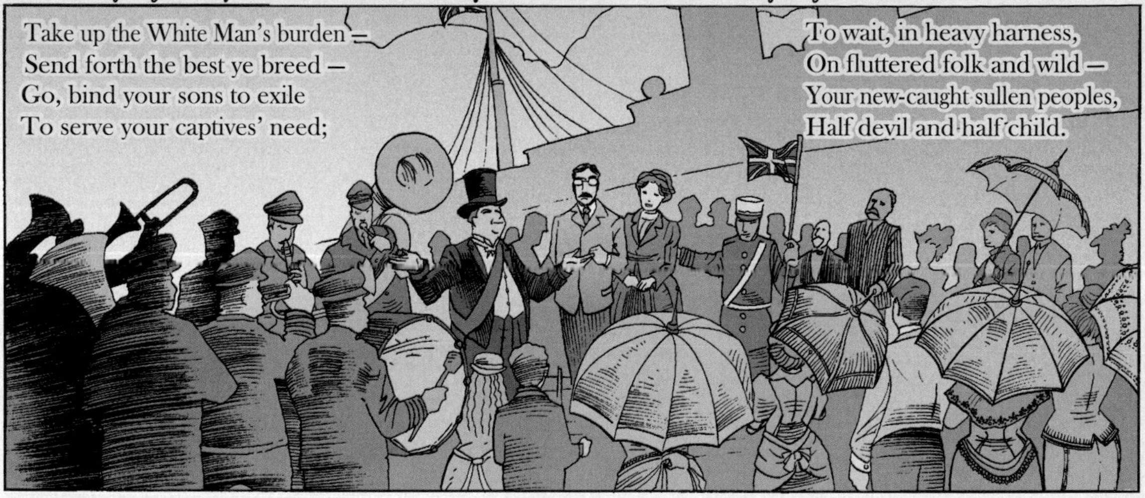
Take up the White Man's burden –
Send forth the best ye breed –
Go, bind your sons to exile
To serve your captives' need;
To wait, in heavy harness,
On fluttered folk and wild –
Your new-caught sullen peoples,
Half devil and half child.

I had a mission – to preach my gospel of empire to the nations of Earth. This was my boom time. I was hailed as the voice of England, and I was welcomed wherever England's writ extended. South Africa. Canada. India. New Zealand.

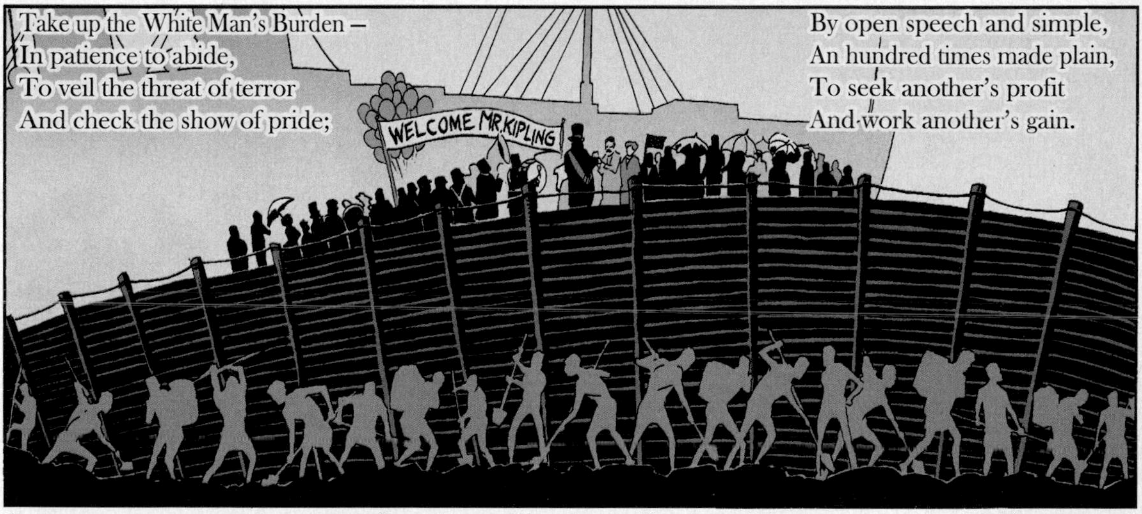
Take up the White Man's Burden –
In patience to abide,
To veil the threat of terror
And check the show of pride;
WELCOME MR. KIPLING
By open speech and simple,
An hundred times made plain,
To seek another's profit
And work another's gain.

My message was a stern one. Bend your backs to this mighty work, men of Albion, and ask no reward except the work itself.

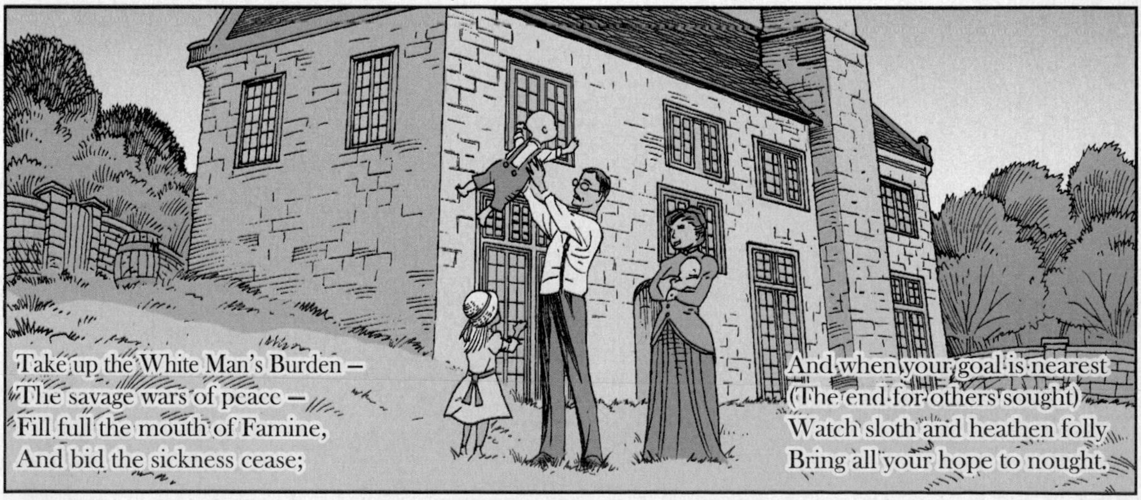
Take up the White Man's Burden –
The savage wars of peace –
Fill full the mouth of Famine,
And bid the sickness cease;
And when your goal is nearest
(The end for others sought)
Watch sloth and heathen folly
Bring all your hope to nought.

But I was rewarded. Carrie Balestier gave me her love, and then – more precious even than that – three children. Josephine, Elsie and John. Three lives. Three human beings, at large in this world because of me. My small, domestic empire – which in short time indeed became an anarchist state, for I doted on them and capitulated to all their demands.

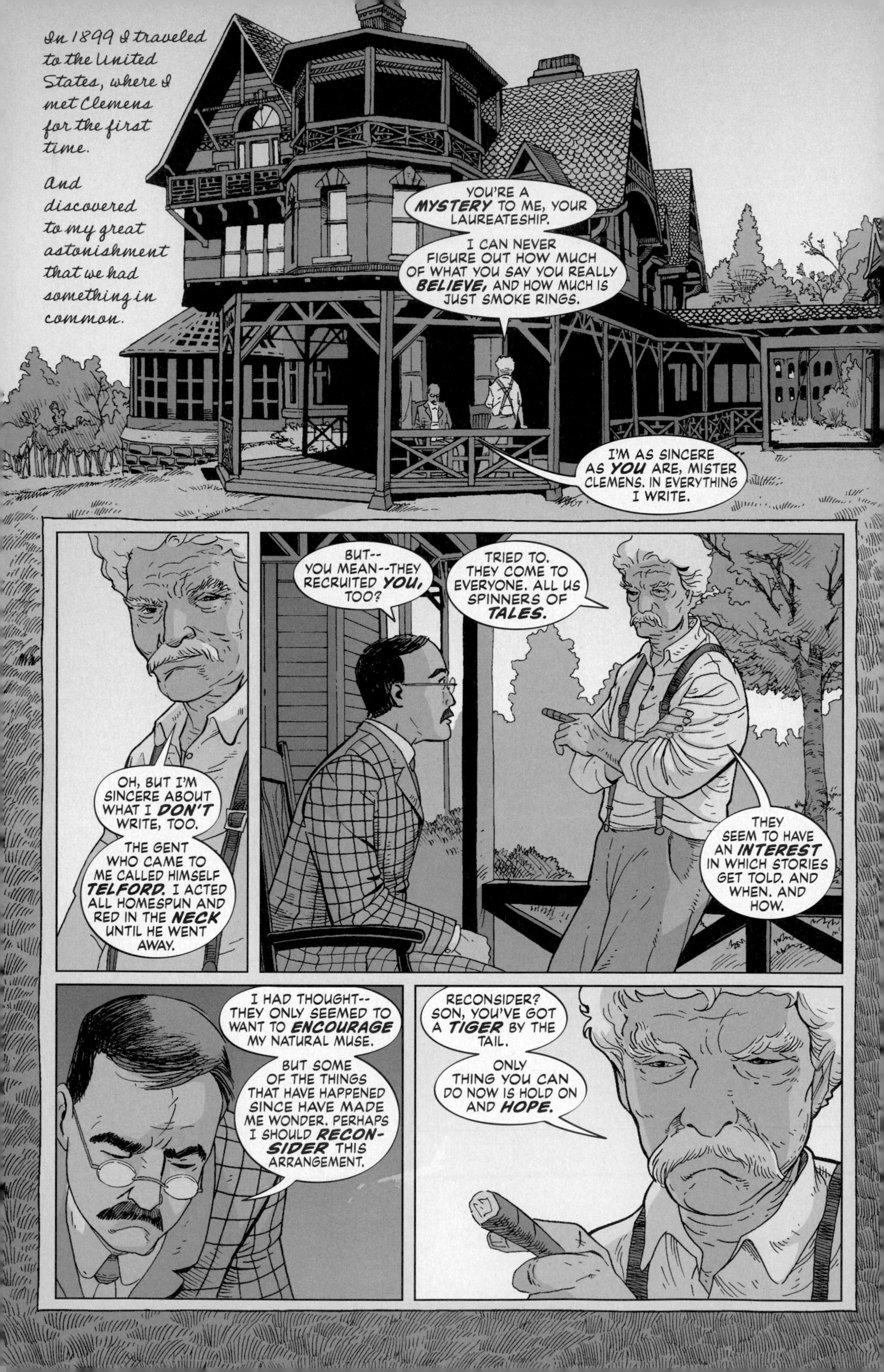
In 1899 I traveled to the United States, where I met Clemens for the first time.
And discovered to my great astonishment that we had something in common.
YOU'RE A MYSTERY TO ME, YOUR LAUREATESHIP.
I CAN NEVER FIGURE OUT HOW MUCH OF WHAT YOU SAY YOU REALLY BELIEVE, AND HOW MUCH IS JUST SMOKE RINGS.
I'M AS SINCERE AS YOU ARE, MISTER CLEMENS. IN EVERYTHING I WRITE.
OH, BUT I'M SINCERE ABOUT WHAT I DON'T WRITE, TOO.
THE GENT WHO CAME TO ME CALLED HIMSELF TELFORD. I ACTED ALL HOMESPUN AND RED IN THE NECK UNTIL HE WENT AWAY.
BUT-- YOU MEAN--THEY RECRUITED YOU, TOO?
TRIED TO. THEY COME TO EVERYONE. ALL US SPINNERS OF TALES.
THEY SEEM TO HAVE AN INTEREST IN WHICH STORIES GET TOLD. AND WHEN. AND HOW.
I HAD THOUGHT-- THEY ONLY SEEMED TO WANT TO ENCOURAGE MY NATURAL MUSE.
BUT SOME OF THE THINGS THAT HAVE HAPPENED SINCE HAVE MADE ME WONDER. PERHAPS I SHOULD RECON- SIDER THIS ARRANGEMENT.
RECONSIDER? SON, YOU'VE GOT A TIGER BY THE TAIL.
ONLY THING YOU CAN DO NOW IS HOLD ON AND HOPE.

MISTER KIPLING! A BRACING DAY, IS IT NOT? AND A BRACING **COUNTRY**.

YES, IT'S IMPRESSIVE.

MISTER LOCKE, I WANT TO **ASK** YOU ABOUT SOME OF OUR PREVIOUS TRANSACTIONS.

WHY YOU, AND THE **FACTION** YOU REPRESENT, INVOLVE YOURSELVES IN--

WE'VE DECIDED YOU SHOULD **STAY** IN AMERICA.

CHRONICLE THE **NEW** EMPIRE THAT'S STRUGGLING TO BE BORN, RATHER THAN THE OLD ONE THAT'S **DYING**.

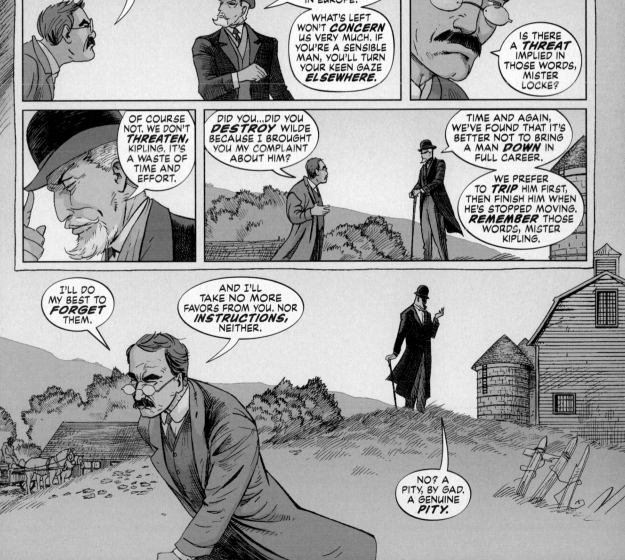

DYING? WH-WHAT DO YOU MEAN?

ENGLAND AND GERMANY ARE ABOUT TO TEAR EACH OTHER **APART**, FIRST IN AFRICA AND THEN IN EUROPE.

WHAT'S LEFT WON'T **CONCERN** US VERY MUCH. IF YOU'RE A SENSIBLE MAN, YOU'LL TURN YOUR KEEN GAZE **ELSEWHERE**.

IS THERE A **THREAT** IMPLIED IN THOSE WORDS, MISTER LOCKE?

OF COURSE NOT. WE DON'T **THREATEN**, KIPLING, IT'S A WASTE OF TIME AND EFFORT.

DID YOU...DID YOU **DESTROY** WILDE BECAUSE I BROUGHT YOU MY COMPLAINT ABOUT HIM?

TIME AND AGAIN, WE'VE FOUND THAT IT'S BETTER NOT TO BRING A MAN **DOWN** IN FULL CAREER.

WE PREFER TO **TRIP** HIM FIRST, THEN FINISH HIM WHEN HE'S STOPPED MOVING. **REMEMBER** THOSE WORDS, MISTER KIPLING.

I'LL DO MY BEST TO **FORGET** THEM.

AND I'LL TAKE NO MORE FAVORS FROM YOU. NOR **INSTRUCTIONS**, NEITHER.

NO? A PITY, BY GAD. A GENUINE **PITY**.

We were booked to leave the United States three days later, on the 3rd of March.

But we were forced to postpone our voyage when our oldest child, Josephine, fell ill with influenza.

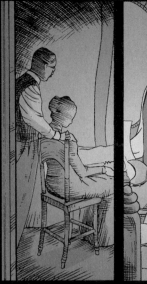

The prophet of empire! I cut a pathetic figure right then, assailed by doubts and fears that my rational mind balked at.

Could Locke and his shadowy associates command invisible legions of germs, as well as men? There was Wheeler's malaria, after all...

I kept vigil at my little girl's bedside, and tried my hand at a story extolling the virtues of new, Western frontiers.

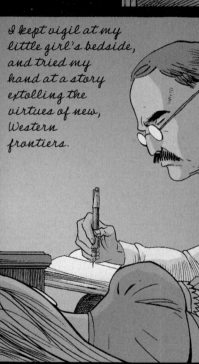

They would not come.

The words would not come.

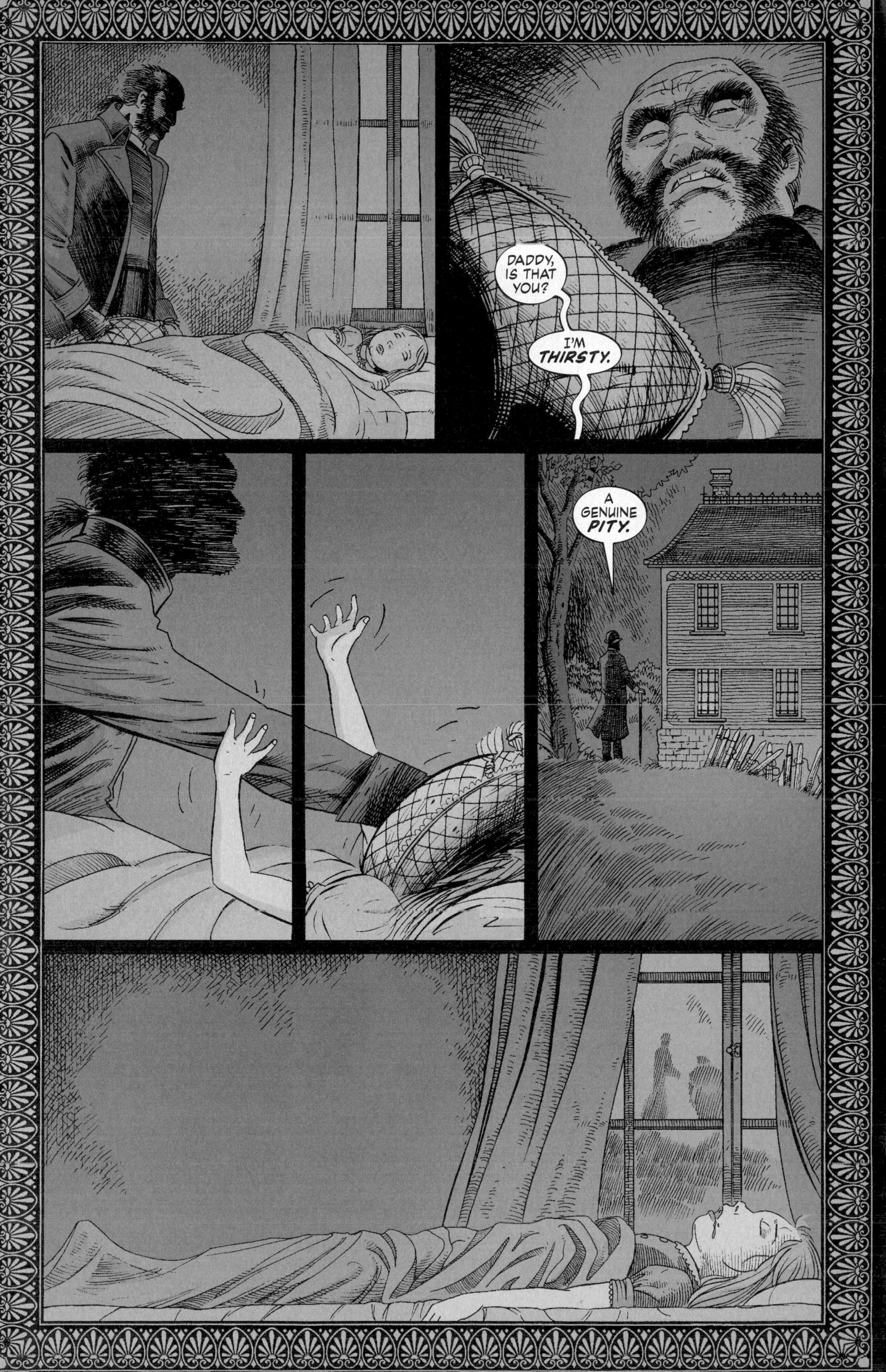
DADDY, IS THAT YOU?
I'M THIRSTY.
A GENUINE PITY.

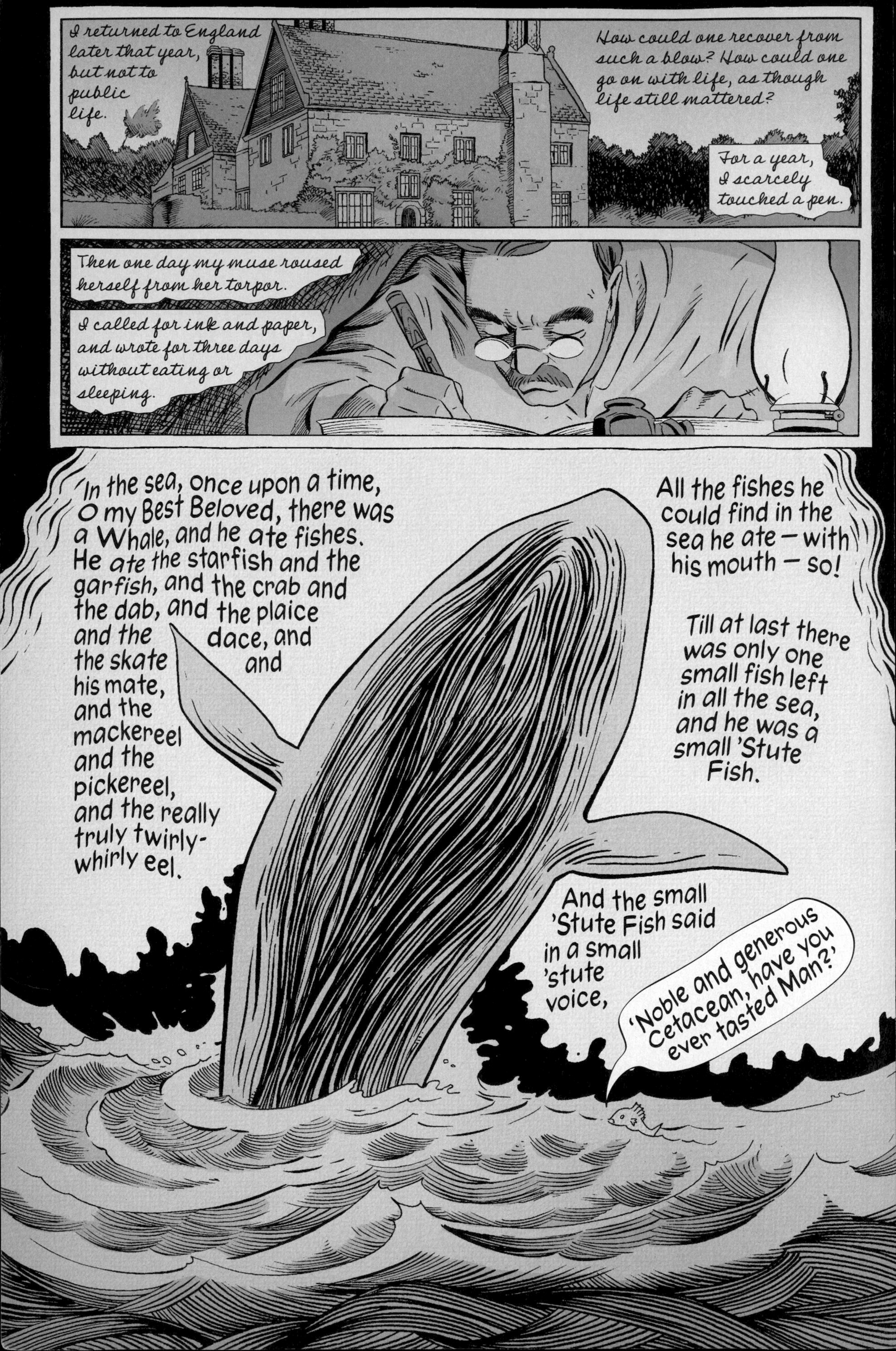
I returned to England later that year, but not to public life.
How could one recover from such a blow? How could one go on with life, as though life still mattered?
For a year, I scarcely touched a pen.
Then one day my muse roused herself from her torpor.
I called for ink and paper, and wrote for three days without eating or sleeping.
In the sea, once upon a time, O my Best Beloved, there was a Whale, and he ate fishes. He ate the starfish and the garfish, and the crab and the dab, and the plaice and the dace, and the skate and his mate, and the mackereel and the pickereel, and the really truly twirly-whirly eel.
All the fishes he could find in the sea he ate — with his mouth — so!
Till at last there was only one small fish left in all the sea, and he was a small 'Stute Fish.
And the small 'Stute Fish said in a small 'stute voice,
'Noble and generous Cetacean, have you ever tasted Man?'

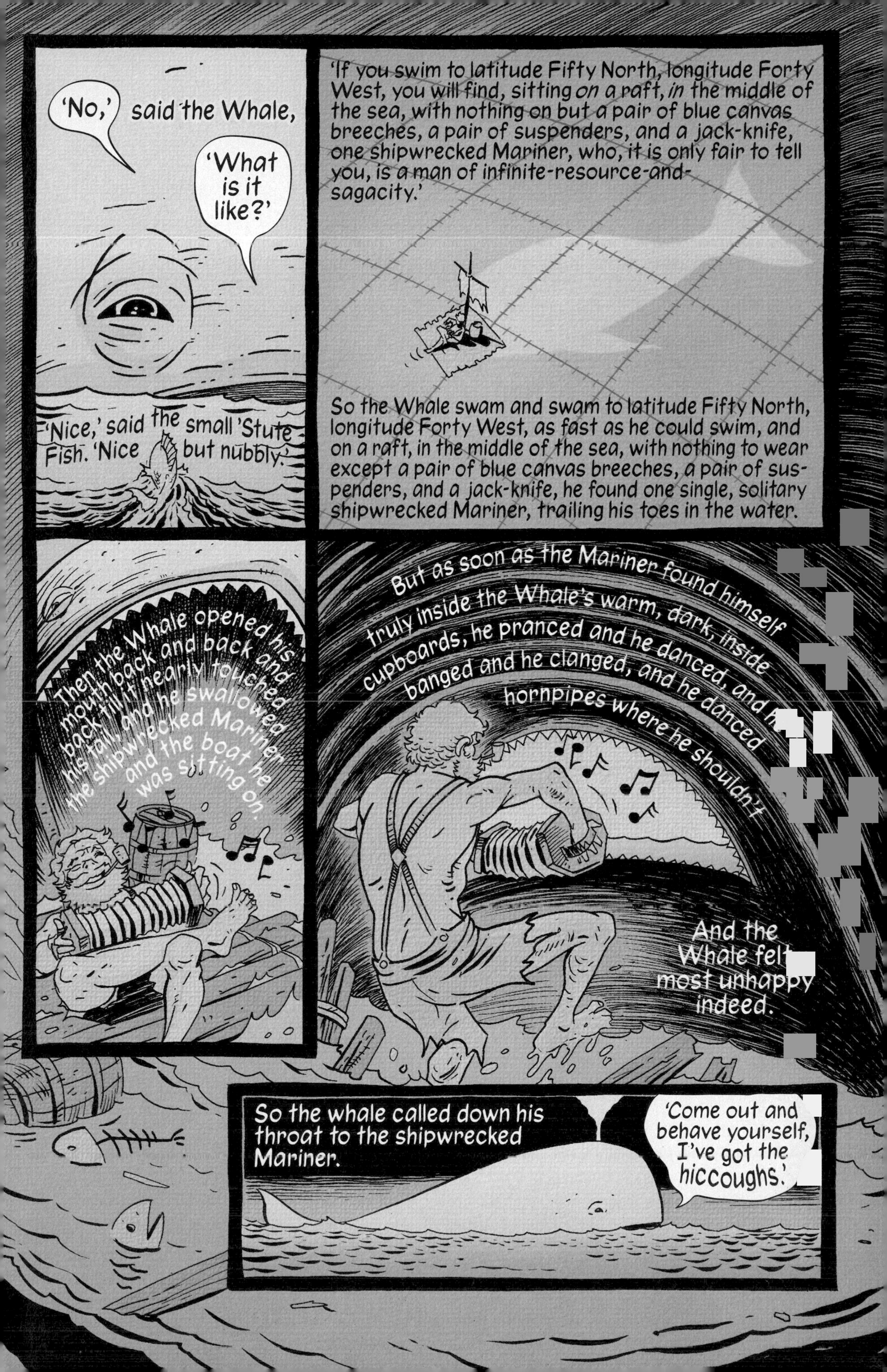
'No,' said the Whale,
'What is it like?'
'Nice,' said the small 'Stute Fish. 'Nice but nubbly.'
'If you swim to latitude Fifty North, longitude Forty West, you will find, sitting *on a raft*, *in* the middle of the sea, with nothing on but a pair of blue canvas breeches, a pair of suspenders, and a jack-knife, one shipwrecked Mariner, who, it is only fair to tell you, is a man of infinite-resource-and-sagacity.'
So the Whale swam and swam to latitude Fifty North, longitude Forty West, as fast as he could swim, and on a raft, in the middle of the sea, with nothing to wear except a pair of blue canvas breeches, a pair of suspenders, and a jack-knife, he found one single, solitary shipwrecked Mariner, trailing his toes in the water.
Then the Whale opened his mouth back and back and back till it nearly touched his tail, and he swallowed the shipwrecked Mariner and the boat he was sitting on.
But as soon as the Mariner found himself truly inside the Whale's warm, dark, inside cupboards, he pranced and he danced, and he banged and he clanged, and he danced hornpipes where he shouldn't
And the Whale felt most unhappy indeed.
So the whale called down his throat to the shipwrecked Mariner.
'Come out and behave yourself, I've got the hiccoughs.'

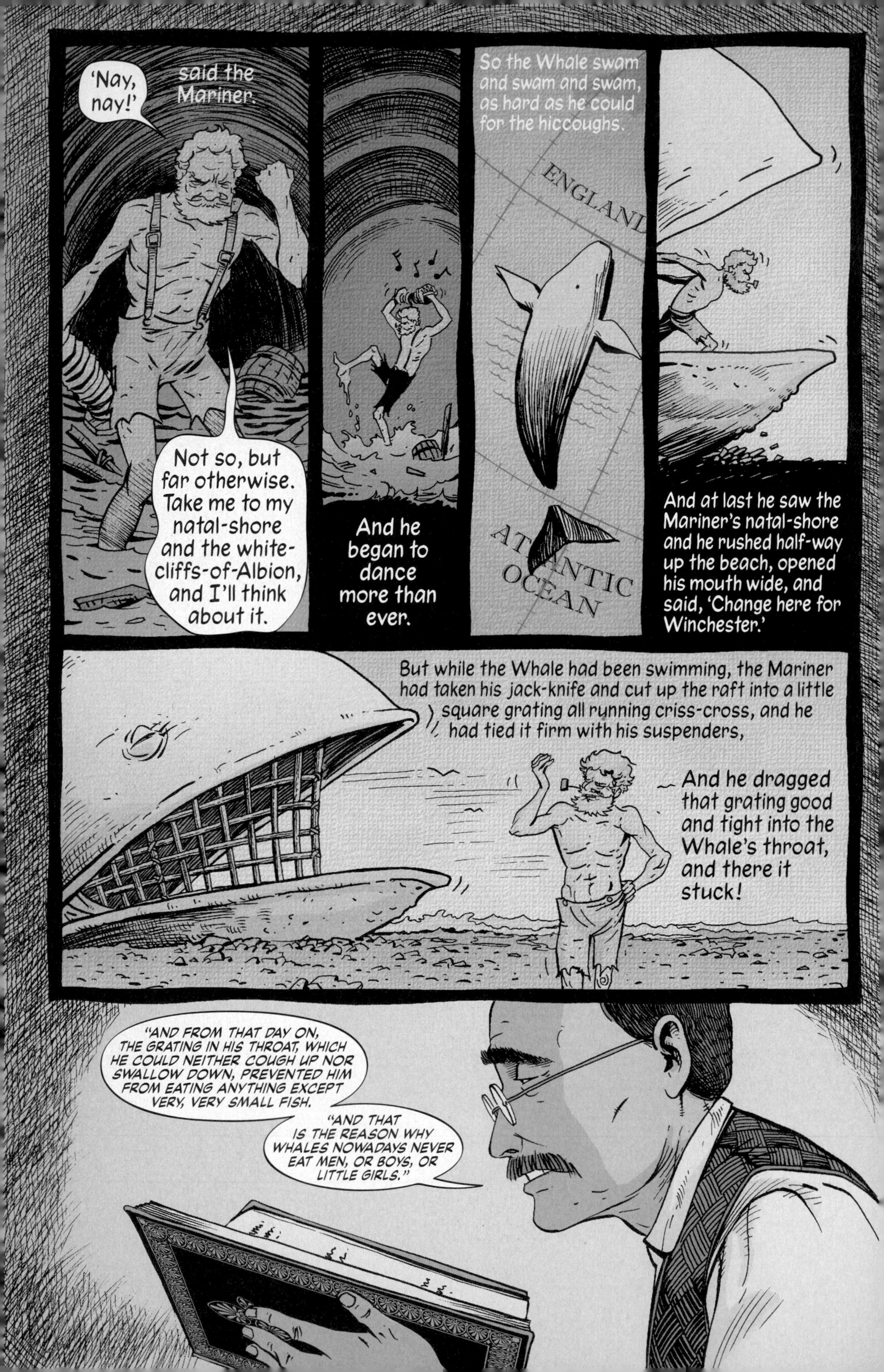
'Nay, nay!'
said the Mariner.
Not so, but far otherwise. Take me to my natal-shore and the white-cliffs-of-Albion, and I'll think about it.
And he began to dance more than ever.
So the Whale swam and swam and swam, as hard as he could for the hiccoughs.
ENGLAND
ATLANTIC OCEAN
And at last he saw the Mariner's natal-shore and he rushed half-way up the beach, opened his mouth wide, and said, 'Change here for Winchester.'
But while the Whale had been swimming, the Mariner had taken his jack-knife and cut up the raft into a little square grating all running criss-cross, and he had tied it firm with his suspenders,
And he dragged that grating good and tight into the Whale's throat, and there it stuck!
"AND FROM THAT DAY ON, THE GRATING IN HIS THROAT, WHICH HE COULD NEITHER COUGH UP NOR SWALLOW DOWN, PREVENTED HIM FROM EATING ANYTHING EXCEPT VERY, VERY SMALL FISH.
"AND THAT IS THE REASON WHY WHALES NOWADAYS NEVER EAT MEN, OR BOYS, OR LITTLE GIRLS."

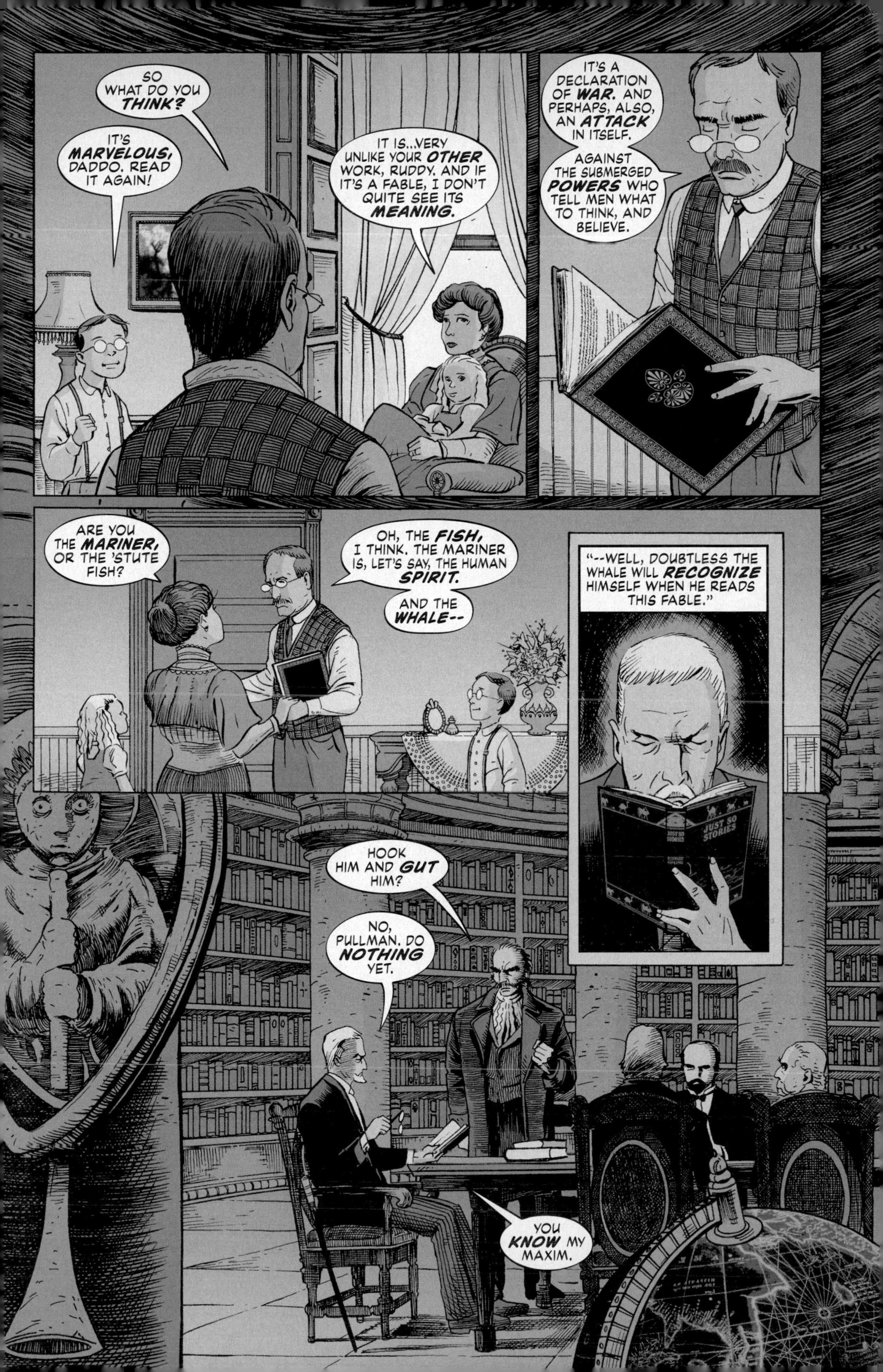
SO WHAT DO YOU THINK?
IT'S MARVELOUS, DADDO. READ IT AGAIN!
IT IS...VERY UNLIKE YOUR OTHER WORK, RUDDY. AND IF IT'S A FABLE, I DON'T QUITE SEE ITS MEANING.
IT'S A DECLARATION OF WAR. AND PERHAPS, ALSO, AN ATTACK IN ITSELF.
AGAINST THE SUBMERGED POWERS WHO TELL MEN WHAT TO THINK, AND BELIEVE.
ARE YOU THE MARINER, OR THE 'STUTE FISH?
OH, THE FISH, I THINK. THE MARINER IS, LET'S SAY, THE HUMAN SPIRIT.
AND THE WHALE--
"--WELL, DOUBTLESS THE WHALE WILL RECOGNIZE HIMSELF WHEN HE READS THIS FABLE."
JUST SO STORIES
HOOK HIM AND GUT HIM?
NO, PULLMAN. DO NOTHING YET.
YOU KNOW MY MAXIM.

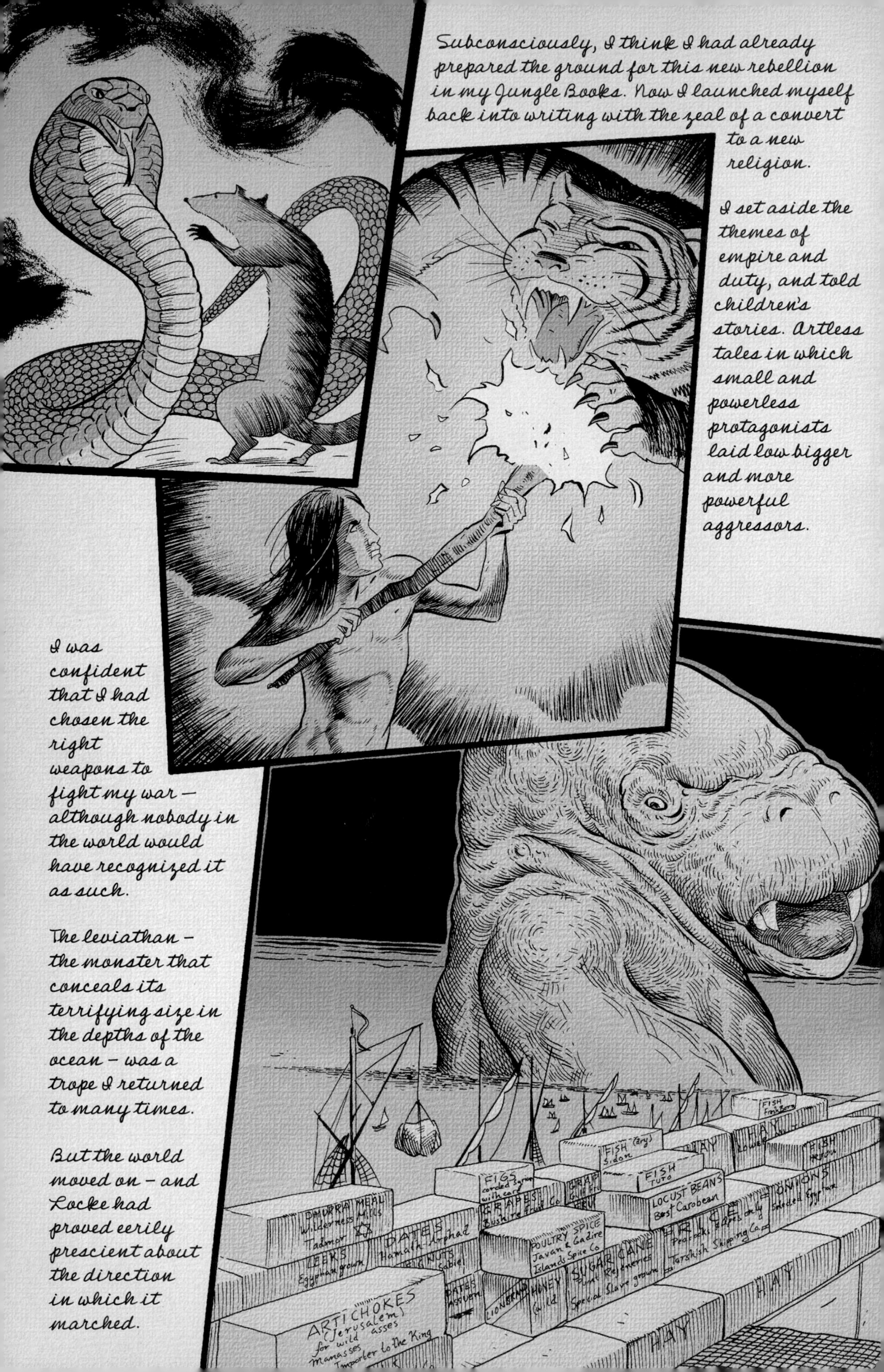
Subconsciously, I think I had already prepared the ground for this new rebellion in my Jungle Books. Now I launched myself back into writing with the zeal of a convert to a new religion.
I set aside the themes of empire and duty, and told children's stories. Artless tales in which small and powerless protagonists laid low bigger and more powerful aggressors.
I was confident that I had chosen the right weapons to fight my war — although nobody in the world would have recognized it as such.
The leviathan — the monster that conceals its terrifying size in the depths of the ocean — was a trope I returned to many times.
But the world moved on — and Locke had proved eerily prescient about the direction in which it marched.
FISH
FISH (dry)
Sidon
HAY
FISH
Tyre
FIGS
LOCUST BEANS
Best Carobean
ONIONS
Selected Egyptian
DHURRA MEAL
Wilderness Mills
Tadmor
DATES
Hamath-Arphad
POULTRY SPICE
Javan & Gadire
Islands Spice Co
Peacocks Apes only
Tarshish Shipping Co.
LEEKS
Egyptian grown
SUGAR CANE
Special Slave grown
HONEY
(wild
LION BRAND
HAY
ARTICHOKES
(Jerusalem)
for wild asses
Manasses
Importer to the King
HAY

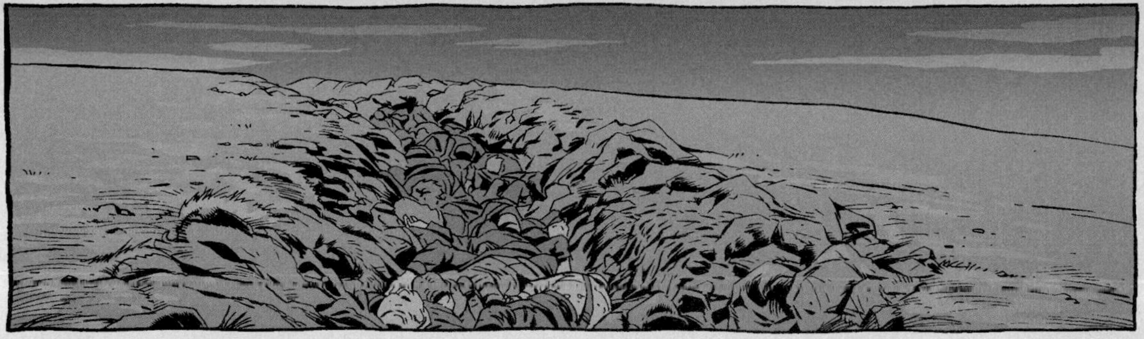

In South Africa. Boer farmers shot British soldiers with the blessing of the German Kaiser...

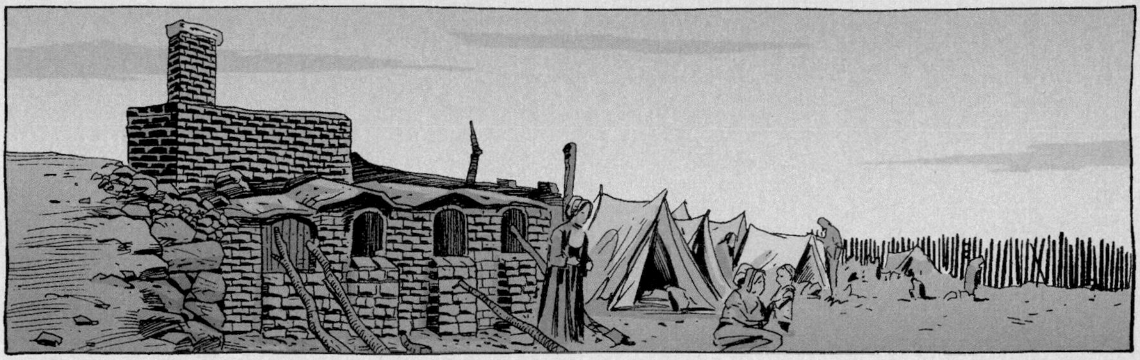

...and the empire I loved responded by locking up the farmers' wives and children to starve behind wooden stockades. I cannot describe how it felt. My words had not conjured these events into being, but still I felt complicit in them. Sullied by them.

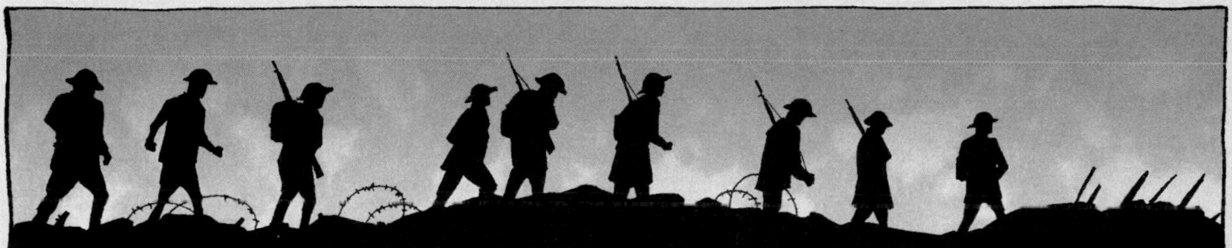

And then came the final twist of the knife. At the age of seventeen, John, my only son, enlisted in the Irish Guards. The war in France had already begun, and he knew where his duty lay. Duty, after all, was a word that had become synonymous with my name. Which was his name, too...

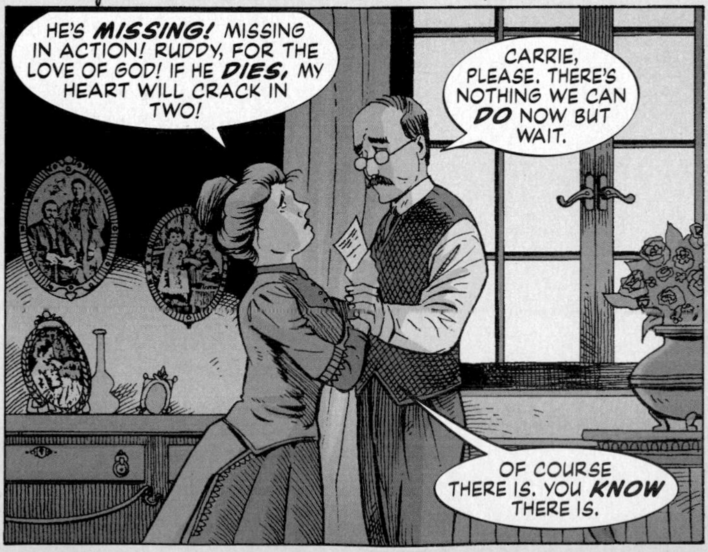
HE'S **MISSING!** MISSING IN ACTION! RUDDY, FOR THE LOVE OF GOD! IF HE ***DIES,*** MY HEART WILL CRACK IN TWO!
CARRIE, PLEASE. THERE'S NOTHING WE CAN ***DO*** NOW BUT WAIT.
OF COURSE THERE IS. YOU ***KNOW*** THERE IS.

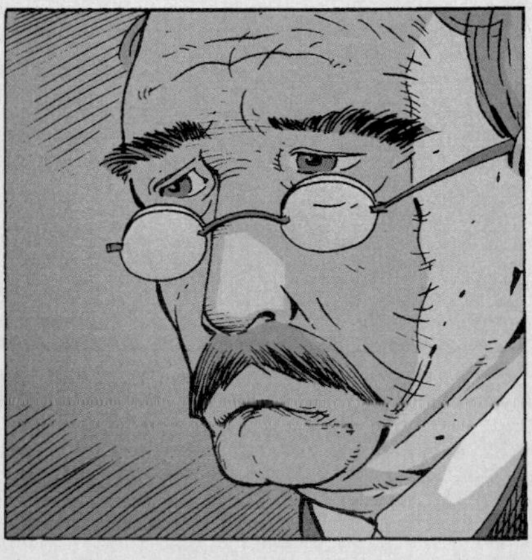

We seldom spoke his name, but I knew she meant that I should go to Locke. And once she said it, I knew that I had no choice.

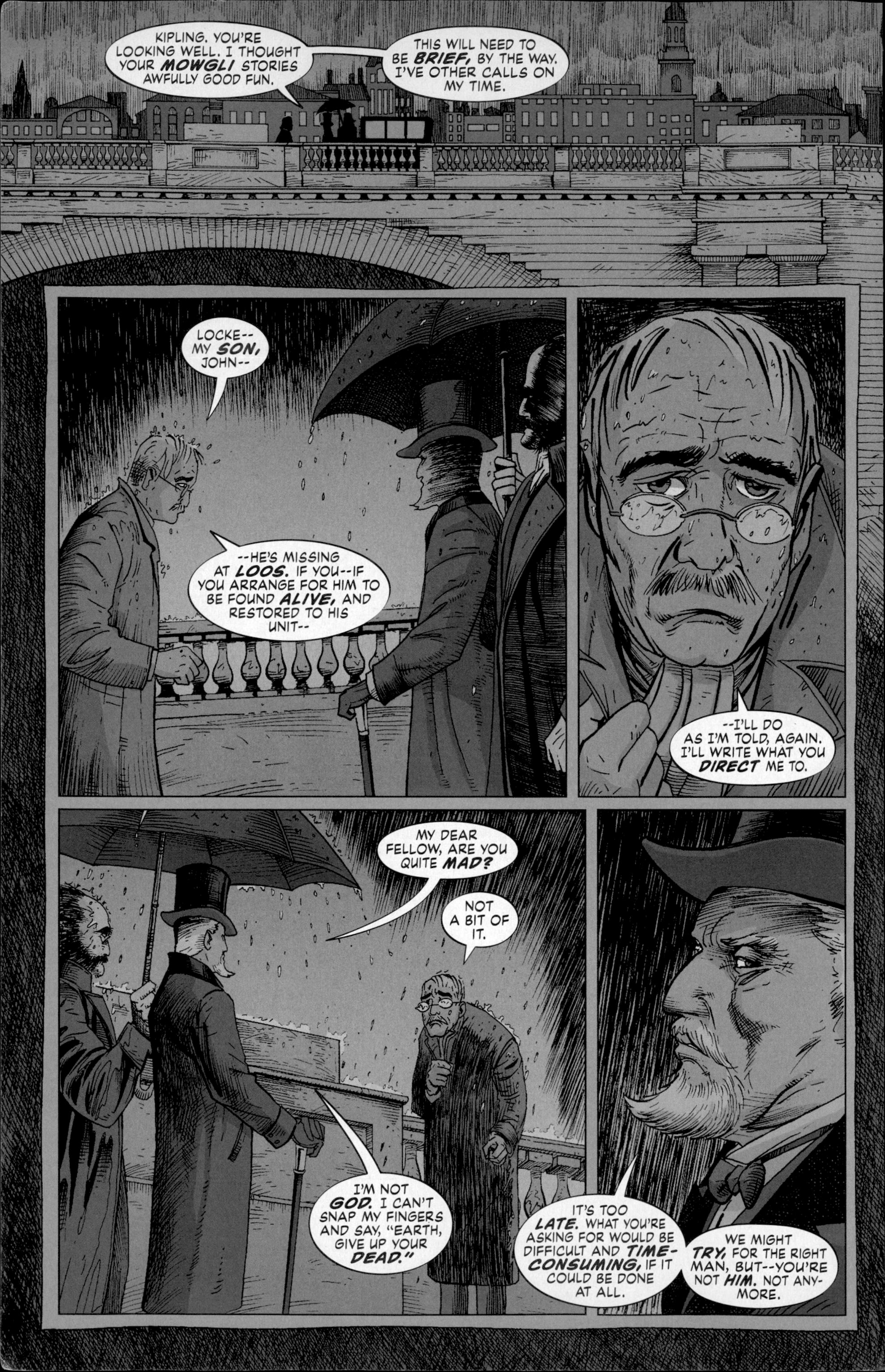
KIPLING. YOU'RE LOOKING WELL. I THOUGHT YOUR MOWGLI STORIES AWFULLY GOOD FUN.
THIS WILL NEED TO BE BRIEF, BY THE WAY. I'VE OTHER CALLS ON MY TIME.
LOCKE-- MY SON, JOHN--
--HE'S MISSING AT LOOS. IF YOU--IF YOU ARRANGE FOR HIM TO BE FOUND ALIVE, AND RESTORED TO HIS UNIT--
--I'LL DO AS I'M TOLD, AGAIN. I'LL WRITE WHAT YOU DIRECT ME TO.
MY DEAR FELLOW, ARE YOU QUITE MAD?
NOT A BIT OF IT.
I'M NOT GOD. I CAN'T SNAP MY FINGERS AND SAY, "EARTH, GIVE UP YOUR DEAD."
IT'S TOO LATE. WHAT YOU'RE ASKING FOR WOULD BE DIFFICULT AND TIME-CONSUMING, IF IT COULD BE DONE AT ALL.
WE MIGHT TRY, FOR THE RIGHT MAN, BUT--YOU'RE NOT HIM. NOT ANY-MORE.

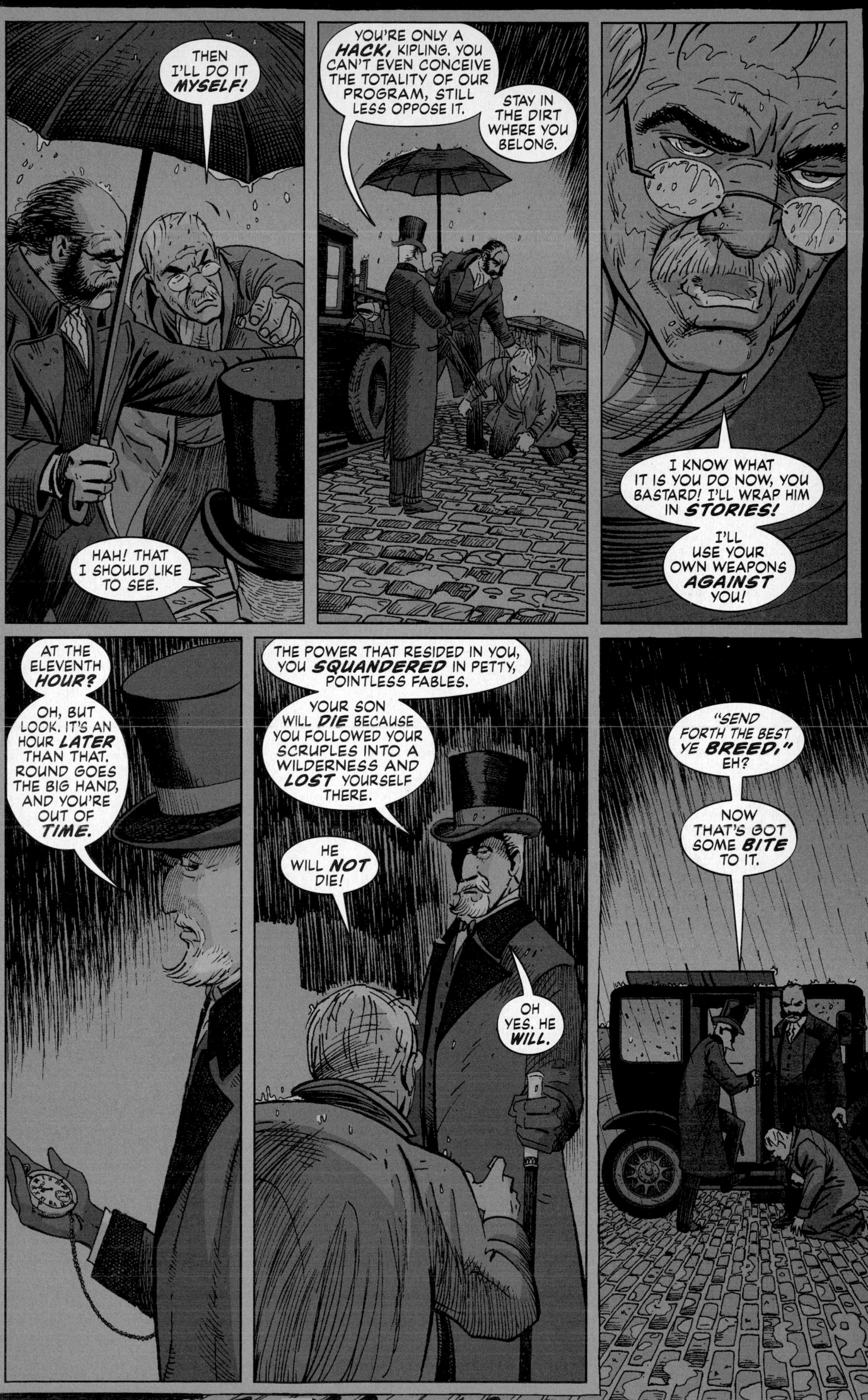
THEN I'LL DO IT MYSELF!
HAH! THAT I SHOULD LIKE TO SEE.
YOU'RE ONLY A HACK, KIPLING. YOU CAN'T EVEN CONCEIVE THE TOTALITY OF OUR PROGRAM, STILL LESS OPPOSE IT.
STAY IN THE DIRT WHERE YOU BELONG.
I KNOW WHAT IT IS YOU DO NOW, YOU BASTARD! I'LL WRAP HIM IN STORIES!
I'LL USE YOUR OWN WEAPONS AGAINST YOU!
AT THE ELEVENTH HOUR?
OH, BUT LOOK. IT'S AN HOUR LATER THAN THAT. ROUND GOES THE BIG HAND, AND YOU'RE OUT OF TIME.
THE POWER THAT RESIDED IN YOU, YOU SQUANDERED IN PETTY, POINTLESS FABLES.
YOUR SON WILL DIE BECAUSE YOU FOLLOWED YOUR SCRUPLES INTO A WILDERNESS AND LOST YOURSELF THERE.
HE WILL NOT DIE!
OH YES. HE WILL.
"SEND FORTH THE BEST YE BREED," EH?
NOW THAT'S GOT SOME BITE TO IT.

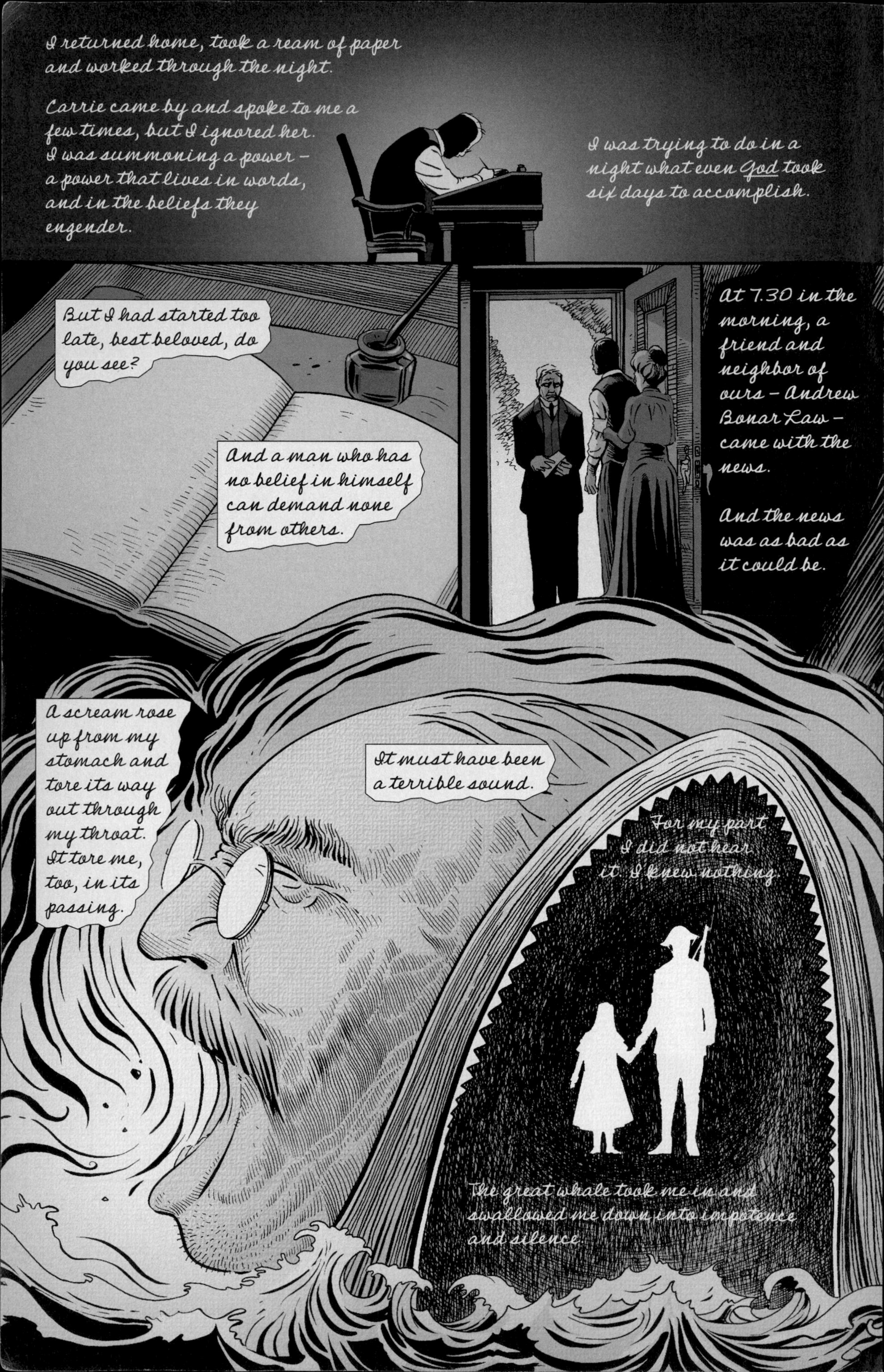
I returned home, took a ream of paper and worked through the night.
Carrie came by and spoke to me a few times, but I ignored her. I was summoning a power – a power that lives in words, and in the beliefs they engender.
I was trying to do in a night what even God took six days to accomplish.
But I had started too late, best beloved, do you see?
And a man who has no belief in himself can demand none from others.
At 7.30 in the morning, a friend and neighbor of ours – Andrew Bonar Law – came with the news.
And the news was as bad as it could be.
A scream rose up from my stomach and tore its way out through my throat. It tore me, too, in its passing.
It must have been a terrible sound.
For my part I did not hear it. I knew nothing.
The great whale took me in and swallowed me down into impotence and silence.

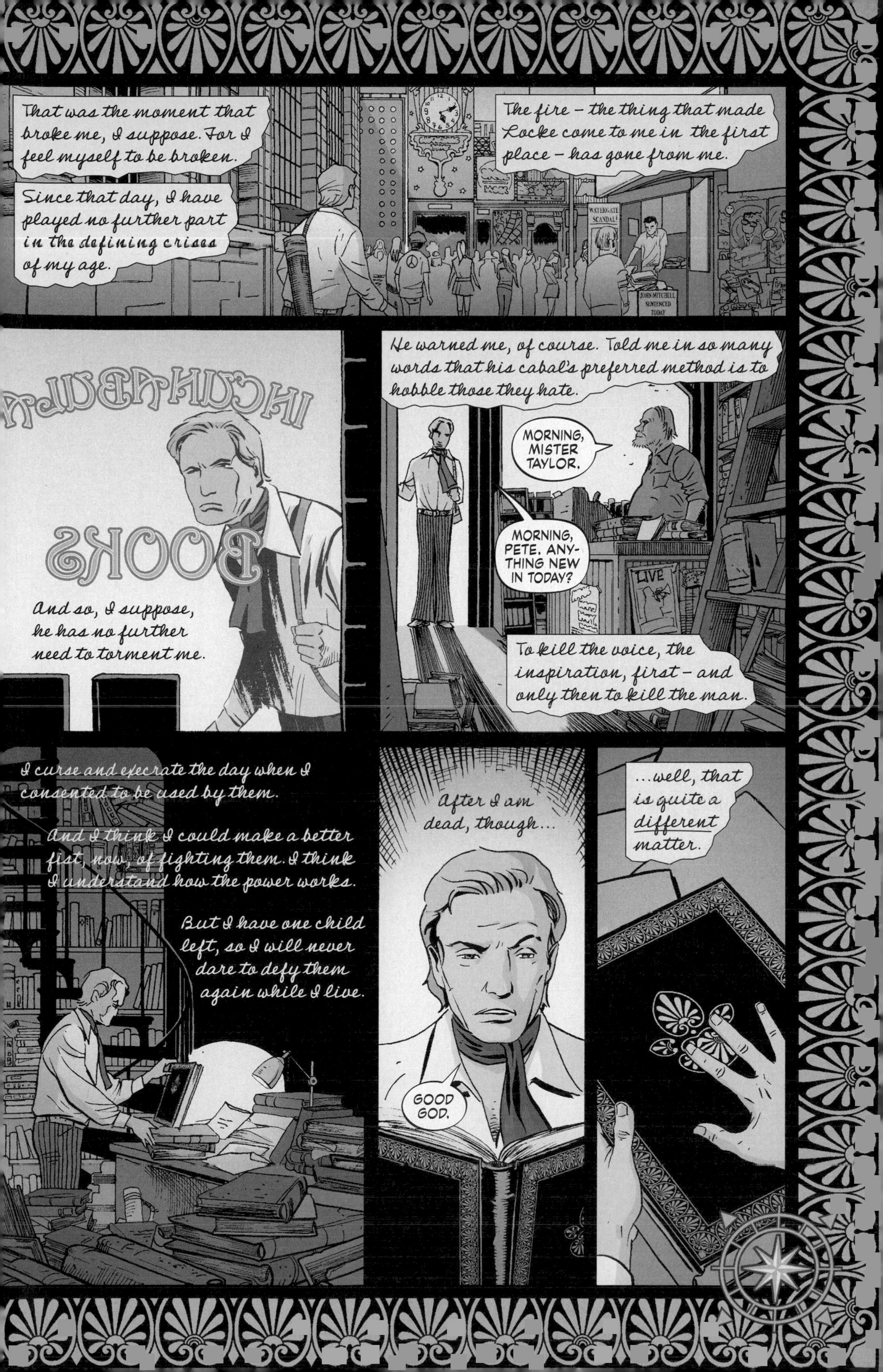

That was the moment that broke me, I suppose. For I feel myself to be broken.
Since that day, I have played no further part in the defining crises of my age.
The fire – the thing that made Locke come to me in the first place – has gone from me.
WATERGATE SCANDAL!
JOHN MITCHELL SENTENCED TODAY
INCUNABULA
BOOKS
And so, I suppose, he has no further need to torment me.
He warned me, of course. Told me in so many words that his cabal's preferred method is to hobble those they hate.
MORNING, MISTER TAYLOR.
MORNING, PETE. ANYTHING NEW IN TODAY?
LIVE
To kill the voice, the inspiration, first – and only then to kill the man.
I curse and execrate the day when I consented to be used by them.
And I think I could make a better fist, now, of fighting them. I think I understand how the power works.
But I have one child left, so I will never dare to defy them again while I live.
After I am dead, though...
GOOD GOD.
...well, that is quite a different matter.

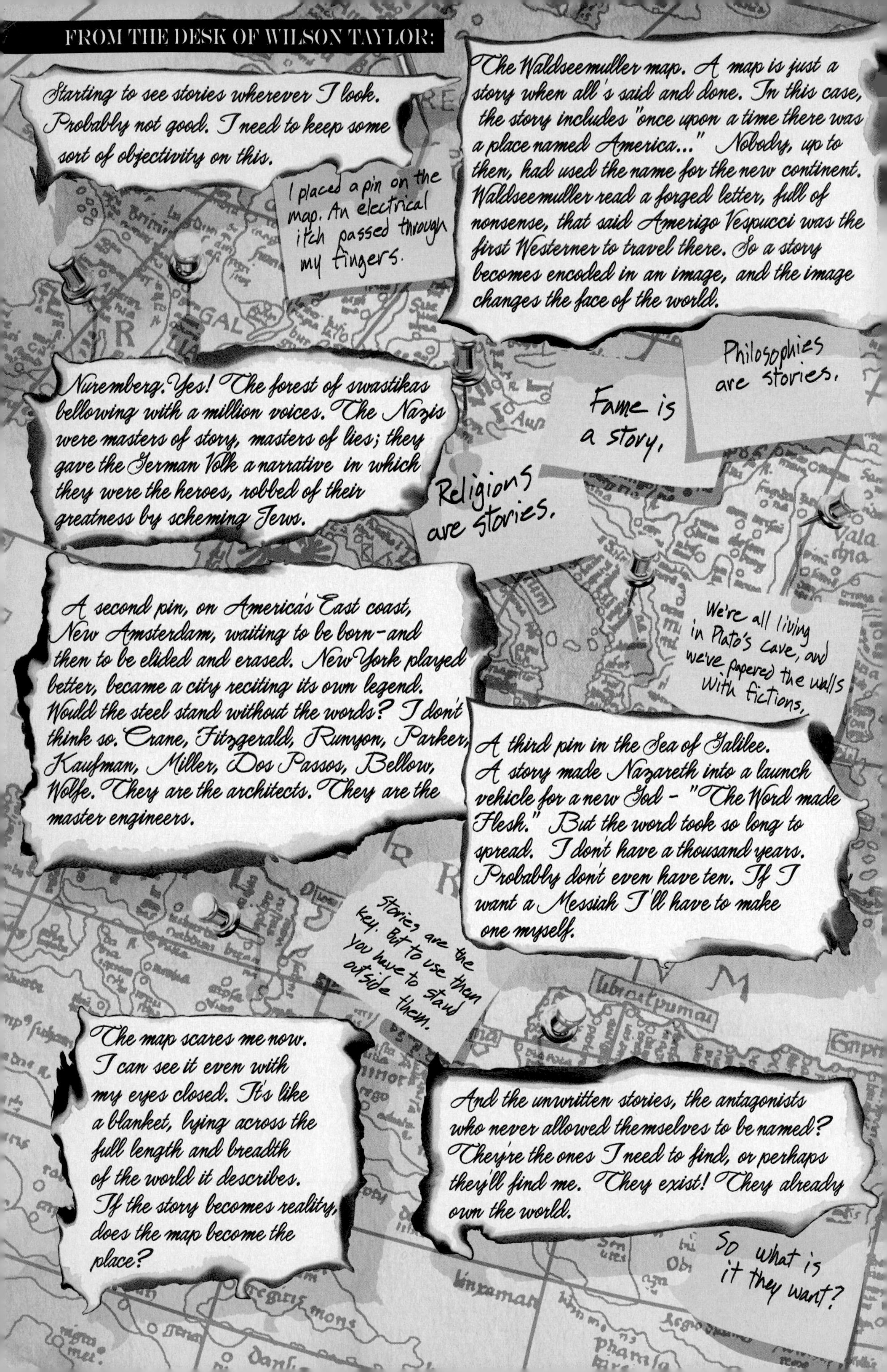
FROM THE DESK OF WILSON TAYLOR:
Starting to see stories wherever I look. Probably not good. I need to keep some sort of objectivity on this.
I placed a pin on the map. An electrical itch passed through my fingers.
The Waldseemuller map. A map is just a story when all's said and done. In this case, the story includes "once upon a time there was a place named America..." Nobody, up to then, had used the name for the new continent. Waldseemuller read a forged letter, full of nonsense, that said Amerigo Vespucci was the first Westerner to travel there. So a story becomes encoded in an image, and the image changes the face of the world.
Nuremberg. Yes! The forest of swastikas bellowing with a million voices. The Nazis were masters of story, masters of lies; they gave the German Volk a narrative in which they were the heroes, robbed of their greatness by scheming Jews.
Fame is a story.
Philosophies are stories.
Religions are stories.
A second pin, on America's East coast, New Amsterdam, waiting to be born - and then to be elided and erased. New York played better, became a city reciting its own legend. Would the steel stand without the words? I don't think so. Crane, Fitzgerald, Runyon, Parker, Kaufman, Miller, Dos Passos, Bellow, Wolfe. They are the architects. They are the master engineers.
We're all living in Plato's cave, and we've papered the walls with fictions.
A third pin in the Sea of Galilee. A story made Nazareth into a launch vehicle for a new God - "The Word made Flesh." But the word took so long to spread. I don't have a thousand years. Probably don't even have ten. If I want a Messiah I'll have to make one myself.
Stories are the key. But to use them you have to stand outside them.
The map scares me now. I can see it even with my eyes closed. It's like a blanket, lying across the full length and breadth of the world it describes. If the story becomes reality, does the map become the place?
And the unwritten stories, the antagonists who never allowed themselves to be named? They're the ones I need to find, or perhaps they'll find me. They exist! They already own the world.
So what is it they want?

THE UNWRITTEN
MISCELLANEA

TURN IT INTO COMICS

The first issue of THE UNWRITTEN was originally intended to open with the book within the book in order to bring readers directly into the world of Tommy Taylor. But after Mike Carey wrote the opening sequence, he and Peter Gross reconsidered and wondered if several pages of straight prose was the best way to sound the opening fanfare for their very ambitious new series.

Peter was confident that he could turn Mike's prose into comics but still have it presented recognizably as a novel: the comics version of "reading" Wilson Taylor's book.

Here for the first time is the original prose passage that was written for the series opening, and the adaptation process that Peter used to turn into comics.

Peter stared in awe at the Gossamoks' bodies, lying around the ancient stone altar in twisted heaps. It was not the fact that they were dead that astonished him: it was their solidity. In life the creatures had been half-ghost, half-devil, but Tommy's spell had made them entirely solid: had dragged them flailing and screaming into the physical world, and the trauma of that crossing had utterly destroyed them.

"Peter!" Sue exclaimed, startling him from his reverie. "Over there!"

She was pointing at the temple doors, which had been ripped from their hinges and were lying on the valley floor as though some Cyclops child had picked them up to examine them, then grown bored and tossed them aside. "They're in there," he said. "Tommy, and Ambrosio — alone. And Ambrosio has the trumpet. If he sounds the last note..."

Sue didn't finish the sentence. She didn't have to. They'd seen for themselves what the first six notes had done: the seventh would end everything, and the Count would finally achieve his dream of being the only sentient thing on the face of the earth.

They sprinted across the rubble-strewn ground to the cavernous doorway and stepped inside, into the huge and forbidding space that Sue had seen so often in her dreams. It seemed so strange to be standing here, at last: so strange to find that her feet actually echoed on the stone, and that the cold air actually touched her skin.

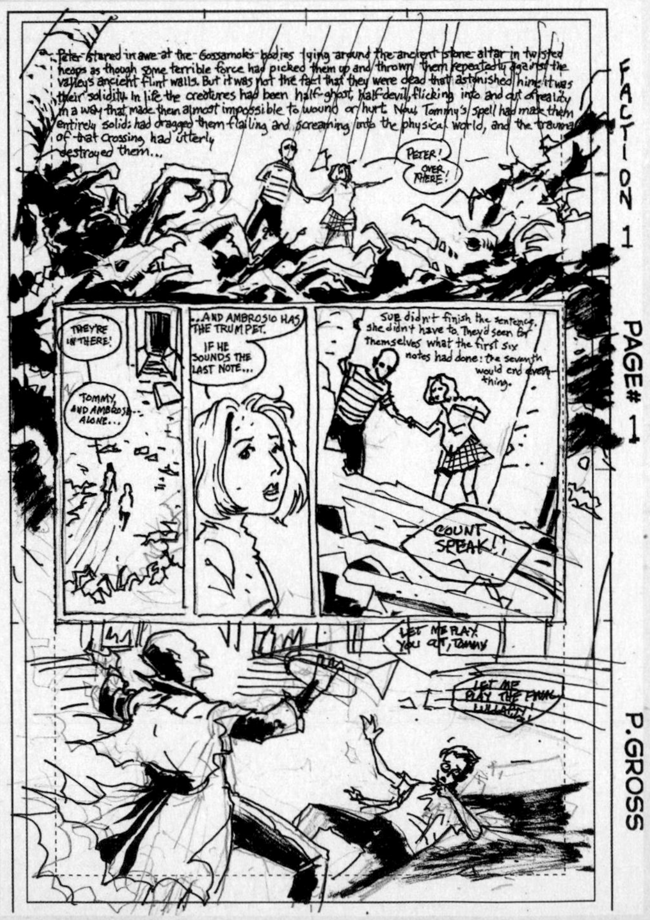
Peter stared in awe at the Gossamoks bodies lying around the ancient stone altar in twisted heaps as though some terrible force had picked them up and thrown them repeatedly against the valley's ancient flint walls. But it was not the fact that they were dead that astonished him: it was their solidity. In life the creatures had been half-ghost, half-devil, flicking into and out of reality in a way that made them almost impossible to wound or hurt. Now Tommy's spell had made them entirely solid: had dragged them flailing and screaming into the physical world, and the trauma of that crossing had utterly destroyed them...
PETER! OVER THERE!
THEY'RE IN THERE!
TOMMY, AND AMBROSIO... ALONE...
...AND AMBROSIO HAS THE TRUMPET.
IF HE SOUNDS THE LAST NOTE...
Sue didn't finish the sentence. She didn't have to. They'd seen for themselves what the first six notes had done: the seventh would end everything.
COUNT SPEAK!
LET ME PLAY YOU OUT, TOMMY
LET ME PLAY THE FINAL
FACTION 1
PAGE# 1
P.GROSS

The Count was standing over Tommy's sprawled body; he had the trumpet in his hands. They could see that Tommy was wounded, and that although he was trying to sit up he kept falling back again, his strength sapped by the vampire-king's terrible bite. He lifted one trembling hand, as if to pull the golden instrument from Ambrosio's grasp.

The Count laughed – triumphantly, even melodiously. "Let me play you out, Tommy," he cried. "Let me play the final lullaby." His chest inflated as he sucked in a lungful of air. He touched the trumpet to his lips.

At that moment, Tommy spoke the last three words of the unicorn's blessing. *"Niath turbal erohain!"*

The shock wave knocked both Sue and Peter off their feet, threw them back across the temple's threshold and slammed them down hard. Within it there was a sound, compressed and flattened by the tortured air. It was a word: a single, spoken word. *"Goodbye."*

It was a long while before Sue and Peter could move. Slowly, painfully, they found their feet and limped into the great hall again. They found the two enemies together, and both their hopes and their fears were realized to the full.

Count Ambrosio had turned to stone at the exact moment when he raised the golden trumpet to his lips. His head was tilted back; his mouth was half-open, and the mouthpiece of the instrument rested

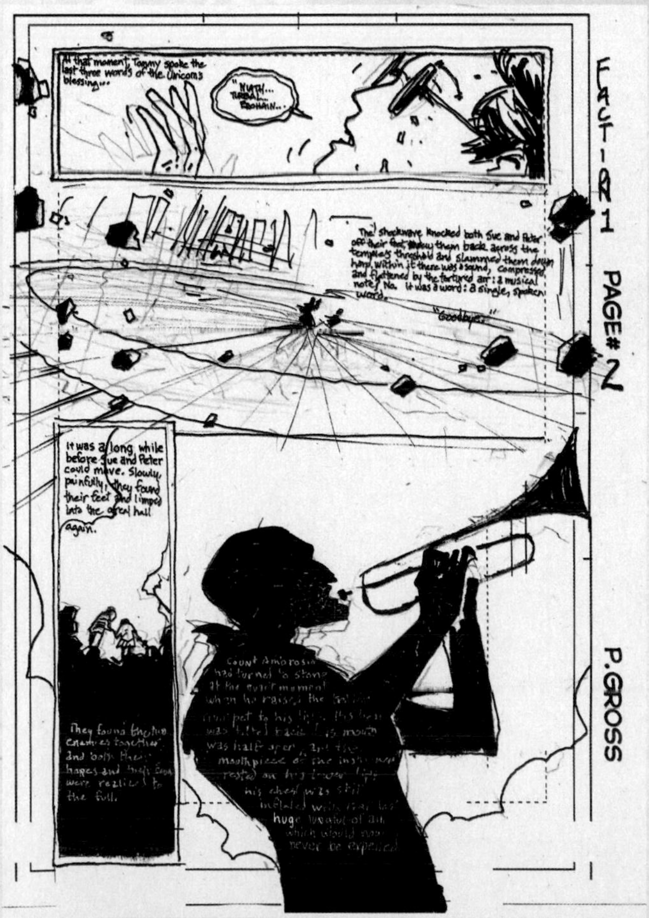

At that moment, Tommy spoke the last three words of the Unicorn's blessing...
"NIATH... TURBAL... EROHAIN..."
The shockwave knocked both Sue and Peter off their feet, threw them back across the temple's threshold and slammed them down hard. Within it there was a sound, compressed and flattened by the tortured air: a musical note? No. It was a word: a single, spoken word.
"Goodbye."
It was a long while before Sue and Peter could move. Slowly, painfully, they found their feet and limped into the great hall again.
They found the two enemies together, and both their hopes and their fears were realized to the full.
Count Ambrosio had turned to stone
FACT-R 1 PAGE#2
P.GROSS

on his lower lip; his chest was still inflated with that last, huge lungful of air, which would never now be expelled.

Tommy lay on the floor at the Count's feet. His eyes were closed, his face as pale as death, and he didn't rouse when his two friends called his name. The little winged cat, Mingus, sat beside him, miawling plaintively.

"Oh Tommy! Tommy!"

Sue scooped him up in her arms. Still he didn't move or speak. But Peter's gaze had fallen on the trumpet, and his heart began to hammer as the thought came to him.

There was a way. There *was* a way.

How had that part of the prophecy gone? *When the horn sounds, he will pass beyond the veil of legend, and live again.*

Behind him, the sound of Sue's sobbing filled the great hall.

What would happen if he blew the horn? Would the world end? Or would the other six notes not count at all, since a different player held the trumpet now? There was only one way to find out.

Peter Price lifted the golden trumpet to his lips and blew the final, irrevocable note.

4
KALI #
PAGE# 3
P.GROSS
Tommy lay on the floor at the Count's feet. His eyes were closed, his face as pale as death, and he didn't rouse when his two friends called his name. The little winged cat, Mingus, sat beside him, plaintively lapping at his cheek and miawling in complaint that he didn't sit up and stroke her.
OH, TOMMY!
TOMMY!
She scooped him up in her arms but still he didn't move or speak. But Peter's gaze had fallen on the trumpet and his heart began to hammer as the thought came to him.
There was a way.
There was a way
He crossed to Count Ambrosio's body. Queasily, trying not to touch the clammy stone, which he saw now was crazed across with a million tiny cracks, he eased the instrument from the Count's hands and held it in his own.
How had that part of the prophecy gone? When the maiden weeps, the horn shall sound. And one shall pass beyond the veil of legend, to live again after death's sting has found him.
Behind him, the sound of Sue's sobbing filled the great hall.
What would happen if he blew the horn? Would the world end? Or would the other six notes not count at all, since a different player held the trumpet now? There was only one way to find out.
Peter Price lifted the golden trumpet to his lips and blew the final, irrevocable note.

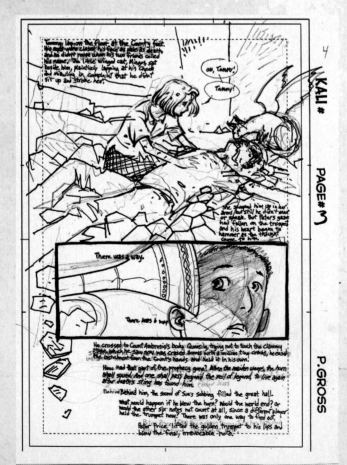

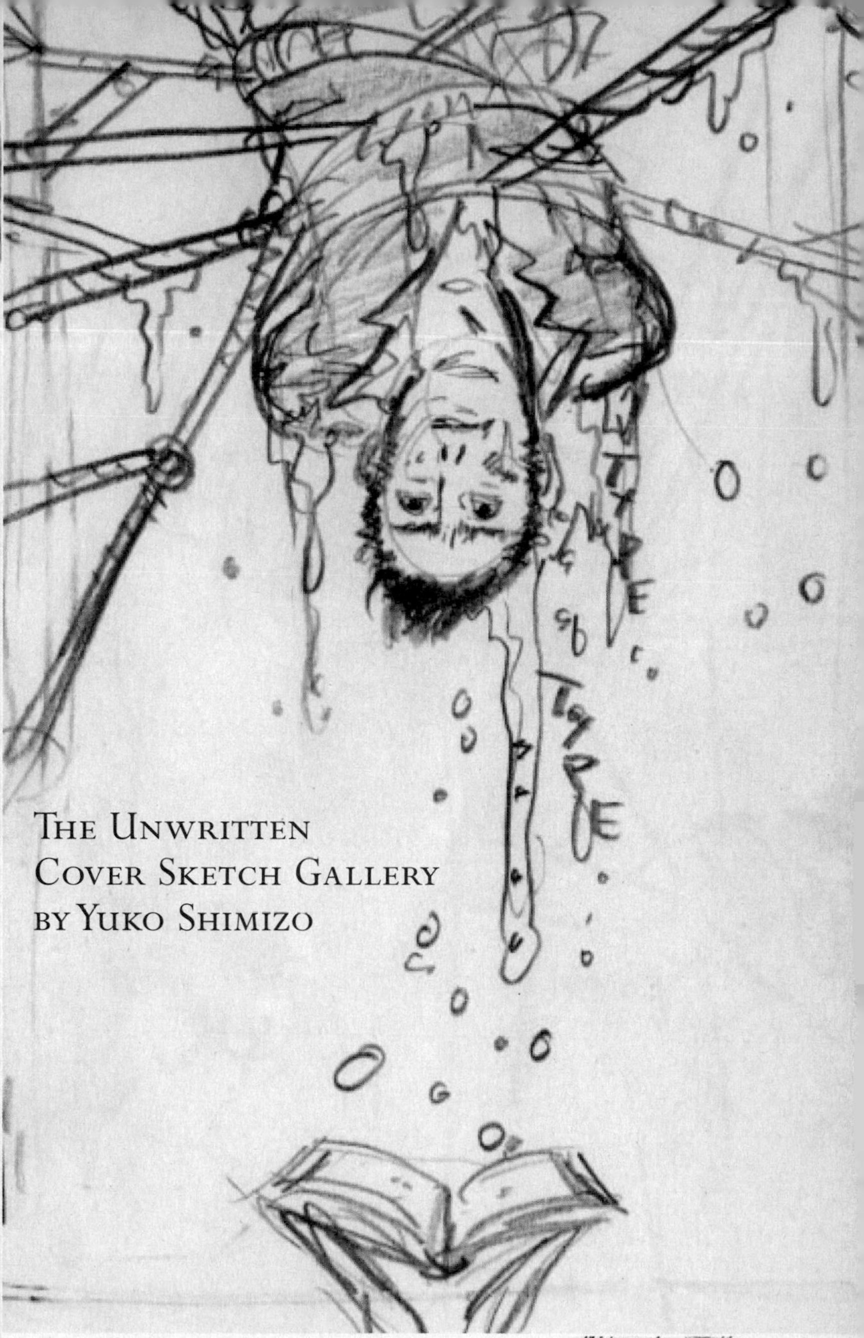

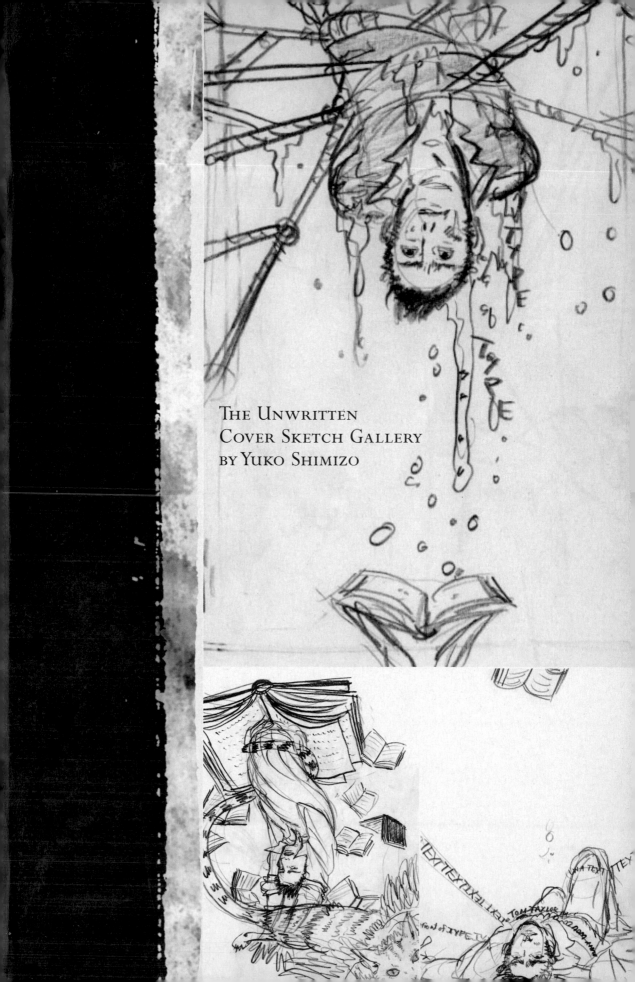

The Unwritten Cover Sketch Gallery by Yuko Shimizo

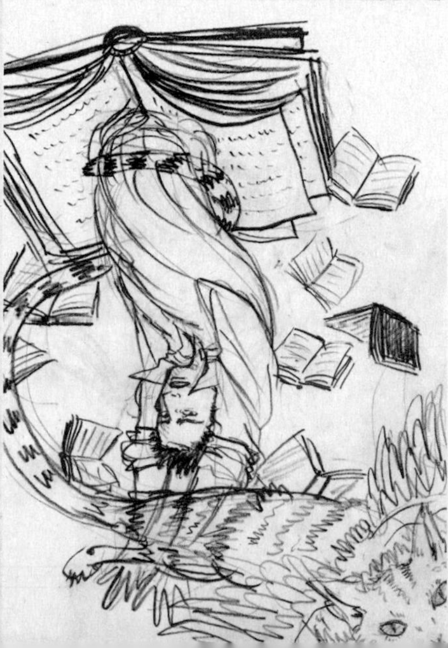

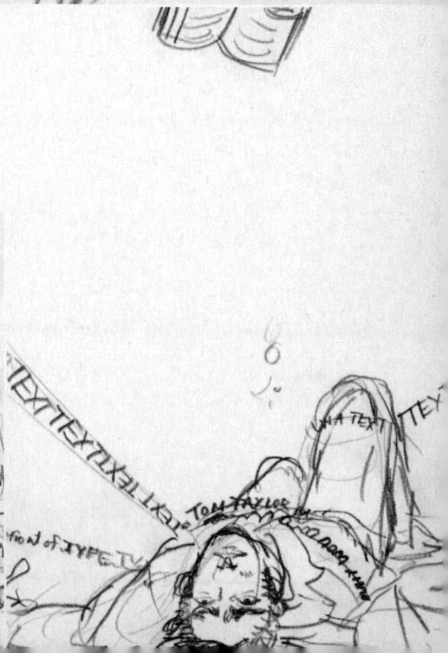

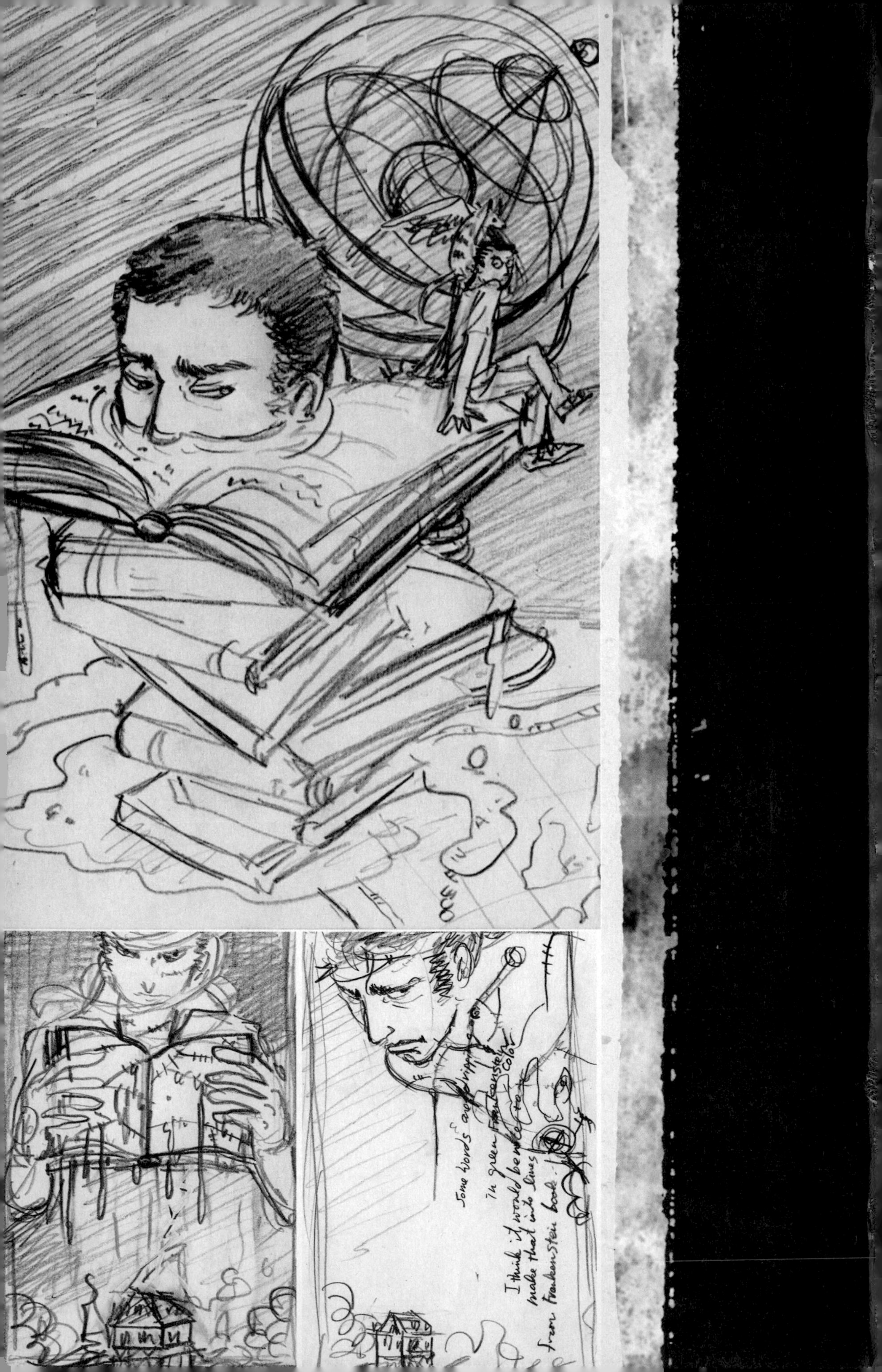
Some words are dripping
In green Frankenstein color
I think it would be nice to
make that into lines
from Frankenstein book.

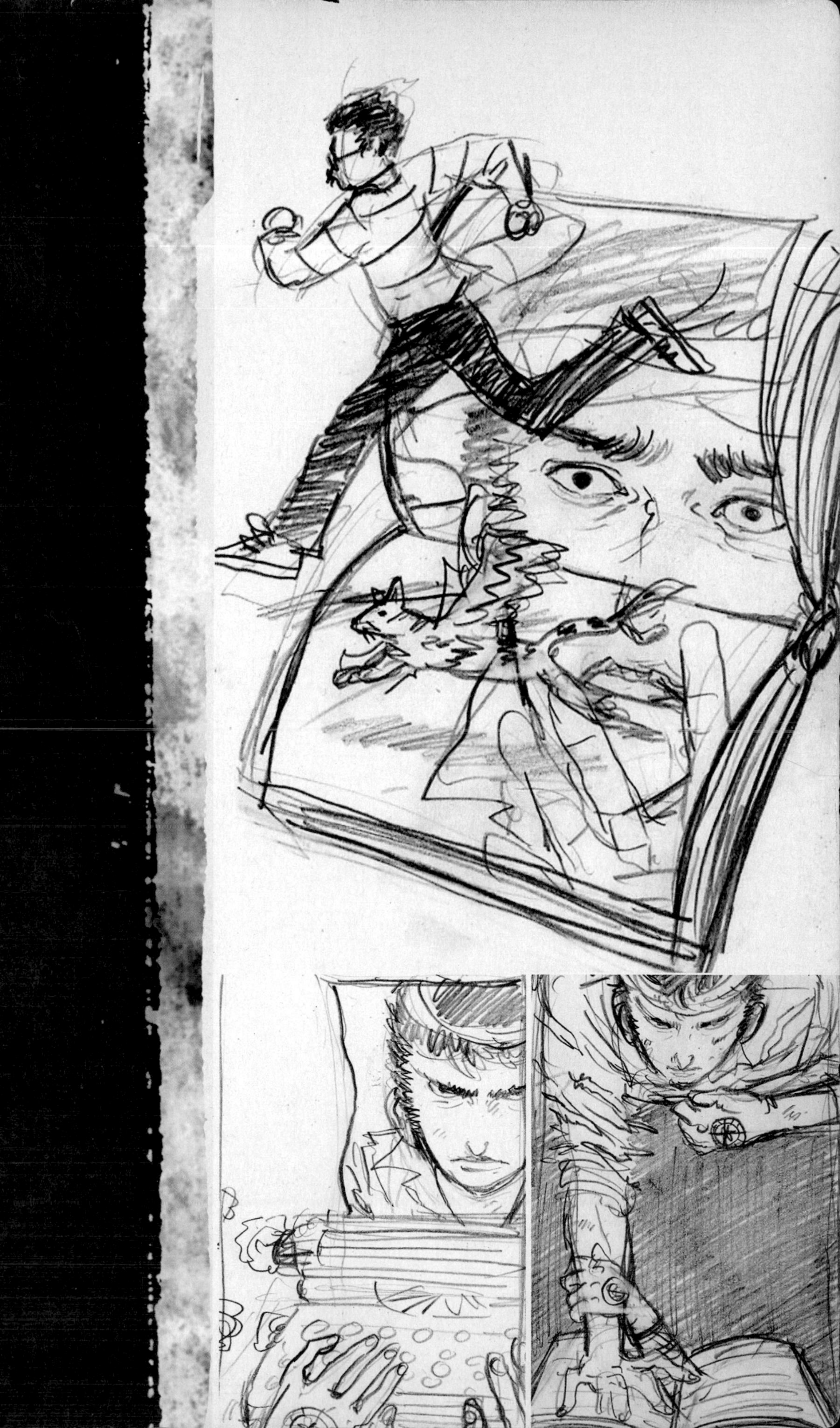

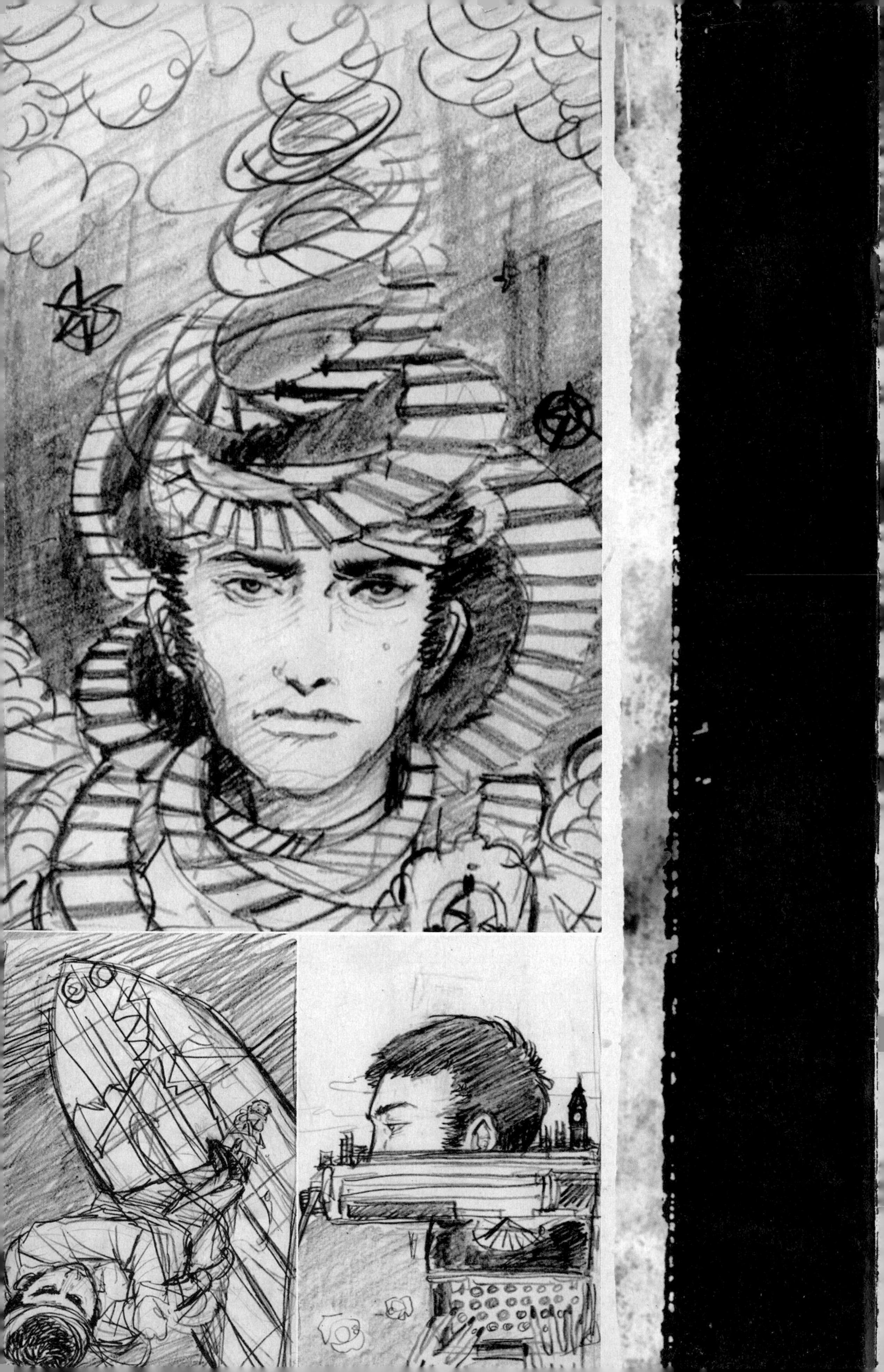